Evaluation of Library Collections, Access and Electronic Resources

EVALUATION OF LIBRARY COLLECTIONS, ACCESS AND ELECTRONIC RESOURCES

A Literature Guide and Annotated Bibliography

Thomas E. Nisonger

160401

LIBRARIES
U N L I M I T E D

A Member of the Greenwood Publishing Group

Westport, Connecticut • London

Library of Congress Cataloging-in-Publication Data

Nisonger, Thomas E.
    Evaluation of library collections, access and electronic resources :
    a literature guide and annotated bibliography / Thomas E. Nisonger.
        p. cm.
    Includes bibliographical references.
    ISBN 1–56308–852–5 (alk. paper)
    1. Collection development (Libraries)—Evaluation—Bibliography.
I. Title.
Z687.N57   2003
025.2′1—dc21   2003053877

British Library Cataloguing in Publication Data is available.

Library of Congress Catalog Card Number: 2003053877
ISBN: 1–56308–852–5

First published in 2003

Libraries Unlimited, Inc., 88 Post Road West, Westport, CT 06881
A member of the Greenwood Publishing Group, Inc.
www.lu.com

Printed in the United States of America

The paper used in this book complies with the
Permanent Paper Standard issued by the National
Information Standards Organization (Z39.48–1984).

10   9   8   7   6   5   4   3   2   1

This book is dedicated to my daughter,
Suzanne Marie Nisonger.

Contents

Acknowledgments

I would like to acknowledge a number of people who contributed to the completion of this book. My wife, Claire Nisonger, showed remarkable patience throughout the duration of my writing efforts. Edward M. Kurdyla, Jr., the Libraries Unlimited Vice President and Publisher, read my sample submission and provided helpful feedback. Martin Dillon, Libraries Unlimited Director of Acquisitions, served as my editor, and Mary Beth Dunning, Impressions Book and Journal Services, was Project Coordinator for publication of my book. Kira Barnes, Erik Estep, Vanessa Davis, Jason Cooper, and Leah Broaddus, my graduate assistants at Indiana University's School of Library and Information Science (SLIS) during various times, provided important assistance by photocopying articles, requesting items through Interlibrary Loan or document delivery, or proofreading citations. I also thank for their help numerous individuals from the Indiana University Bloomington Libraries Document Delivery Services, the Indiana University Bloomington Reference Department, Libraries Unlimited, Greenwood Press, and Impressions Book and Journal Services, who assisted me in a variety of ways. I am especially grateful to the staff of the Indiana University SLIS Library whose extraordinary service extended to forgiving overdue items. Any deficiencies of this volume are, of course, my own responsibility.

Introduction

This book's objective is to provide an annotated bibliography and literature guide to the English language collection evaluation literature of the decade 1992 through 2002 pertaining to all types of libraries. The primary audience is professional librarians whose job responsibilities include collection management and/or collection development, while the secondary audience is library and information science faculty, students, and researchers.

The author's original intention was to publish a second edition of his *Collection Evaluation in Academic Libraries: A Literature Guide and Annotated Bibliography,* which would repeat the most important entries while adding additional items published beginning in 1992. However, it rapidly became apparent that the amount of relevant collection evaluation literature published since 1991 warrants a completely separate book. This volume, which may be viewed as a sequel to the author's earlier work, differs from the first book in four key respects:

- No entries from the earlier book are repeated in this volume.

- The chronological focus is on works published from 1992–2002 rather than 1980–91.

- Instead of restriction to academic libraries, coverage is expanded to all types of libraries (i.e., public, school, and special).

- Chapters dealing with the evaluation of access and electronic resources have been added.

This bibliography concentrates on evaluation of library collections in general, serial collections, electronic resources, and library performance in accessing needed materials as well as the use of journal rankings and citation data in evaluation. Items whose primary focus deals with nonevaluative collection development/collection management issues, such as weeding, approval plans, gifts and exchange, budget allocation, and preservation, are generally excluded from this literature guide. Also excluded are non-English items, doctoral dissertations, master's theses, ERIC (Educational Resource Information Center) and National Technical Information Service documents, in-house library publications, and unpublished conference presentations or proceedings. Secondary reports of conference presentations written by someone other than the original presenter are generally, but not always, excluded. As one would expect, most of the entries are journal articles, but some books, book chapters, and conference proceedings are included.

The primary emphasis is on material published in the major Anglo-American countries (i.e., the United States, Canada, the United Kingdom, Australia, and New Zealand), yet—when identified—pertinent English language items published anywhere in the world have been included. Because items published in India, Malaysia, the Netherlands, Nigeria, Singapore, South Africa, and Sweden are included, a total of twelve different countries are represented. Note, however, that the coverage is generally limited to entries that can be identified through the standard indexing and abstracting resources available in North America.

As with the author's initial book, this bibliography is neither comprehensive nor highly selective. Inclusion of an item does not necessarily mean endorsement of its quality per se but rather that it offers information of value or interest to readers or helps fill a niche in the literature. Also note that more entries could have been included except for space limitations.

ORGANIZATION

Following the introduction, the book is organized into twelve chapters. The initial chapter covers items offering overviews of collection evaluation as well as bibliographies and literature reviews. Chapter 2 is devoted to traditional, collection-centered evaluation, including the Online Computer Library Center (OCLC)/ Amigos Collection Analysis CD and overlap studies, while chapter 3 is devoted to the Conspectus. Chapter 4 covers client-centered approaches, such as availability studies and document delivery tests, combinations of client and collection-centered techniques, and reference collection evaluation. Chapter 5 contains entries about evaluation at the multilibrary and national collection level. Chapter 6 deals with performance measures and standards. Serials, including evaluation of serial collections, serial decision models, and serials cancellation projects, are covered in chapter 7. Evaluation of the use of periodicals and books as well as methodological issues concerning usage studies are addressed in chapter 8. Chapter 9 annotates items dealing with the use of citation analysis for serials management, collection evaluation, and studying the structure of subject areas. Next, chapter 10 is devoted to journal ranking studies. Chapter 11 covers the evaluation (from a content or collection management perspective) of Web pages, full-text databases, electronic journals, and other electronic resources as well as their use. Finally chapter 12, focuses on the evaluation of access, including methodological issues, interlibrary loan and document delivery performance, and the cost-effectiveness of access versus serial subscription.

Each chapter begins with a brief introduction, covering its organization and scope. These introductory sections often outline major issues and, when necessary, contain cross-references to other chapters with related coverage.

The citation (and other formats) conform to the University of Chicago *Manual of Style.* The print version is cited for journal articles originally published in that format, although many of these articles are now available electronically through *Science Direct, Emerald, Ebsco Host,* and so on. The Web address is given for items originally published in all-electronic journals. The journal article rather than the book chapter is cited for the numerous Haworth Press items simultaneously published as a journal issue and a monograph. The annotations, usually ranging in length from 100 to 200 words, are based on direct examination of the item. In all instances an original annotation has been written by the author rather than using an abstract accompanying the work. Methodologies and significant research findings are emphasized in the annotations.

METHODOLOGY

The following methods were used to identify entries for this bibliography:

- Searching (through a Web interface) the standard library and information science indexing and abstracting databases: *Library Literature and Information Science, Library and Information Science Abstracts,* and *Information Science Abstracts*

- Searching, also through the Web, indexing and abstracting databases from related disciplines (e.g., *ERIC*)

- Using other resources on the Web, either freely available or provided by the Indiana University Bloomington Libraries to its patrons: *Web of Science, UnCover, Amazon.com,* and *AcqWeb*

- Reviewing previously published bibliographies

- Reviewing the notes and references in all items identified for inclusion in this volume

- Shelf-scanning of major journals in the Indiana University School of Library and Information Science Library

- Drawing on the author's own knowledge of the subject area, based on teaching and research

PREVIOUS BIBLIOGRAPHICAL RESEARCH

More than half a dozen bibliographies pertaining to collection evaluation in its entirety or to a substantial extent have been published during the last three decades.

In 1971 Signe Ottersen's "A Bibliography on Standards for Evaluating Libraries," annotated 138 entries dealing with standards and collection evaluation published between 1933 and 1970 with a major but not exclusive focus on academic libraries.[1] In 1982 Thomas E. Nisonger supplemented and updated Ottersen with his "An Annotated Bibliography of Items Relating to Collection Evaluation in Academic Libraries, 1969–1981," which contained 97 items.[2] This work was updated by Nisonger in 1992 with a booklength annotated bibliography *Collection Evaluation in Academic Libraries: A Literature Guide and Annotated Bibli-*

ography containing 617 entries mostly published between 1980 and 1991.[3] As previously noted, *Evaluation of Library Collections, Access, and Electronic Resources: A Literature Guide and Annotated Bibliography* is an updated and expanded sequel to Nisonger's 1992 bibliography. Thus, one may observe a linear development from Ottersen's 1971 bibliography to the works of Nisonger in 1980 and 1992 to this present volume.

A number of other bibliographical works should be mentioned. In 1976 Samuel E. Ifidon's short bibliography, "Qualitative/Quantitative Evaluation of Academic Library Collections: A Literature Survey," annotated 19 items published from 1956 to 1974.[4] A highly selective book-length work by Irene P. Godden, Karen W. Fachan, and Patricia A. Smith, *Collection Development and Acquisitions, 1970–1980: An Annotated, Critical Bibliography,* published in 1982, contained a section on collection evaluation that annotated 84 entries (dealing with all library types but placing a heavy emphasis on academic libraries) published during the 1970s.[5] In 1991 the American Library Association's Reference and Adult Services Division issued *Collection Evaluation Techniques: A Short, Selective, Practical, Current Annotated Bibliography 1980–1990* compiled by Cynthia Stewart Kaag with Sharon Lee Cann and others.[6] Emphasizing evaluation techniques, this pamphlet annotated 58 entries published from 1980 to 1990. Michael R. Gabriel's book *Collection Development and Collection Evaluation: A Sourcebook,* published in 1995, contained a collection evaluation bibliography listing approximately 350 items published between 1940 and 1991.[7] The 1991 ALA bibliography was updated in 1999 with *Collection Evaluation Techniques: A Short, Selective, Practical, Current, Annotated Bibliography, 1990–1998,* edited and compiled by Bonnie Strohl.[8] Annotating 110 items, Strohl's work was the most current collection evaluation bibliography prior to the publication of this volume.

Why is another bibliography and guide to the literature of collection evaluation necessary? The identification of more than 600 entries for inclusion in this volume testifies to the interest in the topic. Collection management's increasing complexity caused by the current emphasis on access and the unresolved challenges posed by electronic resources enhances the need for evaluation to insure client information needs are being met effectively and cost-efficiently. The greater stress on accountability in higher education and society also requires evaluation of library effectiveness. Finally, as indicated by the preceding review, this volume will be the most current and comprehensive annotated bibliography available on the topic and the only one that covers, to a significant extent, evaluation of access and electronic resources.

KEY DICHOTOMIES IN COLLECTION EVALUATION

In order to help explain this book's structure and illuminate some fundamental collection evaluation theory, a number of dichotomies for classifying evaluation methods are outlined below.

Collection-Centered versus Client-Centered

This is probably the most frequently used approach for classifying collection evaluation methods. A collection-centered method focuses on the collection itself. According to the ALA's *Guide to the Evaluation of Library Collections,* "techniques are employed to determine the size, scope, or depth of a collection, or segment thereof, often in comparison with an external standard, the National Shelflist Count, for example, or the holdings of a library known to be comprehensive in the subject area being compared."[9] Examples would include the check-list method (i.e., checking a list of desired items against a library's catalog), direct examination, holdings statistics, and the Conspectus. In contrast, a client-centered, or use-centered, (both terms are employed) method focuses on the actual use of information resources and those using them. The *Guide to the Evaluation of Library Collections* states these techniques "determine whether or not library users can identify and locate the items they need, whether specific items are indeed available, what unmet needs exist, and who the users are."[10] Shelf availability studies, document delivery tests, circulation statistics, and patron surveys serve as examples. Investigations of interlibrary loan and commercial document delivery vendor performance, although not strictly collection evaluation techniques, are clearly client-centered.

Quantitative versus Qualitative

This distinction is now used less frequently than the collection-centered/client-centered dichotomy, but nevertheless it is important for understanding evaluation methods. A quantitative evaluation technique counts measurable units. Typically a quantitative collection-centered method addresses the size of holdings or expenditures for information resources. Examples are data on current serial subscriptions or total volumes held for a single library; comparative holdings statistics among a group of libraries; or formulas, such as Clapp-Jordan, that determine if an academic library's collection is of adequate size considering the curriculum plus the number of faculty and students. Studies of availability, circulation, or in-house use serve as examples of quantitative client-centered methods. A qualitative method (depending on how the term is used) addresses the collection's quality or uses qualitative research methods to determine patron assessments of the collection or related information services. Direct examination of the collection by a subject expert or the checklist method (which presumes the listed items are high quality) are qualitative collection-centered approaches. Patron surveys, questionnaires, and interviews, as well as focus groups, are qualitative client-centered techniques.

Inputs versus Outputs

This dichotomy is receiving increasing attention in the evaluation literature of the last decade. A significant emphasis of traditional collection evaluation concerned inputs (what the community or parent institution puts into the library). *Inputs* (staff, information resource materials, facilities, and equipment) are purchased with the financial resources invested in the library by its community. Statistics or evaluative methods relating to these categories are considered *input measures.* Examples of input measures relevant to collections would be the size of the holdings, the number of current periodical subscriptions, or the volumes added in a year. Indeed, collection-centered evaluation methods, such as checklists or the Conspectus, measure inputs. In contrast, *outputs* are received by the community or parent institution in return for the investment made in the library. Literally, the term refers to what the library puts out. Reference questions correctly answered, registered patrons with library cards, and children attending story hours represent outputs. Within this book's scope, use of the collection and patrons finding sought after items on the shelves or receiving them through document delivery are considered outputs. In fact, user- or client-centered collection evaluation methods generally measure outputs.

Outputs versus Outcomes

Recently, there has been a trend away from outputs, which have been explained in the previous section, and toward outcome measures, which concern how a library affects its environment, that is, what difference does the library really make? Outcomes-related evaluation research addresses such questions as the following: How well does a school library promote information literacy? How does an academic library impact faculty research and student learning? One should mention Peter Hernon's and Robert E. Dugan's *An Action Plan for Outcomes Assessment in Your Library,* which is not annotated here because it does not directly address collection evaluation issues.[11] Likewise, considerable attention is now being given to service quality, especially on the part of large academic libraries.

Microevaluation versus Macroevaluation

There are two concepts to the microevaluation versus macroevaluation distinction. In one concept, as described by Baker and Lancaster, who cite the work of King and Bryant, macroevalation measures an overall performance level, whereas microevaluation analyzes reasons for deficient performance.[12] For illustration, the "title fill rate" from *Output Measures for Public Libraries* represents macroevaluation as it only indicates the proportion of time patrons can locate a desired book title on the shelf.[13] In contrast, Kantor's Branching Method is an example of microevaluation because it not only measures an overall availability rate but also measures the reasons for an item's nonavailability, such as it was never acquired by the library or in circulation. In another and more frequently used concept, microevaluation refers to evaluation of a specific information resource (i.e., a book, serial, or whatever) while macroevaluation refers to evaluation of an entire category or group of resources. In a practical sense, most microevaluation is actually selection.

SUMMARY

One should note that a particular evaluation study can combine different approaches. In light of the profession's current emphasis on access and the growing importance of electronic resources as alternatives to large library holdings, trends toward client-centered rather than collection-centered methods, as well as outputs and outcomes instead of inputs, are readily apparent and can reasonably be expected to continue in the future. Many methods for evaluation of print collections have been developed and tested for validity over the last half century. A major challenge for the library profession early in the third millenium is the identification of evaluation methods (through modification of existing techniques or the development of new ones) appropriate to the hybrid library, incorporating both print and electronic resources. The author hopes this book will contribute to that objective by providing a record of the most relevant collection evaluation literature published during the previous ten years.

NOTES

1. Signe Ottersen, "A Bibliography on Standards for Evaluating Libraries," *College & Research Libraries* 32 (March 1971): 127–44.

2. Thomas E. Nisonger, "An Annotated Bibliography of Items Relating to Collection Evaluation in Academic Libraries, 1969–1981," *College & Research Libraries* 43 (July 1982): 300–311.

3. Thomas E. Nisonger, *Collection Evaluation in Academic Libraries: A Literature Guide and Annotated Bibliography* (Englewood, CO: Libraries Unlimited, 1992).

4. Sam E. Ifidon, "Qualitative/Quantitative Evaluation of Academic Library Collections: A Literature Survey," *International Library Review* 8 (June 1976): 299–308.

5. Irene P. Godden, Karen W. Fachan, and Patricia A. Smith, with Sandra Brug, comps., *Collection Development and Acquisitions, 1970–1980: An Annotated, Critical Bibliography* (Metuchen, NJ: Scarecrow Press, 1982).

6. Cynthia Stewart Kaag et al., *Collection Evaluation Techniques: A Short, Selective, Practical, Current Annotated Bibliography 1980–1990* (Chicago: Reference and Adult Services Division, American Library Association, 1991).

7. Michael R. Gabriel, *Collection Development and Collection Evaluation: A Sourcebook* (Metuchen, NJ: Scarecrow Press, 1995).

8. Bonnie Strohl, comp. and ed., *Collection Evaluation Techniques: A Short, Selective, Practical, Current, Annotated Bibliography, 1990–1998* (Chicago: Reference and User Services Association, American Library Association, 1999).

9. Barbara Lockett, *Guide to the Evaluation of Library Collections* (Chicago: American Library Association, 1989), 3.

10. Lockett, *Guide to the Evaluation of Library Collections*, 9.

11. Peter Hernon and Robert E. Dugan, *An Action Plan for Outcomes Assessment in Your Library* (Chicago: American Library Association, 2002).

12. Sharon L. Baker and F. W. Lancaster, *The Measurement and Evaluation of Library Services,* 2d ed. (Arlington, VA: Information Resources Press, 1991), 8–9.

13. Nancy A. Van House, et al., *Output Measures for Public Libraries: A Manual of Standardized Procedures,* 2d ed. (Chicago, American Library Association, 1987), 50–52.

Abbreviations and Acronyms

AACSB	American Assembly of Collegiate Schools of Business
AASL	American Association of School Librarians
ABA	American Bar Association
ACI	autonomous citation indexing
ACL	Association of Christian Librarians
ACLIS	Australian Council of Libraries and Information Services
ACOLAM	Advisory Committee on Latin American Materials (in U.K.)
ACRL	Association of College and Research Libraries (a division of ALA)
AECT	Association for Educational Communications and Technology
AFSAAP	African Studies Association of Australia and the Pacific
AHCI	*Arts and Humanities Citation Index*
ALA	American Library Association
ALIA	Australian Library and Information Association
ANOVA	ANalysis of VAriance between groups
APSA	American Political Science Association
ARL	Association of Research Libraries
ARLIS/NA	Art Libraries Society of North America
ARMMS	Atkins Reference Materials Management System
ASLIB	Association of Special Libraries and Information Bureaux.
ASU	Arizona State University
AT&T	American Telephone and Telegraph Company (former name; the initials are now the company's legal name)
B & T	Baker and Taylor
BCL3	*Books for College Libraries,* 3d edition (1988)
BGSU	Bowling Green State University
BIDS	Bath Information and Data Services
BIP	*Books in Print*
BL	British Library
BLDSC	British Library Document Supply Centre

BODOS	BIDS Online Document Ordering System
BPO	*Business Periodicals Ondisc*
BRD	*Book Review Digest*
BRJ	Benefit Ratio of Journal
BRS	Bibliographic Retrieval Service
BYU	Brigham Young University
CACD	Collection Analysis Compact Disc (from OCLC/AMIGOS)
CACUL	Canadian Association of College and University Libraries
CARL	Colorado Association of Research Libraries
CAS	Current Alerting Service
CBLJ	Cited by Leading Journal
CCCD	Coordinated Cooperative Collection Development
CCD	Cooperative Collection Development
CDAA	Canadian Dental Assistants' Association
CDS Method	Chisnell-Dunn-Sittig Method
CI	Capability Index (from Orr's Document Delivery Test) or Core Influence from Allen's journal ranking method.
CIF	Constructed Impact Factor
CINAHL	*Cumulative Index to Nursing and Allied Health Literature*
CISTI	Canada Institute for Scientific and Technical Information
CJA	Cost per Journal Article
CODES	Collection Development and Evaluation Section (of ALA's RUSA)
CONSER	Cooperative Online Serials Project
CSU	Colorado State University
CSULB	California State University at Long Beach
CUNY	City University of New York
DBMS	Database management system
DDC	Dewey Decimal Classification
DDT	Document Delivery Test
DENI	Department of Education for Northern Ireland
DIF	Discipline Impact Factor
EACR	Estimated Annual Citation Rate
e-book	electronic book
EBSCO	the Elton B. Stephens Company

e-collections	electronic collections
e-content	electronic content
E-Index	Excellence Index (for Australian public libraries)
e-journal	electronic journal
e-mail	electronic mail
e-print	electronic preprint or electronic print
e-resource	electronic resource
ERIC	Educational Resource Information Center
FAQ	Frequently Asked Questions
FE	further education (in the U.K.)
FSCS	Federal-State Cooperative System
FTE	full time equivalent
GMRLC	Greater Midwest Research Libraries Consortium
GNN	Global Network Navigator
HAPLR	Hennen's American Public Library Rating
HEFCE	Higher Education Funding Council for England
HEFCW	Higher Education Funding Council for Wales
HTML	Hyper Text Markup Language
IAC	Information Access Corporation
IAMSLIC	International Association of Aquatic and Marine Science Libraries and Information Centers
IAS	Individual Article Supply
ICAS CD	Interactive Collection Analysis System CD-ROM (from OCLC/WLN)
ICOLC	International Coalition of Library Consortia
IDEAL	International Digital Electronic Access Library
IFLA	International Federation of Library Associations and Institutions
ILL	Interlibrary loan
INSPEC	Information Services in Physics, Electronics, and Computers
IP	Internet Protocol
ISBN	International Standard Book Number
ISI	Institute for Scientific Information
ISSN	International Standard Serial Number or International Standard Serials Number
IVLS	Illinois Valley Library System

JCR	*Journal Citation Reports*
JISSI	*Journal of the International Society for Scientometrics and Informetrics*
JMU	James Madison University
JSTOR	Journal STORage
K	Kindergarten
LALINC	Louisiana Academic Library Information Network Consortium
LAMDA	London and Manchester Document Access
LC	Library of Congress
LIBER	*Ligue des Bibliothéques Européennes de Recherche*
LINCC	Library Information Network for Community Colleges (in Florida)
LIS	Library and information science
LLA	Louisiana Library Association
LMC	Library Media Center
LNS	Library of Natural Sciences (at the Russian Academy of Sciences)
LRC	Learning Resources Center
LSCA	Library Services and Construction Act
LSU	Louisiana State University
LSUMC-S	Louisiana State University Medical Center at Shreveport
MARC	Machine Readable Cataloging
MAS	*Magazine Articles Summaries* (from EBSCO)
MBA	Master of Business Administration
METRO	Metropolitan Reference and Research Organization (in New York)
MIS	Management Information Systems
MIT	Massachusetts Institute of Technology
MLA	Medical Library Association
MMU	Manchester Metropolitan University (in U.K.)
MSW	Master of Social Work
NAAB	National Architectural Accrediting Board
NAAL	Network of Alabama Academic Librarians
NASIG	North American Serials Interest Group
NCIP	North American Collections Inventory Project

NEA	National Education Association
NEERI	National Environmental Engineering Research Institute (in India)
NLM	National Library of Medicine
NMJC	New Mexico Junior College
NOTIS	Northwestern Online Total Integrated System
NSC	National Shelflist Count (now renamed the North American Title Count)
NSW	New South Wales
NTIS	National Technical Information Service
OAB	Outstanding Academic Books (from *Choice*)
OCLC	OCLC Online Computer Library Center
OLUC	Online Union Catalog (of OCLC)
OPAC	Online public access catalog
OSU	Ohio State University
PAD	Periodicals Analysis Database (developed at Wichita State University)
PCR	Primary Collecting Responsibility
PDF	Portable Document Format
PEAK	Pricing Electronic Access to Knowledge
PILLR	Prism Interlibrary Loan Reports (from OCLC)
POM	production and operations management
PSU	Pennsylvania State University
RILA	*Répertoire international de la littérature de l'art*
RLG	Research Libraries Group
RLIN	Research Libraries Information Network
RRL	Regional Research Laboratory (in Jorhat, India)
RUSA	Reference and User Services Association (of ALA)
S & T	Science and Technology
SAIS	Southern African Interlending Schemes
SALALM	Seminar on the Acquisition of Latin American Library Materials
SCI	*Science Citation Index*
SDI	Selective Dissemination of Information
SHEFC	Scottish Higher Education Funding Council
SIM	Simple Index Method (for identification of core journals)

SCOLMA	Standing Conference on Library Materials on Africa (U.K.)
SCONUL	Standing Conference of National and University Libraries (U.K.)
SCOUG	Southern California Online Users' Group
SLIS	School of Library and Information Science
SPEC	Systems and Procedures Exchange Center
SPIRES	Stanford Public Information Retrieval System
SSCI	*Social Sciences Citation Index*
STM	Science, Technology, and Medicine
SUNY	State University of New York
TAMU	Texas A & M University
TGA	The Genuine Article
TOC	table of contents
TTU	Texas Tech University
UAM	University of Agriculture Makurdi (in Nigeria)
UCLA	University of California at Los Angeles
UCRI	Usage/Cost Relational Index
UCSB	University of California at Santa Barbara
UI	University of Iowa
UIUC	University of Illinois at Urbana-Champaign
Ulrich's	*Ulrich's International Periodicals Directory*
UMI	University Microfilms International
UNH	University of New Hampshire
UOP	University of the Pacific
UT	University of Texas
UTK	University of Tennessee at Knoxville
WIU	Western Illinois University
WJ	Worth of Journal
WLN	Western Library Network
WPC	William Patterson College

1

Overviews of Evaluation

This chapter covers materials that introduce collection evaluation through discussion of its purpose, the process itself, the major approaches and techniques, and the published literature. Included are textbook chapters, introductory surveys, and bibliographical research. Note that previous bibliographical research relating to collection evaluation is reviewed, in essay format, in this book's introduction. The overview and survey literature typically cover such topics as:

- The purpose of collection evaluation

- Steps in the collection evaluation process

- Evaluation's role in collection development or collection management

- The techniques that can be used for collection evaluation

- The advantages and disadvantages of the available methods

- The application of collection evaluation methodology to a particular type of library or context

- Previously published literature concerning collection evaluation

The remainder of this chapter is organized into three sections: overviews and surveys, bibliographies, and literature reviews.

OVERVIEWS AND SURVEYS

Alire, Camila A. "Evaluation: 'Where's the Beef' in Collections?" In **Community College Reference Services: A Working Guide for and by Librarians,** edited by Bill Katz, 293–311. Metuchen, NJ: Scarecrow Press, 1992. ISBN 0-8108-2615-1.

Following introductory material, this chapter analyzes the applicability of five basic techniques to community college collection evaluation: list-checking, quantitative analysis, direct examination, standards, and use studies. A figure illustrates a planning cycle for collection evaluation. Drawing upon the work of Karen Krueger, Alire outlines a three-step collection evaluation process for community college libraries: data collection and analysis, data interpretation, and writing a plan for collection development.[1] In step one, the collection can, at the evaluating library's discretion, be divided into 20, 119, or 507 subject areas (the numbers are based upon the Conspectus). Data is then gathered on size of holdings, each subject's holdings as percentage of the total collection, availability, median age, subject distribution and median age of circulating items, and subject distribution of the previous year's acquisitions. This entry offers a praiseworthy overview of collection evaluation from a community college perspective.

Clayton, Peter, and Gary E. Gorman. "Collection Evaluation and Review." In **Managing Information Resources in Libraries: Collection Management in Theory and Practice,** 160–78. London: Library Association Publishing, 2001. ISBN 1-85604-297-9.

In this chapter the authors argue that accountability is an important reason for collection evaluation and that the perception of a library's performance is more important than the reality. Seven "essential steps" in implementing a collection evaluation are discussed: setting the objectives, reviewing earlier research, determining methodology and data to be collected, selecting a population sample, conducting a pilot study, data analysis, and facilitating replication. Clayton and Gorman state that user-centered approaches "are increasingly the methods of choice." Accordingly, they discuss in detail the pros and cons of use and user studies, document delivery tests, shelf availability tests, circulation studies, in-house use studies, and qualitative measures of user opinion. Observing that collection-centered methods can be used "in exceptional circumstances," the authors also cover *verification studies* (their term for the checklist method) and citation analysis. They conclude that the evaluation should focus on five "elements": size, utilization, access, age, and condition. Note that this fairly recent textbook is titled "Managing Information Resources," but only subtitled "Collection Management."

Dillon, Ken. "Collection Evaluation." In **Providing More with Less: Collection Management for School Libraries,** edited by Ken Dillon, James Henri, and Joy McGregor, 261–98. 2d ed. Wagga Wagga, Australia: Centre for Information Studies, Charles Sturt University, 2001. ISBN 0-949-060-99-2, and in *Collection Management for School Libraries,* edited by Joy McGregor, Ken Dillon, and James Henri, 245–80. North American ed. Lanham, MD: Scarecrow Press, 2003. ISBN 0-8108-4488-5.

This annotation is based on the Australian edition, which was published first. Dillon begins his chapter by emphasizing that collection analysis should be "planned, systematic, and continuous" instead of a "series of isolated, random events." Incorporating previously published literature, he lists numerous reasons why collection evaluation is important for school library collection management (e.g., assessing how the collection is supporting the school's educational goals). A bullet outline approach is used to list advantages and disadvantages of checking lists, direct examination/expert opinion, compiling statistics, standards, circulation studies, citation analysis, in-house use studies, and user surveys, all of which have "varying degrees of relevance" for school libraries. The author suggests that David V. Loertscher's collection mapping (see entry in next chapter) may be "the queen of methodologies" in a school library context. He then refutes such frequent criticisms of collection mapping as its time-consuming nature and focus on ownership at the expense of access. Dillon stresses that collection mapping should be preceded by curriculum mapping, which is the use of content analysis to systematically describe what is actually being taught, originally published by Fenwick English.[2] Although originally published in Australia, this entry has universal application to school library collection evaluation.

Dobson, Cynthia, Jeffrey D. Kushkowski, and Kristin H. Gerhard. "Collection Evaluation for Interdisciplinary Fields: A Comprehensive Approach." **Journal of Academic Librarianship** 22 (July 1996): 279–84.

This thoughtful essay addresses the problems of collection evaluation in interdisciplinary fields. Citing Michael Keresztesi, the authors observe that information resources vary during the three stages of an interdisciplinary field's development: "pioneering," "elaboration and proliferation," and "establishment."[3] Because of variation among interdisciplinary fields, one must consider a field's relationship to its parent discipline, the number of parent disciplines, and the interdisciplinary field's age. The authors propose a three-level model for interdisciplinary materials: interdisciplinary core resources; closely related, interdisciplinary resources; and related resources from traditional disciplines. Dobson, Kushkowski, and Gerhard contend that traditional evaluation methods do not work for interdisciplinary fields because the focus may be on a specific subject, scholars "may lack a broad understanding of the interdisciplinary field as a whole," reference resources may be unavailable for immature fields, and the Library of Congress (LC) classification ranges may be widely scattered. Thus, they recommend familiarity with both the interdisciplinary area itself and the local program, definition of the user group, use of the Internet and CD-ROMs to identify resources, and evaluation beyond the local holdings by investigation of existing cooperative collection development agreements and the library's ability to deliver unowned materials.

Doll, Carol A., and Pamela Petrick Barron. "Gathering and Analyzing Collection Data." In **Managing and Analyzing Your Collection: A Practical Guide for Small Libraries and School Media Centers,** 15–58. Chicago: American Library Association, 2002. ISBN 0-8389-0821-7.

This chapter, comprising almost half the book, offers both an overview of evaluation methods for school libraries and practical advice on implementing them. The authors explain use of simple, stratified, and systematic random sampling for cases in which data can not be extracted from an automated circulation or cataloging system. They then outline techniques for calculating the collection's subject dispersion by Dewey classes; its average age; the subject dispersion and average age of circulating materials; as well as for checking standard bibliographies, textbooks, or periodical indexes against the holdings. They discuss the ben-

efits of evaluating a "limited area." Step-by-step processes are outlined for calculating the cost of increasing the collection's average age (i.e., making it more current, and fulfilling unmet teacher requests). Finally, a section addresses evaluation
of information in different formats and reviews eight evaluative criteria (e.g., currency, depth of overage, authority, etc.). More than thirty bar graphs, pie charts,
spreadsheet print-outs, and forms are used for illustration. In summary, school
librarians would be well advised to consult Doll and Baron's excellent guide.

Evans, G. Edward. "Evaluation. " In **Developing Library and Information Center Collections,** 401–26. 3d ed. Englewood, CO: Libraries Unlimited, 1995.
ISBN 1-56308-183-0 (cloth); 1-56308-187-3 (paper).

Evans, G. Edward, with the assistance of Margaret R. Zarnosky. "Evaluation." In
Developing Library and Information Center Collections, 429–53. 4th ed.
Englewood, CO: Libraries Unlimited, 2000. ISBN 1-56308-706-5 (paper);
1-56308-832-0 (cloth).

These chapters from variant editions of the best-known collection development textbook are grouped together with the annotation based on the fourth edition. The chapter begins by noting the 1990s were the "decade of evaluation."
Twenty-nine reasons for collection evaluation are outlined, including internal
ones (for collection development and budgeting needs) and external reasons (to
meet local institutional plus extra-organizational needs). Most of the chapter is
devoted to a thoughtful and balanced discussion concerning the relative merits
of the major approaches to collection evaluation. Separate sections are devoted
to list checking, expert opinion, comparative use statistics, and collection standards (collection-centered techniques) as well as circulation studies, customer
perceptions, interlibrary loan (ILL) statistics, and citation studies (use-centered
methods). Several tables illustrate the OCLC/Amigos Collection Analysis CD,
while availability studies are mentioned. A brief section on electronic resources
forecasts "over time we will development as many, if not more, methods for
evaluating e-collections as we have for print-based collections." Appended is a
useful unannotated bibliography listing more than seventy items published from
1976 to 1999. Evans and Zarnosky offer a solid state-of-the-art overview of collection evaluation methodology at the end of the twentieth century.

Everhart, Nancy. "Collections." In **Evaluating the School Library Media Center: Analysis Techniques and Research Practices,** 91–117. Englewood, CO:
Libraries Unlimited, 1998. ISBN 1-56308-085-0.

This chapter from a school library evaluation textbook begins "the collection
is perhaps the most evaluated area of the entire program." About 20 percent of this
entry reproduces a document from the Maryland State Department of Education
concerning analyzing student, teacher/administrator, and parent information
needs; outlining key issues; and listing student records, informal conversations,
school and community publications, and surveys as sources. Nevada and Pennsylvania state standards on holdings size and expenditures are reprinted to assist
quantitative evaluation. Fourteen criteria for qualitative evaluation of individual

items (such as authority, appropriateness, and scope) are listed from the second edition of Phyllis J. Van Orden's book, *The Collection Program in Schools.* Drawing upon a North Carolina state document, Everhart has outlined content, organization, objectivity, scope, authenticity, appeal, format, construction, and uses as "points to consider" in evaluating audiovisual resources. She lists fifteen bibliographies that can serve as checklists and provides two sample questionnaires for surveying student and faculty opinion. In short, this chapter offers a helpful tool kit for evaluating school library media center collections.

Gabriel, Michael R. "Collection Evaluation." In **Collection Development and Collection Evaluation: A Sourcebook,** 77–137. Metuchen, NJ: Scarecrow Press, 1995. ISBN 0-8108-2877-4.

Explaining that he is drawing upon the "seminal" works of George Bonn, F. W. Lancaster, and Paul H. Mosher, the author reviews the collection evaluation literature and critiques some of the leading techniques.[4] Five major approaches outlined by Bonn (compiling statistics, list checking, obtaining user opinion, directly examining the collection, and applying standards) are discussed in detail. The pros and cons of citation analysis, the Conspectus, and correlating the curriculum with the holdings are also examined. An online public access catalog's (OPAC) potential role in collection evaluation is stressed: it tells whether an item is checked out; facilitates analysis by age, language, and format; and provides speedy keyword searching to determine the number of items supporting a particular course. Gabriel offers a reasonably balanced overview, but he relies too much on older resources.

Gorman, Gary E. "Collection Evaluation in Australian Theological Libraries." **Australian & New Zealand Theological Library Association Newsletter** no. 18 (December 1992): 3–17.

This article's focus is succinctly explained by the title. Following a discussion of problems associated with collection development policies in Australia, eleven specific reasons for collection evaluation are listed and four basic collection evaluation assumptions (for example, use is a measure of value) are critiqued. A considerable portion of this entry is devoted to problems of use studies: reported variations in use may really be variations in interpreting the word "use," demand rather than need is measured, and theological librarians may lack the training needed to implement them. Accordingly, Gorman recommends three collection-centered approaches for Australian theological librarians: list checking, collecting statistics, and direct examination of the collection. An overview is offered for each of these techniques while the advantages and disadvantages are listed in outline format. Gorman's analysis would be useful for readers beyond the ostensible audience of Australian theological librarians.

Gorman, Gary E., and J. Kennedy. "Methods of Collection Evaluation." In **Collection Development for Australian Libraries,** 161–72. 2d ed. Wagga Wagga, Australia: Centre for Information Studies, Charles Sturt University-Riverina, 1992. ISBN 0-949060-16-X.

This textbook chapter's purpose is to discuss "how collections can be evaluated." Eight questions that should be answered at the project's beginning are listed, such as, "what is the goal of the study?" Evaluation measures are classified into three categories: "user-oriented," "collection-oriented," and "non-quantifiable." The first category, according to Gorman and Kennedy, is based on the implicit assumption that use indicates value. Document delivery tests and studies of shelf availability, circulation, and in-house use are discussed as examples. Verification studies (an Australian term for the checklist approach) and "citation analysis," that is, using citations as a checklist, are discussed under the "collection-oriented" rubric. Here a "stimulus-response" approach to user need is assumed. Finally, they state nonquantifiable measures "rely on opinions rather than on counting" and examine user surveys. The benefits and drawbacks of each approach are analyzed, and in many instances, published studies from the literature are cited. The authors offer a beneficial survey of traditional collection evaluation methods from an Australian perspective.

Gorman, Gary E., and J. Kennedy. "Procedures for Collection Evaluation." In **Collection Development for Australian Libraries,** 127–38. 2d ed. Wagga Wagga, Australia: Centre for Information Studies, Charles Sturt University-Riverina, 1992. ISBN 0-949060-16-X.

The first half of this chapter provides an analysis of basic collection evaluation issues. Eleven aims of collection evaluation are listed in priority order with the caveat that understanding the collection's current state "underpins" all other aims. The authors offer some thought-provoking observations, asserting that whether a library service is actually any good is less significant than its being perceived as good and that ease of access is more important to users than the information's accuracy or currency. The second half outlines the "essential steps" in designing either a user-centered or collection-centered evaluation:

- Set purpose and objectives

- Review previous research

- Select data to be collected and methodology

- Select population sample

- Analyze data

- Facilitate replication

Several paragraphs are devoted to each stage of the procedure. Gorman and Kennedy note these steps "differ in no important respect from the requirements for any respectable piece of research."

Gorman, Gary E., and Ruth H. Miller. "Changing Collections, Changing Environments." In **International Yearbook of Library and Information Manage-**

ment **2000–2001: Collection Management,** edited by Gary E. Gorman, 309–38. London: Library Association Publishing, 2000. ISBN 1-85604-366-5.

Gorman and Miller begin with a perceptive review of traditional collection evaluation methods covering collection-centered approaches, the Conspectus, and user-centered methods. They then argue "a more flexible paradigm" is needed and discuss five "outcomes based" variables that impact evaluation "in the current environment": quantity, access, quality, appropriateness, and duplication. Next, they analyze how such phenomena as electronic journals, electronic books, full-text databases, and the Internet are influencing evaluation. For example, they ask how one can count holdings and use for mixed print-electronic resources and note the need for guides for evaluation of title coverage in full-text databases. Twelve evaluation criteria for Internet resources, including ease of use and relation to other resources, are listed with bullets. A substantial amount of literature is incorporated into this thoughtful essay. Advocating "rethinking evaluation methods," the authors cite Nitecki and Franklin's (see entry in chapter 6) assertion that service quality, user satisfaction, and the number of service interactions are "indicators of the library's impact." In summary, Gorman and Miller do an excellent job of pointing out the challenges of evaluation in the newly emerging electronic environment.

Gorman, Gary E., and Ruth H. Miller. "Collection Evaluation: New Measures for a New Environment." **Advances in Librarianship** 25 (2001): 67–96

Nearly 40 percent of this item, a follow-up to the preceding entry, addresses four factors that shape the current collection development environment: patron demand for remote access, aggregated databases, digitization, and e-books. The authors believe collection evaluation is still important because data is needed to support budgeting, to understand client needs, and to assist selection. However, traditional evaluation methods require substantial revision. Gorman and Miller argue that integrated automated system reports, citation data, and transaction log analysis from Web sites and databases are "new measures" that can identify users and their needs. The authors conclude that three questions must constantly be asked:

- What to measure

- How to measure it

- How to use the data

The final sentence of the essay reads, "It is essential that we devise new means of evaluating our collections while there is still a chance that such evaluation can have a positive impact on collecting activities." More than fifty other publications are cited in this perceptive essay.

Gottlieb, Jane, ed. **Collection Assessment in Music Libraries**. Canton, MA: Music Library Association, 1994. 93p. ISBN 0-914954-47-4.

This book is comprised of papers presented at a plenary session of the Music Library Association's 1991 annual meeting. In the introduction, Gottlieb observes that music collection evaluation is complicated by the multiple formats (scores, sound recordings, archival material, etc.) that must be assessed. Then Peggy Daub provides a detailed description of the Music Conspectus. Her informal survey of twenty-five (mostly) music librarians discovered that eleven considered the Music Conspectus "not very useful." Elizabeth Davis describes the development of Supplemental Guidelines for the Music Conspectus by the Metropolitan Reference and Research Organization (METRO) library consortium in New York (for further details see entry by Underwood in chapter 3). Next, Sherry L. Vellucci recounts the application of technology to music library collection evaluation, focusing primarily on the OCLC/Amigos Collection Analysis CD. Finally, Lenore Coral maintains that alternatives to the Conspectus are needed. While offering a variety of perspectives, this book is skewed toward collection-centered evaluation of music materials.

Hawks, Carol Pitts. "In Support of Collection Assessment: The Role of Automation in the Acquisitions and Serials Departments." **Journal of Library Administration** 17, no. 2 (1992): 13–30.

The author, now named Carol Pitts Diedrichs, reviews the use of automated serials and acquisitions products in collection assessment as of the early 1990s. She begins with a literature review focusing on expert systems and the Bibliographer's Workstation, developed at Southwest Missouri State University library. Hawks explains how the Ohio State University (OSU) library used *Books in Print (BIP) Plus* for approval plan evaluation. She also describes and analyzes the potential collection assessment applications of automated acquisitions systems, B & T (Baker and Taylor) Link, Blackwell North America's retrospective approval plan, OCLC Collection Analysis CD, and other products. This entry illustrates the serendipitous use of technology, that is, technology beyond its ostensible purpose such as when products designed to perform specific functions are also employed for evaluation, (but note that Hawks does not use the term "serendipitous"). The author does an excellent job of achieving her stated objectives.

Intner, Sheila S. "Objectifying Subjectivity." **Technicalities** 21 (January/February 2001): 3–7.

This entry, written in an informal, first-person style, focuses on how subjective collection evaluation decisions can be made more objectively. The author observes that collection-centered methods are "somewhat passé," but asserts that collection size is still "one of the best methods." She notes that the use method "fell out of favor" after the "infamous" Pittsburgh Study. In order to make meaningful quantitative comparisons among different size libraries, Intner recommends calculating the ratio of volumes held to the population served, the collection's size divided by the number of years of its existence to determine the average number of volumes acquired annually, and the proportion of the total library budget devoted to collections. Intner also states "I like...comparing the proportion of collections held in each subject area of interest to the library's user population with the proportion of the user population likely to want it." The importance of performance measures is emphasized so long as they are established before the data is gathered. This article admirably achieves its intended purpose.

Intner, Sheila S., and Elizabeth Futas. "Evaluating Public Library Collections: Why Do It, and How to Use the Results." **American Libraries** 25 (May 1994): 410–12.

Written by two well-known library and information science educators and once used in a collection development course pack at Indiana University's SLIS, this article contents "evaluation is the process of the '90s" due to the emphasis on accountability and the economic environment. The pros and cons of a "do-it-yourself" approach, using an outside consultant, or combining the former and latter are discussed. The authors explain that four factors should be considered before making any decisions based on evaluation data: the community, material use, shelf allocation, and user views. This is a short but useful justification for collection evaluation in public libraries.

Kachel, Debra E. **Collection Assessment and Management for School Libraries: Preparing for Cooperative Collection Development**. Westport, CT: Greenwood Press, 1997. 205p. ISBN 0-313-29853-X.

Authored by a practicing librarian, this is one of the relatively few books with a primary focus on collection evaluation. The first chapter describes a five-stage collection management process, consisting of needs assessment, collection assessment, selection, acquisition, and making the resources accessible. Note that on page 97, collection assessment is defined as "an organized process for systematically analyzing and describing a library's collection." Chapter 2 reviews specific techniques, such as calculation of collection size, growth rate, age, and subject breakdown plus items per pupil; visual inspection; circulation, in-house use, and ILL statistics; relative use by subject; and user surveys. The third chapter explains how the Conspectus approach can be adopted to school libraries, including a "quick list" of techniques to be used and a sample timetable for project completion. Chapter 4 addresses collection development policies, and chapter 5 explains cooperative collection development. The conclusion observes that assessment can help match the collection to the curriculum. About half the book is devoted to appendices, which include numerous collection assessment worksheets. There is a short but useful glossary of collection evaluation terminology. This entry provides both an assessment action plan and a synopsis of collection evaluation's overall role in school libraries.

Kelley, Shirley A. "A Comparison of Methods for Evaluating Curricular Support: Two Studies." **Christian Librarian** 39 (January 1996): 18–22.

In early 1995 Kelley sent a list of nine collection evaluation techniques to the directors of twenty-five small academic libraries in North Carolina (68 percent responded) asking whether the method was used in their library, and if so, for them to rate its effectiveness on a 1 (low) to 5 (high) scale. She found that surveying the faculty to determine the collection's adequacy was the most frequently employed method (used by 100 percent of respondents) and also deemed the most effective. She replicated her survey with a more diverse group of 30 librarians at an Association of Christian Librarians (ACL) conference workshop at Lakeland, Florida, in June 1995, using a modified list of eleven methods. In this second survey "direct contact with faculty" (one of the two methods added to the original list of nine) was discovered to be the most frequently used (by 93.3 percent) and was also rated as most effective. While not methodologically rigorous, this study is worth noting.

Lancaster, F. W. "Evaluation of the Collection: Formulae, Expert Judgment, and Bibliographic Checking." In **If You Want to Evaluate Your Library . . .**, 21–50. 2d ed. Champaign, IL: University of Illinois, Graduate School of Library and Information Science, 1993. ISBN 0-87845-091-2.

This excellent chapter focuses on three collection-centered evaluation methods: size and growth rate formulas, expert opinion, and the checklist method. Lancaster uses his own observations and detailed analysis of the literature to explain and, more frequently, point out the pitfalls of these approaches. For example, "books per capita," often used by public libraries, is termed "simplistic," and formulas, such as Clapp-Jordan, possibly suffer from imprecise definition of the term "volume." Growth rate is more validly measured by the number of volumes added than by percentages, although a collection's size may reach "saturation" whereby increases in acquisitions do not result in a proportionate increase in use. A presumed expert may be biased or unfamiliar with the subject's literature. Seven sources of checklists (standard lists, monographs, textbooks, indexing/abstracting tools, journals, faculty publications, and bibliographic searches) are analyzed while it is emphasized that variant results can be obtained from different lists. A brief final section addresses the use of overlap studies for comparing the collections of different libraries. The final paragraph comments that these techniques do not consider the collection's use.

MacEwan, Bonnie. "An Overview of Collection Assessment and Evaluation." In **Collection Management for the 1990s: Proceedings of the Midwest Collection Management and Development Institute, University of Illinois at Chicago, August 17–20, 1989,** edited by Joseph J. Branin, 95–104. Chicago: American Library Association, 1993. ISBN 0-8389-0608-7

This item was originally presented at one in a series of successful collection development institutes during the late 1980s/early 1990s. About two-thirds of the text is devoted to the National Shelflist Count (NSC) (note that this has been renamed the North American Title Count; see Grover in chapter 4 for a description and example of its use) and the Association of Research Libraries' (ARL) North American Collections Inventory Project (NCIP), based on the Conspectus. MacEwan observes that the Conspectus "can provide more information" than the NSC because it is both qualitative and quantitative while the latter is only quantitative. Interestingly, she notes that forty to seventy hours are required for a library to gather its NSC data. Short sections describe the OCLC/Amigos Collection Analysis CD, course and faculty research profiles, comparing holdings with *Books for College Libraries,* 3rd edition *(BCL3),* and use methods for public library assessment. An unannotated bibliography of approximately forty items, organized under seven headings, is appended.

MacEwan, Bonnie. "Report of the Amigos Special Workshop: The Reality of Collection Evaluation; Facts, Myths, and Practices." **Library Acquisitions: Practice & Theory** 16, no. 1 (1992): 51–55.

A two-day workshop in Dallas in 1991 sponsored by Amigos is summarized by one of the two main speakers. George Soete began by addressing managerial aspects of collection assessment. Next, MacEwan's synopsis of client-centered methods differentiated "use" and "user" studies and listed eight methods (interviews, citation analysis, etc.) for gathering information. MacEwan then turned to collection-centered methods, focusing on the benefits and drawbacks of the NSC. She also listed eight types of information (holdings size, age of collection, etc.) for assessing public library collections. In the final session, Soete discussed the Conspectus, which was being used in the NCIP. This report provides an overview of collection evaluation at the beginning of the 1990s.

Richards, Daniel T., and Dottie Eakin. "Collection Assessment." In **Collection Development and Assessment in Health Sciences Libraries,** 181–98. Vol. 4 of **Current Practices in Health Sciences Librarianship.** Lanham, MD: Medical Library Association and Scarecrow Press, 1997. ISBN 0-8108-3201-1.

This textbook chapter takes a concise but systematic summary of health science library collection assessment. A bullet approach is used to list sixteen reasons for assessment, nine steps in planning an assessment program, ten project focuses (i.e., subject, format, language, etc.), and eight steps in writing a report. Drawing upon Barbara Lockett's guide, the advantages and disadvantages of checking lists, expert review, circulation studies, user surveys, and citation studies are outlined.[5] A brief literature review about serials cancellation projects in health sciences libraries reveals that use and cost were the most frequent criteria. A long table outlines a generic serials review project plan, covering goals, project guidelines, and methodology. Then a major section addressing collection assessment to determine if the library can support new institutional programs explains the following three steps: understanding the program, understanding the field's literature, and identifying other available resources. In short, the authors make a commendable effort to explain fundamental collection evaluation concepts in the context of health sciences libraries.

Roy, Loriene. "Collection Evaluation as Research." **Journal of Youth Services in Libraries** 5 (spring 1992): 297–300.

After briefly reviewing some quantitative and subjective approaches to evaluating collections for youth, a library and information science (LIS) educator maintains that local library data on holdings and circulation can be used in evaluation research. For illustration, Roy cites four studies: Therese Bissen Bard and John E. Leide, who compared circulation and user characteristics in an elementary school library during five years; Kathleen Garland's analysis of circulation patterns in a public library and a school library media center during one academic year; Carol A. Doll, who examined overlap between the public and school library collections in four communities; and Mary Jo Detweiler's investigation of the correlation between collection size and circulation rate in 101 public libraries.[6] This entry's major contribution lies in its summary of four earlier studies.

Russell, Jill. "Collection Profiling." **SCONUL Newsletter** 16 (spring 1999): 26–30.

Drawing on the University of Birmingham's (in the United Kingdom) experience, the author provides an overview of "collection profiling." Information from the shelves, the OPAC, and other sources is used to create subject profiles based on the Conspectus worksheets. The purpose of profiling and staffing implications are discussed. Thirteen profiling criteria are outlined, including age of collection, size of holdings, balance, international coverage, use, ILL requests, and nonprint formats. The piece concludes with a brief discussion of nine "pertinent issues" regarding profiling, such as the required time, priority changes, price versus quality, teaching versus research, and access versus holdings. This entry provides a British perspective and uses the term "collection profiling" for what, as Russell notes, could otherwise be called "collection assessment" or "collection evaluation."

Van Fleet, Connie. "Evaluating Collections." In **Library Evaluation: A Casebook and Can-Do Guide,** edited by Danny P. Wallace and Connie Van Fleet, 117–28. Englewood, CO: Libraries Unlimited, 2001. ISBN 1-56308-862-2 (paper).

This chapter in a practitioner-oriented library evaluation guidebook offers an interesting taxonomy of collection evaluation techniques. They are organized into five categories according to their focus:

1. The "extent" of the collection by measuring size. Examples are holdings counts; ratios, such as volumes per capita; formulas, such as Clapp-Jordan; and the Conspectus.

2. "Efficiency" by measuring cost. Examples are ratios, such as expenditure per capita or weighted systems, such as the Hennen's American Public Library Rating (HAPLR) Index.

3. "Quality." The checklist method, citation analysis, and impressionistic judgment fall into this category.

4. "Performance" to measure achievement of goals. This approach is divided into three subcategories:

    a. Use measures, such as circulation, in-house use, aging studies, Web server logs, and weeding techniques

    b. User satisfaction, through surveys, interviews, and focus groups

    c. Availability, based on fill rates, response time, and ILL ratios

5. "Effectiveness" to analyze the relationship between performance and efficiency. Cost-benefit analysis is the main example.

Each technique is briefly described while the advantages and disadvantages of the major approaches are discussed. For appended case studies illustrating reference collection evaluation, list checking, and citation studies, respectively, see the entries by Kahn in chapter 4, Halliday in chapter 2, and Barkett in chapter 9.

Van Fleet offers a succinct summary of the available methods at the beginning of the twenty-first century.

Van Orden, Phyllis J. "Evaluating the Collection." In **The Collection Program in Schools: Concepts, Practices, and Information Sources,** 278–303. 2d ed. Englewood, CO: Libraries Unlimited, 1995. ISBN 1-56308-120-2 (cloth); 1-56308-334-5 (paper).

Van Orden, Phyllis J., and Kay Bishop with the assistance of Patricia Pawelak-Kort. "Evaluating the Collection." In **The Collection Program in Schools: Concepts, Practices, and Information Sources,** 275–98. 3d ed. Englewood, CO: Libraries Unlimited, 2001. ISBN 1-56308-980-7 (cloth); 1-56308-804-5 (paper).

This annotation is based on the third edition's chapter, which is not remarkably different from that in the second edition. A figure illustrates four evaluation process phases: problem identification, establishment of the methodology, data collection and interpretation, and reporting information. Van Orden and Bishop make a useful distinction between evaluation, "determining worth," and measurement, "identifying extent or quantity." Citing Baker and Lancaster, five evaluation barriers are discussed, including lack of staff time and lack of knowledge.[7] Most of the chapter is devoted to twelve specific evaluation methods organized into three broad categories: checking lists, direct examination, age analysis, comparative statistics, and standards under the heading "collection-centered measures;" circulation studies, in-house use studies, user surveys, shelf availability studies, and ILL statistical analysis under "use-centered measures;" plus citation studies and document delivery tests as "simulated-use studies." A separate section for each method lists advantages plus disadvantages and then discusses the technique's application to school library collection evaluation, drawing upon the published literature or apparently hypothetical examples. An excellent summary of the basic collection evaluation methods in the context of school libraries is offered here.

Zweck, Trevor. "Collection Evaluation for Theological Libraries: Planning and Implementation." **Australian & New Zealand Theological Library Association Newsletter** no. 28 (April 1996): 18–29.

Zweck's objective is "to take away some of the mystique surrounding collection evaluation." He proposes a collection evaluation plan for the Lohe Memorial Library (which serves the Luther Seminary, Luther School of Theology, and Luther Teachers College in North Adelaide, South Australia). Three methods would be used: a document delivery test; a verification study (his terminology for what is usually called the checklist method); and visual appraisal. Sections of the article are devoted to steps in implementing the process: population samples, that is determining which lists to check and documents to use in the document delivery test (DDT); data analysis; facilitating replication; and utilization of results. The item's most significant contribution is a fairly thorough literature review, from the theological library perspective, of the major collection evaluation approaches: document delivery tests, shelf availability tests, circulation studies, in-house use studies, verification studies (checklists), citation analysis, standards, and qualitative methods such as expert opinion. Zweck draws upon and complements earlier work by Gorman.

BIBLIOGRAPHIES

Allen, Barbara McFadden. "RLG and NCIP: A Brief Overview and Selected Bibliography." **Collection Building** 13, nos. 2–3 (1994): 11–12.

The Research Libraries Group (RLG) Conspectus and the North American Collections Inventory Project (in which, beginning in 1983, ARL libraries used the Conspectus to inventory their collections) are briefly introduced. Allen then provides an unannotated alphabetical list of fourteen articles, chapters, or books published between 1981 and 1992, which she describes as "outstanding documents" on the Conspectus and NCIP. This is a highly select bibliography.

Auer, Nicole. "Bibliography on Evaluating Internet Resources." **Emergency Librarian** 25 (May/June 1998): 23–24. Updated version available on the Web at http://www.lib.vt.edu/research/libinst/evalbiblio.html, accessed August 26, 2003.

Originating from a regional conference in Wisconsin, this unannotated bibliography emphasizes the teaching of Web evaluation skills. The print version, published in a periodical for school librarians, is organized into two major parts. The first list more than forty Web sites (all accessed by Auer during the late 1990s) and the second part lists more than forty print items, mostly articles published between 1995 to 1997. It also gives addresses for seven "useful listservs." The Web version, updated as of April 25, 2003, includes direct links to more than seventy documents on the Web and about a dozen sites created for teaching Web evaluation to high school and college students, as well as sample evaluation forms, humorous sites, and hoax sites. More than sixty print articles and books published during the 1990s are also listed. A major portion of these entries relate to content evaluation. Auer stresses that her bibliography is "by no means comprehensive."

Bauer, Kathleen. "Resources for Library Assessment: Tools for a New Era." **College & Research Libraries News** 62 (January 2001): 12–14, 28.

This Webliography lists (along with the URL) and annotates thirteen World Wide Web sites that contain information pertinent to library assessment. The sites are organized under six headings: Web analysis software; demographics; economic benchmarks; library benchmarks; measuring usage of electronic resources; and statistical resources, including statistical software. Particularly useful sites include the ARL Statistics and Measurement Program and the National Center for Education Statistics Library Statistics Program.[8] Bauer offers a useful introduction to Web-based resources that can assist in the evaluation of both print and electronic collections.

Gabriel, Michael R. "Comprehensive Bibliography on Collection Evaluation." In **Collection Development and Collection Evaluation: A Sourcebook,** 114–37. Metuchen, NJ: Scarecrow Press, 1995. ISBN 0-8108-2877-4.

Gabriel's unannotated bibliography lists in a single alphabetical sequence almost 350 English language items (mostly journal articles with a few books included) published between 1940 and 1991. Unfortunately, this bibliography is disappointing for a variety of reasons: there is no introduction defining the criteria for inclusion; it is not truly comprehensive; journals are sometimes listed by their abbreviation rather than full titles; and, in a few cases, the abbreviations are incorrect. Also, although published in 1995, the majority of entries date from the 1970s and 1980s with only a few from 1990 or 1991. On the positive side, this work may have some historical value because it cites a number of noteworthy items from the 1940s, 1950s, and 1960s.

Hérubel, Jean-Pierre V.M., and Anne L. Buchanan. "Citation Studies in the Humanities and Social Sciences: A Selective and Annotated Bibliography." **Collection Management** 18, nos. 3–4 (1994): 89–137.

In a brief introductory discussion, Hérubel and Buchanan observe that social science and humanities citation studies are more pertinent to collection development than those conducted for the sciences and technology. Then more than 210 English language articles, theses, dissertations, monographs, book chapters, and conference proceedings published between 1952 and 1991 are annotated in a single alphabetical sequence. Note that most of the entries are journal articles published during the 1970s or 1980s. A major portion of the items relate to collection development and/or collection evaluation issues, such as the age, format, or subject of items cited in various disciplines or journal evaluation. However, some of the covered topics, authorship gender and institutional affiliation for example, are not directly relevant to collection evaluation. The introduction notes that items focusing on mathematical and statistical procedures are beyond the bibliography's scope. The descriptive annotations are concise but informative. The authors successfully achieve their stated goal of providing a "useful and selective survey of citation analysis devoted to . . . the humanities and social sciences."

Nisonger, Thomas E. **Collection Evaluation in Academic Libraries: A Literature Guide and Annotated Bibliography.** Englewood, CO: Libraries Unlimited, 1992. 271p. ISBN 0-87287-925-9.

As noted in the introduction, the present volume is a sequel to this book. Six hundred seventeen English language items dealing with academic library collection evaluation are annotated here. The vast majority of entries, mostly published between 1980 and 1991, are journal articles, with a number of books, book chapters, and conference proceedings also covered. Among the twelve chapters, separate ones are devoted to methods and methodology, case studies, use studies, availability and document delivery tests, overlap studies, the Conspectus, citation studies, serials, journal ranking, and the application of automation to evaluation. There is a glossary as well as author-title and subject indexes. Because of the possibility of bias, praise for this work will be restrained.

Schoen, David M., and Suzette M. Hino. "Building Psychology Collections Using Core Journal Lists: An Annotated Bibliography." **Behavioral & Social Sciences Librarian** 17, no. 1 (1998): 55–61.

Schoen and Hino annotate approximately twenty English language articles, books, and book chapters published between 1986 and 1997 that identify core psychology journals. This short bibliography is organized into two sections: "core journal lists" (which are based on subjective judgment) and "citation analyses." Although ostensibly compiled to support collection building, this item could assist in the evaluation of psychology journal collections.

Seay, Jerry. "The Conspectus: A Selected Annotated Bibliography." **Acquisitions Librarian** no. 7 (1992): 177–89.

Nearly eighty items covering the Conspectus, mostly journal articles published between 1982 and 1990 are listed here. The bibliography is restricted to English language items published in the United States, Canada, Australia, and New Zealand, although, interestingly, the author states he identified "much" pertinent material in French and German. Only about twenty of the entries are annotated, so this bibliography's title is something of a misnomer. Seay implies that the unannotated entries were unavailable to him, but many of the unannotated entries are in readily available journals such as *College and Research Libraries*. The author also states that several of his annotations were directly taken, with permission, from *ERIC*. Although worth including because it lists the most important literature of the 1980s dealing with the Conspectus, this is a haphazardly done bibliography.

Strohl, Bonnie, comp. and ed. **Collection Evaluation Techniques: A Short, Selective, Practical, Current, Annotated Bibliography, 1990–1998,** sponsored by the Collection Evaluation Techniques Committee, Collection Development and Evaluation Section (CODES). Chicago, Reference and User Services Association, American Library Association, 1999. 30p. (RUSA Occasional Papers, no. 24). ISBN 0-8389-8019-8.

One hundred ten items listed in a single alphabetical sequence are annotated in this update to an earlier bibliography edited by Kaag.[9] While collection evaluation is broadly conceptualized, there is an emphasis on the application of techniques. Public and school libraries are covered, although inevitably a larger number of entries deal with academic libraries. The primary focus is on journal articles with a small number of books, conference proceedings, Ph.D. dissertations, and Web sites also included. Foreign language material and secondary reports of conferences are excluded. A short glossary defining ten terms and a subject index are appended. Prior to the publication of the volume in the reader's hands, this was the most current collection evaluation bibliography.

Whiteside, Ann. "Recent Publications on Collection Evaluation." **Art Documentation** 15, no. 1 (1996): 53–56.

Published under the aegis of the Art Libraries Society of North America (ARLIS/NA) Collection Development Committee, Whiteside's bibliography annotates more than thirty items published between 1990 and 1995. After a brief introduction, it is organized into three parts: articles, book chapters, and books. The bibliography is slanted toward academic libraries and emphasizes tools, methods, and budgeting, but only one item is exclusively devoted to art libraries. Some of the most important collection evaluation literature published during the first half of the 1990s is reviewed here.

LITERATURE REVIEWS

Altmann, Klaus G., and Gary E. Gorman. "Usage, Citation Analysis, and Costs as Indicators for Journal Deselection and Cancellation: A Selective Literature Review." **Australian Library Review** 13 (November 1996): 379–92.

As suggested by its title, this essay reviews the literature concerning the application of usage, citation, and cost data in serials cancellation decision. The primary focus is on academic libraries. Close to 100 items, mostly published during the 1980s and the first half of the 1990s (the earliest dates to 1974) are cited in the footnotes. The authors emphasize the methodological shortcomings of the various approaches, concluding that "no single indicator" is "infallible." Altmann and Gorman note that use is the "most important factor" employed by librarians in deselection and that journal price has variously been used as a ratio to the following: thousand words, thousand characters, *Journal Citation Reports (JCR)* "source items," impact factor, total citations, use, and the number of relevant articles. This entry offers a sophisticated synthesis of a fairly extensive literature.

Butkovich, Nancy J. "Use Studies: A Selective Review." **Library Resources & Technical Services** 40 (October 1996): 359–68.

Butkovich's review of use studies focuses on measurement methodology. Most of this entry is composed of seven sections devoted to the following: core lists and opinion surveys, reshelving studies, non-use studies, circulation, patron observation, citation studies, and ILL analysis. Each section explains various permutations of the approach, cites salient studies, and points out methodological issues. More than forty use studies published between 1975 and 1995 are incorporated into the review. This useful synthesis stresses that each technique has "strengths and weaknesses" and that different methods should be used in combination with each other because each measures different aspects of use.

Caswell, Thomas Reed. "Studies on Government Publications' Use, 1990–1996." **Government Information Quarterly** 14, no. 4 (1997): 363–71.

Caswell's literature review is a follow-up to earlier reviews of government document use by Terry L. Weech in 1971 plus Beth Postema and Weech in 1991.[10] Recapitulations of nine studies (three citation studies, two surveys of professional librarians regarding use, and four user studies) are interwoven into a textual narrative. All the studies focus on the United States and were written or co-authored by academic librarians. Whereas Postema and Weech found twenty-seven studies published during twelve years, Caswell notes a "severe decline" to nine between 1990 and 1996. Moreover, not a single study addressed the use of electronic government information. Caswell concludes by advocating a standardized methodology for future studies. The small number of items limits the utility of this review.

Medina, Sue O. "Duplication and Overlap Among Library Collections: A Chronological Review of the Literature." In **Advances in Collection Development and Resource Management,** vol. 1, edited by Thomas W. Leonhardt, 1–60. Greenwich, CT: JAI Press, 1995. ISBN 1-55938-213-9.

The author reviews 73 overlap studies published between 1906 and 1993. Note that an overlap study investigates the duplication rate among the holdings of a group of libraries. Medina calculates that 56 of the inquiries were conducted in the United States and 7 in Australia with the remainder in the United Kingdom, South Africa, Canada, and Germany, while 46 "primarily" involved academic libraries, 14 different types of libraries, 5 school and 3 public libraries. Detailed description of these studies is provided in chronological order of publication. An appended six-page table summarizes the findings from each investigation. The bibliographical researcher concludes that collection size, the holdings' age, and library type influence the overlap rate.

Nisonger, Thomas E. "Accessing Information: The Evaluation Research." **Collection Management** 26, no. 1 (2001): 1–23.

This article synthesizes the findings from approximately seventy-five items published during the 1990s concerning the evaluation of ILL and commercial document delivery performance. It is based on the first draft, completed in the fall of 2000, of chapter 11 in the book, *Evaluation of Library Collections, Access, and Electronic Resources*. Three tables tabulate specific results from the various studies concerning delivery time, fill rate, and cost per document accessed for both ILL and commercial document delivery. Separate sections analyze findings about the cost-effectiveness of access versus ownership, user satisfaction, and the percentage of requested items already held in the collection. Nisonger concludes, among other things, that commercial document delivery is both speedier and more expensive than traditional ILL and that access is more cost-effective for infrequently used titles contrasted to ownership for heavily used journals.

NOTES

1. Karen Krueger, *Coordinated Cooperative Collection Development for Illinois Libraries,* 2d ed, 3 vols. (Springfield: Illinois State Library, 1983).

2. Fenwick English, "Re-Tooling Curriculum with On-Going School Systems," *Educational Technology* 19, no. 5 (1979): 7–13.

3. Michael Keresztesi, "The Science of Bibliography: Theoretical Implications for Bibliographic Instruction," in *Theories of Bibliographic Education,* edited by Cerise Oberman and Katina Strauch (New York: R. R. Bowker, 1982), 13–21.

4. George Bonn, "Evaluation of the Collection," *Library Trends* 22 (January 1974): 265–304; F. W. Lancaster, *The Measurement and Evaluation of Library Services* (Washington, D.C.: Information Resources Press, 1977); Paul H. Mosher, "Collection Evaluation or Analysis: Matching Library Acquisitions to Library Needs," in *Collection Development in Libraries: A Treatise,* pt. B, edited by Robert D. Stueart and George B. Miller, Jr. (Greenwich, CT: JAI Press, 1980), 527–45.

5. Barbara Lockett, ed., *Guide to the Evaluation of Library Collections* (Chicago: American Library Association, 1989).

6. Therese Bissen Bard and John E. Leide, "Library Books Selected by Elementary School Students in Hawaii As Indicated by School Library Circulation Records," *Library & Information Science Research* 7 (April/June 1985): 115–43; Kathleen Garland, "Chil-

dren's Materials in the Public Library and the School Library Media Center in the Same Community: A Comparative Study of Use," *Library Quarterly* 59 (October 1989): 326–38; Carol A. Doll, "A Study of Overlap and Duplication Among Children's Collections in Selected Public and Elementary School Libraries," *Library Quarterly* 54 (July 1984): 277–89; Mary Jo Detweiler, "The 'Best Size' Public Library," *Library Journal* 111 (May 15, 1986): 34–35.

7. Sharon L. Baker and F. W. Lancaster, *The Measurement and Evaluation of Library Services,* 2d ed. (Arlington, VA: Information Resources Press, 1991).

8. Association of Research Libraries, *ARL Statistics and Measurement Program.* Available: http://www.arl.org/stats/ (accessed August 26, 2003); National Center for Education Statistics, *Survey and Program Areas.* Available: http://nces.ed.gov/surveys (accessed August 26, 2003).

9. Cynthia Stewart Kaag et al., *Collection Evaluation Techniques: A Short, Selective, Practical, Current Annotated Bibliography 1980–1990* (Chicago: Reference and Adult Services Division, American Library Association, 1991).

10. Terry L. Weech, "The Use of Government Publications: A Selected Review of the Literature," *Government Publications Review* 5, no. 2 (1978): 177–84; Beth Postema and Terry L. Weech, "The Use of Government Publications: A Twelve Year Perspective," *Government Publications Review* 18 (May/June 1991): 223–38.

2

Collection-Centered Approaches to Traditional Collection Evaluation

As noted in this volume's introduction, collection evaluation methods have been traditionally classified as collection-centered or client-centered. This chapter annotates items that take a primarily collection-centered approach. Well-known collection-centered techniques include the checklist method (in which a list of presumably high-quality items is checked against a library's holdings), compilation of holdings data, comparative holdings among libraries, calculation of the collection's average age, and the Conspectus—arguably the most frequently used collection-centered method of the last decade.

The earliest recorded instance of collection evaluation in a North American library utilized the checklist method. Charles Coffin Jewett checked the citations in a number of leading ethnography, chemistry, international law, and commerce textbooks of the mid-nineteenth century to reach his conclusion that the Smithsonian and other leading U.S. libraries fell short of their European counterparts.[1] Paul H. Mosher indicates that the checklist approach was used in a major collection evaluation project at the University of Chicago during the 1930s when over 200 bibliographies were checked.[2] In subsequent decades, numerous evaluations using the checklist technique were reported in the literature. Availability studies and document delivery tests may be viewed as sophisticated versions of the checklist method because each item sought on the shelf or for document delivery is analogous to a checklist entry. Also, checklists have been used in Conspectus "verification studies."

"Overlap studies" comprise a distinct type of collection-centered evaluation methods. These studies compare the holdings of a group of libraries, often in a geographical area or consortium, to analyze "overlap," (titles held by two or more libraries) and "uniqueness," (titles held by only one library in the group). Most overlap studies focus on books, but a few have addressed serials. These studies have been conducted, among several reasons, to investigate opportunities for cooperative collection development (CCD), as a high rate of overlapping titles might suggest the participating libraries are needlessly duplicating each others collecting efforts, and to identify the core (i.e., high overlap titles held by multiple institutions). Medina (see entry in chapter 1) reports that 73 overlap studies were published between 1906 and 1993. The number of published overlap studies declined during the last decade, presumably because of an increasing interest in client-centered approaches, access, and electronic resources.

The OCLC/Amigos Collection Analysis CD may be viewed as an elaboration of the overlap approach. This product was jointly developed during the 1980s by OCLC and the Amigos Bibliographical Council as a collection-centered approach to evaluation of monographic holdings. The system used software to analyze a CD-ROM database containing ten years of OCLC monographic records (initially totaling about 1.8 million) for more than one thousand academic libraries. Each year a new CD-ROM was issued, containing an updated ten years of records. In essence, the system compared a library's holdings with those of peer group member. The libraries were organized into fourteen peer groups based on size and admissions standards, but evaluating libraries could also create their own peer groups. Data was gathered for the total collection as well as 32 broad and 500 specific segments of the Library of Congress Classification System. The Collection Analysis compact disc (CACD) produced numerous statistical reports, including holding counts and size of holdings compared to the average peer group member. It also generated bibliographies listing "gap" titles (held by peer institutions but not the evaluating library), "unique" titles held by a single library, and "overlap" titles held in common by several libraries plus books owned by the evaluating institution. Note that this description is based, to a significant extent, on direct examination of the OCLC/Amigos CACD database created in June 1989, covering 1977–87. The system was frequently used during the 1990s, but discontinued toward the end of the decade.

Following this introduction, chapter 2 is organized into three sections covering the following: collection-centered approaches in general, overlap studies, and the OCLC/Amigos Collection Analysis CD. Items addressing the use of the OCLC/Amigos Collection Analysis CD to evaluate a specific library or consortium collections are included in this chapter while articles that depict its use to analyze national collecting patterns are annotated in chapter 5. The Conspectus, arguably the best-known collection-centered methodology, is dealt with in chapter 3. Studies that combine collection-centered and client-centered methodologies are included in chapter 4.

COLLECTION-CENTERED APPROACHES

Bergen, Phillip L., and Delores Nemec. "An Assessment of Collections at the University of Wisconsin–Madison Health Sciences Libraries: Drug Resistance." **Bulletin of the Medical Library Association** 87 (January 1999): 37–42.

This item reports an in-depth collection evaluation of drug resistance (an increasingly important medical topic as germs build resistance to antibiotics) completed in December 1997 by the University of Wisconsin at Madison Health Science Libraries. The primary emphasis falls on four steps, adapted from traditional approaches, used in the project:

- The OPAC was searched to count the relevant holdings published between 1993 and 1997

- The Big Ten universities, the University of Chicago, the University of California at San Francisco, and the National Library of Medicine (NLM) were identified as benchmark libraries for comparison purposes

- Thirty-eight books held by at least two benchmark libraries, determined by checking their OPACs, were considered a standard list

- Sittig's method (see entry in chapter 7) was used to identify thirty core serials

The authors found their library held 63.2 percent of the standard monographs and 86.7 percent of the core serials while their 156 total holdings (in all formats) were twice the average peer size and nearly as strong as the NLM.[3] Bergen and Nemec conclude by outlining a six-step collection evaluation process that adds client-centered techniques (analysis of ILL/document delivery and circulation data plus user surveys) to their methodology.

Bhola, Lalitendu K., and Sanjay Mishra. "Dependency Quotient: A Tool for Collection Evaluation." **Herald of Library Science** 34, nos. 1–2 (January/April 1995): 62–65.

Published in an Indian library science journal, this entry introduces a formula, termed the "dependency quotient," for evaluating the collection's strength in a particular subject. First, "matter strength" is calculated by assigning one point for each title held in the area. "Material strength" considers multiple copies with the first valued at 1, the second 0.5, the third 0.25, and so on, so three copies equal a 1.75 score. "Matter strength" and "material strength" are added and divided by 100 to derive the "dependency quotient." Bhola and Mishra claim "this method could be of great help for comparative evaluation of library collection[s] in a subject." Although possibly applicable to small collections, there is no evidence this measure has been applied in North American libraries.

Carpenter, Kathryn Hammell. "Evaluating Library Resources for Accreditation: Results of a Study." **Bulletin of the Medical Library Association** 80 (April 1992): 131–39.

A self-study evaluation, conducted in 1990 by the University of Illinois at Chicago's Health Sciences Library for accreditation by the National League for Nursing, is described by Carpenter. About half the article is devoted to an evaluation of the collection's "scope" (defined as the range of subjects collected) and "coverage," that is, "the extent to which each subject is acquired" on the program's three sites. The checklist method revealed that the Chicago site, housing the research collection, held from 76.47 percent to 96.21 percent of the items on ten book lists, 58.81 percent and 92.44 percent of two periodical lists, but less than 3 percent of the items on two audiovisual lists. The percentages for the Peoria and Urbana sites were smaller because they are not primarily research collections. Holdings data for selected Conspectus categories found that all sites held 4,558 retrospective monographs compared to 9,581 by the NLM. The *Annual Statistics of Medical School Libraries in the United States and Canada* provided comparative data on volumes held, volumes added, current periodical subscriptions, and expenditures. The collection was concluded to be "research-level." About half this article is devoted to collection development organization, liaison work, fund allocation, selection criteria, user services, and so on, thus informing the reader that the nursing accreditation process focuses on more than the collection itself.

Coe, D. Whitney. "Global Perspectives: Evaluating Collections at Seoul National University Library, Part 1." **Technicalities** 15 (April 1995): 1,13; "Global Perspectives: Evaluating Collections at Seoul National University Library, Part 2—Collections and Colleagues." **Technicalities** 15 (June 1995): 1, 12–13.

Writing in an informal, first-person style, Coe, a Princeton University Anglo-American bibliographer, relates his experience during the 1993–94 academic year visiting the Seoul National University library and evaluating its Western language social sciences and humanities collection. The following techniques were applied: comparing serial subscriptions with a list developed at the Princeton University libraries, using direct shelf examination, statistically profiling collection growth, and comparing title counts with *BCL3*, the Tokyo National University library, and selected North American ARL libraries. After finding many older titles, Coe concluded, "The collection had suffered from...minimal budgets, random acquisitions via gifts and exchange, the vagaries of faculty selection and lack of systematic collecting policies." The library itself and the collection's history are among the other topics described here. Even though more detail could have been provided, this two-part item serves as an interesting example of international collection evaluation activity by an American specialist.

Dennison, Russell F. "Quality Assessment of Collection Development Through Tiered Checklists: Can You Prove You Are a Good Collection Developer?" **Collection Building** 19, no. 1 (2000): 24–26.

Drawing upon Winona State University library's experience, Dennison explains the use of tiered checklists, predicated on the assumption that higher tier entries are more valuable than those in lower tiers. The author states that any three lists of presumed equal value can be combined to create three tiers of items: those on all three lists, two lists, or one list only. Alternatively, lists may already be organized into tiers. For example, Winona State owned 68.1 percent of the "essential," 46.0 percent of the "highly recommended," 37.5 percent of the "recommended," and 32.1 percent of the "listed" books in *Library Recommendations for Undergraduate Mathematics*.[4] Similar holdings data is presented for mathematics journals from the above source and nursing journals based on combining a two-tiered list with a nontiered list. Because the percentage differences among the tiers were statistically significant for mathematics books and nursing journals, the author concludes Winona State selected the best quality material. Although not related to the tiered approach, Winona State, during the summer of 1989, owned 38.9 percent of the books in *BCL3*. In summary, an important variation on the checklist approach is described here.

Doll, Carol A. "Quality and Elementary School Library Media Collections." **School Library Media Quarterly** 25 (winter 1997): 95–102.

This article by an LIS educator focuses on average collection age as an evaluation technique for elementary school library collections. The necessary data are obtained by calculating the mean copyright date for a randomly selected sample of the holdings. Using data for thirty-five libraries from several previously published studies from 1980 through 1995, Doll consistently found an average collection age of approximately twenty years. She also discovered that the average age of recommended items in the current *Children's Catalog* was eleven years and nine years in the *Elementary School Library Collection;* weeding guides recommend considering for removal titles five to ten years old; and that in standard bibliographies fiction is older than nonfiction, but in library collections nonfiction is older. Doll suggests careful attention to collection age in recently revised curriculum areas. She concludes children's collections are probably "too old." Three tables and an appendix concisely summarize the data on collection age. This item represents well-done research of value to elementary school librarians.

Flaherty, Brian. "Assessing Legal Collections: Trying to Eke Out a Method from the Madness." **Against the Grain** 14 (February 2002): 66–68, 70.

The methodology used in an ongoing collection evaluation project at the Suffolk University Law Library (in Boston) is recounted in this witty piece. Each librarian was assigned to evaluate the collection in a specific area and numerous general and specialized bibliographies were checked against the catalog. A major portion of the article describes the use of *EndNote* bibliographic software to access OCLC's WorldCat to compare Suffolk University's holdings in specific subjects with those of another library—in this instance an institution facetiously called Joe Schlabotnik University. Flaherty acknowledges his library's approach focuses on print resources and that a "systematic" method for evaluation of electronic resources is needed. Nevertheless, this item is significant because it illustrates how modern technology can support a traditional collection evaluation technique.

Graham, Rata. **Collection Profile, Acquisitions, Budget Manual**. North Shore City, New Zealand: North Shore Libraries, 1992. 327p. ISBN 0-9597936-6-6.

This manual, developed from Graham's Conspectus training experience in the Auckland vicinity, provides a framework for data gathering to support collection management and evaluation in public libraries. Most of Graham's manual is devoted to worksheets that are organized by broad subject categories and subdivided according to the Dewey Decimal System. They are used to tabulate holdings size and median age for adult, young adult/juvenile (the term "junior" is used), and reference materials. Each subject division also has worksheets for serials. Separate sections contain worksheets dealing with large print, adult fiction, young adult fiction, juvenile fiction, and budget reconciliation. Although intended for use by New Zealand public librarians, this item is occasionally cited in the North American assessment literature.

Griffin, Patricia S. "Faculty Surveys of Collections, Roanoke Bible College, May-September 1995." **Christian Librarian** 39 (January 1996): 25–27, 30.

During the summer of 1995, twelve faculty members at Roanoke Bible College evaluated the library holdings supporting 66 courses by applying a 0 to 3 scale (0 = not applicable, 1 = more than adequate, 2 = adequate, and 3 = inadequate) to each of five areas: bibliographic resources, reference works, books, periodicals, and audiovisual materials. The faculty were given forms (examples of which are shown) with Dewey Decimal numbers and subject headings on which to enter their ratings and suggest new resources for inadequate areas. While many evaluation studies solicit faculty input, this case is noteworthy in that the faculty actually conducted the evaluation itself.

Halliday, Blane. "Identifying Library Policy Issues with List Checking." In **Library Evaluation: A Casebook and Can-Do Guide,** edited by Danny P. Wallace and Connie Van Fleet, 140–52. Englewood, CO: Libraries Unlimited, 2001. ISBN 1-56308-862-2 (paper).

A practical application of the checklist approach is demonstrated in this case study from a recent library evaluation text. Halliday begins by listing six steps typically used in implementing this method:

1. Identification of an area for evaluation

2. Selection of appropriate lists

3. Definition of terms (i.e., what constitutes holding an item)

4. Checking lists against holdings

5. Analysis of results for trends

6. Decision-making

The popular music recording section at an unidentified "major urban public library" was evaluated by checking, during June through October 1998, sections from three standard discographies (including *A Basic Music Library*) and samples from the *Billboard* 200 bestselling album charts.[5] Altogether more than 1,500 items were checked. Several tables analyze the library holdings by decade (the 1950s though the 1990s) and by genre (rock as well as rhythm and blues). Not counting missing items, the percentage of titles held was 33, 31, and 42 for the discographies and 89 for the bestseller list. Halliday detected a bias toward collecting current titles without regard to long-term artistic merit. This entry does a good job of illustrating one of the oldest collection evaluation approaches.

Leng, Yeap Lay. "The Development of the Book Collection is Not Well Planned: Practising Collection Evaluation." **Singapore Libraries** 24 (1995): 20–31.

Writing for a Singapore audience, the author observes that a school library collection can be qualitatively evaluated through questionnaires, interviews, or comparison with the holdings of the Singapore National Library. However, Leng advocates a quantitative approach termed "collection review," which she illustrates for School X in mathematics. Numerous tables, graphs, and charts present evaluative data for School X, including: total holdings; mathematics books as a percentage of total holdings, nonfiction, and science books; the balance among mathematics subareas such as geometry, fractions, and so on; mathematics books added per year; circulation statistics; and comparative data with School Y. The author stresses that "systematic" collection evaluation is vital for "well-planned" collection development. Offering a complex approach, Leng concludes that using a simple pupil to book ratio for collection evaluation is a "trap" that can conceal "serious inadequacy" in specific subjects.

Loertscher, David V. **Collection Mapping in the LMC: Building Access in a World of Technology.** San Jose, CA: Hi Willow Research and Publishing, 1996. 104p. ISBN 0-931510-58-9.

Loertscher's collection mapping technique, first published in 1986, is probably the best-known collection evaluation method for school libraries and has even been used in academic libraries.[6] In the original approach, a collection is mapped by calculating the items held to pupils ratio for the basic collection, "general emphasis areas" corresponding to courses such as U.S. history, and "specific emphasis areas" corresponding to course units such as the Civil War. This book offers guidance on collection mapping to school library media specialists and updates the approach by addressing the question of access. Three types of access are introduced:

- "Instant access" "at elbow's length"

- "Access nearby" at the Library Media Center (LMC)

- "Referral to" for items obtained in ILL from other libraries

There are chapters on data gathering, drawing a map, and creating a collection map as well as on such collection development issues as budgeting, acquisitions, and policy making. Note that an accompanying computer disk contains practice files and templates to assist the evaluation process. In summary, a national expert has written an important book explaining a major school library collection evaluation method.

Morrison, Carol, et al. "School Library Snapshots: A Brief Survey of Illinois School Library Collections in Three Areas of Science." **Illinois Libraries** 76 (fall 1994): 211–19. Also published in **School Library Media Annual**, vol. 12, edited by Carol Collier Kuhlthau, 207–27. Englewood, CO: Libraries Unlimited, 1994. ISBN 1-56308-317-5. ISSN 0739-7712.

This research project, reported in both sources cited above, profiles the holdings of Illinois K-12 school library collections in three scientific areas: astronomy, biology/ecology, and human anatomy/physiology. The investigation is based on an early 1990s survey of 800 Illinois School Library Media Association members, to which 409 responded. More than thirty tables or bar graphs tabulate the results, which include expenditure data and holdings by format, level of school, subject, and age. Perhaps the most noteworthy finding is the fact that during 1991–92 nearly two-thirds of Illinois school libraries could not afford to buy one book per student. The authors conclude "the majority of school libraries in Illinois have woefully inadequate book collections in three vital areas of science education," while noting many books are outdated or inaccurate. They attribute the problem to "lack of money." A somewhat negative picture is depicted of school library collections in a state often perceived as progressive in librarianship.

Rao, Sushella N. "Meeting Modern Demands of Collection Evaluation: A New Approach." **Collection Building** 13, no. 1 (1993): 33–36.

Rao writes about the methodology used at the University of Wisconsin at Oshkosh to evaluate the collection supporting a newly introduced statistics program. The size of the holdings (based on checking appropriate subject headings in the catalog) in nine topical areas of statistics were calculated and compared to those of other institutions with similar programs. To track collection growth, the number of books published since 1980 and 1985, respectively, was counted for the nine areas. Then, to ascertain the collection's currency, the percentage of titles listed in *Books in Print (BIP)* was calculated for samples of the holdings in six subject areas. Core lists were checked, but the results were not reported. Three tables summarize the findings, of which the most noteworthy table compares the nine statistical topics' holdings size at the University of Wisconsin at Oshkosh with those of the University of Wisconsin at Green Bay. This entry is worth mentioning because of its methodology. However, the article appears hastily prepared as table 2 contains a glaring mathematical error.

Senkevitch, Judith J., and James H. Sweetland. "Evaluating Public Library Adult Fiction: Can We Define a Core Collection?" **RQ** 36 (fall 1996): 103–17.

Seeking to investigate whether OCLC holdings data can identify an adult fiction core list for public libraries, the 406 adult fiction titles most frequently held by public libraries in OCLC in August 1994 were checked against nine major lists, including *Fiction Catalog, Best Books for Public Libraries,* and the *Publishers Weekly* bestsellers list. None of the 406 appeared in eight or nine sources and only one was listed in seven. Of the nine lists, only the *Fiction Catalog* contained a "large majority," (i.e., 370 of the 406 titles) suggesting it might "be useful in evaluating a fiction collection." Bar graphs illustrate the findings and reveal 96 percent of the titles were published in 1980 or later. Senkevitch and Sweetland acknowledge their approach tells nothing about actual use in libraries. An appendix supplies bibliographic citations for the nine sources searched and another appendix lists the top 99 adult fiction titles by holdings in OCLC. The authors conclude, "It is not yet clear to what extent the list of widely held titles may be useful as an evaluation tool." See the next entry for additional research.

Senkevitch, Judith J., and James H. Sweetland. "Public Libraries and Adult Fiction: Another Look at a Core List of 'Classics.'" **Library Resources & Technical Services** 42 (April 1998): 102–12.

As a follow up to their previous research (see the previous entry), the authors test the year-to-year stability, that is, consistency, of the 400 adult fiction titles most frequently held in OCLC by public libraries. Consistency would indicate validity as a potential evaluation tool, while low stability would have the opposite implication. A list of the 409 most frequently held titles, compiled in August 1995 (when 4,700 public libraries, representing 43 percent of the U.S. total, participated in OCLC) was compared with the list of 400 titles generated in August 1994. The authors discovered that 13 titles dropped from the 1994 list and 16 titles were added to the 1995 list for an overall change of approximately 3.2 percent. The average title dropped 24 ranking positions from 1994 to 1995 while the largest decline was 96 positions and the largest increase 107 positions. A table, listing in rank order the thirty most frequently held adult fiction titles in 1995, indicates the top title was held by 1,090 libraries. Because the list is "relatively stable over time" (a complete turnover would take an estimated thirty years), Senkevitch and Sweetland conclude it is "suitable for public library collection evaluation"—presumably as a checklist. This is an especially well-done piece of research.

Sweetland, James H. and Peter G. Christensen. "Developing Language and Literature Collections in Academic Libraries: A Survey." **Journal of Academic Librarianship** 23 (March 1997): 119–25.

This research articles investigates two separate but related issues regarding Wisconsin academic library collections: selection practices for language and literature and holdings of *Choice's* "Outstanding Academic Books" (OAB). A spring 1995 survey of 33 libraries, resulting in a 67 percent usable response rate, revealed that the medium expenditure for language and literature books was 5 percent of the materials budget even though the area produced 18.6 percent of the academic titles published in North America. Curricular relevance and faculty requests were the two most frequent reasons for selection (which was primarily English titles), while only four responding libraries used approval plans. Next, the holdings by all Wisconsin academic libraries of 85 *Choice* 1993 *Outstanding Academic Books* (OAB) books were checked in OCLC and the Wisconsin Union Catalog in March 1995. The number of libraries holding each title ranged from 4 to 23 with the average at 10. Further analysis of OAB data found a delay in adding books to collections, which Sweetland and Christensen attribute to reliance on faculty recommendations. The authors pessimistically conclude that Wisconsin academic libraries collect to support teaching but not research.

Sweetland, James H., and Judith J. Senkevitch. "Evaluating Public Library Fiction Collections: Is There a Core List of Classics?" **Annual Review of OCLC Research 1994** (Dublin, OH: OCLC, 1995): 59–61.

This brief item introduces the authors' then ongoing research project concerning the application of OCLC holdings data to the evaluation of adult fiction collections in public libraries that led to their articles in *RQ* in 1996 and *Library Resources and Technical Services* in 1998 (see entries by Senkevitch and Sweetland). They initially identified 498 fiction titles held by the largest number of 1,400 public libraries, but the total was pared to 407 after manual checking eliminated children's and young adult books. Checking these titles against lists of recommended books found that the *Fiction Catalog* contained 91 percent and *Best Books for Public Libraries* contained 98.8 percent, thus implying some recommended lists predict which books public libraries will buy. However, only 2 of 407 titles were on four or more lists. Sweetland and Senkevitch conclude that additional research is required before an evaluation tool can be developed.

Twiss, Thomas M. "A Validation of Brief Tests of Collection Strength." **Collection Management** 25, no. 3 (2001): 23–37.
    This study investigates the validity of White's "brief test" methodology (see the following entry for an explanation). The test was implemented twice in Soviet history in five libraries: the University of Pennsylvania, the University of Virginia, Temple University, the Free Library of Philadelphia, and the Jefferson-Madison Regional Library in Charlottesville, Virginia. The results of the two tests were compared with each other, with a previous test in one of the libraries, and with librarian evaluations of their own collections. As expected, the three academic libraries scored higher than the two public libraries. The researcher reports spending twenty hours, but states a brief test in a single library could be done in less than ten hours. Using four criteria of validity suggested by White (intelligible results, sensible results, consistent results, and correspondence with librarians' own evaluations) Twiss concludes that his study offers "strong evidence" of the methodology's validity.

White, Howard D. **Brief Tests of Collection Strength: A Methodology for All Types of Libraries.** Westport, CT: Greenwood Press, 1995. 191p. ISBN 0-313-29753-3.
    One of the nation's top information science scholars introduces a quick and efficient evaluation method termed a "brief test," which is tied to Conspectus collection levels and OCLC holdings counts. Bibliographies of 40, 80, or 120 books (he experimented with different numbers) were developed for use as checklists and organized into four collecting levels of ten, twenty, or thirty titles each:

- Minimal level, comprised of books held by 751 or more libraries in the OCLC database

- Basic levels, made up of books held by 401–750 libraries

- Instruction level, composed of books held by 151–400 libraries

- Research level, containing books held by 1–150 libraries.

The evaluating library's collection is assumed to be capable of supporting all levels for which it contains half the titles. The technique was tested 268 times in 76 subjects by the author's Drexel University students and in eight subjects, such as American history, French literature, and genetics, by the Bryn Mawr, Haverford, and Swarthmore College libraries. This research monograph is organized into three parts covering the methodology, the results, and OCLC holdings counts with major attention given to those for titles used in the test samples. Although ostensibly associated with Conspectus verification studies, White's "brief test" can stand on its own as a collection evaluation tool. The researcher offers both a major scholarly work and a practical tool for librarians.

Womboh, Benki S. H. "Collection Evaluation in Africa: A Case Study of a University Library." **Collection Management** 17, no. 4 (1993): 79–94.

This entry reports an evaluation of the University of Agriculture Makurdi (UAM) library's ability to support its newly decreed (by the Nigerian "military government") mission emphasizing agricultural research. A significant portion of the article is devoted to the organization and interesting history of UAM. The study is structured around a ten-question survey (reproduced in an appendix) sent to all forty faculty members, of which 50 percent responded. The author found that 95 percent of the responding faculty felt that the library could not "effectively support" the new program. Asked whether the collection could support their subject area, 35 percent responded "to a large extent," 45 percent "to a small extent," and 20 percent "the least effect." Womboh discovered the library could support the new mission at "45 percent of optimal effectiveness," a somewhat ambiguous concept that is not further explained. In addition, 90 percent supported a special allocation from the Vice-Chancellor for library acquisitions, 95 percent favored the creation of a materials selection task force, but only 30 percent supported a book buying trip by the head librarian to the United States and the United Kingdom (too bad!).

OVERLAP STUDIES

Felder-Hoehne, Felicia, and Carolyn Sellers Ashkar. "The African-American Collection at the University of Tennessee: Does It Measure Up? An Overlap Study." **Behavioral & Social Sciences Librarian** 12, no. 2 (1993): 37–61.

This article describes the use of an overlap study to evaluate the African-American collection at the University of Tennessee at Knoxville. Random samples of 100 items (divided approximately equally among religion, history, and literature) were selected from the dictionary catalogs of four other libraries known for the strength of their African-American holdings (Fisk University, the Chicago Public Library, Howard University, and the New York Public Library's Schomburg Collection) and checked against the University of Tennessee at Knoxville's (UTK's) catalog. The results showed that UTK, compared to the four other collections, held from 62 percent to 70 percent of the total sampled items. The percentage of held items ranged from 36 percent to 52 percent in religion, 70 percent to 76 percent in history, and 74 percent to 97 percent in literature. A similar statistical analysis was applied to four areas of literature: novels, drama, poetry, and nonfiction. A number of methodological issues, such as selecting the samples, are discussed in detail. Most overlap studies analyze the holdings of a consortium or group of libraries in a geographical area, but this study uses overlap for evaluation of a single library's collection.

German, Richard N., Tony Kidd, and Gordon Pratt. "Serials Overlap in the Higher Education Institution Libraries in Glasgow." **New Review of Academic Librarianship** 3 (1997): 115–38.

German, Kidd, and Pratt report an investigation of serials overlap among twelve higher education institutions in the Glasgow area, including Glasgow University and Strathclyde University as well as specialized schools such as the Argyll and Clyde College of Nursing. The analysis was based on self-reported serial subscriptions during the final quarter of 1996. The research revealed that 58.5 percent of the 17,295 total (a title received by two libraries counting twice) subscriptions were unique, whereas 41.5 percent were held by at least two libraries. Of 12,903 individual (a title received by two libraries counted as one) subscriptions, 78.43 percent were unique to only one library. Many tables and graphs summarize the findings for each library and illustrate overlap among the twelve institutions in both absolute numbers and percentage terms. In both large universities and small specialized institutions, a high percentage of the subscriptions were unique. Because most overlap is among core titles the authors perceive limited opportunities for cooperative collection development, although they use the British term "rationalization." The authors state overlap was less than "anticipated," but, after a literature review, decide it was "consistent" with earlier studies of book overlap.

Hardesty, Larry L. "Collection Development and Bibliographic Instruction: A Relationship." In **Bibliographic Instruction in Practice: A Tribute to the Legacy of Evan Ira Farber,** edited by Larry L. Hardesty, Jamie Hastreiter, and David Henderson, 129–36. Ann Arbor, MI: Pierian Press, 1993. ISBN 0-87650-328-8.

The title is somewhat misleading, as this item focuses on overlap in college library book collections. OCLC-provided data for 64 Oberlin Group libraries (described as "the better liberal arts colleges around the country") revealed that nearly half (49.4 percent) of 3,246,738 titles were held by only one library, while only 1.5 percent were held by a majority of the Oberlin Group institutions. Next, OCLC/Amigos CACD data for 473 academic libraries with holdings between 100,000 and 299,999 showed that 35.2 percent of the American history and 38.2 percent of the social science books published between 1979 and 1989 were in the collections of only a single library, and, in both subjects, far less than 1 percent of the titles were in a majority of the 473 collections. Hardesty repeatedly states that the data demonstrate small library collections are "highly distinctive." Accordingly, he concludes one library's collection might not support bibliographic instruction assignments developed at other institutions.

Hardesty, Larry L., and Collette Mak. "Searching for the Holy Grail: A Core Collection for Undergraduate Libraries." **Journal of Academic Librarianship** 19 (January 1994): 362–71.

A follow-up to the previous entry begins by reviewing core book lists for college libraries (from the 1931 Shaw List to *BCL3* in 1988) and previously published overlap studies. Data concerning overlap among the Oberlin Group is repeated here. Then OCLC/Amigos CACD data on the 1980–90 holdings of 427 "modest-sized" college libraries revealed that 28.55 percent of more than 600,000 titles were held by only one library while less than half of a percent (0.46) were held by a majority. Analysis of American history, American literature, and the social sciences found the same pattern. In contrast, CACD data for ARL institutions showed that 11.4 percent of American history titles were contained in a majority of their collections, suggesting a higher overlap rate among larger libraries. The researchers decide that the undergraduate library core, if defined as those titles owned by most college libraries, "is *extremely* small." Hardesty and Mak make a significant contribution by illustrating the potential role of overlap studies in addressing issues regarding the core collection.

Heath, Fred. "An Assessment of Education Holdings in Alabama Academic Libraries: A Collection Analysis Project." In **Cooperative Collection Development: Proceedings of the June 1991 ASCLA Multi-LINCS Preconference,** compiled by Diane Macht Solomon, 37–61. Chicago: Association of Specialized and Cooperative Library Agencies, 1992. ISBN 0-8389-7611-5.

Heath describes a pilot study, completed in 1989, of education holdings overlap in the Network of Alabama Academic Libraries (NAAL), whose seventeen members included Alabama A & M University, Auburn University, and the University of Montevallo. Citing the earlier work of the Association for Higher Education of North Texas,[7] the author explains that Amigos software was used to analyze the participating libraries' complete OCLC cataloging records for education books. It was found that 50.95 percent of 66,921 titles were unique to one library and only 2.3 percent were held by ten or more institutions. Further analysis showed a "surprisingly low" duplication rate of 2.6 volumes for each title, a "strong" 0.60 correlation between collection size and the number of unique titles, that geographic proximity is not a factor in overlap, and that smaller collections have "significant holdings" of unique items. Health believes the high rate of uniqueness indicates Alabama libraries were supporting the local curriculum.

Schaffner, Ann C., Marianne Burke, and Jutta Reed-Scott. "Automated Collection Analysis: The Boston Library Consortium Experience." In **Advances in Library Resource Sharing,** vol. 3, edited by Jennifer Cargill and Diane J. Graves, 35–49. Westport, CT: Meckler, 1992. ISBN 0-8873-6826-3.

The twelve library member Boston Library Consortium, which included Brandeis University, Massachusetts Institute of Technology (MIT), and the Boston Public Library, analyzed in two groups nearly one million bibliographical records for books, scores, sound recordings, and microfilms (but not serials) published between 1981 and 1988. Amigos provided the programming, and the findings were broken down according to the Pacific Northwest Conspectus. A considerable portion of this entry discusses methodological considerations, technical processing issues, and project administration. Sixty-two percent of the books were held by simply one library, whereas "very few" were held by all consortium members. The observation from William Gray Potter's "landmark" study that larger collections hold more unique titles was confirmed, even though all twelve institutions contributed "significant unique titles."[8] Law, physical education, and agriculture had the highest percentage of unique titles, and the physical sciences had the lowest percentages. A detailed analysis of 3,197 unique mathematics titles revealed that 52 percent were popular computer manuals and 3 percent juvenile (mostly held by the Boston Public Library) while 38 percent were English language research books and 7 percent non-English books. Schaffner, Burke, and Reed-Scott note that creation of "a tool for communication" was one of the exercise's main benefits.

THE OCLC/AMIGOS COLLECTION ANALYSIS CD

Ciliberti, Anne C. "Collection Evaluation and Academic Review: A Pilot Study Using the OCLC/Amigos Collection Analysis CD." **Library Acquisitions: Practice & Theory** 18 (winter 1994): 431–45.

This item reports the OCLC/Amigos CACD's use in a four-phase collection evaluation project at William Patterson College (WPC), in New Jersey, during the early 1990s. A pilot study was conducted for the Department of Special Education and Counseling with 37 Mid-Atlantic region state colleges serving as a predefined peer group. Due to the department's interdisciplinary character, it was necessary to undertake a programming "workaround" to generate data for eighteen appropriate segments of the LC classification system for the years 1979–89. The 1,641 titles held by the WPC library represented 36 percent of the 4,567 separate titles acquired by the entire peer group and compared favorably to the average peer member size of 123.4. Only 3 percent of the library's titles were unique, that is, they were not held by any other peer group library. Ciliberti's insightful analysis concludes with the observation that the CACD "provided a perspective on the collection that would not otherwise have been available."

Dole, Wanda V. "Myth and Reality: Using the OCLC/Amigos Collection Analysis CD to Measure Collections Against Peer Collections and Against Institutional Priorities." **Library Acquisitions: Practice & Theory** 18 (summer 1994): 179–92.

As a consequence of a strategic planning exercise, the SUNY at Stony Brook libraries used the OCLC/Amigos CACD to compare their 1980–90 book acquisitions with those of two self-defined peer groups: a "mythical" group of fifteen high-ranking ARL libraries and a "realistic" group of 29 ARL institutions with rankings similar to Stony Brook's. It was found that the State University of New York (SUNY) at Stony Brook library acquired 168,589 titles during the ten-year period compared to 249,534 by the "mythical" peer group and 185,297 by the "realistic" group. An analysis by subject discovered that third priority academic programs were, compared to the two peer groups, better supported than first or second priority programs (a recently completed Collection Analysis Project had classified the universities academic programs into three priority categories). Accordingly, a committee was appointed to review the allocation system. Numerous graphs and tables illustrate the results in various subjects.

Dole, Wanda V., and Sherry S. Chang. "Consortium Use of the OCLC/Amigos Collection Analysis CD: The SUNY Experience." **Library Resources & Technical Services** 41 (January 1997): 50–57.

The authors assert, apparently correctly, that theirs is the first article dealing with the use of the CACD by a consortium. In February and March of 1996, the 1984 to 1994 holdings of SUNY at Stony Brook were compared with the three other SUNY Center Libraries (those granting doctoral degrees): Albany, Binghamton, and Buffalo. At the same time the average holdings for the four SUNY Center libraries were compared with four peer groups: the 80 ARL libraries on OCLC, the 18 largest ARL libraries on OCLC, the next 23 largest ARL libraries on OCLC, and the 99 largest academic libraries with holdings exceeding one million volumes. It was discovered that the SUNY libraries acquired fewer titles than the average member of all four peer groups. When compared with each other, Binghamton had acquired more humanities and social science titles than the other three and Stony Brook more science titles. Graphs created by spreadsheets showed that some areas were being collected at higher levels than specified in the collection development policy. Dole and Chang "recommend the use of computer-based tools" for consortial collection evaluation.

Findley, Marcia. "Using the OCLC/Amigos Collection Analysis Compact Disk to Evaluate Art and Art History Collections." **Technical Services Quarterly** 10, no. 3 (1993): 1–15.
　　Loyola Marymount University library's use of the OCLC/Amigos CACD to evaluate the art and art history holdings, as well as fill in gaps, is depicted by Findley. These areas' 1979–89 monographic holdings were compared with a self-defined peer group of 40 "thought to be similar" libraries. The Collection Development Department found their collection of 1,435 fine arts titles was 73.44 percent of the size of the average peer group member and that their 55 unique titles compared to 254 by the average peer group member. Comparative collection size (with the peer group average) is given for several specialty areas, including 80.74 percent in visual arts, 41.53 percent in architecture, and 76.73 percent in sculpture. A total of 176 books held by peer libraries was added to the collection. Findley reports that "despite inherent problems" (e.g., duplicate editions of the same titles were identified as lacking from the collection) her library will continue to use the system.

Gaylor, Randall H. "Collection Analysis at a Junior College Library: The OCLC/Amigos CACD." **OCLC Systems & Services** 10 (spring 1994): 9–12.
　　In this candidly written piece, Gaylor reflects upon the New Mexico Junior College Library's (NMJC's) use of the OCLC/Amigos CACD to assist with a certification review of the medical licensed technology program during the fall of 1993. Because NMJC may have been the first junior college to use the system, it was necessary to define two peer groups: two-year colleges in the region with allied health programs and two-year colleges in the Western United States. The CACD demonstrated the "relative strength" of the NMJC program compared to its peers, identified titles for selection, that is, those held by peers, and "provided a wealth of data." Nine steps in the decision-making process for acquiring new materials based on the CACD are outlined using bullets. Inaccuracies in the LC classification system and the possibility peers may not have selected correctly represent potential problems. The program cost "slightly" more than $5,000. In

final summary, Gaylor believes the CACD is not a "silver bullet" but a 'useful tool" for community college libraries.

Gyeszly, Suzanne D., Gary Allen, and Charles R. Smith. "Achieving Academic Excellence in Higher Education Through Improved Research Library Collections: Using OCLC/Amigos Collection Analysis CD for Collection Building." In **Academic Libraries; Achieving Excellence in Higher Education: Proceedings of the Sixth National Conference of the Association of College and Research Libraries, Salt Lake City, Utah, April 12–14, 1992**, edited by Thomas Kirk, 197–206. Chicago: American Library Association, 1992. ISBN 0-8389-7622-0.

    As part of strategic planning for a Texas A & M University (TAMU) five-year plan (1990–95), academic departments were surveyed in January 1991 concerning their current and projected teaching and research needs. Responses were received from forty-three departments for a 71.7 percent return rate. For forecasted areas of emphasis, the CACD was used to compare the main library's holdings of 1978 to 1988 imprints with a peer group of ten, including the University of Arizona, the University of Georgia, and Purdue. Several tables present data concerning the TAMU collection and the CACD analysis. The library's total size equaled 87 percent of the average peer group member's size. Books held by 80–90 percent of the peer group libraries but not TAMU were listed for the "highest" acquisition priority. The authors believe the CACD "worked well," but regret that only ten years of acquisitions data are included. This entry is significant for its use of the CACD in conjunction with strategic planning.

Harrell, Jeanne. "Use of the OCLC/Amigos Collection Analysis CD to Determine Comparative Collection Strength in English and American Literature: A Case Study." **Technical Services Quarterly** 9, no. 3 (1992): 1–14.

    Like the preceding entry, this article also addresses use of the CACD at the Texas A & M University library. The case study compared the 1977–87 English and American literature holdings with those of fourteen "first quartile" ARL libraries and the same self-defined ten-member peer group mentioned-above. English literature accounted for 3.4 percent of the TAMU collection but 3.0 percent of the total holdings of both peer groups, while American literature comprised 4.4 percent of the TAMU collection compared to 2.8 percent for first quartile ARL libraries and 3.2 percent for the self-defined peer group. The author discusses the CACD's benefits ("easy to use") and weaknesses, noting, among several points, that American and British imprints of the same title would be counted as two records. However, Harrell recommends the CACD as "a valuable tool."

Joy, Albert H. "The OCLC/Amigos Collection Analysis CD: A Unique Tool for Collection Evaluation and Development." **Resource Sharing & Information Networks** 8, no. 1 (1992): 23–45.

    This entry's author offers a careful description of the OCLC/Amigos CACD along with an unbiased assessment of its strengths and weaknesses. Joy incorporates the experiences of the University of Vermont library to explain its potential uses and limitations, with separate sections covering accreditation and grant writing, collection level review and budget planning, verification of collection development goals, and cooperative collection development. The library found the number of its unique items was "striking," subject areas holding 80 percent of the published output were "rare," and, as expected, it was "weak" in children's literature. Joy candidly discusses several drawbacks, such as restriction of the data to ten years of monographic records, lack of a Dewey Decimal system version, and unsuitability for interdisciplinary fields. Yet, the CACD supports collection building by generating lists of titles held by peer institutions and, in the final analysis, is "worthy of use and further investigation."

Vellucci, Sherry L. "OCLC/Amigos Collection Analysis CD: Broadening the Scope of Use." **OCLC Systems & Services** 9 (summer 1993): 49–53.

Here a library science educator explains the CACD's potential applications. Vellucci perceives a two-stage process with the CACD's statistical reports providing quantitative assessment and generated book lists offering qualitative assessment. Most of the article is devoted to describing how consortia, specific libraries, and individuals might use the product. She explains a consortium could create its own self-defined peer group and apply the findings in cooperative collection development decisions. A library could conduct longitudinal studies of collection growth over a period of years and incorporate the holdings data into a management information system along with other statistics. Libraries can also use the Gap Report to build a desiderata list and Uniqueness Reports to assist preservation decisions. Three categories of individuals can use the CACD system: faculty for creating lists of books supporting their courses; librarians for conducting personal research; and citing her own experience, library educators as a teaching tool.

Webster, Michael G. "Using the Amigos/OCLC Collection Analysis CD and Student Credit Hour Statistics to Evaluate Collection Growth Patterns and Potential Demand." **Library Acquisitions: Practice & Theory** 19 (summer 1995): 197–210.

The University of Central Arkansas library's history collection was evaluated with data on the following: comparative holdings from the CACD (a collection-centered method), student enrollment (a use-centered technique representing "potential demand"), and current acquisitions. Comparison of the library with Peer Group 9 (124 institutions, listed in an appendix, with holdings between 300,000 and 699,999) found that its general and Old World history holdings were 98.53 percent of the average member's size, while the corresponding figure for American history stood at 110.23 percent. An examination of history subareas found several lower than 65 percent of the peer group average, which was the minimally acceptable threshold agreed upon by the History and Acquisitions Departments. Analysis of the study's other variables revealed ancient history generated 7 percent of upper-division and graduate student credit hour enrollment during 1992–93 but produced only 3.6 percent of the History Department books orders, whereas Asian history had approximately the same credit hour enrollment but four times the book orders. Detailed findings are presented in the eight appendices. As a consequence of this study, the History Department revamped its selection procedures and budget allocation method. Webster concludes with the pithy observation that collection assessment is "more art than science."

Wood, Richard J. "Building a Better Library Collection: The CACD Way." **Library Software Review** 15 (spring 1996): 4–24.

Wood provides an excellent overview of the OCLC/Amigos CACD. He comments the system evolved from an Amigos automated tape analysis of the Association of Higher Education of North Texas libraries' holdings in 1984 while the software and database was developed by OCLC. The holdings reports generated by CACD are explained and illustrated as are the 14 standard peer groups. Sixteen "general uses" are enumerated, from number 1, ongoing assessment, to number 16, serving as the basis for cooperative collection development. Outlined with bullets are eight "limitations and disadvantages," for example, serials/journals are excluded and the system can not readily be used by public and school libraries (because data is excluded for libraries using the Dewey Decimal System). A final section covers cost and sales information. This article clearly meets its stated objective of describing the CACD's "features, uses, benefits, and weaknesses."

NOTES

1. Charles Coffin Jewett, "Report of the Assistant Secretary Relative to the Library, Presented December 13, 1848," in *Third Annual Report of the Board of Regents of the Smithsonian Institution to the Senate and House of Representatives* (Washington, DC: Tippin and Streeper, 1849), 39–47.

2. Paul H. Mosher, "Collection Evaluation in Research Libraries: The Search for Quality, Consistency, and System in Collection Development," *Library Resources & Technical Services* 23 (winter 1979): 18.

3. These percentages are Nisonger's calculation from the raw data.

4. Lynn Arthur Steen, ed., *Library Recommendations for Undergraduate Mathematics* (Washington, DC: Mathematical Association of America, 1992).

5. Elizabeth Davis, ed., *A Basic Music Library: Essential Scores and Sound Recordings,* 3d ed. (Chicago: American Library Association, 1997).

6. David V. Loertscher and May Lein Ho, *Computerized Collection Development for School Library Media Centers* (Castle Rock, CO: Hi Willow Research and Publishing, 1986); Loertscher, "The Elephant Technique of Collection Development," *Collection Management* 7 (fall 1985/winter 1985–86): 45–54.

7. Thomas E. Nisonger, "Editing the RLG Conspectus to Analyze the OCLC Archival Tapes of Seventeen Texas Libraries," *Library Resources & Technical Services* 29 (October/December 1985): 309–27.

8. William Gray Potter, "Studies of Collection Overlap: A Literature Review," *Library Research* 4 (spring 1982): 3–21.

3

The Conspectus

Chapter 3 covers the Conspectus approach to collection evaluation. Meaning "summary" or "outline," the Conspectus was designed to provide a synopsis of collection strengths and weaknesses. The RLG Conspectus was developed by the Research Libraries Group during the late 1970s and the 1980s. In 1990 the Western Library Network (WLN) began sponsoring an alternate version known as the WLN Conspectus, which evolved from the Pacific Northwest Conspectus (a modification of the original Conspectus by librarians in that region).

The RLG Conspectus is organized according to a three-level subject hierarchy from the general to the specific: divisions, corresponding to disciplines or broad areas of knowledge, such as history; subject categories, such as history of the United Kingdom; and, finally, subject groups or descriptors, such as nineteenth-century Serbian history. (A corresponding Library of Congress classification range is indicated for each subject descriptor.) There is a separate worksheet for each division. Note that various sources occasionally use variant terminology for the Conspectus subject breakdown.

Libraries implementing the Conspectus originally assigned for each subject descriptor a 0 to 5 collecting level code (0 = out of scope, 1 = minimal level, 2 = basic information level, 3 = instructional support level, 4 = research level, and 5 = comprehensive level) to two worksheet columns representing density (the cumulative collection strength) and intensity (current collecting activity). Libraries were later offered the option of a ten-point scale, created by adding subcategories for levels 2 and 3. Language codes (E = English, F = selected non-English, W = wide selection of languages, and Y = one non-English language) can be used in conjunction with the collecting level codes. An alternative set of language codes was established by Canadian libraries where French-language holdings are a major concern. Also, additional collection-level codes have been developed for fiction and children's collections.

The WLN Conspectus varies from its RLG counterpart in a number of key respects. The subject organization is somewhat different, and collecting levels are assigned for four columns, representing density, intensity, the goal level, and preservation commitment. Libraries, when assessing their collections, are offered the option of omitting the third, most-detailed level of the subject hierarchy, as well as using worksheets tied to either the Library of Congress or Dewey classification with the choice presumably depending upon the classification system in their own library.

During the 1980s, "Supplemental Guidelines" were published for many Conspectus divisions to help librarians assign collecting levels accurately. That decade also witnessed the origin of "verification studies" to ascertain that collecting levels were assigned consistently among different libraries. In such studies the results of checking the same subject list against the holdings of multiple libraries are compared in order to identify (and presumable correct) obvious anomalies, for example when a level 3 collection held 50 percent of the items and a level 4 collection held 40 percent. Note that a number of manuals, several of which are annotated in this chapter, have been issued to assist with Conspectus implementation. The WLN also offers Conspectus software for keeping track of collecting codes and other pertinent data.

The ARL libraries, beginning in 1983, used the Conspectus to evaluate their collections in an endeavor known as the North American Collections Inventory Project (NCIP). In 1989 and again in 1996, the American Library Association (ALA) recommended use of the Conspectus framework in writing collection development policies to facilitate standardization and comparison among libraries.

The Conspectus has also been used throughout the world, especially in the English-speaking democracies. For example, in 1989 the Australian Council of Libraries and Information Services' (ACLIS') National Task Force on the Conspectus recommended that Australian librarians implement the Pacific Northwest Conspectus, and in 1990 the National Library of Australia appointed a Conspectus Officer.[1] The Conspectus has also been used in New Zealand, Canada, the United Kingdom, and various continental European nations.

The Conspectus's ostensible purpose was to lay the groundwork for cooperative collection development. Libraries with strong collections in a subject would be identified and agree to assume "primary collecting responsibility," thus allowing other libraries to ease their collecting efforts for the subject. A consensus seems to exist that Conspectus implementation did not generally result in successful cooperative collection development endeavors. Nevertheless, the literature reports numerous other practical uses for the Conspectus, including evaluation of individual library collections, budgeting, setting preservation priorities, staff education and training, and supporting grant applications.

The Conspectus has always been controversial. Criticisms relate to the following: the impressionistic nature of the collection level assessments, concerns about accuracy and consistency among libraries in assignment of collection levels, a pro-American bias in the subject breakdown, questions as to whether the effort expended in Conspectus implementation justifies the benefits, and its focus on the print holdings at the expense of electronic resources as well as print items that can be accessed through ILL or commercial document delivery.

In 1997 the RLG discontinued support for its version of the Conspectus. However, the WLN version is still supported by the recently merged OCLC-WLN bibliographic utility and a WLN Conspectus users group continued to convene at ALA meetings at the beginning of the twenty-first century.

This chapter is divided into six sections dealing with overviews of the Conspectus, case study reports concerning Conspectus implementation, commentary on the Conspectus, the Conspectus's use in countries other than the United States, Conspectus manuals, and miscellaneous issues regarding the Conspectus.

OVERVIEWS OF THE CONSPECTUS

Blake, Virgil L. P., and Renee Tjoumas. "The Conspectus Approach to Collection Evaluation: Panacea or False Prophet?" **Collection Management** 18, nos. 3–4 (1994): 1–31.

The first half of this article, which cites an extensive literature, covers the Conspectus's historical evolution. The authors observe that the ARL's adoption of the Conspectus for the NCIP was a critical development. Then the Conspectus subject organization and collecting codes are described, and five implementation steps from the *Manual for the North American Inventory of Research Library Collections* are outlined:[2]

1. Preparatory investigation of the library and institution

2. Assessment of the collection through traditional methods such as shelf scanning

3. Completion of the worksheets

4. Reporting results to the project coordinator

5. Conduct of a verification study

"Uniform and concise" data recording is the Conspectus's "primary advantage," whereas incomplete LC classification numbers, variations between the LC and Dewey versions, and the methodology's subjectivity are considered "problems." Blake and Tjoumas decide the "Conspectus is a sophisticated but paradoxical instrument."

Bushing, Mary. "The Conspectus: Possible Process and Useful Product for the Ordinary Library." **Acquisitions Librarian** 7 (1992): 81–95.

As the title indicates, this entry maintains the Conspectus is "well-suited" for medium-sized and small libraries. Bushing offers valuable practical advice on the successful implementation of the Conspectus, stating administrative skills are as important as assessment techniques. Of four assessment methods (shelflist counts, calculation of collection age, list-checking, and shelf-scanning), she notes the latter is especially suited to nonresearch libraries because of their smaller size. Regarding statistics, Bushing observes "avoid unnecessary 'bean counting.'" She discusses six elements necessary for a successful Conspectus project: correct application of the methodology, a statement of Conspectus goals, a commitment of resources, a skilled and energetic project manager, staff training, and communication concerning the Conspectus process. Eight responsibilities of a project manager are listed, including "provide leadership," "administer detailed procedures," and "exercise authority." The author believes that nonresearch libraries are "more likely" than their research counterparts to have most of the elements required for a successful Conspectus project.

Clayton, Peter, and Gary E. Gorman. "Conspectus." In **Managing Information Resources in Libraries: Collection Management in Theory and Practice,** 37–51. London: Library Association Publishing, 2001. ISBN 1-85604-297-9.

This textbook chapter begins with an overview of the Conspectus along with its benefits and limitations. The authors observe the Conspectus is an assessment rather than an evaluation method and subjective rather than "scientific." An inset "case study" discusses the Australian National University Library's use of the Conspectus in preparing a collection development policy. Clayton and Gorman stress there is no "viable alternative" to the Conspectus but that it "urgently needs" updating to take into consideration electronic resources. Accordingly, they propose a revised set of collection level definitions in which the terminology "the library provides access to" is substituted for "the collection contains." Due to the "ephemeral" nature of electronic resources, the authors assert their revised definitions would be more useful for depicting current collecting activity and the goal rather than established collection strength. The fact that a fairly recent collection management textbook devotes an entire chapter to the Conspectus testifies to its continuing relevance.

Coffey, Jim. "The RLG Conspectus: What's in the Numbers." **Acquisitions Librarian** no. 7 (1992): 65–80.

The author begins by emphasizing that correct assignment of Conspectus collecting levels requires knowledge about the subject and its resources as well as the institution's collecting objectives. Then, "expanded explanations" of Conspectus collecting levels 0 through 5 are given. Sequential steps in Conspectus implementation are discussed:

- Take shelflist counts and scan the shelves

- Check bibliographies and subject lists

- Inspect the Supplemental Guidelines

- Consult faculty subject specialists

- Finally, apply the collecting levels

About half the article is devoted to a discussion of "problems with the process:" implementation is time-consuming, verification studies indicate inaccurate assignment of collecting levels, subject bibliographies can be difficult to locate, level 3 is hard to understand, and the Supplemental Guidelines are often inconsistent and ambiguous. Finally, Coffey stresses that the Conspectus is "difficult to apply" in nonresearch libraries.

Coleman, Jim. "The RLG Conspectus: A History of Its Development and Influence and a Prognosis for Its Future." **Acquisitions Librarian** no. 7 (1992): 25–43.

This item provides a useful sketch of the Conspectus's historical development through the early 1990s. Coleman calls the Conspectus a *"de facto lingua franca"* for collection description. A "Time Line" outlines twenty-two key events from the creation of the RLG Collection Management and Development Committee (which initially developed the Conspectus) in 1979 to the 1990 RLG meeting at the International Federation of Library Associations and Institutions (IFLA) to review worldwide Conspectus efforts. In the early 1980s, verification studies and Supplemental Guidelines were developed to improve the accuracy of Conspectus assessments. The author discusses four models for drawing verification study samples: expertly selected; randomly drawn; randomly drawn, stratified; and mixed. Other sections discuss the following: the Conspectus Online database, set up in 1982; the Conspectus's expansion beyond the United States; and consortial uses of the Conspectus. Coleman speculates that in the future the Conspectus will be important for local library decision-making, but its role in national level policy making is "less clear."

Davis, Burns. "How the WLN Conspectus Works for Small Libraries." **Acquisitions Librarian** no. 20 (1998): 53–72.

This somewhat lengthy essay, frequently using bullets to list points, analyzes the Conspectus's role in collection assessment for small libraries. Davis stresses that the Conspectus offers small libraries the advantage of simplicity because fewer people and fewer resources will be involved. Data collection, data reports, and potential uses are discussed. Separate sections explain how small libraries can use the Conspectus to establish a collection management plan, develop a budget, evaluate collection management performance, and achieve cooperative agreements. Another section illustrates how an unnamed public library serving a community of 9,700 created customized Conspectus worksheets for adult fiction, juvenile fiction, and reference works. The conclusion emphasizes the Conspectus's "flexibility" and that it can be customized for often unclassified resources such as biography, large type, or local interest collections.

Grant, Joan. "The Conspectus: An Important Component of a Comprehensive Collection Management Program." **Acquisitions Librarian** no. 7 (1992): 97–103.

Arguing that assessment is "the foundation for all other collection development activities," Grant explains the Conspectus's overall role in collection development. Six sequential collection development components are outlined: assessment, policy statements, budgeting and funding, selection, preservation, and resource sharing. Beyond its obvious assessment function, Grant notes that the ALA has recommended the Conspectus as a framework for collection development policies. Assessment of collection strengths and weaknesses via the Conspectus can inform budget allocation, selection decisions, and setting priorities for preservation. Finally, one of the Conspectus's original purposes was to lay the groundwork for resource sharing and cooperative collection development. The author observes that the Conspectus's implementation requires "an investment of staff time" in return for "wide reaching" effects on collection management.

Lange, Janice, and Richard J. Wood. "The Conspectus: A Tool for Collection Assessment and Description." **Encyclopedia of Library & Information Science** 66, supplement 29 (2000): 65–78.

This lengthy encyclopedia article provides an overview of the Conspectus at the turn of the millennium and, incidentally, approximately twenty years after its origin. Although descriptive rather than prescriptive, the authors observe the Conspectus is both collection-centered (describing existing strength plus current activity) and client-centered (establishing goals based on user need). The sections dealing with the Conspectus's history and structure note that in August 1997, the RLG discontinued support for its version of the Conspectus. Also in 1997, a task force headed by Columbia University's Tony Ferguson revised the WLN collecting level definitions to reflect electronic resources and the language code definitions to reduce English language bias. The traditional uses of the Conspectus (collection development policy making, budget justification, resource sharing, communication, training, etc.) are discussed. "Difficulties" include the facts that the Supplemental Guidelines, issued between 1983 and 1990, are outdated; subject fields such as computer science have changed rapidly since the Conspectus was written; and Web-based electronic resources are often unclassified (and thus are difficult to tie to the Conspectus system). Taking a generally favorable attitude, this entry offers a relatively current in-depth analysis of the Conspectus.

Loken, Sally. "The WLN Conspectus." **Collection Building** 13, nos. 2–3 (1994): 31–42.

Written by a nationally known authority, this entry provides a useful introductory overview of the WLN Conspectus as of the mid-1990s. The WLN Conspectus's historical evolution, its organizational structure, collecting levels, language codes, and uses are briefly covered. Ten steps for implementing the Conspectus are listed, beginning with "plan and prepare" and ending with entering the assessments into a database. An important section describes the WLN automated services for collection assessment, including *Conspectus Software Version 5.0* for maintaining assessment levels and other data dealing with circulation, budgets, and so on. Eight pages of appended material include blank LC and Dewey worksheets, completed worksheets from the Anchorage Municipal Libraries, the University of Alaska at Fairbanks, and Montana State University, as well as a WLN Collection Analysis report for an unnamed library.

Wood, Richard J. "The Conspectus: A Collection Analysis and Development Success." **Library Acquisitions: Practice & Theory** 20 (winter 1996): 429–53.

Synthesizing a fairly extensive literature, Wood provides a broad overview of the Conspectus and explains why he believes it is an "effective tool." He begins by citing his own informal 1993 survey showing that 63 of 100 librarians were unfamiliar with the Conspectus. Then the Conspectus's history and structure are described. A lengthy discussion of numerous benefits states the Conspectus "is as objective a tool as has been developed." Wood notes that his institution, Sam Houston State University, added to the worksheets columns for preservation decisions and circulation data. Included in this section are ten "intangible" benefits listed with bullets, such as reducing selector bias and "strategic planning/funding." "Barriers to use" include the lack of new services and immediate rewards. Excerpts from the Illinois State Library and the National Library of Medicine collection development policies are used to illustrate the Conspectus's role in policy writing. One tends to feel optimistic about the Conspectus after reading this entry.

Wood, Richard J. "A Conspectus of the Conspectus." **Acquisitions Librarian** no. 7 (1992): 5–23.

This entry's goal, in Wood's own words, is to provide "a general, nontechnical overview of the Conspectus." Separate sections explain the Conspectus's structure, collection intensity codes, and RLG language codes. Then a section on assessment techniques discusses the pros and cons of six approaches: shelflist analysis, list checking, shelf scanning, expert opinion, client-centered methods such as circulation and ILL data, and such computer-centered methods as the OCLC/Amigos Collection Analysis CD. Inconsistencies in assigning collecting levels among a consortium can be minimized by cooperative training, central administration, and running preliminary test evaluations. Seven benefits of the Conspectus, including assistance with approval plans, grants, and long range goals, are listed. Finally, Wood recommends a five-part organizational scheme for Conspectus summary reports: introduction; curriculum, special programs; results and analysis; recommendations/conclusions; and appendix. For a more in-depth analysis of the Conspectus written four years later by the same author, see the preceding entry.

CASE STUDIES OF CONSPECTUS IMPLEMENTATION

Benaud, Claire-Lise, and Sever Bordeianu. "Evaluating the Humanities Collections in an Academic Library Using the RLG Conspectus." **Acquisitions Librarian** no. 7 (1992): 125–36.

This essay presents the perceptions of four humanities selectors (art, architecture, and photography; English and American literature; French; and Classics) concerning their experience implementing the Conspectus at the University of New Mexico library during 1989. Salient observations are listed below:

- Several disadvantages are associated with the Conspectus's tie to the LC classification.

- The verification studies are "inadequate."

- One selector found the Supplemental Guidelines "useful" but another did not.

- The Conspectus is not useful for "relatively small collections."

Only the art selector shared results with the faculty. Most faculty did not consider the results "relevant," and "a vocal minority dismissed them as useless."

This entry is beneficial because it offers subjective impressions from the grass-roots level.

Bushing, Mary. "Insights from One Public Library: Birmingham Public Library's Conspectus Project, Part 1." **WLN Participant** 15, no. 1 (winter 1995): 15–18; part 2, **WLN Participant** 15, no. 2 (spring 1996): 13–15.

This two-part item transcribes Bushing's interview with Linda Cohen, the Birmingham Public Library's collection management librarian, concerning her library's use of the WLN Conspectus. Challenged by their use of four classification systems (LC, Dewey, SuDoc, and a local system), the library administration wished to find out "what is in the collection" and how it relates to user needs in order to prepare a collection development policy, described as the "BIG goal." The project (to be completed in 1997) was actually ahead of schedule! Cohen emphasizes that her library was interested in the WLN Conspectus because of its flexibility and observed that Conspectus implementation in public libraries differs from academic libraries due to the former's collecting focus on fiction plus juvenile and popular materials. She perceptively commented, "Ambiguity is not comfortable for librarians and collection assessment is full of ambiguity." Upbeat in tone, these entries offer insightful perspectives concerning the Conspectus's applicability to a large public library.

Ebersole, W. Dale, Jr. "Using Online Catalogs to Evaluate Science Collections for a Group of Institutions." **Science & Technology Libraries** 18, no. 1 (1999): 105–13.

Most of this entry is devoted to a discussion of using OPACs to gather collection assessment data in support of cooperative collection development and the problems inherent in science collection evaluation. Ebersole then reports a project, carried out in 1995, in which a group of OhioLINK librarians used the Conspectus approach to evaluate their physics collections. The consortium's online catalog was used to gather institutional holdings data according to the Conspectus breakdown. They also found that 98.1 percent of 415 physics journals recommended in a standard source were held by one or more Ohio libraries.[3] Sixty hours were spent gathering and presenting the data. The reader is cautioned that the Conspectus approach may give "erroneous information" when making comparisons among different size institutions with diverse programs.

Faries, Cindy. "Collection Evaluation in Women's Studies: One Model for Learning the Process." **Collection Building** 13, no. 4 (1994): 1–7.

Faries analyzes the implementation of the RLG Conspectus at the Penn State library during the fall of 1990 for women's studies, a field presenting challenges due to its interdisciplinary nature. Sarah Pritchard's *RLG Conspectus: Supplemental Guidelines for Women's Studies* was consulted to determine the appropriate collecting levels to be assigned based on the percentages held in seven bibliographies that were list checked. The OPAC was checked to calculate the number of items the library owned in each LC class range on the 44 page worksheet. Selectors in overlapping disciplines with women's studies were also consulted. The author asserts the Conspectus was useful for assessing the book and serial collections, but not microforms, audiovisuals, or archival resources. Conspectus implementation for a novice was, according to Faries, "a daunting task" (requiring three to four hours of daily work for four to five weeks) that resulted in "better knowledge of the collection." This entry is notable for its discussion of methodological issues regarding use of the Conspectus in interdisciplinary areas.

Palestrant, Zelma G., and Elizabeth W. Carter. "Library Statistics and Conspectus Data Elements: The Citadel Model." **Acquisitions Librarian** no. 7 (1992): 115–23.

A statistical gathering and reporting system developed at the library of the Citadel is described here. Holdings and current acquisitions data was entered into a LOTUS 1-2-3 spreadsheet searchable by department, LC class range, and Conspectus heading. Several tables illustrate the title and volume statistics that can be produced. Contrasted to such labor-intensive methods as shelflist scanning or call number searches in the OPAC, this system offered benefits "greater than anticipated," providing data that supported assignment of Conspectus collecting levels and other collection assessment purposes. The authors claim the "Citadel Model" for recording statistics can be used by other libraries. In any case, this entry illustrates use of the Conspectus format to assist statistical compilation for collection assessment.

Pinnell-Stephens, June. "A Management Information System Using the WLN Conspectus Software." **WLN Participant** 11 (November/December 1992): 12–14.

Pinnell-Stephens uses the experience of the Fairbanks North Star Borough Library in Alaska to explain the Management Information File in the WLN Conspectus software. The file offers fifteen predefined and ten user-defined data fields for gathering data at the Conspectus division, subject, or category levels with fields and levels chosen at the implementing library's discretion. The author's library gathered data in the predetermined circulation, ILL, and acquisitions fields and created optional fields for reference holdings data, juvenile holdings, and selector names. The fact the available data was not organized according to the Conspectus subject breakdown posed a problem. The benefits are that multi-variable data can be compiled, compared to collecting levels, and used for benchmarking.

Pinnell-Stephens, June. "Shared Futures: Cooperative Collection Development and Management in Alaska." **Collection Building** 13, nos. 2–3 (1994): 57–61.

The Conspectus's role in cooperative collection development in the state of Alaska is recounted by the Coordinator of the Alaska Conspectus Consortium. The article begins by describing Alaska's "very poor" library resources and the efforts of the Alaska Collection Development Project, begin in 1982, to rectify the situation. To assist collection assessment as a prelude to cooperative collection development agreements, the Conspectus was modified to meet the needs of smaller libraries. Pinnell-Stephens refers to this revision as the "Alaska model" from which the Northwest Conspectus—forerunner of the WLN Conspectus—borrowed. A major section is devoted to a management information system, beta tested in Alaskan libraries, that incorporates data on holdings, clientele, circulation, mission, and curriculum. This system became part of the WLN Conspectus Database Software. The author observes, "In the beginning, adoption of the Conspectus methodology was a leap of faith," but the participating libraries "discovered" the "benefits" of collection assessment.

Powell, Nancy. "Using Collection Assessments to Justify Budget Requests." **WLN Participant** 11 (November/December 1992): 10–12.

Written by the co-author of a WLN Conspectus manual, this item offers a short but convincing illustration of how the Conspectus can be used in budget justification. The Nicholls State University library in Louisiana, where the Conspectus was implemented during 1992–93, needed budget projections for an upcoming accreditation visit. The following steps, illustrated in a table, were used to calculate the minimum annual dollar figure required to support the assigned Conspectus collection goal level for each division:

1. The annual book publication output in the division was obtained from the *Bowker Annual.*

2. The recommended percentage of book output for the assigned collecting level was obtained from the Conspectus manual.

3. The required number of annual acquisitions was calculated from the above data.

4. The average cost per book was obtained, available from the library's automated system or the *Bowker Annual.*

5. The results from steps 3 and 4 are multiplied to derive a total cost figure for the division.

Powell emphasizes that supporting a level 3b collection at the division level requires 7.5 times the amount of money needed for a level 2a collection.

Powell, Nancy. "Using the WLN Conspectus in a Non-Automated Environment." **Collection Building** 13, nos. 2–3 (1994): 43–56.

This piece candidly reflects on the Conspectus's use at Nicholls State University library. In the fall of 1992, the library choose the WLN Conspectus to assess the collection in order to assist with budget allocation, request additional funding, and help write a collection development policy for an upcoming accreditation study. As suggested by the title, data gathering in the library's non-automated environment was time-consuming, but interpreting the data was even more difficult. A significant portion of the article is devoted to the collection assessment narrative summary reports compiled for academic departments in conjunction with the Southern Association accreditation self-study in 1993. The four-page report for psychology is appended along with sample worksheets. These reports included the following elements:

- Description of the program

- Description of the monographic collection

- Description of the serials collection

- Description of other formats

- Description of other types of support (i.e., interdisciplinary, ILL, off-campus, etc.).

- Present collection level

- Goal level

- Summary of needed collection management action to achieve goal

Powell concludes the Conspectus was "an effective tool." This entry offers a worthwhile case study of the WLN Conspectus's implementation in a medium-sized academic institution.

Siverson, Scott E. "Fine-Tuning the Dull Roar of Conspectors: Using Scaled Bibliographies to Assess Collection Level." **Acquisitions Librarian** no. 7 (1992): 45–64.

Following a detailed review (drawing upon approximately sixty previously published items) concerning the Conspectus's role in internal collection evaluation and checking bibliographies to help assign collecting levels, Siverson concludes that Conspectus collecting levels tend to be assigned based on the quantity of holdings (often determined by checking a bibliography) rather than the type of holdings. To remedy this situation, he proposes a four-point scale for weighting bibliographic items:

1. "*Essential* items that define a collection's main concentration"

2. "Special items that support minor concentrations"

3. "General items that are broadly related to the collection"

4. "Peripheral items" that are tangential

Siverson reports application of this scaling technique at the University of Florida library in African archaeology and prehistory and Yoruba Language and Literature. This is a praiseworthy attempt to render the Conspectus more useful as a tool for evaluating a particular library's collection.

Stephens, Dennis. "Multi-Type Library Collection Planning in Alaska: A Conspectus-Based Approach." **Acquisitions Librarian** no. 7 (1992): 137–56.

The use of the Conspectus for cooperative collection development in Alaska through the early 1990s is narrated here. A Steering Committee, founded in 1982 to provide overall direction to the process, grappled with such issues as reconciling Dewey and LC versions and deciding how acquisitions decisions can be based on Conspectus findings. The collection intensity indicators (termed the Alaska Expansion) were revised and a twenty-fifth Conspectus division was developed for Polar Regions materials. As of this writing, the WLN Conspectus database included data from 16 libraries, and 14 libraries had agreed to assume primary collecting (level 3a or higher) or secondary (level 2a or higher) responsibility within 20 completed Conspectus divisions. The Conspectus was also used for local agreements between the Fairbanks North Star Borough and the University of Alaska at Fairbanks libraries and in Juneau among the State Library, the University of Alaska Southeast library, and the Juneau Public library. Appendices illustrate Conspectus reports and worksheets. Stephens states the Conspectus "enabled Alaska librarians to view all the state's collections as one large resource."

Thweatt, Elizabeth. "Using the WLN Conspectus to Assess a Law Library Collection." In **Advances in Collection Development and Resource Management,** vol. 2, edited by Thomas W. Leonhardt, 81–91. Greenwich, CT: JAI Press, 1996. ISBN 0-7623-0097-3.

Use of the Law division of the WLN Conspectus to assess the Gonzaga University Law Library is analyzed here. WLN automated services were used to compare the holdings with those of seventeen other medium-sized law libraries. Of 129,818 different titles in the seventeen libraries, 18.5 percent were held by Gonzaga, 1.4 percent were "close matches," and 80.1 percent were not held. Other data gathering methods included investigating the collection's age and subject dispersion through the OPAC, checking bibliographies (both described as labor-intensive), studying ILL records, and directly examining the collection. A number of worksheets are reproduced in an appendix. Thweatt perceptively comments that collection assessment is "not judgmental...but descriptive."

Williams, Pauline, and Rosemary Arneson. "Using the Automated OCLC/WLN Conspectus at a Small University." **Against the Grain** 13 (April 2001): 1, 18, 20, 22, 24, 26.

This entry depicts the use of the OCLC/WLN automated Conspectus along with other evaluation approaches at the University of Montevallo library in Alabama. In anticipation of an accreditation visit, the library ordered the age and subject analysis services, as well as the *BCL3,* OAB (from *Choice)* and *Booklist* comparisons, which report the percentage of items in these sources held by the library. The Interactive Collection Analysis System CD-ROM (ICAS CD) was modified to allow analysis of the number of books on each Conspectus line by 5 (rather than the original 14) publication date ranges. It was found *inter alia* that: the library held a yearly average of 3,830 books published between 1970–74 contrasted with 1,692 for 1995–99 and held 74 percent (counting close matches) of the music titles in *BCL3.* Lists of unheld *BCL3* and OAB items will be used in collection building. The journal collection was assessed with the help of Katz's *Mag-*

azines for Libraries and by asking faculty to rate journals in their discipline on a 1–5 scale. This item helps introduce the OCLC/WLN collection assessment services as of 2001.

COMMENTARY ON THE CONSPECTUS

Atkinson, Ross. "In Defense of Relativism." **Journal of Academic Librarianship** 17 (January 1992): 353–54.

Atkinson's contribution to a symposium on research and library education defends the Conspectus against criticisms by David Henige.[4] This essay is organized around five major points with a separate section devoted to each. First, completing the Conspectus serves as a "declaration of cooperative intent." Second, collection theory is supported by confronting fundamental questions concerning the meaning of a collection. Third, in addition to allowing comparisons of collection strength among institutions, the Conspectus allows comparison of different subjects at the same institution. Fourth, the Conspectus is an "inter-institutional communications vehicle." Fifth, the Conspectus is necessary but not sufficient for cooperative collection development. This short piece offers thoughtful insight into the Conspectus by a seminal collection development thinker.

Ferguson, Anthony W. "Philosophical Arguments and Real Shortcomings." **Journal of Academic Librarianship** 17 (January 1992): 350–51.

Taking part in the same symposium with Atkinson, Ferguson refutes four specific criticisms of the Conspectus in a previously published article by Henige.[5] First, he responds to criticism about the Conspectus's subjectivity with the assertion that subjective judgments make it an "invaluable" training tool. Secondly, Ferguson says Henige is playing "epistemological games" when he claims the Conspectus definitions are "ill-defined." Third, Ferguson states that Henige's suggestion the "Conspectus is susceptible to deception" could be applied to other methods as well. Fourth, to Henige's claim that the National Shelflist Count is better than the Conspectus, he argues that the NSC data is skewed by uncataloged collections and does not offer qualitative assessments. Ferguson's final sentence states, "The problem with the Conspectus is not the data itself, it is that we have done nothing significant with the data."

Hazen, Dan C. "The Latin American Conspectus: Panacea or Pig in a Poke?" In **Latin American Studies into the Twenty-First Century; New Focus, New Formats, New Challenges: Papers of the Thirty-Sixth Annual Meeting of the Seminar on the Acquisition of Latin American Library Materials; University of California, San Diego and San Diego State University, San Diego, California, June 1–6, 1991,** edited by Deborah L. Jakubs, 235–47. Albuquerque, NM: SALALM Secretariat, General Library, University of New Mexico, 1993. ISBN 0-917617-38-X.

As hinted by the title, this entry offers, to use the author's words, "rather curmudgeonly remarks" about the Conspectus. Among his numerous observations, Hazen, a Latin American specialist at the Harvard Libraries, maintains the Conspectus approach is "flawed in both concept and methodology" while the results have been "mixed." Considerable attention is devoted to the "Latin American Update," a Conspectus division developed during 1985–86 but "folded" by the RLG in 1989. This "Update" was "long and complicated" and tied to the LC classification, in which terms many important Latin American collections "are not even minimally understandable." Moreover, no Latin American verification studies or cooperative collection development agreements resulted from the Update. Because there are less than twenty-five "significant" Latin American collections, local collection guides might be preferable to the Conspectus. However, Hazen concedes the Conspectus forced librarians "to think and work together" regarding collections.

THE CONSPECTUS OUTSIDE THE UNITED STATES

Gorman, Gary E. "African Studies, Australian Conspectus, and Cooperative Acquisitions." **Australian Library Review** 11 (November 1994): 459–63.

Although acknowledging "shortcomings" in the Conspectus's treatment of Africa, Gorman argues that the Conspectus can lay the foundation for a national cooperative collection development plan for African studies in Australia. The University of Western Australia's application of the Conspectus to its African materials is cited as an example to be emulated by other Australian libraries. The author proposes the creation of an Area Specialization Scheme, modeled upon the United States' defunct Farmington Plan or the United Kingdom's Standing Conference on Library Materials on Africa (SCOLMA), which would be administered by the African Studies Association of Australia and the Pacific (AFSAAP). Six points offering details for implementation of the proposed scheme are outlined. This entry provides a forward looking approach for the Conspectus's potential use at the national level.

Gorman, Gary E., and J. Kennedy. "Conspectus and the Distributed National Collection." In **Collection Development for Australian Libraries,** 203–14. 2d ed. Wagga Wagga, Australia: Centre for Information Studies, Charles Sturt University-Riverina, 1992. ISBN 0-949060-16-X.

The Conspectus in Australia and its role in the Australian Distributed National Collection are discussed in this textbook chapter. The ACLIS National Task Force on Conspectus in 1989 recommended adoption of the Pacific Northwest version in order to facilitate cooperative collection development. Seven ways the Conspectus can promote resource sharing are listed. The authors emphasize the Conspectus is an instrument for "describing" rather than "assessing" collections. Although Australian librarians have been "generally uncritical" of the Conspectus, Gorman and Kennedy note the following disadvantages: a pro-North American bias even in the Australianized version, the cost and labor of implementing it, the subjectivity of the assessments, and its unsuitability for special libraries using specialized classification schemes. The chapter's final portion focuses on the Distributed National Collection, defined as "the aggregation of all collections in Australia." The Conspectus can promote a formal national system of coordinated collection development by providing better knowledge of existing collections. This item provides a useful Conspectus overview from an Australian viewpoint.

Gray, Andrea. "An Evaluation of Selected Users' Experience of Conspectus in New Zealand." **New Zealand Libraries** 47 (June 1994): 194–99.

The twelve New Zealand libraries that had contributed assessments by June 1993 to the Conspectus New Zealand Database were surveyed by Gray in September-October 1993 concerning their perceptions about the Conspectus and all responded. She found that the implementation process supported staff professional development and validated "intuitive beliefs" about the collection. However, staff understood their collections better due to the evaluation process per se rather than because of the collected data. Respondents perceived that the major benefit of the Conspectus would be derived from internal library decision-making rather than from national cooperative collection development agreements, although "small scale ventures are feasible." Most of the surveyed libraries "remain optimistic" about the potential benefits of the Conspectus.

Sridhar, M.S. "Role of Conspectus in Collection Management and Resource Sharing." **Library Science with a Slant to Documentation & Information Studies** 34 (June 1997): 91–99.

This essay's stated objective is to inform Indian LIS professionals about the Conspectus methodology. Following a basic description it is explained the Conspectus can be used for collection evaluation, resource sharing, fund raising, accreditation, and setting retrospective conversion priorities among other functions. The "cost efficiency" of implementation, the questionable precision and validity of assigned collecting levels, and difficulties with the LC classification scheme are discussed as "pitfalls." The approach is termed "soft" because the Conspectus values are "expressions of opinion" rather than data. Verification studies and Supplemental Guidelines are noted as possible solutions to these problems. Sridhar observes that during the preceding fifteen years, the Conspectus was not "conspicuous in India." Although this entry offers an Indian perspective, the footnotes indicate the analysis is based on reviewing the North American literature.

Wade, Ann. "European Approaches to the Conspectus." In **Latin American Studies into the Twenty-First Century; New Focus, New Formats, New Challenges: Papers of the Thirty-Sixth Annual Meeting of the Seminar on the Acquisition of Latin American Library Materials; University of California, San Diego and San Diego State University, San Diego, California, June 1–6, 1991,** edited by Deborah L. Jakubs, 258–64. Albuquerque, NM: SALALM Secretariat, General Library, University of New Mexico, 1993. ISBN 0-917617-38-X.

Wade, the U.K. National Conspectus Officer in the British Library, offers an historical overview of the Conspectus in Europe through the early 1990s. The British Library implemented the Conspectus in 1985 and entered the results in Conspectus Online. The Conspectus was also used by a consortium of Scottish libraries for cooperative collection development and by the National Library of Wales during the late 1980s. In 1987 Ligue des Bibliothéques Européennes de Recherche (LIBER), a European research library consortium, set up the Conspectus Working Group to create a framework for implementing the Conspectus in continental Europe. Conspectus developments in France, Portugal, the Netherlands, Sweden, and Germany are briefly reviewed. Adapting the worksheets to a European context and translation of worksheets, code definitions, and the Supplemental Guidelines into one or more European languages are deemed "major tasks." Wade observes that interest in the Conspectus "varies markedly" among European countries, but "most" are in the "early stages" of planning Conspectus use.

Waters, David. "The Distributed National Collection, Conspectus, Resource Sharing and Cooperative Collection Development." **Australian Academic & Research Libraries** 23 (March 1992): 20–24.

Waters begins by noting that the 1988 Australian Libraries Summit recommended the concept of a Distributed National Collection and that the ACLIS and National Library coordinate the Conspectus's use for collection assessment and collection development policies in Australian libraries. Two perceived "problem areas" with the Conspectus are the costs and the reliability of the assessments. Waters observes that an "inaccurate map" of the strengths and weaknesses of Australian library collections is better than no map. The five assessment techniques outlined in Henty's *Australian Conspectus Manual* (see entry in next section) are acknowledged to have "shortcomings," but it is asserted that "the quality of assessments seems to depend less on the reliability of the techniques than on the knowledge and judgment of the librarians who carry them out."

CONSPECTUS MANUALS

Bushing, Mary, Burns Davis, and Nancy Powell. **Using the Conspectus Method: A Collection Assessment Handbook.** Lacey, WA: WLN, 1997. 200p. ISBN 0-9633700-1-6.

This handbook, organized into five parts, is intended to support use of the Conspectus method in "all types and sizes of libraries." Part 1 discusses the role of assessment in collection management. The second part offers a detailed overview of the WLN Conspectus, covering the method, structure, collecting levels, and the WLN Conspectus software. Part 3, the longest section, focuses on the assessment project, covering project management, assessment techniques, and data interpretation. Next, part 4 explains how Conspectus results can be used in reports, collection plans, budgeting, policy, accreditation, disaster preparedness, reassessment, and resource sharing. The fifth part includes a formula for relating collecting levels to book publishing output as well as list checking sources in about twenty-five subject areas. Finally, a useful glossary and a fairly extensive unannotated bibliography are appended. Numerous illustrations of reports, worksheets, and so on, are interspersed throughout the text. Of the half dozen or so Conspectus manuals, this is the most current and most thorough.

Henty, Margaret, comp. **Australian Conspectus Manual: A Collection Assessment Guide.** Canberra, Australian Capital Territory: Australian Council of Libraries and Information Services, 1992. 102p. ISBN 1-875351-10-8.

Henty, Margaret, comp. **Australian Conspectus Manual: A Collection Assessment Guide.** Canberra, Australian Capital Territory: National Library of Australia, 1992. np. ISBN 0-64210-574-X.

Henty, Margaret, comp. **Australian Conspectus Manual: A Collection Assessment Guide.** Preliminary Ed. Canberra, Australian Capital Territory: National Library of Australia, 1991. 1. V. (loose-leaf) ISBN 0-64210-510-3.

Although bibliographical searching identified citations for three separate versions of the manual, this annotation is based on direct examination of the one listed first. The National Library of Australia's Conspectus Officer revised Nancy Powell's *Pacific Northwest Collection Assessment Manual,* third edition, in order to assist Australian librarians with implementing the Conspectus worksheets.[6] The Conspectus's organization, collecting levels, and worksheets, including Australianization of the LC and Dewey versions, are explained. Five assessment techniques (shelflist measurement, shelf scanning, list checking, expert evaluation, and citation analysis) are discussed. A separate section addresses issues such as divided collections, uncataloged material, and validation studies. More than a third of the volume is devoted to eight appendices, including a bibliography of bibliographies and indexes that can be used in list checking and a summary of estimated publishing output statistics in various subject areas (both to help assign collecting levels). This manual fulfills its intended purpose.

Powell, Nancy, and Mary Bushing. **WLN Collection Assessment Manual**. 4th ed. Lacey, WA: WLN, 1992. 89p. ISBN 0-9633700-0-6.

This "new, refined, and enlarged" edition of Powell's *Pacific Northwest Collection Assessment Manual* is intended to serve as a "reference tool" for librarians "with a wide diversity of sophistication and skills" using the Conspectus methodology.[7] A section on the assessment process offers detailed information on five techniques: examining shelflist data, direct examination of the holdings, checking lists, use of outside experts, and citation analysis. Nearly 40 percent of the manual is devoted to the WLN Conspectus framework, explaining the methodology, structure, codes, worksheets, and so on. Other sections discuss collection management, collection development policies, and cooperative collection development. Worksheets, publishing output data, and bibliographies for list checking are appended.

Weech, Terry L. **CCM in Illinois: A Resource Book.** 2d ed. Springfield: Illinois Cooperative Collection Management Coordinating Committee, 1992. 40p.

Although the title suggests a focus on cooperative collection management, this manual actually addresses collection evaluation using the Illinois Conspectus. (The Illinois State Library licensed the WLN software for use by select Illinois libraries to create a statewide online collection assessment database termed the "Illinois Conspectus.") This approach, Weech stresses, combines qualitative assessment based on judgment with quantitative assessment using shelflist measurement or title count. A lengthy chapter explains the WLN Conspectus and its implementation with separate sections offering "tips" for academic, public, special, and school libraries as well as special collections and formats. Then, eleven steps in implementing the Conspectus methodology are listed. An appendix presents samples of completed worksheets in a public library, school library, and a museum archive.

MISCELLANEOUS ISSUES

Clayton, Peter, and G. E. Gorman. "Updating Conspectus for a Digital Age." **Library Collections, Acquisitions, & Technical Services** 26 (Fall 2002): 253–58.

Reemphasizing some themes from the Conspectus chapter in their 2001 collection management textbook (see entry in this chapter), Clayton and Gorman stress that the Conspectus "urgently needs to be updated" because it was developed in the predigital age. They maintain that the Conspectus should consider resources a library provides access to in addition to its present focus on what is owned, that is, it should be "resource access-centered" rather than "collection-centered." A revised set of Conspectus collecting level definitions that take into account Internet and other electronic resources (actually the same set published in the above-mentioned chapter) is presented. The authors conclude that either a new instrument must be developed for assessing the resources available in and through libraries or the Conspectus must be revised to meet this need.

Davis, Burns. "Using Local Marketing Characteristics to Customize the Conspectus for Fiction Assessment." **Acquisitions Librarian** no. 19 (1998): 29–44.

In essence, Davis argues the Conspectus can be customized to correspond with shelf arrangement by genre or format (apparently assumed to reflect a library's marketing strategy) when evaluating a public library fiction collection. The author outlines three approaches for using the WLN Conspectus software for fiction assessment: using the existing Dewey or LC Conspectus classifications, entering keywords into the worksheets' notes area then generating customized reports with the software, and creating local divisions based on genre or format. Drawing upon the experience of the same unnamed public library in the above article, examples of customized reports and a locally created three-level subject hierarchy for fiction are listed. There is some overlap in content and wording between this and the preceding entry.

Dorner, Daniel G. "A Study of the Collection Inventory Assessments for Psychology in the Canadian Conspectus Database and an Analysis of the Conspectus Methodology." **Library & Information Science Research** 16 (fall 1994): 279–97.

Dorner compared the assigned collecting levels for established collection strength and current collecting intensity in the fifty-one subdivisions of the Psychology Conspectus (gathered from the Canadian Conspectus database in November 1993) with data on expenditures during 1987–90 and total holdings as well as current periodical subscriptions in 1990 (obtained from the *American Library Directory*) for eighteen Canadian university libraries and the National Library of Canada. One subdivision, "Memory" was examined for sixteen libraries, correlating the current collecting intensity with the number of relevant items held. The author found Conspectus collecting levels and the other data were often inconsistent among libraries, that is, a library with higher expenditures and holdings might have a lower collecting level. Moreover, in the Memory subdivision the correlation between the current collecting intensity and the number of relevant volumes owned was not even statistically significant. Thus, he concludes the assigned collecting levels are unreliable as consequences of flaws in the methodology. Dorner explains that Conspectus collecting levels represent "category scaling," a method used in LIS research since the 1960s and dating back to the ancient Greek Astronomer Hipparchus, who developed a six-point scale to assess a star's brightness. He points out a number of biases in category scaling that help explain problems with the Conspectus (i.e., people tend to pick the middle categories while avoiding the extremes).

Drummond, Rebecca C., and Mary H. Munroe. "Including Access in Conspectus Methodology." In **Advances in Collection Development and Resource Management,** vol. 2, edited by Thomas W. Leonhardt, 63–79. Greenwich, CT: JAI Press, 1996. ISBN 0-7623-0097-3.

Drummond and Munroe decide the Conspectus, supporting the "old paradigm" of ownership, focuses on size of holdings without considering a library's ability to access unowned materials. They also note the Supplemental Guidelines for assigning collecting levels based on ownership are "vague and ambiguous." A large section discusses access issues, including speed, reciprocal borrowing, Internet resources, informing patrons about access methods, and cost and asks "when evaluating a collection, would more weight be given to the library that subsidizes more of the cost?" The authors conclude with five recommendations:

1. The Conspectus worksheets should be revised by adding collecting levels for access.

2. The Supplemental Guidelines should be revised because most were written before access became a major issue.

3. A core of materials should be established (based on overlap and verification studies) for each Conspectus collecting level.

4. Standards for "what constitutes acceptable access" should be defined.

5. Collecting responsibilities should be defined with greater flexibility (i.e., finite periods and duplicate Primary Collecting Responsibility (PCR) assignments).

Ferguson, Anthony W. "The Conspectus and Cooperative Collection Development: What It Can and Cannot Do." **Acquisitions Librarian** no. 7 (1992): 105–14.

This essay explores the Conspectus's role in cooperative collection development. The author surmises that Conspectus-based cooperative collection development agreements have been "illusive" because implementing the Conspectus became an end in itself. Further, competitiveness among libraries, their desire for autonomy, and the ownership paradigm have been barriers to cooperation. Yet, "The Conspectus is the only systematic collection development tool available which allows libraries to map their strengths and weaknesses at narrow subject levels and then communicate this picture to each other." The Conspectus can, according to Ferguson, best be used for cooperative collection development in areas of high current need but low resources. He contends that two "concepts," that is, categories for assigning collecting levels, need to be added to the Conspectus: "desired collecting goals" and "cooperative collecting responsibility." Ferguson's opinion carries authority because he was among the collection development librarians that spent thirteen years developing the Conspectus.

Ferguson, Anthony W. "The Conspectus as an On-Site Training Tool." In **Recruiting, Educating, and Training Librarians for Collection Development,** edited by Peggy Johnson and Sheila S. Intner, 171–81. Westport, CT: Greenwood Press, 1994. ISBN 0-313-28561-6.

Ferguson stresses that the Conspectus can analyze the collection at three levels: what is needed, what is on the shelf, and what is currently being acquired. Eight assessment factors are outlined: curricular support, publication dates, periodical subscriptions, monographic acquisitions, foreign language materials, reference works, databases, and authors. Shelflists, expenditure reports, circulation data, and subject headings in the library catalog are listed as information sources. As spin-offs to Conspectus implementation, selectors become familiar with literature guides, develop an *esprit de corps,* have a communication device with faculty, and "become involved with the collection as a physical object." Remedies are suggested for four weaknesses of the Conspectus: its "time-consuming nature," implementation becoming an end in itself, the subject headings, and imprecise collection-depth definitions. Drawing upon Powell and Bushing's *WLN Collection Assessment Manual,* Ferguson makes specific suggestions relating to training (e.g., develop an action calendar). The author emphasizes "the Conspectus is a tool for helping selectors understand their collections … [but] it is more than a training tool."

Kachel, Debra E. "Look Inward Before Looking Outward: Preparing the School Library Media Center for Cooperative Collection Development." **School Library Media Quarterly** 23 (winter 1995): 101–13.

This article discusses how a Conspectus approach can support cooperative collection development among school libraries. Kachel explains that "resource sharing" shares existing materials, whereas "cooperative collection development" plans future acquisitions. She states the Conspectus "provides a process for systematically analyzing and describing a collection on a subject-by-subject basis."

Modified Conspectus worksheets for the Ephrata Senior High School Media Center, in Pennsylvania, illustrate the compilation of holdings, current acquisitions, growth rate, age, use, and collecting level data (mostly generated from an automated circulation system) in order to assess the local collection. "Considerable computer power" is required to build a regional database of local collection information that can assist CCD. Research is cited showing school libraries in a region "contain significantly different materials" (despite a common assumption they hold the same core items) thus facilitating the opportunities for cooperative collection development. A final section lists nine levels of CCD from listing unique collections to each library collecting specific subjects. Note that the modified Conspectus approach described here differs considerably from the original RLG Conspectus.

Olson, Georgine. "The Conspectus as a Tool for (Cooperative) Collection Management." **Collection Building** 13, nos. 2–3 (1994): 87–90.

This relatively short piece introduces two charts, termed "Olson Overview Charts," for assessing library collections. The Non-fiction Overview Chart is based on thirty broad subject categories adapted from the first level of the Illinois Conspectus. The Fiction Overview Chart contains sixteen categories (i.e., horror, mystery, romance, etc.) developed in the Fiction Assessment Project (see entries by Baker, "Quality and Demand: The Basis for Fiction Collection Assessment," in chapter 4, and Olson in chapter 4). For each subject category, ten types of evaluative data are entered, including the number of titles held, the assigned Conspectus acquisition level, the number of titles in nonbook format, and the year the collection was last weeded as well as assessments concerning the level of ILL requests, reference questions, and user requests in the area. The charts are "primarily" intended for small libraries, but Olson says they can be adapted for all library types and sizes. This assessment approach may be viewed as a notable permutation of the Conspectus method.

Reed-Scott, Jutta. "The Implications of the Conspectus for Western European Studies." **Collection Management** 15, nos. 3–4 (1992): 509–15.

A well-known Conspectus expert discusses its utility for Western European Studies. She observes the Conspectus structure "works well" for specific country studies, but "poses difficulties" for cross-national studies (e.g., trade imbalances) or micro-topics (the Medici in Florence). Many of her specific illustrations relate to Italy. The Conspectus online database indicated forty-five level 5 collections in Western European Studies, mostly relating to England, France, and Germany, and in "narrowly-focused" areas such as French folklore at Indiana University. The author notes there have been fifty assignments of Primary Collecting Responsibility in Western European Studies, primarily to the Library of Congress, but overall there are "grave problems" in North American coverage of European materials. Reed-Scott stresses that the Conspectus can not support cooperative collection development in Western European Studies until two conditions are met: "broader" Conspectus implementation by North American and European research libraries and expansion of the Conspectus structure for European countries similar to what was done for Canada.

Underwood, Kent. "Developing Supplemental Guidelines for Music: A Case Report." **Acquisitions Librarian** no. 7 (1992): 157–68.

Underwood describes the development of the Supplemental Guidelines for the Music Conspectus. The guidelines were drawn up by the four-member Music Task Force, working from 1989 to 1991, of METRO, a 300 member multitype library consortium in New York City and the surrounding area. The author stresses that Supplemental Guidelines are an important part of the evaluation process because they provide "benchmarks" that promote consistent assignment of collecting levels among libraries. It was decided that music collections should be evaluated according to four separate formats: books, periodicals, scores, and recordings. The latter were further subdivided into "Western classical music," "jazz and popular music," and "world music." Benchmarks are provided for each of these formats. For example, a level 2 collection should contain 20 percent to 50 percent of the music books in *BCL3*. In addition the task force proposed a revision of the Music Conspectus, the main features of which are summarized in a postscript. Instead of tying the Conspectus to a classification system, such as LC or Dewey Decimal Classification (DDC), there would be "one universal Music Conspectus." Also, periodicals could be assessed separately and additional chronological and geographic terms would be added. This is one of a relatively small number of items that address Supplemental Guidelines (an aspect of Conspectus implementation whose significance is often unappreciated).

NOTES

1. Gary E. Gorman and J. Kennedy, *Collection Development for Australian Libraries,* 2d ed. (Wagga Wagga, Australia: Centre for Information Studies, Charles Sturt University-Riverina, 1992), 204.

2. Jutta Reed-Scott, *Manual for the North American Inventory of Research Library Collections,* 1985 ed. (Washington, DC: Association of Research Libraries, 1985).

3. Nisonger's calculation from Ebersole's raw data; Dennis Shaw, *Information Sources in Physics,* 3d ed. (London: Bowker Saur, 1994).

4. David Henige, "Epistemological Dead End and Ergonomic Disaster? The North American Collections Inventory Project," *Journal of Academic Librarianship* 13 (September 1987): 209–213.

5. Ibid.

6. Nancy Powell, comp. and ed., *Pacific Northwest Collection Assessment Manual,* 3d ed. (Salem: Pacific Northwest Collection Development Program, Oregon State Library Foundation, 1990).

7. Ibid.

4

Client-Centered and Combination Approaches to Traditional Collection Evaluation

Chapter 4 concentrates on evaluation studies based on client-centered methods as well as on investigations that combine the client- and collection-centered approaches. As explained in the introduction, a client-centered approach focuses on the collection's use rather than its content per se. Some of the leading client-centered approaches should be briefly explained.

An availability study, as suggested by its name, tests whether items are available for patron use. Mansbridge identifies an availability study conducted in Iowa as far back as the 1930s.[1] The best-known approach to the investigation of availability is the so-called Branching Method, developed by Paul B. Kantor during the 1970s.[2] Kantor identified four branches, or barriers, to the patron locating a desired item: acquisitions (the item was not acquired by the library), circulation (its checked out to another patron), library operations (the book is not on the correct shelf location), and the user (the patron can not locate a correctly shelved item). Numerous subsequent researchers have used modified forms of Kantor's technique, often by adding additional branches. The majority of availability studies have been based on surveying patrons as they leave the library concerning whether they located sought-after items. Simulated studies, which check the ownership, circulation status, and shelf availability of a list of items presumed to represent patron information needs, have also been conducted.

A document delivery test (DDT) measures accessibility, in order words, how much time is required to place a needed document in the patron's hands. The best-known document delivery test was developed during the 1960s by Richard H. Orr and his colleagues and is frequently termed Orr's DDT.[3] First, one measures the time needed to obtain each document from a sample of approximately 300 citations, presumed to simulate patron information needs. Then a five-point scoring system (1 = less than ten minutes, 2 = between ten minutes and two hours, 3 = two to twenty-four hours, 4 = one day to one week, 5 = more than a week) is applied to the result for each item. Finally, the scores are averaged and a Capability Index, ranging from 0 (no document procured within a week) to 100 (every document obtained in less than ten minutes), is calculated.

Other client-centered methods include surveys, interviews, focus groups, analysis of interlibrary loan statistics, citation studies, circulation studies, and in-house use studies. Thus, for full treatment of client-centered approaches the reader is referred to chapter 8, which covers evaluation of use, chapter 9, which deals with citation analysis, and chapter 12, which addresses evaluation of interlibrary loan and document delivery.

Numerous authoritative sources, including the ALA's *Guide to the Evaluation of Library Collections,* advocate the use of multiple evaluation methods (to compensate for the potential deficiencies of a single approach).[4] Consequently, client-centered techniques are commonly used in combination with collection-centered methods. Chapter 4 thus contains a section on the use of client-centered methods in combination with collection-centered techniques.

A voluminous literature addresses the evaluation of reference question answering, a topic clearly beyond this book's scope. While a sizeable amount has been written about reference collection development, publications focusing primarily on the evaluation and use of reference collections are relatively sparse. This chapter includes a section about reference collection evaluation, covering both collection-centered and client-centered methods as well as use studies. Note, however, that the evaluation of specific reference resources, such as indexing services, is not included.

The remainder of this chapter is divided into three segments: availability studies and document delivery tests, combinations of client and collection-centered methods, and evaluation of reference collections.

AVAILABILITY STUDIES AND DOCUMENT DELIVERY TESTS

Ciliberti, Anne, et al. "Empty Handed? A Material Availability Study and Transaction Log Analysis Verification." **Journal of Academic Librarianship** 24 (July 1998): 282–89.

An availability study, conducted at random times during a three-week period in an unspecified fall semester at Adelphi University, is reported here. A modified form of Kantor's Branching Method was used to analyze the outcome of about 400 OPAC searches and 200 searches in a CD-ROM journal index. The success rate was 61 percent for known-item searches in the OPAC and 60 percent for subject searches, whereas the rate was 45 percent for journal index searches. There is detailed statistical analysis concerning the status of searchers, the types of searches conducted, and the success rate at each branch. It is noteworthy that in only 1 percent of the cases did the user locate the item on the shelf and decide it was inappropriate. The use of transaction log analysis to verify patron self-reports regarding unsuccessful OPAC searches found that most reports were accurate (thus validating earlier studies based on self reports). The four authors conclude that availability studies can result in "informed future planning," citing ten changes made by the library as a result of their investigation.

Jacobs, Neil A. "Book Availability Surveys." In **Academic Library Surveys and Statistics in Practice: Proceedings of a Seminar Held at Loughborough University, 2–3 June 1997,** edited by David Spiller, 43–46. Loughborough, U.K.: Library and Information Statistics Unit, Loughborough University, 1998. ISBN 1-9017-8601-3.

Writing in an informal, first-person style, Jacobs reflects upon the implementation of two availability studies at the University of Sussex (see subsequent entries by Jacobs for further details). The paper is organized around five specific "lessons" learned from the experience:

1. Know why you are doing the survey

2. Design the methodology based on the survey's purpose

3. Estimate sample size based on the survey's purpose

4. Be "willing and able" to act on the results

5. Publicize your success

Jacobs notes that a researcher planned the survey and analyzed the findings, six library staff spent an hour a day following up on unfound books, students distributed questionnaires, and a £10 gift voucher was given each day to encourage patron cooperation. Being on loan accounted for about half the unavailability of all books, 79 percent of the unavailability of six-week loan books; and 26 percent for four-day loan and reserve titles. This entry is useful for its focus on nitty-gritty organizational and methodological issues.

Jacobs, Neil A. "The Evaluation and Improvement of Book Availability in an Academic Library." **New Review of Academic Librarianship** 1 (1995): 41–55.

Jacobs describes two book availability studies conducted at the University of Sussex (in the United Kingdom) during the spring of 1994 (based on 4,103 books sought) and the autumn term of the same year (1,585 books sought). Kantor's Branching Method was expanded to include eight branches:

1. "A good citation"

2. "Acquired by library"

3. "Found in catalog"

4. Not in circulation

5. "Not 'mislaid.'" (i.e., the item could not be located)

6. "Not 'temporarily absent,'" (i.e., the item could be located by the next morning)

7. "Not 'slightly misfiled,'" (i.e., the item could be located within a few minutes)

8. A correctly shelved book not found by user

The overall availability rate was 62.54 percent. Changes were then made in six areas of library policy (the OPAC, signage and guides, stack maintenance, user education, the reserve collection, and circulation). Availability increased to 71.7 percent in the second study using seven branches when "good citation" and "acquired by the library" were collapsed into a single branch. However, Jacobs cautions this improvement can not be completely attributed to the library policy changes. This exceedingly sophisticated study developed a strategy for address-ing multiple copy issues (i.e., one copy is checked out and another lost).

Jacobs, Neil A., and R. C. Young. "Measuring Book Availability in an Academic Library: A Methodological Comparison." **Journal of Documentation** 51 (September 1995): 281–90.

This article compares two approaches to measuring availability used at the University of Sussex during the same two-week period in the spring of 1994: Kantor's patron survey method and data derived from the OPAC. A custom-written software program analyzed 99,778 title searches in the Geac 9000 OPAC and identified 24,652 instances whereby the title was unavailable because all copies were checked out. This 24.7 percent failure rate due to circulation was sig-nificantly higher than the 15.1 percent circulation failure rate indicated by patron surveys. Jacobs and Young believe that patrons often perceived that their failed OPAC searches were not "sufficient[ly] important to merit reporting." Analysis of the percentage distribution of unavailable titles among thirty-four subject groups revealed no statistically significant difference between the two availability meth-ods for all but four subjects. The authors thus conclude that OPAC-derived avail-ability data can substitute for survey-derived data with two limitations: relative unavailability by subject rather than an absolute level of unavailability is indi-cated and reasons for nonavailability other than the book circulating are not addressed.

Kaske, Neal K. "Materials Availability Model and the Internet." **Journal of Aca-demic Librarianship** 20 (November 1994): 317–18.

In this brief opinion piece, Kaske contends that the traditional availability test "is no longer useful." It is, he argues, based on the "just-in-case" model and does not consider material accessed "just-in-time" nor the fact that patrons use online gateways to external information resources rather than limiting their search to one library. The author advocates a "collaborative effort...to create a new valid mea-sure of materials availability" incorporating at least three new elements: search-ing multiple libraries, the time waited for the information, and type of information needed. His identification of patron time spent waiting for information as a key measure reminds one, although not explicitly acknowledged by Kaske, of a docu-ment delivery test. He concludes that we may need both a new model of materials availability and a model "for user satisfaction with the digital library."

Lancaster, F. W. "Shelf Availability." In **If You Want to Evaluate Your Library...,** 129–46. 2d ed. Champaign, IL: University of Illinois, Graduate School of Library and Information Science, 1993. ISBN 0-87845-091-2.

Lancaster begins by distinguishing between a simulated study, in which library staff check the shelf availability for a list of citations, and a real study, based on surveying actual users. He offers a detailed methodological discussion concerning the technical pitfalls of various methods of drawing citations (i.e., from the shelflist, circulation records, or published sources). User surveys can be based on questionnaires or interviews. A discussion of scoring methods explains the calculation of Orr's Capability Index, ranging from 0 (no item available within a week) to 100 (every item available within ten minutes). Finally, citing Michael K. Buckland, Lancaster explains that an item's popularity, the number of copies, and the loan period's length are the three major factors affecting availability.[5] Doubling the number of copies or reducing the loan period in half will increase, but not double, the number of copies. This entry is useful for both its practical advice and methodological insights.

Mitchell, Eugene S., Marie L. Radford, and Judith L. Hegg. "Book Availability: Academic Library Assessment." **College & Research Libraries** 55 (January 1994): 47–55.

A book availability study conducted in 1989 at an unidentified "medium-sized public college library in New Jersey" is recounted here. A modification of Kantor's original method, the investigation was a follow-up to a previously published 1986 study.[6] The authors analyze the success rate in each of six branches for sixty-one known item searches:

1. Bibliographic error (i.e., patron has incorrect bibliographic citation)

2. Selection error (i.e., library did not acquire desired book)

3. Catalog use error (i.e., patron cannot identify call number)

4. Circulation error (i.e., book is on loan or "hold")

5. Library malfunction error (i.e., book is missing, misshelved, etc.)

6. Retrieval error (i.e., patron can not locate correctly shelved book)

They also analyze the success rate in a different set of six branches for fifty subject searches:

1. Matched query error (i.e., the patron can not find a subject heading matching the information need)

2. Catalog use error

3. Circulation error

4. Library malfunction

5. Retrieval error

6. Appropriate title error (i.e., identified titles are unsuitable for patron information need)

The overall success rate was 64 percent. Detailed comparisons are made with the 1986 study, which had a final success rate of 54 percent.

Norton, Mick, Sheila Lynne Seaman, and Michael Joseph Sprankle. "Measuring Book Availability: A Monthly Sampling Method." **College & Undergraduate Libraries** 3, no. 1 (1996): 101–15.

A random method for assessing book shelf availability, developed at the College of Charleston, is described in this entry. Each month fifty bar code numbers for books were randomly selected by a shelving assistant, who checked their on-shelf status and the reason why missing books were absent. Written in the language of systems theory and quality control, this article focuses on the methodology and only presents sketchy results. From September 1991 through June 1995, the mean number of missing books per month was 1,348. Note that books in circulation were not considered missing. A table lists seven expected reasons for absent books, such as shelver error, patron reshelving error, or stolen books, and the corrective action. Four unexpected causes were identified, including book truck breakdowns and student hoarding of personal collections using an incorrect call number. Although useful as a shelf inventory method, this technique does not address nonacquisition, in-circulation, or user inability to locate the item as causes of nonavailability.

Rehman, Sajjad Ur, and Shaheena Bashir. "Comparative Measurement of Book Availability in Academic Libraries." **International Information & Library Review** 25 (September 1993): 183–93.

Rehman and Bashir describe the implementation of Kantor's method in the Punjab University library in Lahore, Pakistan. The study was based on 300 books sought at the main library during December 1990 through January 1991. The overall availability rate was 41.3 percent. A comparison with four studies using Kantor's approach in developed country libraries found availability ranged from 58.9 percent to 63 percent. In only one branch, circulation, did the Punjab library perform better than the four other libraries. The Punjab University library's weakest branch was library operations (a 65.7 percent success rate). Among other reasons, many books had been transferred to branch libraries without updating the catalog. The user branch (an 82.4 percent success rate) was the next weakest, reflecting the lack of effective user education and the absence of a signage system.

Salter, Elaine. "How Good Is the Library Provision in FE Colleges?" **Library Association Record** 95 (June 1993): 348–49.

This short item describes a document availability test carried out at Acton College (a further education college in Greater London) during the fall of 1991.

Note that further education (FE) is a British term for post secondary education not considered higher education.[7] Citing her MLib thesis, Salter observes this was the only availability or document delivery test reported to have been conducted in thirty further education colleges in the Greater London area.[8] Data for this study was gathered from 9 A.M. to 5 P.M. on five days beginning in October 1991. The final success rate was 70 percent, calculated from 500 patron completed forms. Among the four traditional barriers, the largest failure rate (12 percent) was in circulation. The author offers considerable practical advice. Noting she once had to interrupt handing out forms because students were setting off firecrackers, Salter humorously exclaims "It's a bit like that in FE." Nevertheless, Salter believes that availability studies "can be done with minimum disruption to services."

Shaw-Kokot, Julia, and Claire de la Varre. "Using a Journal Availability Study to Improve Access." **Bulletin of the Medical Library Association** 89 (January 2001): 21–28.

The authors write about a study of journal availability at the University of North Carolina at Chapel Hill's Health Sciences Library. The investigation was modeled on a 1989 study at the University of New Mexico library, which used a modified form of Kantor's Branching Method. Library patrons were surveyed on twelve days (once a week) during the fall semester of 1997. Overall availability was 80.9 percent for 2,056 journal article searches. The success rate at the weakest branch—Library Operations—was 90.9 percent, where 38 percent of 150 failures were because the item was in intermediate reshelving, 34 percent were at the bindery, and 15 percent were missing. Further analysis indicated graduate students were the largest user group and that use was heaviest during the semester's first three weeks. The project required 160 staff hours plus ten hours a week by a library science graduate student. Seven specific recommendations, such as improved signage, were made to increase availability. This is one of the few availability studies to focus exclusively on journal articles.

Steynberg, Susan, and S. F. Rossouw. "The Availability of Research Journals in South African Academic Medical Libraries." **South African Medical Journal** 83 (November 1993): 837–39.

This entry's primary focus is on the implementation of Orr's Document Delivery Test and Kantor's Branching Method (the authors use the term "availability index") in the University of Cape Town Medical Library during August 1990. The study found that 69.4 percent of a 307 item sample was immediately available on the shelf, 19.5 percent were accessible in one to five days, 8.1 percent in six to ten days, and 2.9 percent in eleven to fifteen days.[9] The overall Capability Index was 88.86 (on a scale of 0 to 100). Applying Kantor's methodology, 74.92 percent of the sample had been acquired by the library, but 69.38 percent were available on the shelf. The availability rates at six other unnamed South African medical libraries ranged from 59.3 percent to 84.0 percent. For details about the DDT methodology and the results in seven unnamed South African medical libraries, see Steynberg and Rossouw entry in chapter 5.

Wall, Terry, and Jan V. Williams. "Availability, Accessibility, and Demand for Recommended Books in Academic Libraries." **Journal of Librarianship & Information Science** 31 (September 1999): 145–51.

This rigorous quantitative study investigates the effect that loan period has on the use and availability of books. The relative use of one-day and one-week loan copies of identical law and business titles at Cardiff University in the United Kingdom was compared, using a variety of statistical analyses, based on actual usage and computer-simulated estimated use. The authors demonstrated that one-day loan items were underutilized because readers preferred one-week loans. An availability study of law books at Cardiff University, cited from Williams's MSc. dissertation, found an 84 percent availability rate for 480 items.[10] Significantly, in about one-quarter of the failures, a one-day copy was available but not taken off the shelf because the user wanted a one-week copy. While it is often assumed that a reduced loan period increases use and availability of materials, Wall and Williams caution this may not be a correct assumption. Almost as an afterthought, the authors conjecture that "electronic short loans" might increase availability. This item is noteworthy for challenging the conventional lore that a reduced loan period increases availability.

Zondi, Lindiwe E. "Measuring Availability and Non-Availability Rates at the University of Zululand Library." **South African Journal of Library & Information Science** 64 (June 1996): 108–13.

Zondi reports an availability study carried out at the University of Zululand. A pilot study conducted in September 1994 had found a 55 percent success rate for fifty titles. In the actual investigation, questionnaires, asking information about the books sought and the patrons themselves, were distributed to students during the twelve-week period from March through May 1995. The methodology and implementation procedure are discussed. Overall, 50.42 percent of 353 desired titles were successfully located on the shelf. A user analysis found no statistically significant differences in the success rates among full-time, part-time, or evening students nor among undergraduate and post-graduate students. A user-education program for students was initiated as a result of this study.

COMBINATIONS OF COLLECTION-CENTERED AND CLIENT-CENTERED APPROACHES

Anderson, James H. "Assessment of the Seismology and Volcanology Collection, Geophysical Institute Library, University of Alaska Fairbanks." In **Finding and Communicating Geoscience Information: Proceedings of the Twenty-Eighth Meeting of the Geoscience Information Society, October 25–28, 1993, Boston, Massachusetts,** vol. 24, edited by Connie Wick, 99–110. Alexandria, VA: Geoscience Information Society, 1994. ISBN 0-934485-22-4.

A comprehensive evaluation of the seismology and volcanology collection at the University of Alaska at Fairbanks' Geophysical Institute Library, conducted by a Brigham Young University LIS master's student, is depicted here. Three approaches were used: compiling holdings statistics, the checklist method, and surveying users. The collection contained 549 books representing five major subject divisions. Checking an "authoritative bibliography," compiled from four sources including *GeoRef* and the *BIP Subject Guide,* found that 44 percent of 273 items were held by the Geophysical Institute Library, 12 percent by the main library, and 44 percent were not held on campus. The "held" and "not held" items were further analyzed by age, format, and publisher. A survey of thirteen faculty and ten graduate students (response rate not given) revealed that 54 percent of the former and 40 percent of the latter rated the collection as "very good" for instructional purposes, while 62 percent and 60 percent deemed the collection "very good" for research. A table lists the twenty-six journals most frequently read by the respondents. Anderson suggests nine issues for additional research. This item, written in a concise, well-organized style, contains more detailed information than can easily be summarized.

Baker, Sharon L. "A Product-Analysis Approach to Collection Evaluation." In **The Responsive Public Library Collection: How to Develop and Market It,** 167–232. Englewood: CO: Libraries Unlimited, 1993. ISBN 0-87287-911-9.

Baker, Sharon L., and Karen L. Wallace. "Collection Evaluation: A Product Analysis Approach." In **The Responsive Public Library: How to Develop and Market a Winning Collection,** 197–246. 2d ed. Englewood, CO: Libraries Unlimited, 2002. ISBN 1-56308-648-4.

This annotation is based primarily on the second edition of Baker's well-known text on marketing library collections. The chapter is organized around a four-pronged approach to public library collection evaluation:

1. Identification of heavily used currently owned titles: methods include examination of reserve lists, circulation records for specific titles, and total circulation patterns

2. Identification of currently owned titles that are not used: circulation and in-house use studies are recommended

3. Identification of unowned items likely to receive use: ILL records, unanswered reference questions, solicitation of patron suggestions, solicitation of suggestions from experts and community groups, patron questionnaires, focus groups, and checking lists are discussed as possible information sources

4. Identification of other barriers to collection use: an availability study is recommended and, based on Kantor, four barriers to access are explained: acquisitions, circulation, library errors, and patron errors

This chapter is useful for its practical approach. Step-by-step outlines are given for techniques such as determining turnover rate, calculating relative use by class, and conducting an availability study.

Baker, Sharon L. "Quality and Demand: The Basis for Fiction Collection Assessment." **Collection Building** 13, nos. 2–3 (1994): 65–68.

The author begins by reviewing the "quality" (advocated by Murray Bob) versus "demand" (promoted by Nora Rawlinson) debate concerning selection of books for public libraries.[11] Using a four-quadrant analysis, Baker recommends the following: "purchase in largish quantities" for high-quality, high-demand works; "purchase... in smaller quantities... and promote" high-quality, low-demand titles; purchase in smaller numbers low-quality, high-demand items; and "refrain from purchasing" low-quality, low-demand books. Drawing upon the quality versus demand issue, Baker describes what she terms the "fiction collection assessment tool," created for various-sized public libraries in Illinois. For details about this tool, see the next entry. This is one of the relatively small number of published items devoted to the evaluation of public library fiction collections.

Baker, Sharon L. project coordinator, and Patricia J. Boze, ed. **Fiction Collection Assessment Manual.** Champaign, IL: Lincoln Trail Libraries System, 1992. 76p.

A Library Services and Construction Act (LSCA) grant supported the development of this manual during 1991 in ten rural public libraries serving population of less than 10,000 in Illinois's Lincoln Trail Libraries and Corn Belt Library Systems. A three-page introductory chapter advocates assessment of fiction by format (hardback, paperback, large print, videotape, and books-on-tape), reading level (picture book, easy, juvenile, young adult, and adult), and genre (i.e., general, mystery, romance, etc.). Chapter 2 is organized into three parts. The first, "material-centered evaluation," addresses data-gathering on collection size and growth plus the checklist method and recommends use of classical fiction, award winners, and bestseller lists plus the ALA "List of Notable Books." The second section briefly discusses the Illinois Conspectus. Another section, "use-centered evaluation," explains a fiction availability survey as well as utilization of reserve lists, ILL requests, and focus groups to identify high-demand titles. The third and final chapter contains more than a dozen forms or worksheets (along with instructions) for fiction assessment, including estimating collection depth and size, recording the growth rate, and calculating the stock turnover rate. The preface asserts this tool can be used in libraries of any size.

Bunner, Kimberly. "The Krueger Manuals: A Case Study." **Collection Building** 13, nos. 2–3 (1994): 19–23.

The author reflects upon the implementation during the early 1980s of what she terms "the Krueger Manuals" in four Illinois libraries: East Peoria Community High School, Bradley University, Peoria Public Library, and Peoria Heights Public Library.[12] She briefly describes the implementation of the Krueger method's five components in the Peoria Heights Public Library, although specific results are not reported:

1. Shelflist measurement

2. Availability of a random sample from the shelflist

3. Analysis of circulation and in-house use statistics

4. Acquisitions statistics analysis

5. ILL statistics analysis

In addition, the "Materials Availability Survey" from *Output Measures for Public Libraries* was used. Bunner believes the Krueger approach was "ahead of the times" in its emphasis on availability and application to all types of libraries. Several criticisms of this method are noted: libraries felt "overwhelmed," there was concern about uniform application throughout the state, too much focus was placed on percentages rather than raw numbers, and questions arose about the collected data's usefulness. Bunner offers a balanced assessment of the Krueger method as well as a thoughtful perspective on collection evaluation in a small public library.

Carpenter, David, and Malcolm Getz. "Evaluation of Library Resources in the Field of Economics: A Case Study." **Collection Management** 20, nos. 1–2 (1995): 49–89.
A multifaceted evaluation of the economics collection at Vanderbilt University is reported here. A detailed table analyzing holdings data for 87,610 monographs reveals that 54.96 percent had circulated since 1986, 9.3 percent were published after 1989, 63.3 percent were published in North America, and 89.3 percent were in English. The collection contained 88.72 percent of the economics titles in *BCL3*. Analysis of books held by peer institutions, as indicated in the OCLC/Amigos Collection Analysis CD, identified Type I selection errors (titles that should have been acquired but were not), while data on noncirculating titles indicated Type II errors—books that were acquired but should not have been. The library had current subscriptions to 24 of the 25 most cited journals in Laband and Piette's study (see chapter 10), 47 of the 48 journals most cited by Vanderbilt faculty from 1980–93 (based on a search of the *Social Sciences Citation Index [SSCI]*), 63.7 percent of the journals in *Econlit*, 59.2 percent in *ABI/Inform Ondisc*, and 87.2 percent of the economics titles plus 85.3 percent of business titles in Katz's *Magazines for Libraries*. Scatter plots showed no relationship between journal cost and quality as indicated by citation measures. Data is also presented on expenditures. Electronic resources for economics are discussed, but it was "not possible" to evaluate them due to a "lack of tools" and their rapidly changing nature. This was an exceedingly thorough evaluation.

Crawley-Low, Jill V. "Collection Analysis Techniques Used to Evaluate a Graduate-Level Toxicology Collection." **Journal of the Medical Library Association** 90 (July 2002): 310–16.
This article depicts an evaluation, using a multifaceted approach, of the University of Saskatchewan library toxicology collection. The evaluation methods include the following:

- Checking a standard bibliography (*Information Resources in Toxicology*, 3d ed, edited by Philip Wexler and published by Academic Press in 2000) and the monographs listed in *Annual Review of Pharmacology and Toxicology* from 1997 to 1999 against the holdings

- Calculating the cost per use for twenty toxicology serial titles

- Checking the toxicology journals covered in the 1999 *JCR* against the library's holdings

- Creating a "classified profile" that calculated the number of the collection's books supporting each of eight graduate-level toxicology courses

- Analysis of ILL requests from September 1999 through March 2000 and monographs that circulated during a two-year period ending in March 2001.

Although some results are reported, the entry is notable for its careful discussion of the pros and cons of the various methodological approaches. Crawley-Low decides that list checking and the classified profile technique were the "simplest to use" and "easiest to interpret."

Curl, Margo Warner. "Collection Assessment of the CONSORT Collections." **Against the Grain** 14 (December 2002/January 2003): 54, 56–7.
Curl describes an assessment conducted by the Five Colleges of Ohio Consortium (Denison University, Kenyon College, Oberlin College, Ohio Wesleyan University, and the College of Wooster that share an online catalog named CONSORT) to prepare the groundwork for cooperative collection development. The OCLC/WLN service offering automated checking of *BCL3* and *Choice's* OAB found that the consortium collectively owned 78 percent of the titles with the percentage owned by individual libraries ranging from 43 percent to 52 percent. She explains how data on holdings, collection age, and circulation were obtained from the Innopac automated system. It was discovered that 46.57 percent of the Consortium's monographs had circulated during the preceding six years, with the figure ranging from 34.4 percent to 49.1 percent among the institutions. Other methods included checking the lists provided by Howard D. White (see entry in chapter 2). Candidly reflecting on the experience, the author writes, "If I were to start over now, I would start with a better sense of what was needed and why, [and] of what skills were needed to manipulate and analyze the data."

Davis, Burns. **Collection Assessment Manual for Small- and Medium-Sized Libraries.** Lincoln, NE: Nebraska Library Commission, 1993. 52p.

Davis, Burns. **Collection Assessment Manual for Small- and Medium-Sized Libraries.** Rev. ed. Lincoln, NE: Nebraska Library Commission, 1994. 52p.
These two entries will be covered in one annotation since they are essentially the same. The manuals were compiled to assist all types of small and medium-sized libraries in Nebraska, focusing on four areas:

1. The collection's size, age, and physical condition

2. Acquisitions

3. Circulation, reference, and ILL use

4. The budget

It is emphasized that collection assessment should be part of an ongoing process termed the "collection management cycle" that includes community analysis, planning/budgeting, selection/acquisitions, weeding, and so on. Step-by-step outlines are given for planning the assessment project, collecting data, completing the WLN Conspectus worksheets, analyzing data and setting priorities, and preparing the materials budget. Examples of worksheets are included, and a separate section is devoted to assessment of fiction. Davis acknowledges drawing upon Baker and Boze's *Fiction Collection Assessment Manual* (see entry in this chapter) and WLN Conspectus tools.

Davis, Burns. "Designing a Fiction Assessment Tool: The Customer Service Approach." **Collection Building** 13, nos. 2–3 (1994): 69–82.

Davis depicts a fiction assessment tool developed for small and medium-sized public and school libraries in Nebraska to be used in conjunction with the WLN Conspectus. The author emphasizes in a detailed outline that this approach is flexible, comprehensive, simple, and shareable. The article illustrates, and is based upon, three lengthy worksheets:

- The Median Age Tally Sheet: used to calculate the age of the holdings in various genres and formats

- The Fiction Assessment Data Worksheet: in which seventeen types of collection-centered and use-centered data as well as the Conspectus line number, recommended action, and notes are entered for thirteen genres

- The Assessment Data Worksheet Summary: follows the above organization but covers fiction and nonfiction

The worksheets can be formatted as Excel spreadsheets to generate reports and "set up predictive scenarios." Ten steps are listed for recording quantitative (shelflist numbers) and qualitative (based on observation) data. This entry is useful for readers interested in fiction assessment, but is verbosely written.

Davis, Frances. "A Plan for Evaluating a Small Library Collection." **College & Research Libraries News** 54, no. 6 (June 1993): 328–29.

The author briefly describes the plan and methodology used to evaluate the Owensboro Community College collection during a three-week period in February-March 1992. Faculty were assigned a segment of the LC classification system and asked to complete a five-question worksheet pertaining to that segment concerning topics missing from the collection or needing broader coverage as well as naming titles from course textbooks that should be included. No specific results are reported. This short piece is worth noting because items relating to community college collection evaluation are relatively sparse in the literature.

Ephraim, P. E. "A Review of Qualitative and Quantitative Measures in Collection Analysis." **Electronic Library** 12 (August 1994): 237–42.

After reviewing the quantitative versus qualitative argument in collection evaluation, Ephraim advocates "a mix" of these approaches. The majority of this article is devoted to recapitulation of two studies from the 1970s: a collection-centered evaluation at Gonzaga University described by Robert L. Burr and a combination collection and client-centered analysis of four Nigerian University libraries (Ibadan, Lagos, Ahmadu Bello, and Obafemi Awolowo) by Samuel E. Ifidon.[13] The final section, a brief discussion of software packages, seems disjointed from the rest of the article. This item may disappoint some readers because it does not fully deliver what the title suggests—a thorough review of both qualitative and quantitative collection evaluation measures.

Erbes, Bill, and adapted by Georgine Olson. "Illinois Valley Library System and the Development of the Krueger Method." **Collection Building** 13, nos. 2–3 (1994): 15–18.

Taking an historical approach, this entry is a revised version of an earlier article from *Illinois Libraries.*[14] King Research, Inc., was contracted in 1980 to assist cooperative collection development in the Illinois Valley Library System (a 90 member multitype consortium). A five-point plan includes assessment of the consortium library's existing collection strengths. A significant portion of this article addresses collection evaluation goals and methods. Four data gathering objectives are outlined:

1.   Identification of subject strengths

2.   Identification of subjects where demand exceeds supply

3.   Identification of subject strength overlap among libraries

4.   Use of the results to plan cooperative collection development

After considering "library self-nomination of strengths," expert review, and the checklist method, King Research recommended the subject, publication date, and last circulation date be analyzed for samples from the shelflist and stacks. Moreover, the samples' subject breakdowns would be analyzed for circulation, holdings, and ILL. The remainder of the paper describes the development of Karen Krueger's three-volume assessment manual (the basis of the "Krueger method") that was tested in seventeen libraries of the Illinois Valley Library System and 6 libraries of the Rolling Prairie Library System.[15]

Green, Lucia. "Evaluating a Corporate Library Collection." **Journal of Interlibrary Loan, Document Delivery & Information Supply** 6, no. 1 (1995): 49–61.

Green describes a collection evaluation project at the Federal Reserve Bank in Cleveland, modeled on two previously published studies. First, the Collection Balance Indicator of Gary D. Byrd, D. A. Thomas, and Katherine E. Hughes, which compares an area's percentage of current acquisitions with its percentage of ILL borrowing, was calculated for twenty-one segments of the LC classification.[16] ILL and acquisitions data for six nonconsecutive months from November 1989 through May 1990 were used. Next, drawing upon Robert Peerling Coale's classic study at the Newbery Library, the author found the Cleveland Federal Reserve Bank's collection held 78 percent of items cited in its recently published papers and 73 percent of cited items in papers from the Atlanta and Minneapolis Banks plus the Federal Reserve Board.[17] Green then discusses why 15 percent of all the cited monographs were unpublished. This entry serves as a useful example of collection evaluation in a special library.

Grover, Mark L. "Large Scale Collection Assessment." **Collection Building** 18, no. 2 (1999): 58–66.

Grover describes the use of National Shelflist Count data and, to a lesser extent, circulation data to assess the foreign language and area studies collection at the Brigham Young University (BYU) library. (The National Shelflist Count, issued at five-year intervals, presents holdings data for sixty U.S. academic and research libraries according to 624 segments of the LC classification.) Several tables present data on BYU's holdings in numerous LC class ranges (and the percentage of total holdings devoted to the range) compared with average data for five other university libraries: Chicago, Texas at Austin, California at Davis, Pennsylvania, and New York University. BYU circulation data from an automated system was also analyzed for 1992 through 1994. The major findings were the following: the size of BYU's area and foreign language holdings were 78 percent of the other five libraries compared to 112 percent for the total collection, BYU ranked fifteenth in total holdings but twenty-fourth in area studies, and 23 percent of the total collection circulated while 17 percent of area studies did so. Grover thus contents BYU has placed a lower priority on foreign languages and area studies than on the rest of the collection, despite the perception these areas' budget was "too high." One senses this article was written in response to internal political conflicts over budget allocation.

Intner, Sheila S., and Elizabeth Futas. "The Role and Impact of Library of Congress Classification on the Assessment of Women's Studies Collections." **Library Acquisitions: Practice & Theory** 20 (fall 1996): 267–79.

This entry's analysis evolved from the authors' experience evaluating the Smith College Women's Studies collection. Separate sections describe the historical development of Women's Studies and the Library of Congress classification system. Intner and Futus then explain that collection evaluation of Women's Studies is hindered by the field's dispersal throughout the LC classification (thus assessment techniques can not be applied to a single segment). They review major tools affected by this problem: the RLG Conspectus (which has 200 lines devoted to Women's Studies), the National Shelflist Count, and the Amigos Collection Analysis CD. To resolve the dilemma, the authors recommend librarians use the

Internet to compile their own Women's Studies bibliographies for use as evaluation checklists. Specifically, course syllabi from universities around the country, available on listservs, could be combined for this purpose. Tragically, Elizabeth Futas, an illustrious leader in library and information science education, died prior to the article's publication.

Lawal, Olu Olat, and Jonathan A. Ocheibi. "An Analysis of World Bank Depository Publications Collection: Case Study of University of Calabar Library." **Collection Building** 21, no. 1 (2002): 6–9.

This brief case study describes the evaluation of the World Bank depository publications collection at the University of Calabar library in Nigeria. A number of tables and charts analyze the regional and subject coverage of books received between October 2000 and June 2001. They show that 46.9 percent of 1,812 titles deal with Asia, 27.6 percent Latin America, and 23.3 percent sub-Saharan Africa. Lawal and Ocheibi observe that the book authors are often "foreign" to the area they write about and "[t]his can be disadvantageous . . . where there is racial bias." A subject breakdown revealed that 16.7 percent of the volumes address poverty, 15.6 percent agriculture, and 13.3 percent corruption. Interviews with thirty users found that 82 percent were "very satisfied with the collection" and 87 percent found the publication "of high relevance to their research."

Leighton, H. Vernon. "Course Analysis: Techniques and Guidelines." **Journal of Academic Librarianship** 21 (May 1995): 175–79.

Relating course subject content to holdings, expenditures, or circulation data, termed "course analysis" by Leighton, is occasionally used as a client-centered evaluation method in academic libraries. Three sources for obtaining course information are depicted: course descriptions in college or university catalogs, reading lists and syllabi, and interviews with faculty. Most of the article is devoted to techniques for representing the course information for further use. The pros and cons of classification schedules, subject headings, and Boolean keyword expressions are discussed. The author advocates a "heterogeneous model" that mixes the three formats. Previously published examples of the application of course analysis to collection evaluation, dating to the initial work written and co-authored by William E. McGrath in the late 1960s, are integrated into the analysis.[18] This entry makes a notable contribution to the literature through its methodological insights.

Lochstet, Gwenn S. "Course and Research Analysis Using a Coded Classification System." **Journal of Academic Librarianship** 23 (September 1997): 380–89.

An evaluation method developed at the University of South Carolina termed the "Studies—Collection Classification System" is illustrated here. The technique was implemented for the Physics, Mathematics, and Statistics Departments using data from the 1994–95 and 1995–96 academic years. "Studies" data coded each time a topic was mentioned in a university catalog course description or a departmental Web page statement of faculty research interest. "Collection" data coded coverage of the topic in a book order or an item already cataloged. Each topic's percentage of "Studies" and "Collection" within a department were calculated and compared to each other on the assumption the two should be equal. If the

"Studies" percentage was higher, the topic was considered to be undersupported; if the "Collection" percentage was higher the topic was deemed oversupported. In about 85 percent of the cases (399 of 468), the percentage difference between "Studies" and "Collection" was less than 5 percent. As noted by the authors, this technique can be applied in other departments. This approach is significant because it addresses balance of collection support for topics within a department rather than balance among different departments.

Lotlikar, Sarojini D. "Collection Assessment at the Ganser Library: A Case Study," **Collection Building** 16, no. 1 (1997): 24–29.

Lotlikar, Sarojini D. "A Collection Assessment Model: A Case Study at the Ganser Library." In **Advances in Collection Development and Resource Management,** vol. 2, edited by Thomas W. Leonhardt, 93–104. Greenwich, CT: JAI Press, 1996. ISBN 0-7623-0097-3.

These two entries both describe a comprehensive evaluation of the Millersville University library, in Pennsylvania, political science collection. The shelf count was used to measure total political science holdings. The political science sections of *BCL3* were used as a checklist for books while journal subscriptions were checked against the basic political science list in *Magazines for Libraries,* by Katz and Katz, and the most cited political science, area studies, and international relations journals in the 1993 *SSCI JCR* as well as other core lists. The online circulation module provided circulation statistics on all 1970–88 imprints and, on a sample basis, 1920 through 1970 imprints in political science, law, and public administration. That the collection held 77 percent of the 1970–88 political science imprints in *BCL3* and that 36 percent had circulated at least once are noteworthy findings. Lotlikar stresses "an online catalog should be recommended for qualitative and quantitative collection assessment in libraries."

Nevin, Susanne. "Evaluating the Children's Literature Collection: A College Library's Experience." **Collection Management** 19, nos. 1–2 (1994): 127–33.

Nevin reports on the evaluation of the children's literature collection at Gustavus Adolphus College during the spring of 1992. Using Herbert Goldhor's "inductive method" (which checks a sample of the holdings against recommended book lists), every third English language title, published from 1981 to 1991, in PZ1 (picture books) and PZ7 (general juvenile literature) was checked in *Book Review Digest (BRD)*.[19] The author defined 67 percent as the threshold for "adequacy" and found that 73 percent of the sample was reviewed in *BRD*. Next, the "Best Children's Books" lists in the *Book Publishing Record* from 1981 to 1989 was checked against the collection's holdings. Here adequacy was defined as 33 percent and the actual result stood at "a little over 30 percent." A survey of students found that about 60 percent rated the collection as "fair" and about 15 percent as "poor." This entry serves as an unusual example of applying the induction method and evaluating a juvenile collection in an academic library.

Olson, Georgine. "Krueger Lives: An Unscientific Exploration." **Collection Building** 13, nos. 2–3 (1994): 25–27.

Olson begins by noting many librarians consider the Krueger method "an antique relic of a long outmoded...experiment" due to the development of the Illinois Conspectus during the preceding decade. This entry briefly recounts five specific instances of the Krueger method's use or adaptation following its development in the first half of the 1980s. In 1987 the Bloomington-Normal Reference Roundtable, in Illinois, "leaned heavily" on Krueger's methodology for a year-long evaluation of reference services and collections. The central Illinois Lincoln Trail and Corn Belt Library system utilized Krueger methodologies in 1991 for creating a fiction assessment tool. That same year the Northwest Regional Cooperative in New Jersey completed a Krueger-based assessment. The Three Rivers Regional Library System in Colorado used the Krueger approach in a three-year Cooperative Collection Development Project involving ninety-five academic, public, and school libraries. In 1987–88 the Southwestern Connecticut Library Council used the method to explore cooperative purchasing. As intended by the author, this entry demonstrates the Krueger method's influence beyond its initial use in Illinois in the mid-1980s.

Senkevitch, Judith J., and James H. Sweetland. "Evaluating Adult Fiction in the Smaller Public Library." **RQ** 34 (fall 1994): 78–89.

This well-done research article provides an exploratory study of adult fiction evaluation practice in small- and medium-sized public libraries in Wisconsin. The analysis is based on a 1992 survey of 195 libraries (representing a 52 percent response rate) plus data from the *Wisconsin Library Service Record.* The authors found that 71 percent of the responding libraries had evaluated their adult fiction collection during the preceding five years and 58 percent during the last two years, while 15 percent had not done so at all. A table lists fifteen different methods used by the 139 evaluating libraries: 98 percent used circulation data, 78 percent analyzed the collection's age, 66 percent used best-seller lists (most frequently the *New York Times*), and 63 percent recommended lists (most frequently *Fiction Catalog*). Approximately 41 percent of responding libraries had conducted a community analysis. It is interesting that 81.4 percent of the 129 libraries adopting one of the eight roles outlined in *Planning and Role Setting for Public Libraries* had chosen "Popular Materials Center," which emphasizes fiction as a primary role.[20] Responses to the questionnaire's open-ended section revealed concern about lack of time for evaluation and weeding (25 comments) and the need for an "easy to use" method (18 comments). Senkevitch and Sweetland also present useful data on the characteristics of the responding libraries.

Weber, Marietta. "Effects of Fiction Assessment on a Rural Public Library." **Collection Building** 13, nos. 2–3 (1994): 83–86.

Writing in the first person, the director of Chatsworth Township Public Library, located in a central Illinois village, describes the evaluation of the fiction holdings during the late 1980s/early 1990s as a prelude to several cooperative collection development agreements. A detailed classification was developed for gathering circulation data. A table outlines fiction classification according to ten genres, such as romance, horror, Western; five reading levels from adult to easy reader; and five formats, for example, hardback, books-on-tape, and so on. Shelflist samples showed a lack of diversity in the collection. The collection growth rate was negative due to a large weeding project a few years earlier. Checking lists of award-winning books and "ALA Notables"—termed "the most valuable" assessment method—showed "inadequacy." As a consequence of these assessments, the library received 200 books from the Corn Belt Library System and entered other cooperative collection development agreements. Although a major thrust of the article is on cooperative collection development, this entry illustrates the role collection evaluation plays in a small rural public library.

White, Gary W. "Building Collections for Accreditation: A Case Study." **Collection Building** 18, no. 2 (1999): 49–57.

The process whereby the business program at Capital College of Pennsylvania State University achieved accreditation from the American Assembly of Collegiate Schools of Business (AACSB) is depicted here. There is a solid literature review concerning library involvement in accreditation efforts. Other sections of the paper describe the library's preparation beginning in 1990 for accreditation, the report submitted to the AACSB in August 1997, and a site visit by the AACSB accreditation team in October 1997. A substantial portion of the article deals with such familiar collection evaluation issues as holdings, periodical subscriptions, materials expenditures, and access to electronic resources. The importance for accreditation of holding materials from the so-called "Baker Collection" (the Baker Library supports Harvard's business school) is strongly emphasized. Nine questions asked by the visiting team, such as what percentage of the Baker core collection is owned and how many business periodicals are subscribed to, are listed. White concludes that advance selection from the Baker Core Collection and creation of an electronic collection development policy were helpful in obtaining accreditation. Library reports to the AACSB are appended.

Willcoxon, Wanda Odom. "Collection Evaluation in a Georgia Elementary School: A Look at the Process and Resulting Change in Teachers' Perceptions of Its Quality and Usefulness." **Knowledge Quest** 29 (May/June 2001): 23–29.

Willcoxon offers a first-person narrative about a collection evaluation and weeding project at the racially/ethnically diverse Kindergarten (K) through 5 Dresden Elementary School Library in DeKalb County, Georgia. As the first step, "recency analysis" from David V. Loertscher's *Collection Mapping in the LMC* (see entry in chapter 2) demonstrated the collection was aging. On February 17, 1999, a survey (appended to this article) adapted from Nancy Everhart's *Evaluating the School Library Media Center* (see entry in chapter 1) and using a 5–1 Likert scale approach, was administered to the faculty. Then, the collection was weeded, the shelf arrangement reorganized, and new books added. A Loertscher collection map was created based on teacher input as well as Fenwick English's and Michael B. Eisenberg's curriculum mapping.[21] After these actions, a second survey, using the same instrument, was taken on April 28, 1999 and indicated "general improvement" in teacher perceptions of the collection. A table lists seventeen areas, such as the collection's currency and holdings size adequacy, in which the second survey indicated significantly better scores. In summary, the author is quite upbeat about the media program's "revitalization" in this useful case study of collection evaluation at the elementary school level.

EVALUATION OF REFERENCE COLLECTIONS

Clark, Juleigh Muirhead, and Karen Cary. "An Approach to the Evaluation of Ready Reference Collections." **Reference Services Review** 23 (spring 1995): 39–43.

Clark and Cary recount an evaluation of the ready reference collection at the Virginia Commonwealth University library during September through December 1991. All the ready reference items were dispersed into the regular reference collection, then an attached tally card was marked to indicate each use. However, because the tally cards fell out and the staff forgot to mark them anyway, perceptions of use rather than raw data were employed in decision-making. Six criteria for inclusion in ready reference, mostly drawn from Elizabeth Futas, were used in the study:[22]

- Items frequently used by reference staff

- Support of telephone service

- Materials requiring interpretation

- Materials relating to special reference functions, such as a computer thesaurus

- Protection from damage

- Provision of temporarily held items

As a result of the study, the ready reference collection was reduced from 210 to 34 titles. An appendix lists the titles included under each of the six criteria. This was not an especially well-done evaluation.

Donnelly, Anna M. "Reference Collection Use." In **The Reference Assessment Manual,** compiled and edited by the Evaluation of Reference and Adult Services Committee, Management and Operation of Public Services Section, Reference and Adult Services Division, American Library Association, 50–52. Ann Arbor, MI: Pierian Press, 1995. ISBN 0-87650-344-X.

Donnelly offers a brief introduction to the evaluation of reference collection use. She explains use means examination of a source for information seeking purposes regardless of whether an answer was found. A major portion of this item addresses the "importance" of reference use studies (to assist selection, weeding, and shelf arrangement). It is emphasized that very few studies of reference use have been conducted. Short paragraphs allude to earlier studies of browsing and in-house use, although not necessarily in a reference context. Although worth mentioning because it is included in a useful reference services assessment manual, this short chapter is disappointing.

Ernest, Douglas J., Joan Beam, and Jennifer Monath. "Telephone Directory Use in an Academic Library." **Reference Services Review** 20 (spring 1992): 49–56, 80.

Following a fascinating historical review of telephone directory collecting by libraries (admittedly some readers may not be fascinated by this topic), the authors report an investigation of telephone directory use at the Colorado State University library. The study was based on 112 questionnaires completed by telephone directory collection users from January through June of 1990. The authors found it interesting that 28.6 percent of the surveyed users were not affiliated with the university. Only 45 percent of telephone directory uses were to find telephone numbers. Other uses included a student looking for his professor, a detective searching for a missing person, and a woman seeking her ex-husband. The "principal use" of the collection was for business information that often could have been provided by other reference sources, such as Dun and Bradstreet's *Million Dollar Directory*. This entry is noteworthy because it analyzes use of a type of information resource that is not extensively discussed in the literature.

Fishman, Diane L., and Megan DelBaglivo. "Rich in Resources/Deficient in Dollars! Which Titles Do Reference Departments Really Need?" **Bulletin of the Medical Library Association** 86 (October 1998): 545–50.

Two reference collection use studies at the University of Maryland Health Sciences Library, both carried out from March 1996 to February 1997, are reported in this article. First, on Mondays through Fridays a reshelving count, termed the "sweep method," was taken for reference volumes excluding the ready reference collection. Overall, 65.5 percent of the volumes were used.[23] Analysis by subject found an inverse relationship between the size of holdings and the percentage used. The ten most frequently used monographic titles, mainly medical textbooks and drug handbooks, are listed in a table. The authors conclude a lengthy study period is necessary if title-level use data is desired. Secondly, 150 patrons were orally surveyed concerning their use of print abstracts and indexes, which did not lend itself to the sweep method due to physical arrangement. Two titles accounted for 68.5 percent of the use. The authors concede that limiting the data collection to Monday through Friday may have skewed the results, but nevertheless they have written a good quality article.

Kahn, Miriam J. "Using Qualitative Criteria to Evaluate Reference Resources." In **Library Evaluation: A Casebook and Can-Do Guide,** edited by Danny P. Wallace and Connie Van Fleet, 131–37. Englewood, CO: Libraries Unlimited, 2001. ISBN 1-56308-862-2 (paper).

Although somewhat inappropriately termed a "case study" in a library evaluation text, this item outlines six criteria for evaluation of reference resources:

- Scope

- Author's or organization's authority

- Currency

- Organization for ready access to information

- Inclusion on standard lists

- Use

The application of these criteria to print materials is illustrated using Val Greenwood's near classic work *The Researchers Guide to American Genealogy.*[24] Then, arguing that "a consistent conceptual framework" can be used to evaluate a single resource and the entire collection, nearly half the entry is devoted to evaluation of the reference collection as a whole. In this section a concise outline approach is taken, with three or four subheadings listed under each criteria. For example, points under use include the following: frequency of use, variation by subject, reasons for non-use, and general use patterns. The author believes that the same criteria can be used for different formats.

Mirkovich, Thomas R. "Investment Information in Academic Libraries: Undergraduate and MBA Students." **RQ** 35 (spring 1996): 382–87.

The author investigates use of library resources by students enrolled in five undergraduate and Master of Business Administration (MBA) investment courses at the University of Nevada at Las Vegas during the 1994 spring semester. During the final two weeks of class, 31 percent of the 120 enrolled students responded to a survey asking, among several questions, which of thirty-five specific library resources they had used during the term. The majority of these resources, named in a table, were reference material. It was found that only eight sources (listed in rank order in another table) were used by at least 50 percent of the respondents, while the remaining sources were used on average by 29 percent. Resources used in the undergraduate course on fundamental investment principles are analyzed in more detail. Also, 17 percent of the students had not used the library during the semester, whereas 14 percent used the library more than six hours. After examining course syllabi and interviewing faculty plus students, Mirkovich concludes library use by investment students is "relatively light" and that sixteen "key resources" currently "meet the bulk of student needs."

Sendi, Karen A. "Assessing the Functionality of the Reference Collection." **Collection Building** 15, no. 3 (1996): 17–21.

This article's primary focus is on the three-part methodology used in a systematic evaluation of the use and users of the University of Toledo library's reference collection in 1994. First, usage based on reshelving counts was calculated for three parts of the reference collection: ready reference, indexes, and regular reference materials. Next, two surveys were conducted to determine who was using the reference collection and their perception of success. One hundred eighty forms (91.1 percent were completed) were randomly passed out from the reference desk, while twenty-four forms placed in eight locations around the library were also turned in.[25] Finally, questionnaires concerning the subjects and types of reference material used were sent to 252 faculty, generating a 60 percent response rate. It was found, among other things, that during 1994, 43 percent of the ready reference collection was unused and 24 percent of the instructors responding to the questionnaire had not used the reference collection. This item is worth including because few use studies of reference material appear in the literature.

Welch, Jeanie M., Lynn A. Cauble, and Lara B. Little. "Automated Reshelving Statistics as a Tool in Reference Collection Management." **Reference Services Review** 25 (fall/winter 1997): 79–85.

A use study of the University of North Carolina at Charlotte's reference collection (excluding ready reference and reserve), conducted from October 1994 to September 1996, is recounted in this entry. A portable bar code reader recorded usage at the time of reshelving, while the results were tabulated in a spreadsheet. The most heavily used reference works tended to be multivolume titles, updated editions (either annually or through loose-leaf), and in education or business. The most frequently used areas, encyclopedias, reference works other than encyclopedias, and printed indexes are also named. The use made of the findings, such as weeding, is also discussed. Five appended bar graphs illustrate usage statistics for various LC classification system ranges, but the text would have benefited by including more specific data.

Welch, Jeanie M., Lynn A. Cauble, and Lara B. Little. "The Evolution of Technology in the Management of Noncirculating Library Collections." **Technical Services Quarterly** 17, no. 4 (2000): 1–11.

The role of technology in the creation of two databases for the management and evaluation of reference materials at the University of North Carolina at Charlotte's Atkins Library is discussed in this entry. A manual file of binding records was converted to a database called the Atkins Reference Materials Management System (ARMMS) that contained 12,000 bibliographical records by April 1994. ARMMS could generate title lists by subject area and holdings counts for accreditation purposes. During the mid-1990s, a portable bar code scanner recorded reshelving statistics that were compiled in a spreadsheet on a monthly, annual, and cumulative basis since October 1994. In 1998 the usage data was mounted onto the Reference Web page. This item contains a number of methodological details about the development of these databases.

Wise, Suzanne. "Making Lemonade; The Challenges and Opportunities of Forced Reference Serials Cancellations: One Academic Library's Experiences." **Serials Review** 19 (winter 1993): 15–26, 96.

Written in an engaging first-person style, this entry provides a reference librarian's observations concerning a project whereby approximately $30,000 worth of reference serials were cancelled at Appalachian State University during the early 1990s. Wise advocates setting priorities to guide decision-making, comparative evaluation of alternative reference tools, soliciting faculty opinion (however, responses to a survey "ranged from the sympathetic to the obnoxious"), and keeping statistics on use of print and electronic resources. She also emphasizes gaining control of the reference budget, cooperative collection development for reference resources, and use of access rather than ownership for "efficient and effective provision of knowledge." Appended is list of reference serials cancelled between 1989 and 1992 and a briefly annotated bibliography of about sixty items, mostly published in the late 1980s/early 1990s dealing with the access model, communication with patrons, electronic resources, resource sharing, use studies, and user surveys, although most do not focus on reference.

NOTES

1. John Mansbridge, "Availability Studies in Libraries," *Library & Information Science Research* 8 (October/December 1986): 299–314.

2. Paul B. Kantor, "Availability Analysis," *Journal of the American Society for Information Science* 27 (September/October 1976): 311–19.

3. Richard H. Orr et al., "Development of Methodologic Tools for Planning and Managing Library Services: II. Measuring a Library's Capability for Providing Documents," *Bulletin of the Medical Library Association* 56 (July 1968): 241–67.

4. Barbara Lockett, *Guide to the Evaluation of Library Collections* (Chicago: American Library Association, 1989), 15.

5. Michael K. Buckland, *Book Availability and the Library User* (New York: Pergamon, 1975).

6. Anne C. Ciliberti et al., "Material Availability: A Study of Academic Library Performance," *College & Research Libraries* 48 (November 1987): 513–27.

7. This definition was provided to the author by the Indiana University Libraries Reference Department.

8. Elaine Salter, "The Evaluation of Library Service Effectiveness with Particular Reference to Further Education" (MLib thesis, University College of Wales, 1992).

9. The percentages are calculated by Nisonger from Steynberg and Rossouw's raw data.

10. Jan V. Williams, "Short Loan Collections—Keeping the Customer Satisfied?" (MSc. diss, University of Bristol, 1998).

11. Murray Bob, "The Case for Quality Book Selection," *Library Journal* 107 (September 15, 1982): 1707–10; Nora Rawlinson, "Give 'Em What They Want," *Library Journal* 106 (November 15, 1981): 2188–90.

12. Karen Krueger, *Coordinated Cooperative Collection Development for Illinois Libraries,* 2d ed., 3 vols. (Springfield, Illinois State Library, 1983).

13. Robert L. Burr, "Evaluating Library Collections: A Case Study," *Journal of Academic Librarianship* 5 (November 1979): 256–60; Samuel E. Ifidon, "A Quantitative Assessment of Nigerian University Library Collections in the Humanities and the Social Sciences in Relation to Postgraduate Research" (Ph.D. diss., University of Ibadan, 1977).

14. Bill Erbes, "If CCD Is Good, CCCD Is Better: The IVLS Approach," *Illinois Libraries* 71 (January 1989): 18–20.

15. Karen Krueger, *Coordinated Cooperative Collection Development for Illinois Libraries,* 2d ed., 3 vols. (Springfield: Illinois State Library, 1983).

16. Gary D. Byrd, D. A. Thomas, and Katherine E. Hughes, "Collection Development Using Interlibrary Loan Borrowing and Acquisitions Statistics," *Bulletin of the Medical Library Association* 70 (January 1982): 1–9.

17. Robert Peerling Coale, "Evaluation of a Research Library Collection: Latin-American Colonial History at the Newberry," *Library Quarterly* 35 (July 1965): 173–84.

18. William E. McGrath, "Determining and Allocating Book Funds for Current Domestic Buying," *College & Research Libraries* 28 (July 1967): 269–72; William E. McGrath and Norma Durand, "Classifying Courses in the University Catalog," *College & Research Libraries* 30 (November 1969): 533–39.

19. Herbert Goldhor, "Analysis of an Inductive Method of Evaluating the Book Collection of a Public Library," *Libri* 23, no. 1 (1973): 6–17; Herbert Goldhor, "A Report on an Application of the Inductive Method of Evaluation of Public Library Books," *Libri* 31 (August 1981): 121–29.

20. Charles R. McClure et al., *Planning and Role Setting for Public Libraries* (Chicago: American Library Association, 1987).

21. Fenwick English, "Re-Tooling Curriculum with On-Going School Systems," *Educational Technology* 19, no. 5 (1979): 7–13; Michael B. Eisenberg, "Curriculum Mapping and Implementation of an Elementary School Library Media Skills Curriculum," *School Library Media Quarterly* 12 (fall 1984): 411–18.

22. Elizabeth Futas, "Issues in Collection Development: Ready Reference Collections," *Collection Building* 3, no. 3 (1981): 46–48.

23. Nisonger's calculation from Fishman and DelBaglivo's data.

24. Val Greenwood, *The Researchers Guide to American Genealogy,* 2d ed. (Baltimore, MD: Genealogical Publishing, 1990).

25. Nisonger's calculation from Sendi's raw data.

5

Collection Evaluation at the National and Multilibrary Levels

The concept of a national collection can be traced at least as far back as the famous but unsuccessful Farmington Plan, begun in the 1940s. The national collection—and concerns about its completeness—may assume greater significance in the current era that emphasizes access. If a nondigital information resource is not available in any of the nation's libraries, access to it will be impeded for all the country's libraries.

Most of the studies reported here do not literally evaluate the holdings of every library in the country—a feat that would be virtually impossible from the methodological perspective. Rather, they analyze the holdings of multiple libraries in order to analyze collecting patterns or trends at the national, regional, or state levels or among a type of library.

Studies addressing the following topics are included in this chapter:

- "Literature loss" (i.e., whether libraries are collecting a smaller proportion of the total output of published literature)

- Serial cancellation patterns among library cohorts, including type of serials cancelled as well as overlap and uniqueness among cancelled titles

- Coverage of a particular subject area or type of material by a group of libraries

- Use of the OCLC/Amigos Collection Analysis CD to analyze national collecting trends and patterns (use of the CACD for evaluation of a single library collection is covered in chapter 2)

Chapter 5 is organized into four sections covering national or multilibrary collection evaluation in Africa, Canada or North America, Europe, and the United States.

AFRICA

Akintunde, Stephen A., and James O. Adelusi. "A Survey of Local History Collections in Nigerian Academic and Research Libraries." **African Journal of Library, Archives & Information Science** 7 (October 1997): 151–61.

In this study two Nigerian librarians evaluate their country's local history collections. The data were gathered from a questionnaire mailed, apparently in the mid-1990s, to the twelve academic and research libraries (eight responded) in the two Central Nigerian states of Bauchi and Plateau. A summary table indicates that the number of a library's local history volumes is not related to the age of the library or the collection's total size. Analysis by format revealed that 55.23 percent of 2,343 held items were books and 12.80 percent were ephemerals such as circulars, programs, and annual reports. The entire local history holdings of all eight libraries were obtained through four methods: acquisitions trips (60.31 percent), gifts (16.77 percent), benefactors (15.28 percent), and legal deposit (7.64 percent). The authors conclude that Nigerian local history collections are "highly underdeveloped" and recommend better bibliographic control, cooperative collection development, and recruitment of librarians with local history backgrounds.

Ifidon, Betty I. "The Effects of Accreditation on University Library Bookstock: The Nigerian Experience." **International Information & Library Review** 28 (March 1996): 1–21.

Ifidon, Betty I. "Recent Developments in Nigerian Academic Libraries: The Effects of Accreditation on University Library Bookstock." **Libri** 45 (September/December 1995): 186–98.

This is essentially the same article published in two places. The author describes the "deplorable" state of the collections in Nigerian university libraries and the attempts to rectify the situation through accreditation standards, outlined for ten disciplines in a four-page table, established by the military dictatorship's National Universities Commission. Separate tables present data on the number of new books and journal subscriptions acquired by each of twenty Federal university libraries in 1994 (a traditional collection-centered, quantitative evaluation approach) after a funding influx. In summary, Ifidon offers an interesting sketch of collection problems in Nigerian university libraries, but her research fails to deliver what the title promises. Data is presented on neither collection size nor growth rate.

Steynberg, Susan, and S. F. Rossouw. "Testing Orr's Document Delivery Test on Biomedical Journals in South Africa." **Bulletin of the Medical Library Association** 83 (January 1995): 78–84.

The authors describe the implementation of Orr's Document Delivery Test (developed in the late 1960s) in seven South African university medical libraries, including the University of Pretoria and the University of Witwatersrand.[1] (Orr's DDT tests how quickly a library can theoretically provide access to a set of citations and then expresses the result as a Capability Index [CI] score between 0 and 100.) A major portion of the paper explains the methodology: 307 citations were randomly selected from a citation pool of 6,298 journal citations in 320 articles (all published in 1989) identified through the South African Medical Database. The test was administered in the seven libraries between August 22 and 31, 1990. Detailed findings for Library A, whose CI was 90.55 (results were reported anonymously), reveal that 79.48 percent of the citations were contained in the collection, 10.10 percent were in other collections on campus, 7.49 percent were available through the national ILL network, and 2.93 percent were unavailable in South Africa. The CI scores for the seven libraries ranged from 81.68 to 92.97. Altogether, 31.6 percent of the test sample was held by all seven libraries, whereas only 2.93 percent were not available in South Africa. This entry is useful not only for its evaluative data concerning South African medical libraries but also for its description of the DDT methodology.

CANADA OR NORTH AMERICA

Rothbauer, Paulette M., and Lynne E. F. McKechnie. "Gay and Lesbian Fiction for Young Adults: A Survey of Holdings in Canadian Public Libraries." **Collection Building** 18, no. 1 (1999): 32–39.

In this study a list of forty English language novels for young adults with explicit gay and lesbian content was checked, in June and July 1998, against the OPACs of forty medium and large public libraries in English-speaking Canada. On average, 40.4 percent of the sample were held by all libraries, whereas the nineteen large libraries held 51.2 percent and the twenty-one medium-sized libraries 30.7 percent. Further analysis revealed no statistically significant correlation between a library's size and the number of titles held, nor between a title's publication data and the number of libraries holding it. A table lists each library along with its service population plus the number and percentage of books held, while another table lists each title and the number of libraries holding it. Rothbauer and McKechnie conclude "some libraries seem to be doing a good job of providing these potentially controversial titles, others are not."

Spence, Alex. "Controversial Books in the Public Library: A Comparative Survey of Holdings of Gay-Related Children's Picture Books." **Library Quarterly** 70 (July 2000): 335–79.

The researcher checked via the Internet a list, compiled from multiple sources, of thirty English language children's picture books with gay content against the holdings of 101 public libraries in the Anglo-American democracies: the United States, Canada, the United Kingdom, Australia, and New Zealand. (This item is annotated in this section because all fifty U.S. states and ten Canadian provinces were represented with a relatively small number of libraries from the other countries.) Spence found the number of titles held ranged from 0 to 24, the number of copies held ranged from 0 to 520, and the number of copies per 100,000 population served ranged from 0 to 39.8. Separate tables identify the leading libraries according to these three criteria. Larger libraries generally held a larger proportion of titles and number of copies. Lengthy appendices identify the thirty titles, the 101 libraries, and the number of copies of each title held by each library.

Spence, Alex. "Gay Young Adult Fiction in the Public Library: A Comparative Survey." **Public Libraries** 38 (July/August 1999): 224–43.
    A list of 99 English language gay young adult fiction titles, compiled by Christine Jenkins, was checked against the holdings of ten U.S. and nine Canadian public libraries serving urban populations ranging from 300,000 to 1 million, as well as six branches of the Toronto Public Library.[2] The percentage of titles held ranged from 23.2 percent to 90.9 percent for the American libraries with a mean of 72.3 percent, while Canadian libraries held a mean of 61.2 percent, ranging from 34.3 percent to 81.8 percent. Further analysis focused on the number of copies held and the ratio of copies held for each 10,000 in the population served. Tables list the seventeen most frequently held and the nine least frequently held titles by both Canadian and U.S. libraries. Several lengthy appendices list the books and libraries in the study, and the number of copies of each book held by each library. Spence observes a "considerable disparity" among library systems as "many libraries have developed substantial collections, while others have not."

EUROPE

Noble, Patricia. "Collection Evaluation Techniques: A British Pilot Study." In **Latin American Studies into the Twenty-First Century; New Focus, New Formats, New Challenges: Papers of the Thirty-Sixth Annual Meeting of the Seminar on the Acquisition of Latin American Library Materials; University of California, San Diego and San Diego State University, San Diego, California, June 1–6, 1991,** edited by Deborah L. Jakubs, 248–57. Albuquerque, NM: SALALM Secretariat, General Library, University of New Mexico, 1993. ISBN 0-917617-38-X.
    Noble describes an investigation, begun in 1990, of Latin American holdings in United Kingdom libraries by a twelve-member working group of the Advisory Committee on Latin American Materials (ACOLAM). The author stresses that in the United Kingdom, only the British Library and Oxford's Bodleian approach the minimum 150,000 to 200,000 Latin American holdings size recommended by Carl Deal.[3] Searching for an evaluation method, the group rejected both the Conspectus and shelf measurement due to the field's interdisciplinary nature and use of subject specialists because of recruitment difficulties. They opted for the checklist approach (using the term "benchmark bibliographies"), deciding that Herbert E. Gooch's *The Military and Politics in Latin America* supplemented by volumes 45, 47, and 49 of the *Handbook of Latin American Studies* would constitute a current, interdisciplinary, research-oriented list.[4] Checking a 328 item sample (drawn from a population of 2,200) the group found the holdings in ten unnamed libraries ranged from 20 percent to 60 percent with a 40 percent average,

while 83 percent were held by at least one library. The results for the ten libraries, further analyzed by age and language, are tabulated in three tables. Approximately 150 hours of staff time were expended on this project.[5]

Voorbij, Henk, and Pieter Douma. "The Coverage by National Libraries of National Imprints: A Study in the Netherlands." **Alexandria** 9, no. 2 (1997): 155–66.

The coverage of Dutch imprints by the depository program of the Netherlands National Library (Koninklijke Bibliotheek) is investigated here. During 1995–96 four categories of national imprints were analyzed: books with ISBNs, academic publications (dissertations and orations, i.e., professors' inaugural and retirement lectures), gray literature, and periodicals. Appropriate lists identified for each category were checked on a sample basis against the Dutch depository collection and the results tabulated as "held," "ordered, not held," and "not held, not ordered." Holdings were well over 90 percent for all categories except orations and gray literature. The authors conclude that coverage had improved since the previous study in 1983, and that mandatory legal deposit is not required for effective coverage (the Dutch system is voluntary).

THE UNITED STATES

Budd, John M., and Catherine K. Craven. "Academic Library Monographic Acquisitions: Selection of *Choice's* Outstanding Academic Books." **Library Collections, Acquisitions, & Technical Services** 23 (spring 1999): 15–26.

Budd and Craven used the OCLC/Amigos CACD to calculate the percentage of academic libraries holding purposive samples of titles from *Choice's* "Outstanding Academic Books" at three five-year intervals: 1984–85, 1990, and 1995. Data were analyzed for four Peer Groups, that is, sizes of libraries, and in the humanities, social sciences, and sciences. Not surprisingly, larger libraries held a greater proportion of books: ARL libraries held 84.17 percent of the titles, large academic libraries held 70.99 percent, medium-sized academic libraries 52.89 percent, and small academic libraries 25.80 percent. All four size categories collected a smaller proportion of books over the five-year intervals. However, "the findings are less clear" when the data were broken down by subject area. There was a statistically significant decline in holdings of humanities books for all peer groups, but not in all size categories for science and social sciences titles. Nevertheless, Budd and Craven believe their findings support Perrault's concerns about the shrinking national collection.

Budd, John M., and Cynthia Wyatt. " Do You Have Any Books On . . . ?: An Examination of Public Library Holdings." **Public Libraries** 41 (March/April 2002): 107–12.

To test the incorporation of Nora Rawlinson's "demand" or Murray Bob's "quality" theories in U.S. public library selection practice, a list of 79 books were checked (via the Internet during February through April 2001) against the holdings of twenty medium-sized public libraries distributed across the country.[6] The list, representing both demand and quality titles, was compiled from multiple sources, including bestsellers, the ten most frequently challenged books according to the ALA Web page, and quality books for academic libraries. All but fifteen books, termed "problematic," were held by at least 70 percent of the libraries. Examination of these fifteen titles found that six were not reviewed in *Book Review Digest* and "some did not receive particularly positive reviews." It seems highly significant that each of the most frequently challenged titles were held by all twenty libraries. Budd and Wyatt decide that U.S. public libraries "consider both quality and popularity when making selection decisions."

Chrzastowski, Tina E. "National Trends in Academic Chemistry Serial Collections, 1992–1994." **Science & Technology Libraries** 16, nos. 3–4, (1997): 191–207.

Chrzastowski uses 1992 through 1994 order and cancellation data from the F. W. Faxon Company's (then a well-known serials subscription agent) database to analyze collection patterns for domestic science serials (with special emphasis on chemistry) in ten U.S. ARL university libraries, including the University of California at Berkeley and Pennsylvania State University. Their collective number of science serial subscriptions declined 23.0 percent from 1992 to 1994. Of the approximately $1.2 million worth of subscriptions cancelled in the three-year period, about $380,000 was for chemistry journals (QD in the LC classification) and $180,000 for physiology (QP). Although the author describes the ten collections as "overwhelmingly homogeneous," they identify a trend toward less homogeneity. The number of unique titles, that is, titles held by only one library, rose over 42 percent from 6.4 percent in 1992 to 9.1 percent in 1994. Furthermore, the number of core chemistry titles (a core title was defined as one held by at least six of the ten libraries) declined from 124 in 1992 to 77 in 1994, leading to the assertion that the core is redefined each year. The authors surmise that duplicate titles are being cancelled resulting in more unique titles.

Chrzastowski, Tina E. and Karen A. Schmidt. "The Serials Cancellation Crisis: National Trends in Academic Library Serial Collections." **Library Acquisitions: Practice & Theory** 21 (winter 1997): 431–43.

This follow-up to the authors' earlier studies uses 1992 through 1994 order and cancellation data from the Faxon Company database to analyze cancellation patterns for domestic serials on the part of ten U.S. ARL university libraries, including the University of California at Berkeley and Pennsylvania State University. It was discovered that: approximately one-third of domestic serial titles were unique (i.e., held by only one library among the ten); a total of 22,370 serials (out of a three-year aggregate of approximately 200,000) were cancelled during the three years, of which 15,897 were unique; and the number of subscriptions declined in all subject areas except law, leading the authors to question the assumption that science titles are most "at risk" for cancellation. Chrzastowski and Schmidt assert, "Libraries generally are forced to cancel serials based on economic indicators rather than on the needs of the users and the collection."

Crawford, Gregory A., and Matthew Harris. "Best-Sellers in Academic Libraries." **College & Research Libraries** 62 (May 2001): 216–25.

The researchers checked a list of 220 bestsellers, selected from *Publishers Weekly* at five-year intervals between 1940 and 1990 and equally divided between fiction and nonfiction, against the holdings of twenty academic libraries in Pennsylvania as indicated in a union catalog. Crawford and Harris found that all but one fiction title was in at least one library and the mean number of libraries owning each was 8.6. However, they were "shocked" that 15 nonfiction titles were not held by a single library, while the average title was held by 7.4 libraries. Tables name the titles and the number of libraries holding each. Generally holdings were higher for older books. The authors fear that important works of American popular culture "may be in danger of becoming lost to future scholars."

Harris, Matthew, and Gregory A. Crawford. "The Ownership of Religious Texts by Academic Libraries." **College & Research Libraries** 63 (September 2002): 450–58.

Harris and Crawford checked a list of 20 "holy books," from Christianity, Judaism, Islam, Hinduism, Buddhism, Scientology, and Satanism as well as a few other religions, against the same union catalog of twenty Pennsylvania academic libraries used in their earlier study (see preceding entry). Eighteen of the twenty libraries owned all four versions of the *Bible* on the checklist (King James, Revised Standard, Jerusalem, and New English). Furthermore, all twenty held the *Koran*, while nineteen owned the *Bhagavad-Gita*. However, only a small number of libraries held original-language versions. A three-page table outlines the specific holy texts held by each library. The authors believe they found an "acceptable" level of diversity in religious text holdings and that their research assumed "new meaning" after September 11 due to the need for discussion of such topics as Islam and the Taliban.

Holleman, Curt. "The Study of Subject Strengths, Overlap, and National Collecting Patterns: The Uses of the OCLC/Amigos Collection Analysis CD and Alternatives to It." **Collection Management** 22, nos. 1–2 (1997): 57–69.

Holleman offers a cogent analysis of the OCLC/Amigos Collection Analysis CD and critique of Perrault's research on the national collection demonstrating that the number of monographic imprints collected by ARL libraries declined 27.76 percent from 1985 to 1989 (see entries by Perrault). After reviewing overlap studies in New York, Wisconsin, and California as well as the CACD, he concludes that automated overlap studies understate overlap by about 15 to 20 percent and overstate uniqueness by the same percentage.[7] Holleman states the OCLC/Amigos CACD is an "excellent framework" for examining overlap but contains three weaknesses:

1. OCLC often contains two different entries for the same book, introducing a 5 percent distortion.

2. Different editions and reprints are not considered matches.

3. Different libraries cataloging new books at variant speeds may distort the results.

The author calls Perrault's study "a good piece of research" containing a "tiny flaw" that renders its conclusions "false" (i.e., many libraries cataloged 1989 imprints after the end of her study). Using the 1995 CACD (Perrault used the 1991 version) Holleman found that the monographic imprints collected by ARL libraries actually increased by 0.56 percent from 1985 to 1989.

Marinko, Rita A., and Kristin H. Gerhard. "Representations of the Alternative Press in Academic Library Collections." **College & Research Libraries** 59 (July 1998): 363–77.
The researchers used OCLC to check the holdings of the 220 periodicals indexed (as of 1996) in the *Alternative Press Index* by 104 U.S. ARL libraries. They found the percentage of titles held by each library ranged from 0 percent to 72 percent with only 12 institutions holding more than 50 percent. Analysis by periodical showed that the percentage of libraries holding each title fell between 0 percent and 88 percent with only 37 titles held by more than 70 percent of the institutions. After a breakdown by subject, Marinko and Gerhard express concern that leftist/Marxist politics and labor are underrepresented. They conclude that alternative viewpoints should be better represented in research libraries in order to promote democratic discussion of issues confronting society.

Olson, Michael P. "The Trip to Venus: New Methods for Evaluating and Comparing Scandinavian Literature Collections." **Journal of Academic Librarianship** 18 (September 1992): 204–10.
The author addresses methodologies for identifying and comparing strong Scandinavian collections at the national level. About half the article is devoted to arguing that neither the Conspectus, the National Shelflist Count, nor Lee Ash and William G. Miller's *Subject Collections* "yield...consequential information on Scandinavian collections" due to inconsistent data and incomplete participation by key institutions. As alternatives, the author proposes three methods for comparing Scandinavian literature collections: "computer analysis," such as the OCLC/Amigos Collection Analysis System; "sampling" items from the *Dictionary of Scandinavian Literature* and checking their holdings in OCLC or Research Libraries Information Network (RLIN); and "survey research," illustrated by using UCLA's ORION OPAC to calculate the library's total holdings for a sample of 161 contemporary authors. Olson maintains these techniques are "economical" and "accurate." Moreover, nationwide assessment facilitates ILL and cooperative collection development. This item, unlike most in the section, focuses on methodological issues instead of reporting results.

Paskoff, Beth M., and Anna H. Perrault. "The Louisiana Academic Libraries Collection Analysis Project: A Report." **LLA Bulletin** 55 (fall 1992): 67–74.
This entry describes the Louisiana Academic Libraries Collection Analysis Project, a further development of a 1984 project at the Louisiana State University (LSU) libraries previous recounted by Paskoff and Perrault.[8] Over the years

1989–91, data was gathered on the subject, age, language, and serial/monographic ratios for fourteen academic library collections in Louisiana, including LSU, Tulane, Loyola, and the University of New Orleans. One should note the following among the major findings: serial titles ranged from 1 to 4 percent of total titles sampled, larger collections had a greater proportion of non-English titles, and there was a "severe decrease in acquisitions in the 1980s as compared to the 1970s." Bar graphs tabulate data for the specific libraries participating in the project. Perrault's work on the national collection appears to be an outgrowth of this project.

Perrault, Anna H. "The Changing Print Resource Base of Academic Libraries in the United States." **Journal of Education for Library & Information Science** 36 (fall 1995): 295–308.

Perrault, Anna H. "The Shrinking National Collection: A Study of the Effects of the Diversion of Funds from Monographs to Serials on the Monograph Collections of Research Libraries." **Library Acquisitions: Practice & Theory** 18 (spring 1994): 3–22.

These two entries are jointly annotated because they both present the findings from the author's award-winning Ph.D. dissertation.[9] The 1991 OCLC/Amigos CACD was used to compare acquisition of 1989 and 1985 imprints by seventy-two ARL libraries assumed to serve as proxies for the national collecting pattern. Overall, the total number of different titles collected by the seventy-two libraries decreased 27.76 percent, from 144,879 in 1985 to 104,664 in 1989, with the largest decline in the humanities followed by the social sciences, then the sciences. The number of titles unique to a single library fell from 36,629 to 26,716 (27.1 percent).[10] The second above-listed article contains a lengthy table showing that total monographic acquisitions and the number of unique titles fell in the vast majority of 108 LC classification system segments. Moreover, English language titles decreased 12.34 percent compared to 43.44 percent for those in other languages. The researcher concludes the national collection is "shrinking" and that ARL libraries are losing diversity by collecting the same core, English language materials.

Perrault, Anna H. "National Collecting Trends: Collection Analysis Methods and Findings." **Library & Information Science Research** 21, no. 1 (1999): 47–67.

The researcher explores methodological issues regarding use of the OCLC/Amigos CACD to discern national collecting patterns and reports additional data from the 1996 edition. Perrault asserts that data for ARL libraries represent national collection patterns because they hold 80 percent of the titles in the database. However, changes in database content have confounded year-to-year comparisons. Implicitly acknowledging one of Holleman's criticisms, Perrault says, "After a period of three to four years, data appear to be reliable." More than a dozen tables and figures present 1986 through 1995 collecting data by year, language, library type, and broad subject category. The basic pattern from her earlier studies holds as the number of books acquired by ARL libraries declined 22 percent from 1986 to 1995. She offers four points in summary:

- The aggregate holdings of U.S. academic libraries are becoming increasingly concentrated in English language titles.

- The impact of the 1980s budget crisis "is still visible."

- Smaller academic libraries have more stable collecting patterns, perhaps because they were less affected by the 1980s budget crisis.

- The 1990s saw "somewhat of a recovery."

This is evidently the most recent article in Perrault's important series on national collecting patterns.

Perrault, Anna H., et al. "An Assessment of the Collective Resources Base of Florida Community College Library Collections: A Profile with Interpretative Analysis." **Resource Sharing & Information Networks** 14, no. 1 (1999): 3–20.

Five authors, including two LIS faculty, use customized programming to analyze, as of March 14, 1996, the subject and age of over 2 million book records held by twenty-eight Florida libraries in the Library Information Network for Community Colleges (LINCC). A table providing holdings counts broken down by decade for twenty-nine segments of the LC classification shows that 30.70 percent of all the libraries' books were published during the 1970s and 26.30 percent in the 1960s, resulting in the conclusion their collections are "out of date." A bar graph demonstrates that about 13 percent of the books were classified in H (economics, business, and sociology) followed by approximately 8 percent in Q (computer science, mathematics, chemistry, physics, and biology). Examination of the data for St. Petersburg Junior College (a large institution), Okaloosa-Walton Community College ("the middle tier"), and Lake City Community College ("the smaller size category") found "similarities and differences" among their collections even though all three displayed "a similar subject profile." The authors assert this is the first reported investigation about the age and subject dispersion of the collective holdings of a community college library network.

Perrault, Anna H., et al. "The Effects of High Median Age on Currency of Resources in Community College Library Collections." **College & Research Libraries** 60 (July 1999): 316–39.

As a follow-up to the previously reported study, the books in twenty-eight Florida community college library collections were analyzed by age and subject based on data extracted from the LINCC database during a later time period: May and June 1998. A major portion of the article is devoted to an especially detailed review of the obsolescence and weeding literature. The results were similar to those of the earlier study. The collective median age was 23.59 years, ranging from 19.19 years for science books to 27.76 for "general" monographs and the median publication year was 1974. Moreover, 36 percent of the collective holdings predated 1970, while only 23 percent were less than fifteen years old. A lengthy table tabulates the collective age for forty-seven subject areas, using seven time intervals from pre-1970 through 1995–98. The authors propose a Continual Update Collection Management Model whereby each year 5 percent of the collection will be weeded and replaced with current books, and they assert this strategy would eventually reduce the median age to 11 years. They acknowledge their proposal is reminiscent of the mid-1970s "no growth" library concept advocated by Daniel Gore.[11] This is topnotch research addressing statewide assessment of community college monographic collections.

Perrault, Anna H., et al. "The Florida Community College Statewide Collection Assessment Project: Outcomes and Impact." **College & Research Libraries** 63 (May 2002): 240–49.

This entry investigates the impact of the multilibrary evaluation, now termed the Florida Community College Statewide Assessment Project, reported in the two previous entries. Directors or collection development specialists from the twenty-eight participating libraries were surveyed in the spring of 2001, receiving an 82 percent response rate. Twelve respondents (52.2 percent) believed the assessment exercise had a "profound effect" on the Florida legislature's decision to appropriate $5 million earmarked for community college library collections. However, only $1,808,500 could be verified as having been allocated to the libraries by the local college administrators (who were not legally required to do so). Twenty-one libraries (75 percent) of those taking part in the project used the evaluation reports to "inform" collection development decisions and in weeding.[12] As it was decided to conduct another collection assessment of the twenty-eight libraries in March 2002, using the 1998 data as a benchmark and incorporating circulation statistics, we can anticipate more good reading.

Reed-Scott, Jutta. "Collecting Patterns of North American Research Libraries." **Journal of Library Administration** 27, nos. 3–4 (1999): 49–60. Also in **Scholarship, Research Libraries, and Global Publishing,** 51–62. Washington, DC: Association of Research Libraries, 1996. ISBN 0-918006-78-3.

North American research library collecting patterns for foreign materials are this item's focus. The author maintains that Western European materials receive the highest priority, followed by East Asia, Eastern Europe, and Latin America, and, finally, Africa, the Middle East, and South and Southeast Asia at the bottom tier. Perrault's research is discussed in detail, and data is synthesized from a variety of sources. For example, the Yale library's coverage of world publishing output declined from 12 percent in the early 1970s to 5 percent in the late 1980s while Library of Congress foreign acquisitions are also declining. It is revealing that in 1994, 72.2 percent of the Cooperative Online Serials Project (CONSER) database serial titles were in English with French, Spanish, and German accounting for about 14 percent. Reed-Scott perceives more emphasis on foreign social science books at the expense of the humanities with "limited" coverage of science. The author asserts that concentration on core titles will result in "more overlap among collections and less coverage of the 'universe' of foreign research materials." Significantly, several of Reed-Scott's and Perrault's perspectives are mutually reinforcing.

Rodriguez, Ketty. "Collection Patterns of Selected Disciplines of Latin American Print and Non-Print Materials." **Collection Building** 17, no. 3 (1998): 129–39.

This research project examines book and nonprint (i.e., films, filmstrips, slides, video, and pictures) collecting patterns by U.S. libraries in Latin American history, anthropology, economic history, and drama. A rather complicated methodology that need not be summarized here was used to extract approximately 70,000 records from the OCLC database, as of 1995–96. A dozen tables and figures tabulate the findings in a variety of ways. The percentage of books ranged from 80.63 percent in history to 90.06 percent in drama, whereas the percentage of nonprint material ranged from 0.88 percent in drama to 9.85 percent in anthropology. (Figures do not add to 100 percent because serials, maps, sound recordings, and computer files were not included in the study.) Analysis of the data during five-year intervals from 1976–80 through 1991–95 found a decline in nonprint materials during 1981–85. Rodriguez attributes the decline to the fact that in a difficult budgetary climate (due to higher telecommunications costs caused by the divestiture of AT&T in January 1984) libraries reduced the acquisition of nonprint items to protect the book collection. The author concludes that "collection emphasis for Latin American materials is slowly shifting to nonprint formats for history, economic history, and drama."

Rowley, Gordon. "Academic Libraries in Iowa Cope with Serials Cutbacks." **Collection Building** 14, no. 2 (1995): 24–28.

The results of two surveys of Iowa academic libraries concerning serial cancellations are reported here by Rowley. Thirty-nine libraries responding to the first survey listed 609 titles cancelled or under consideration for cancellation during the period July 1, 1989, through June 30, 1991. Approximately 5 percent of the titles (33) were listed by more than one library. The second survey, to which eighteen libraries responded, found that 3,175 titles, equally nearly $600,000 in subscription fees, had actually been cancelled between July 1, 1991, and June 30, 1992. Only 92 of these titles were cancelled by more than one library. A table analyzing cancelled titles by LC class indicates that 20.4 percent fell in Q (sciences), 13.4 percent in T (technology), and 10.8 percent in H (social sciences). Another table analyzing costs shows 42.8 percent in Q and 16.8 percent in T. An appendix lists the forty-three libraries that responded to one or both surveys. This is a useful study of serial cancellations in a single heartland state.

Schwartz, Charles A. "Empirical Analysis of Literature Loss." **Library Resources & Technical Services** 38 (April 1994): 133–38.

Schwartz describes the methodology he has used to calculate literature loss in four different subject areas (see the following three entries). "Literature loss" refers to book publication output that is not being collected by the nation's libraries. This article analyzes Judaic Studies for the years 1979–88 by comparing the aggregate holdings of seventy-one ARL libraries, gathered from the OCLC/Amigos CACD, with the number of books cataloged in the LC classification's BM range according to Online Computer Library Center/Online Union Catalog (OCLC/OLUC). A total of 7,100 titles were published, ranging from 599 in 1979 to 846 in 1987 for an annual average of 713. The annual number of titles collected by at least one ARL library ranged between 333 in 1988 and 464 in 1983 for a 393 yearly average. The percentage of total output held somewhere in the ARL declined from 57 percent in the early 1980s to 49 percent by the decade's end. Altogether, about 40 percent of the total 1979–88 book output was not collected by any ARL library. The author asserts that publication growth and price inflation are the two "salient trends" underlying literature loss. After defense of his methodology, Schwartz concludes that his approach "while not precise, has broad reliability."

Schwartz, Charles A. "Gap Analysis of Book Publication and Library Holdings in Psychology." **American Psychologist** 48 (November 1993): 1151–52.

Schwartz used the OCLC database to calculate the number of psychology monographs, restricted to the LC classification's BF section, published between 1979 and 1988. Then he calculated the total number of psychology titles published during each of those years held by seventy-one ARL libraries, as indicated in the OCLC/Amigos CACD. The 25,000 psychology books published during that decade "fluctuated rather narrowly" from 2,459 in 1983 to 2,612 in 1980, averaging 2,516 each year. The number of titles collected by at least one ARL library averaged 991 per year, ranging in number between 876 in 1988 and 1,161 in 1979. The percentage of book production collected by any ARL library fell from 43 percent in the early 1980s to 36 percent in the late 1980s. Altogether, approximately 60 percent of the total psychology output was not collected by any ARL library in the study. The average ARL member held about one-twentieth of the next 20 percent and about half the final 20 percent, termed the "mainstream literature" by Schwartz. This and the next two entries are noteworthy for their publication in non-LIS journals.

Schwartz, Charles A. "Literature Loss in Anthropology." **Current Anthropology** 33 (June 1992): 315–17.

This entry applies Schwartz's methodology for analysis of literature loss to anthropology, focusing on the GN segment of the LC classification for seventy ARL libraries. Approximately 10,000 anthropology books were published during the 1978–87 period, ranging from 934 in 1982 to 1,113 in 1980. The seventy ARL institutions acquired an average of 606 anthropology titles per annum from a low of 507 for 1987 to a high of 694 for 1980. ARL coverage of anthropology declined from 66 percent (i.e., the percentage of books held by at least one library) in the late 1970s to 53 percent during the late 1980s. Forty percent of the 1978 to 1987 output was not held by any of the seventy ARL libraries and another 30 percent was held by only a few. The average ARL institution held roughly a third of the remaining 30 percent, deemed the mainstream literature by Schwartz.

Schwartz, Charles A. "Literature Loss in International Relations." **PS: Political Science & Politics** 25 (December 1992): 720–23.

Schwartz's method for analyzing literature loss is used to investigate international relations in this article. He found that an average of 808 titles were published annually in LC's JX segment, ranging from 601 in 1978 to 904 in 1984. An average of 570 titles were acquired for each publication year, ranging from 525 in 1987 to 662 in 1983. Total ARL coverage decreased from about 75 percent in the late 1970s to 65 percent in the 1980s. In the conclusion, the author summarizes his major findings as follows:

1. Thirty percent of the 1978–87 title output was not held by any of seventy ARL libraries.

2. Forty percent of the title output was held by a single or only a few ARL libraries.

3. The remaining 30 percent may be considered mainstream literature, and the average ARL members holds approximately one-third of it.

4. The average ARL institution holds 13 percent of the total book output.

5. The largest ARL libraries hold about 60 percent of the mainstream literature and 18 percent of the total output.

Sweetland, James H. "Adult Fiction in Medium-Sized U.S. Public Libraries: A Survey." **Library Resources & Technical Services** 38 (April 1994): 149–60.

This well-done investigation reports a spring 1990 survey of 116 medium-sized U.S. public libraries (representing a 57 percent usable response rate) concerning their adult fiction collection and how it was selected. The first part of this article profiles an average collection as containing 110,786 volumes composed of 28 percent adult fiction, of which 66 percent is "light fiction" or entertainment material. A mean of 1,462 titles were purchased in the previous year and 157 "added as gifts," but only 18 were not in English. It is noteworthy that 76 percent of the surveyed libraries acquired no non-English titles and 53 percent acquired fewer than the 1,000 titles recommended by Rawlinson.[13] The discussion and data tabulation concerning adult fiction selection methods in the entry's second half demonstrate that reviews, bestseller lists, and user requests are the most commonly used selection tools, while approval plans plus recommended and award-winning lists are not "highly important." Sweetland also briefly reviews issues in public library fiction selection beginning with the "fiction controversy" begun by George Tichnor in 1852.

Vega García, Susan A. "Racial and Ethnic Diversity in Academic Library Collections: Ownership and Access of African American and U.S. Latino Periodical Literature." **Journal of Academic Librarianship** 26 (September 2000): 311–22.

This entry begins with a review of literature concerning diversity in library and information science. The investigation is based on eighty-seven African American and fifty-two Latino periodicals, identified through Katz's *Magazines for Libraries* and Ulrich's *International Periodicals Directory* and organized into "research" and "leisure" titles. Checking against the holdings of 107 U.S. research libraries, as indicated by OCLC and RLIN, revealed that 49.4 percent of the libraries owned a majority of the research titles; 85.9 percent of ARL institutions owned less than one quarter of the leisure titles; and 65.3 percent owned a majority of the African American research titles whereas only 29.8 percent owned a majority of the Latino ones. Additional data, not lending itself to ready summary, is presented about the holdings of specific libraries and coverage by indexing services, full-text CD-ROM or online availability, and document supplier services. The author concludes that ARL libraries are not well prepared to support Latino studies and that "the role of leisure publications in the collection may need to be reconsidered" because of their weak coverage.

Walden, Barbara, et al. "Western European Political Science: An Acquisition Study." **College & Research Libraries** 55 (July 1994): 286–96.

In 1992 the ACRL's Western European Specialists Section studied the availability of 1990 imprint French, Italian, Swedish, Belgian, Icelandic, and Catalonian political science books in U.S. and Canadian libraries. "Knowledgeable bibliographers" selected the books suitable for large research libraries from the national bibliographies of the studied counties. These titles were checked against OCLC and RLIN on the assumption that these databases represent the holdings of North American research libraries. Of 319 French titles, 15 percent were not contained in any North American library, while 6 percent were held by only one. The cost of the missing titles was about $1,800, and the cost of acquiring the 1990 imprints sufficient for a research level collection was $12,188. Thirty percent of 144 Italian books were not held in the United States or Canada. Their cost would have been approximately $1,500, and a research collection's cost was calculated at $7,140. Fifty-seven percent (costing around $1,000) of 133 Belgian political science books were not in OCLC/RLIN. Interestingly, Yale and Stanford (both claiming level 4 collections in the Conspectus) had only 1 book each. Fifty-five percent of 68 Swedish books, 75 percent of 8 Icelandic titles, and 19 percent of 32 Catalan items, costing $535, $110, and $85 respectively, were also unavailable. The authors quite correctly conclude that factors other than funding influence the findings concerning weak coverage by North American libraries.

NOTES

1. Richard H. Orr et al., "Development of Methodologic Tools for Planning and Managing Library Services: I. Project Goals and Approach," *Bulletin of the Medical Library Association* 56 (July 1968): 235–40; Orr et al., "Development of Methodologic Tools for Planning and Managing Library Services: II. Measuring a Library's Capability for Providing Documents," *Bulletin of the Medical Library Association* 56 (July 1968): 241–67.

2. Christine Jenkins, "From Queer to Gay and Back Again: Young Adult Novels with Gay/Lesbian/Queer Content, 1969–1997," *Library Quarterly* 68 (July 1998): 298–334.

3. Carl Deal, "Latin American Collections: Criteria for Major Status," in *Latin American Frontiers, Borders, and Hinterlands: Papers of SALALM XXXIII, Berkeley, California, June 5–10, 1988,* edited by Paula Ann Covington (Albuquerque, NM SALALM, 1990), 163–68.

4. Herbert E. Gooch, *The Military and Politics in Latin America* (Los Angeles: Latin American Studies Center, California State University, 1979).

5. Nisonger's total from Noble's figures for separate steps in the process.

6. Nora Rawlinson, "Give 'Em What They Want," *Library Journal* 106 (November 15, 1981): 2188–90; Murray Bob, "The Case for Quality Book Selection," *Library Journal* 107 (September 15, 1982): 1701–10.

7. Glyn T. Evans, Roger Gifford, and Donald R. Franz, *Collection Development Analysis Using OCLC Archival Tapes: Final Report* (Albany, NY: SUNY Office of Library Services, 1977). Eric Document ED 152 299; Barbara Moore, Tamara J. Miller, and Don L. Tolliver, "Title Overlap: A Study of Duplication in the University of Wisconsin System Libraries," *College & Research Libraries* 43 (January 1982): 14–21; William S. Cooper, Donald D. Thompson, and Kenneth R. Weeks, "The Duplication of Monograph Holdings in the University of California Library System," *Library Quarterly* 45 (July 1975): 253–74.

8. Beth M. Paskoff and Anna H. Perrault, "A Tool for Comparative Collection Analysis: Conducting a Shelf-List Sample to Construct a Collection Profile," *Library Resources & Technical Services* 34 (April 1990): 199–215.

9. Anna H. Perrault, "The Changing Resource Print Base of Academic Libraries in the United States: A Comparison of Collecting Patterns in Seventy-Two ARL Academic Libraries of Non-Serial Imprints for the Years 1985 and 1989" (Ph.D. diss., Florida State University, 1991).

10. The percentage is Nisonger's calculation from Perrault's data.

11. Daniel Gore, ed., *Farewell to Alexandria: Solutions to Space, Growth, and Performance Problems of Libraries* (Westport, CT: Greenwood Press, 1976).

12. The percentages in this annotation are calculated by Nisonger.

13. Nora Rawlinson, "The Approach to Collection Management at Baltimore County Public Library," in *Collection Management in Public Libraries,* edited by Judith Serebnick (Chicago: American Library Association, 1986), 76–80.

6

Performance Measures and Standards

A performance measure tests how well a library is performing, or, put in other words, the library's effectiveness. The most basic categories of performance measures, inputs, outputs, and outcomes, have been explained in the introduction. The challenge is deciding which performance measures to use. In the past, inputs were used as performance measures. For example, it was once widely (but not universally) assumed that a library containing more volumes would be more effective at meeting information needs than one with a smaller collection. Since at least the 1980s, an increasing interest has developed in outputs as indicators of library effectiveness. An effectiveness measure can, of course, combine both inputs and outputs as does Thomas J. Hennen, Jr.'s American Public Library Rating (HAPLR) index. As we begin the twenty-first century, outcomes are often considered the ultimate test of library effectiveness.

Public libraries have been especially interested in "output measures." During the 1980s, the ALA's Public Library Association published two editions, in 1982 and 1987, of a practical manual for evaluating individual library performance entitled *Output Measures for Public Libraries.*[1] The second edition was part of the Public Library Development program. Similar type of manuals were later published for academic libraries, school libraries (see entry by Frances Bryant Bradburn in this chapter), and for children's and young adults services in public libraries (see this chapter's entries by Virginia A. Walter).[2] There has also been movements toward output measures in such countries as the United Kingdom, Australia, and New Zealand.

A discussion of performance measurements should mention standards, which also address overall library performance and usually contain a component relating to collections. The origin of library standards can be traced to the 1920s, and since then they have been promulgated for many types of libraries. There once was considerable debate concerning quantitative versus qualitative standards, but now the discussion relates to inputs and outputs. Traditionally, most standards tended to be input oriented. One can detect an historical shift from standards to performance measures. The ALA's Public Library Association abandoned national standards in the 1960s and later began emphasizing performance measures.[3] The 1995 Association of College and Research Libraries (ACRL) standard for college libraries counted total holdings whereas the 2000 standards use a combination of input, output, and outcome measures.

Also worthy of mention are a series of so-called "Guidelines." As their name implies, Guidelines are also promulgated by professional organizations but are somewhat less authoritative than standards. Specific examples would be the ACRL Guidelines for distance learning library services, university undergraduate libraries, media resources in academic libraries, and (in draft format) curriculum materials centers.[4] Note that the current ACRL Standards and Guidelines are also available on that organization's Web site.[5] Guidelines are worth mentioning but not annotating because they generally prescribe good practice but seldom include precise evaluative measures.

Chapter 6 annotates material dealing with the measurement of library performance or standards in which a significant portion of the item is relevant to the topics covered in this volume, that is, collections and their use as well as availability and access to information resources. The annotations emphasize points relevant to this book's scope. Generally, published works that do not address these topics to a significant extent, such as those focusing on service quality or outputs such as reference question answering, are excluded. Likewise, U.S. state library standards and standards for countries other than the United States are excluded for the sake of brevity.

Included in this chapter are manuals, research articles, historical surveys, and standards plus guidelines. Performance measures relating to electronic resources are included in chapter 11. The chapter is divided into three sections covering performance measures for public libraries, performance measures for other types of libraries, and standards.

PERFORMANCE MEASURES FOR PUBLIC LIBRARIES

Hennen, Thomas J., Jr. "Building Benchmarks to Craft A Better Library Future: Hennen's American Public Library Rating Index." **Australasian Public Libraries & Information Services** 12 (June 1999): 52–59.

Here Hennen explains the HAPLR Index (see the following entry) to an Australian audience. Noting that media coverage has been "very positive," he acknowledges criticism that his index fails to consider electronic resources and Internet access and can be distorted by inaccurate estimates of a library service area's population. He responds that the Index will incorporate electronic resources and the Internet when such data is available and that the calculation of service area populations by state library agencies needs "refinement." Hennen states an HAPLR Index "could be done," for Australia, but it would be necessary to standardize the data from the three organizational models for Australian public libraries: the centralized, the coordinated, and a combination of these two. He also observes that McIntyre has proposed a similar index for Australia (see entry later in this section). Appended tables illustrate the HAPLR's application to "Anywhere" public library and five other unnamed libraries.

Hennen, Thomas J., Jr. "Go Ahead, Name Them: America's Best Public Libraries." **American Libraries** 30 (January 1999): 72–76.

This entry introduces the HAPLR Index for evaluating U.S. public libraries on a 1 to 1000 scale. A library score is constructed from fifteen weighted variables (six input and nine output measures)—the majority of which relate to collections or circulation, for example, materials expenditures per capita, periodicals per 1,000 residents, circulation per capita, and so on. The necessary data was obtained from the U.S. Department of Education's Federal-State Cooperative System (FSCS). A table lists the fifteen factors, their weights, and scores at the 5, 10, 25, 50, 75, 90, and 95 percentiles for libraries serving population areas between 10,000 and 99,999. The top twenty public libraries are listed in rank order along with their index score for four population categories: over 100,000; 10,000 to 99,999; 2,000 to 9,999; and under 2,000. Hennen's system is intriguing, but some of the factors are not generally accepted quality measures, such as circulation per visit to the library. The author admits his index is "subjective and open to debate."

Hennen, Thomas J., Jr. "Great American Public Libraries: HAPLR Ratings, Round Two." **American Libraries** 30 (September 1999): 64–68.

Hennen emphasizes, "The first HALPR Index received attention from newspapers, magazines, and TV stations throughout the country" and cites more than a dozen examples. This follow-up study is based on preliminary 1997 FSCS data available on the Web (the first index used 1996 data). A two-page table rank orders by index score, the top ten libraries in ten population categories, ranging from "over 500,000" to "999 and under." A table summarizing the average HAPLR index for the fifty states plus the District of Columbia reveals that Ohio ranked number 1 with a score of 669 and Mississippi number 51 with a 292 index. The remainder of the article is devoted to addressing methodological criticisms of the HAPLR: data on electronic resources and Internet access is not considered, population data may be unreliable, too much emphasis on circulation, and libraries emphasizing different roles (research or circulation of popular materials) cannot be compared by a single measurement. While acknowledging limitations to his approach, the author asserts that because some things, such as excellence in research, cannot be measured or compared, it does not follow that "nothing" can be compared.

Hennen, Thomas J., Jr. "Great American Public Libraries: HAPLR Ratings, 2000." **American Libraries** 31 (November 2000): 50–54.

This entry contains the third round or version of Hennen's rankings of American public libraries. The library scores are constructed from "*preliminary* final" (an apparent oxymoron!) 1998 FSCS data available on the Web in June 2000. The format follows that of round two, with the top ten libraries listed in ten population size categories. A state-by-state ranking reveals that Ohio remains first and Mississippi last. Again, a major portion of the article is devoted to fending off criticisms. He claims, rather unconvincingly, that Jim Scheppke (see entry later in this chapter) mis-states his methodology and defends his weightings of the fifteen factors as "advised" by Publib discussion list members. While conceding "there is more to quality library service" than covered by his rankings, he emphasizes they "remain useful comparative tools."

Hennen, Thomas J., Jr. "Great American Public Libraries: The 2002 HAPLR Rankings." **American Libraries** 33 (October 2002): 64–68.

This item represents the fourth round (Hennen uses the term "edition") of the HAPLR rankings and the most current one prior to this book's publication. It is based on FSCS data for 2000, which became available in 2001. Following the format of the previous two rounds, the top ten U.S. public libraries for ten population size categories are listed along with their HALPR Index rating. In a table rating the states by their mean scores, Ohio remains number 1, while the District of Columbia displaces Mississippi in fifty-first place. Once again Hennen defends his system against critics, denying that too much emphasis is placed on circulation.

Immroth, Barbara Froling, and Keith Curry Lance. "Output Measures for Children's Services in Public Libraries: A Status Report." **Public Libraries** 35 (July/August 1996): 240–45.

Immroth and Lance report the results of a September 1993 survey of 187 public library children's librarians (66 percent responded) from fourteen states concerning local data pertinent to *Output Measures for Children's Services in Public Libraries* as well as selected input data. They discovered the average materials expenditure per child (defined as 14 and younger) was $2.14, the mean materials holdings per child (excluding periodicals) was 3.17, and the mean circulation per child 9.3. Note that six tables present the data from each state. For a number of output measures, including in-library use of library materials per child, the results varied so dramatically that the authors considered the data invalid because the library staff probably did not understand the measures. The researchers also found, based on relatively small response rates, the mean children's fill rate was 84 percent, the mean homework fill rate 87 percent, and the picture book fill rate 82 percent. Immroth and Lance recommend, in conclusion, that children's librarians and their supervisors must be convinced that collecting statistics is valuable.

Lance, Keith Curry, and Marti A. Cox. "Lies, Damn Lies, and Indexes." **American Libraries** 31 (June/July 2000): 82–86.

Hennen, Thomas J., Jr. "Go Figure: Thomas J. Hennen Responds." **American Libraries** 31 (June/July 2000): 87.

In these entries two library science researchers offer a sharp critique of the HAPLR Index, and Hennen provides a brief response. Lance and Cox begin by denying the feasibility of a single national standard for public library evaluation as each serves a unique local community. They maintain adequate data does not exist for the HALPR Index to be valid. Moreover, the Index is conceptually "diffuse" and poorly constructed. Two pairs of the fifteen factors are "hypercorrelated" with each other and thus redundant, while six other variables (including volumes per capita and periodicals per 1,000 residents) are "extraneous" because they don't correlate with the other variables. They also state that the weightings are "one of the mysteries" of the Index as 20 percent of the points are for redundant variables and 40 percent for extraneous variables. Finally, they question Hennen's grouping libraries by size of service population because a small city, suburban, and rural library serving the same size population are not peers.

Hennen concedes his Index should be called a "scorecard" and that library data from Federal government agencies needs to be made "better." However, he contends that performance numbers are necessary but not sufficient for library evaluation and emphasizes, "When families move from one community to another, they reasonably expect—and should get—a modicum of consistency in their library service."

McIntyre, Barry. "Measuring Excellence in Public Libraries." **Australasian Public Libraries & Information Services** 7 (September 1994): 135–55.

The first part of this article critiques the 1989 Australian Library and Information Association (ALIA) public library standards. Tables present collective data concerning New South Wales (NSW) and Victoria public library conformance to the standards on holdings, current acquisitions, weeding, and staffing, using 1990–91 data. For example, 38 percent of the NSW libraries failed to hold the stipulated two items for every population member served. Then the author proposes an E-Index ("E" standing for excellence), calculated from totaling standard scores for six variables:

- Items held per capita

- Items added per capita

- Items weeded per capita

- Staffing per capita

- Stock turnover

- Circulation per capita

McIntyre notes the Index does not consider reference services or "community fit" because the necessary data is not available. A lengthy figure illustrates calculation of the E-Index for 71 unnamed NSW public libraries, using the previously mentioned 1990–91 data. Noting the 0.66 correlation between the E-Index and expenditures per capita, the author asserts libraries ranking high on the former and low on the latter offer their communities "'good' value."

Scheppke, Jim. "The Trouble with Hennen." **Library Journal** 124 (November 15, 1999): 36–37.

Drawing upon his knowledge of public libraries in Oregon, Scheppke offers a trenchant critique of the HAPLR Index. The author gives Hennen "As" for effort and for audacity (for selling ratings on his Web site to nearly 9,000 U.S. public libraries for $10 or $15 for rush delivery). Scheppke contends the Index is "less-than-credible." The criteria are "quirky" and redundant as 40 percent relate to circulation.

Indeed, "visits per hour," may reward libraries open fewer hours. Moreover, criteria important to users, such as building spaciousness, access to the Internet, and new books, are not considered. Observing that Oregon's fifth highest ranking library is open fourteen hours a week and served by one 0.35 full time equivalent (FTE) staff member without a professional degree, he proclaims "case closed."

Van House, Nancy A., and Thomas A. Childers. **The Public Library Effectiveness Study: The Complete Report**. Chicago: American Library Association, 1993. 99p. ISBN 0-8389-0619-2.

This complex, large-scale study seeks, among other research questions, to identify the indicators of public library effectiveness. In the late 1980s, 2,689 individuals from seven groups (local officials, community leaders, library managers, library service staff, trustees, library friends organization members, and users) associated with about 100 public libraries throughout the United States were mailed questionnaires (89.8 percent responded) asking them to rate the importance of sixty-one library effectiveness indicators, culled from the literature, on a 1 (low) to 4 (high) Likert scale. Library managers and staff, but not the other groups, were also asked to rate their own library's performance on these indicators. The analysis of the results is quite sophisticated. The most interesting indicators (from this book's perspective) and their relative rank among the sixty-one, based on librarian assessment of their own library's performance, are the following: range of materials (7), circulation (9), materials quality (18), in-library use of materials (22), newness of materials (25), number of materials owned (26), materials turnover (29), interlibrary loan (39), materials availability (45), and materials expenditures (49). The relative rank of the sixty-one indicators according to perceived importance is not given. The authors believe this methodology can be applied to other types of libraries.

Walter, Virginia A. **Output Measures and More: Planning and Evaluating Public Library Services for Young Adults.** Chicago: American Library Association, 1995. 117p. ISBN 0-8389-3452-8.

Part of the Public Library Development Program, this practical guide adopts the approach used in *Output Measures for Public Libraries* to the evaluation of young adult services in public libraries. Part 1 covers the application of planning and role setting to young adult services. Part 2 offers advice on measurement issues such as data collection and interpretation of results. Part 3 provides detailed explanation of the output measures themselves while outlining steps for their implementation. Seven of nineteen measures fall within this literature guide's scope and require little or no explanation:

- Circulation of Young Adult Materials per Young Adult

- Circulation of Materials per Young Adult

- In-Library Use of Young Adult Materials per Young Adult

- In-Library Use of Materials by Young Adults per Young Adult

- Turnover Rate of Young Adult Materials (circulation divided by holdings)

- Young Adult Fill Rate (the percentage of young adult searches for material that are successful)

- Homework Fill Rate (the proportion of searches for homework material that result in success)

A lengthy appendix includes 25 work forms, some of which are in Spanish.

Walter, Virginia A. **Output Measures for Public Library Service to Children: A Manual of Standardized Procedures.** Chicago: American Library Association, 1992. 129p. ISBN 0-8389-3404-8.

This item is quite similar in purpose and organization to the preceding entry, except that it presents performance measures for children's rather than young adult services. Part 1 discusses the measurement process itself. Of the fifteen output measures described in the second part, three relate to materials use (Circulation of Children's Materials per Child, In-library Use of Children's Materials per Child, and Turnover Rate of Children's Materials) and three to availability (Children's Fill Rate, Homework Fill Rate, and Picture Book Fill Rate). Part 3 talks about the role of focus groups and user surveys in assessing library performance. The appendix contains more than twenty forms (with a few in Spanish) for data gathering and tabulation. Both of Walter's manuals offer valuable toolkits for evaluating the performance of a specific library as well as comparing different libraries.

PERFORMANCE MEASURES FOR OTHER TYPES OF LIBRARIES

Bradburn, Frances Bryant. **Output Measures for School Library Media Programs.** New York: Neal-Schuman Publishers, 1999. 95p. ISBN 1-55570-326-7.

The "output measures" approach developed for public libraries has been modified by Bradburn for evaluation of school library media centers. The initial three chapters, comprising approximately two-thirds of the work, explain sixteen different output measures. Materials use measures include:

- Circulation Rate (items circulating in proportion to number of students or teachers)

- In-Library Use Rate (in-house use in proportion to the number of students and teachers

- Electronic Resources Hit Rate (the number of times electronic resources are used)

- Turnover Rate (book uses divided by the number of books in the collection)

Several availability measures should be mentioned:

- Potential Curriculum Support Rate (the number of relevant books held divided by the number needed for a unit)

- Curriculum Support Fill Rate (the percentage of items sought by students and/or teachers to support course work actually found)

- Independent Reading/Information Fill Rate (the percentage of items sought by students for nonclass work actually found)

- Online Resource Success Rate (the percentage of online searches that were successful)

The final three chapters, about one-third the book, illustrate the practical application of these measures. The volume concludes with an unannotated bibliography of about 35 items. Like many Neal-Schuman publications, this book takes a "how-to" approach.

Calvert, Philip J. "Collection Development and Performance Measurement." In **Collection Management for the 21st Century: A Handbook for Librarians,** edited by Gary E. Gorman and Ruth H. Miller, 121–33. Westport, CT: Greenwood Press, 1997. ISBN 0-313-29953-6.

This entry begins by observing that librarians feel "comfortable" with such "traditional" evaluation measures as collection size and growth rate because the data is easily calculated and understood. During the "intermediate stage" of the 1970s and 1980s, a combination of input and output measures were used. In a lengthy section entitled "The Next Generation?" the author recommends the Multiple Constituencies Model for measuring organizational effectiveness. Reviewing previous research employing this model (including this chapter's entry by Van House and Childers), Calvert explains that stakeholders, such as librarians, users, and funders, are surveyed to reach a consensus concerning the key indicators of library effectiveness. Finally, Calvert contends that in the future, performance measures will be needed to ascertain how well the library is meeting patron demands for items from the "anti-collection" (i.e., material not locally held). Calvert offers an insightful essay, not limited by library type, concerning the evolution of approaches for measuring library performance.

Clarke, Tobin de Leon, and Elmer U. Clawson. "Output Measures for Evaluating the Performance of Community College Learning Resources Programs: A California Case Study." **Advances in Librarianship** 17 (1993): 175–202.

The historical development through the early 1990s of output measures for community college libraries in California is traced from 1930s standards for input measures. After the pilot testing of thirteen output measures by sixteen community college libraries during the spring of 1988, the Title Fill Rate and the Subject Fill Rate were collapsed into a single standard called the User Success/Satisfaction Rate (the proportion of time users found and were satisfied with sought after items).

Other measures, all of which are explained in an appendix, include the following: Circulation per FTE user, In-House Use per FTE user, Turnover, and the Interlibrary Loan and Delayed Fill Rate (i.e., the proportion of ILL requests filled within two weeks). A major portion of this entry provides a detailed discussion concerning a survey of 48 California community college libraries (77 percent responded) regarding the final twelve measures. Clark and Clawson conclude that the survey results "validated" the measures because, generally, at least 80 percent of the respondents thought they were "useful" and the directions and definitions "clear."

Doelling, Donna L. "Blueprint for Performance Assessment." **Medical Reference Services Quarterly** 12 (spring 1993): 29–38.

Doelling describes the method and process used in a library effectiveness study carried out at the University of South Florida Health Sciences Center beginning in the fall of 1991. Seven steps in the process are discussed:

- Conducting a literature review

- Setting goals and determining measurement criteria

- Developing a survey instrument

- Establishing a time frame

- "Mobilizing resources," (i.e., organizing materials and manpower)

- Conducting the survey

- Compiling the data.

The survey instrument is appended. Respondents were asked to indicate their "degree of satisfaction" on a 1 (low) to 5 (high) scale with twenty-nine elements organized into five categories including "access/availability" and "resource materials." Specific items relating to collections were "availability of materials on the shelf" and "variety of journal titles." This entry is useful for the concise step-by-step approach.

Joint Funding Councils' Ad-Hoc Group on Performance Indicators for Libraries. **The Effective Academic Library: A Framework for Evaluating the Performance of U.K. Academic Libraries; A Consultative Report to the HEFCE, SHEFC, HEFCW, and DENI by the Joint Funding Councils' Ad-Hoc Group on Performance Indicators for Libraries.** Bristol: Higher Education Funding Council for England, 1995. 44p.

This "consultative report" to U.K. higher education funding authorities proposes a framework for assessing overall library effectiveness. The introduction outlines thirteen "important factors" regarding performance indicators (e.g., they must be clearly defined and not interpreted as standards). Then, it recommends thirty-three performance indicators organized into five broad categories: integration (between institutional and library objectives), user satisfaction, delivery, efficiency, and economy. The performance indicators most pertinent to this book's topics are as follows:

- Overall user satisfaction (under user satisfaction)

- Documents delivered per FTE student (under delivery)

- Volumes in stock per FTE student (under delivery)

- Total library expenditures per documents delivered (under efficiency)

- Total library expenditures per volumes in stock (under efficiency)

- Acquisitions expenditures per FTE student (under economy)

Ten appendices, termed "annexes," include a list of data elements necessary to calculate these performance indicators and summaries of performance indicators from other sources.

Nitecki, Danuta A., and Brinley Franklin. "New Measures for Research Libraries." **Journal of Academic Librarianship** 25 (November 1999): 484–87.

This essay is an outgrowth of a retreat of thirteen directors of ARL libraries (informally termed "the New Measures Group") held in Tucson, Arizona, in January 1999. In place of such traditional input measures as volumes held, volumes added, and current subscriptions, three indicators of library impact were broached:

- Number of service interactions—this might include circulation, reserve use, ILL requests, and reference transactions

- User satisfaction—possibly measured on a Likert scale

- Service quality—defined as user perception of library performance compared to their expectations

Nitecki and Franklin note that most user satisfaction questionnaires have focused on collections, services, facilities, or overall library performance. SERVQUAL is explained and its potential role described. The authors outline eight issues to be addressed, such as how libraries actually are assessing patron satisfaction and service quality plus the need for data-gathering tools and theoretical models. Although not stated here, the ARL New Measures Initiative, begun in October 1999, was an apparent follow-up to the Tucson retreat.

Seavey, Charles A. "Output Measures for the Cartographic Materials Collections of the ARL Libraries: An Exploratory Study." In **Academic Libraries; Achieving Excellence in Higher Education: Proceedings of the Sixth National Confer-**

ence of the Association of College and Research Libraries, Salt Lake City, Utah, April 12–14, 1992,** edited by Thomas Kirk, 221–27. Chicago: American Library Association, 1992. ISBN 0-8389-7622-0.

A performance measurement approach is applied to the cartographic materials (defined as maps, aerial photography, and remote sensing imagery) collections of ARL libraries. Data on FTE student population, map holdings, aerial photo holdings, circulation, square footage, the number of five-drawer map cabinets, and visitors per month (gathered from the *Guide to U.S. Map Resources* and the *ARL Statistics 1988–89*) were used to create "complex statistics," that is, single figures calculated from multiple data points, concerning map collections. Forty-five ARL libraries (the only ones for which all the necessary data were available) are ranked according to the "Overall User Index" based on circulation per capita, annual readers per capita, and turnover rate (circulation divided by holdings). Then seventy-eight ARL institutions are ranked by the "Overall Facilities Index" calculated from the holdings per square foot, square footage per FTE student, and maps per five-drawer map cabinet. Seavey acknowledges that his rankings should not be viewed as "authoritative" due to problems with data reliability as the ARL does not have standards for collecting cartographic materials data.

STANDARDS

Association for Educational Communications and Technology (AECT). Community College Association for Instructional Technology and Association for College and Research Libraries. Community and Junior College Libraries Section. "Standards for Community, Junior, and Technical College Learning Resources Programs [Draft]." **College & Research Libraries News** 55 (May 1994): 274–87.

Association for Educational Communications and Technology and Association for College and Research Libraries. "Standards for Community, Junior, and Technical College Learning Resources Programs: The Final Version Approved by ACRL, ALA, and AECT in 1994." **College & Research Libraries News** 55 (October 1994): 572–85.

This document replaces the 1990 community college standards, but maintains the same emphasis on quantitative input measures such as collection size. The standards are organized around seven areas: objectives, organization and administration, staff, budget, user services, collections, and facilities. The collection standard calls for "an organized collection of materials and information in diversified formats." A formula stipulates the number of holdings for "minimum" and "excellent" collections for ten student body sizes, ranging from fewer than 1,000 FTE students to 17,000–19,000 FTE students. For example, a library supporting 7,000–8,999 FTE students needs total holdings of 109,450 for a "minimum" collection and 161,200 for an "excellent collection." These totals are subdivided with recommended numbers for print volumes, current serial subscriptions, videos and films, and "other items," defined to include microfilms, plus graphic, audio, cartographic, and machine-readable materials. Other quantitative formulas are given for staff size, expenditures, and equipment longevity. Note that the draft version's collection size formula only includes nine student body sizes with the smallest 1,000 to 2,999 FTE students.

Association of College and Research Libraries. College Libraries Section. Standards Committee. "Standards for College Libraries, 1995 Edition, Draft." **College & Research Libraries News** 55 (May 1994): 261–72, 294.

Association of College and Research Libraries. College Libraries Section. Standards Committee. "Standards for College Libraries, 1995 Edition: Final Version Approved by the ACRL Board and the ALA Standards Committee, February 1995." **College & Research Libraries News** 56 (April 1995): 245–57.

The fourth ACRL standards for college libraries (the first three were approved in 1959, 1975, and 1986) continue with the earlier quantitative input-oriented approach. The document is composed of eight standards for the following: mission, goals, and objectives; collections; organization of materials; staff; services; facilities; administration; and budget. The collections standard stipulates the library should contain "all types of recorded information," "promptly" provide "a high percentage of material needed by its users," use Formula A to calculate the print collection's optimal size, and then apply a grading system. The formula is implemented by starting with a base of 85,000 volumes and then adding the following: 100 volumes per FTE faculty, 15 per FTE student, 350 per undergraduate field, 6,000 per master's field with no higher degree offered, 3,000 per master's field with a higher degree, 6,000 per sixth-year specialist degree, and 25,000 per Ph.D. degree. If the collection holds at least 90 percent of the total then the grade is A, 75 to 89 percent a B, 60 to 74 percent a C, and 50 to 59 percent a D. There are two other formulas (B and C) for calculating size of staff and space in the facility. The collection size formula is apparently modeled on the famous Clapp-Jordan formula.[6]

Association of College and Research Libraries. College Libraries Section. Standards Committee. "Standards for College Libraries, A Draft." **College & Research Libraries News** 60 (May 1999): 375–81.

Association of College and Research Libraries. College Libraries Section. Standards Committee. "Standards for College Libraries: The Final Version, Approved January 2000." **College & Research Libraries News** 61 (March 2000): 175–82.

The current ACRL standards "advocate the use of input, output, and outcome measures in the context of the institution's mission statement." Input measures include the following:

- Ratio of volumes held to total number of students and faculty

- Ratio of volumes added per year to student/faculty total

- Ratio of resource expenditures to FTE student/faculty total

Output measures include the following:

- Ratio of circulation to FTE student/faculty total

- Ratio of ILL requests to FTE student/faculty total

- Turnaround, fill rate, and unit cost for ILL/document delivery borrowing and lending

The document suggests that libraries compare their input and output data with those from peer institutions. Surveys, interviews, and tests are recommended for outcomes assessment regarding the achievement of library objectives. Separate sections list questions to be addressed for the following: services, instruction, resources, access, staff, faculties, communication and cooperation, administration, and budget. The nine questions under the resources heading concern selection criteria, the faculty's role in selection, the evaluation program, media and electronic resources, licensing, consortial purchasing, archives, online databases, and weeding. The access section deals primarily with cataloging issues but mentions ILL/document delivery efficiency and consortial borrowing. Compared with the 1995 standards, the shift in emphasis from size of holdings to library performance is obvious.

Crawford, Gregory A., and Gary W. White. "Liberal Arts Colleges and Standards for College Libraries: A Quantitative Analysis." **Journal of Academic Librarianship** 25 (November 1999): 439–44.

Crawford and White test compliance with the 1995 ACRL college library standards, using a randomly selected sample of 60 colleges from 33 states. Data on holdings and staff size were obtained from the U.S. Department of Education and on academic programs from *Lovejoy's College Guide.* They discovered that only 33.3 percent of the college libraries contained the full number of volumes recommended by the collection size formula, while 43.3 percent received an A, 23.3 percent a B, 15.0 percent a C, 8.3 percent a D, and 10.0 percent lower than a D. An identical analysis for the staff size formula found a lower grade distribution. Carnegie BAI colleges had, on average, 2.29 times the recommended collection size, whereas BAII schools had 0.82 of the recommended size. (Note that BAI institutions offer more liberal arts fields and are more selective in admissions than their BAII counterparts.) The researchers conclude by asking "should standards be a goal or a minimum requirement?"

Haycock, Ken, and Robert A. Harrell. "Preface." In **Information Power: Building Partnerships for Learning,** prepared by the American Association of School Librarians and Association for Educational Communications and Technology, v–vii. Chicago: American Library Association, 1998. ISBN 0-8389-3470-6 (paper).

This brief preface offers a succinct synopsis of twentieth-century standards and guidelines for school libraries. In 1920 the National Education Association (NEA) published standards for junior and senior high school libraries, while the

NEA and ALA jointly issued *Elementary School Library Standards* in 1925. The first national K–12 standards, called *School Libraries for Today and Tomorrow,* were published in 1945. The American Association of School Librarians' (AASL's) *Standards for School Library Programs* was issued in 1960. In 1969 the AASL and the NEA's Department of Audiovisual Instruction (now called the AECT) published *Standards for School Media Programs.* AASL and AECT issued *Media Programs: District and School* in 1975 and *Information Power: Guidelines for School Library Media Programs* in 1988. Haycock and Harrell assert that *Information Power: Building Partnerships for Learning,* while evolving from earlier standards and guidelines, stresses the promotion of information literacy and lifelong learning rather than resources. Although not explicitly stated, this represents an outcome-oriented approach.

"Information Access and Delivery." In **Information Power: Building Partnerships for Learning,** prepared by the American Association of School Librarians and Association for Educational Communications and Technology, 83–99. Chicago: American Library Association, 1998. ISBN 0-8389-3470-6 (paper).

Information Power is generally regarded as the de facto national standard or guideline for school library media centers. A dominant theme is the emphasis on information literacy as a key to lifelong learning. This chapter outlines seven principles relating to collections and information access along with subheading "goals" for achieving them. The principles advocate intellectual access to information ("finding, judging and using it"), physical access to information, and intellectual freedom. The most relevant, from this book's perspective, is Principle 5, which states collections should be "developed and evaluated collaboratively to support the school's curriculum and to meet the diverse learning needs of students." Further commentary states the collection should be evaluated on a "continuous" basis with "collaborative" input from teachers and students to whom published evaluations should be circulated. In summary, *Information Power* addresses some collection evaluation issues although it clearly takes a much broader focus.

Walch, David B. "The 1986 College Library Standards: Application and Utilization." **College & Research Libraries** 54 (May 1993): 217–26.

This article compares the 1975 and 1986 standards and reports a survey concerning the 1986 edition's use and effectiveness. A point-by-point comparison found "few substantial changes" between the two editions, but in the 1986 version, audiovisual material and items obtained through ILL or reciprocal borrowing were counted toward meeting the collection size formula's requirements. A survey of 436 libraries (41.8 percent responded) found the standards were applied in accreditation, budget justification, and educating administrators and that "as many as 95 percent" of the respondents found the standards useful. Reported holdings data used to calculate grades according to the collection size formula (essentially the same formula described in the above annotation for the 1992 standards) found that 66.0 percent received an A, 18.2 percent a B, 9.4 percent a C, and 6.4 percent a D. A similar analysis was used for the formulas for staff size and space. Walch judges that the 1986 standards "are of value and are being used," but note that he was a member of the committee that drafted them.

NOTES

1. Douglas Zweizig and Eleanor Jo Rodger, *Output Measures for Public Libraries: A Manual of Standardized Procedures* (Chicago: American Library Association, 1982); Nancy A. Van House et al., *Output Measures for Public Libraries: A Manual of Standardized Procedures,* 2d ed. (Chicago: American Library Association, 1987).

2. Nancy A. Van House, Beth T. Weil, and Charles R. McClure, *Measuring Academic Library Performance: A Practical Approach* (Chicago: American Library Association, 1990).

3. Nancy A. Van House and Thomas A. Childers, *The Public Library Effectiveness Study: The Complete Report* (Chicago: American Library Association, 1993), 5.

4. Association of College and Research Libraries, ACRL Distance Learning Section Guidelines Committee, "Guidelines for Distance Learning Library Services," *College & Research Libraries News* 61 (December 2000): 1023–29; ACRL, University Libraries Section, Ad Hoc Committee to Review Draft Guidelines for University Undergraduate Libraries, "Guidelines for University Undergraduate Libraries: The Final Approved Version," *College & Research Libraries News* 58 (May 1997): 330–33, 341; ACRL, ACRL Media Resources Committee, "Guidelines for Media Resources in Academic Libraries," *College & Research Libraries News* 60 (April 1999): 294–302; ACRL, Education and Behavioral Sciences Section, Ad Hoc Curriculum Materials Centers Standards/Guidelines Committee, "Guidelines for Curriculum Materials Centers: A Draft," *College & Research Libraries News* 63 (March 2002): 207–13.

5. ACRL, *Standards and Guidelines.* Available: http://www.ala.org/acrl/guides/ (accessed August 27, 2003).

6. Verner W. Clapp and Robert T. Jordan, "Quantitative Criteria for Adequacy of Academic Library Collections," *College & Research Libraries* 26 (September 1965): 371–80. Reprinted in *College & Research Libraries* 50 (March 1989): 154–63.

7

Serials Evaluation

The scholarly journal dates to the 1650s when *Journal des Sçavans* was founded in Paris and the *Philosophical Transactions* (of the Royal Society) was launched in London. Serials have posed problems and challenges for librarians ever since! In the late 1970s, an attempt to create a National Periodicals Center ended in failure. By the 1980s, spiraling subscription price inflation coupled with a proliferation of new titles resulted in multiple rounds of serials cancellation projects for many academic libraries. Relatively recent developments that impact serials, including electronic journals, the Web, commercial document delivery services, and full-text databases, present a host of management and evaluation issues.

Chapter 7 covers the evaluation of traditional print serials. Not unexpectedly, the literature is skewed toward academic libraries. During the last decade, librarians have evaluated serials in order to select titles for cancellation, determine how well patron information needs are being met, and develop more cost-effective strategies for providing access to articles. Serials evaluation is complicated because it often combines both micro (focusing on specific titles) and macro (concentrating on the entire serials collection) approaches. Topics that have been addressed in the evaluation literature pertinent to this chapter include the following:

- Assessment criteria and evaluation methods

- Serials cancellation or deselection, especially the criteria and the process itself

- National trends in journal evaluation and cancellation

- The types of serials most likely to be cancelled

- Vendor services that can assist evaluation

- Creation of databases to support serials decision-making

- Identification of the serials important for a specific library

- Identification of the core journals for a discipline or subject area

- Development of models for journal selection and deselection

That at least five other chapters in this book cover literature relevant to serials evaluation illustrates the format's centrality to contemporary librarianship. The reader is referred to chapter 8 for periodical use studies, chapter 9 for citation studies pertinent to serials, chapter 10 for journal ranking, chapter 11 for evaluation issues relating to electronic journals and full-text databases, and chapter 12 for entries addressing the cost-effectiveness of serial subscription versus document delivery. Be aware that items dealing with the increasing costs of serials, explanations for these cost increases, and the associated impact on library budgets are not covered in this book

This chapter is organized into sections covering the evaluation of serials or serial collections, core serial lists (focusing on methodologies for determining the core rather than simple lists of core titles), serials cancellation, and serials decision models.

EVALUATION OF SERIALS OR SERIAL COLLECTIONS

Alexander, Adrian W., and James L. Smith. "Annual Survey of Serials Collection Assessment Programs, Practices, and Policies in Academic Libraries, 1991–1992." **Journal of Library Administration** 17, no. 2 (1992): 133–48.

The authors surveyed collection development, serials, and administrative professionals at fourteen academic libraries, evenly divided between ARL and non-ARL members, concerning serials assessment in their institution. The ten-question instrument (reproduced in an appendix) was designed during November-December 1991 and implemented through telephone interviews in January 1992. Five ARL libraries reported serials cancellation projects during the preceding three years ranging from "under $100,000" to $419,000. The cancellations tended to focus on science titles. Most ARL institutions had used the RLG Conspectus for evaluation, but non-ARL libraries had used the WLN Conspectus, the OCLC/Amigos Collection Analysis Service, or had done no serials assessment. Twelve respondents perceived a future shift from ownership to access and from print to electronic. Detailed responses are given for specific libraries, which are identified by type rather than name. The authors conclude a variety of evaluation approaches are used and that libraries rely heavily on local automated systems for evaluative data. Despite the authors' declared intentions, future surveys were apparently never published.

Black, Steven. "Journal Collection Analysis at a Liberal Arts College." **Library Resources & Technical Services** 41 (October 1997): 283–94.

This entry reports a journal cost-effectiveness study conducted at the College of Saint Rose in Albany, New York. Total journal uses during the 1996 calendar year (measured by marking a shelf label whenever an item was reshelved) were related to 1996 subscription cost and student enrollment data. Subscription cost per use, the number of students enrolled in each department per subscription, and journal use per student were employed as major cost-effectiveness criteria. Among the noteworthy findings, one should mention the following: the median number of uses per journal title was 16; 8.5 percent of the titles were unused; 9.25 percent of the titles could, theoretically, been provided more efficiently through ILL; and cost per use, analyzed by department, ranged from $0.88 for general journals to $44.68 for medical technology, where the larger figure was caused by high journal price and low student enrollment rather than low use per se. Black asserts his data analysis techniques have not previously been published in the literature.

Born, Kathleen. "The Role of the Serials Vendor in the Collection Assessment and Evaluation Process." **Journal of Library Administration** 19, no. 2 (1993): 125–38.

Written by the director of EBSCO's (the Elton B. Stephens Company) Academic Division, this entry describes how serial subscription agents can help librarians assess their serials collection. Born stresses that the agent's database of serial titles contains useful evaluative information, such as price history, language, country of publication, subject coverage, indexing and abstracting data, and whether a title is refereed. The article is organized according to six issues that impact selection/deselection decisions:

- Quality—a subscription agent can generate departmental subscription lists so faculty can rank journals by importance. Also, data concerning the percentage of titles in a particular index subscribed to by the library can be compiled

- Accessibility—indexing and abstracting information can be provided by title or in conjunction with other evaluative criteria

- Manageability—the agent can supply data concerning a journal's past claims history (to identify problem titles) and whether the publisher is registered with the Copyright Clearance Center

- Cost and Budget—three- to five-year price histories can be furnished, future costs projected, and current costs organized by subject area, academic department, publisher, or country of origin

- Availability—subscription agents can serve as a source for individual articles supplied through document delivery

- Usage—the library must conduct its own use studies

This item accomplishes its stated purpose.

Collins, Tim, and Beth Howell. "Journal Accessibility Factor: An Examination of Serials Value from the Standpoint of Access and Delivery." **Collection Management** 21, no. 1 (1996): 29–40.

This entry, co-authored by two EBSCO executives, begins by focusing on EBSCO services in three areas: serial subscriptions; current awareness, abstracting and indexing, and full-text publishing; and document delivery. Collins and Howell observe that EBSCO provides its customers a Collection Management Report, organizing subscriptions by subject, and that most of its CD-ROM products include a software feature for generating journal usage reports. They propose an "Access Factor Report" that incorporates data on "all facets of serials access and delivery" from customer and other information available to EBSCO. Components might include the following:

- Current Awareness Factor—coverage by current awareness services

- Full-Text Quotient—coverage in full-text databases

- Subscription Factor—based on number of subscribers

- Usage Factor—incorporating document delivery data

Data can be obtained for six library types: academic, corporate, medical, public, school, and special. This article would have benefited by providing more specific details about their proposed measures.

Haas, Stephanie C., and Vernon N. Kisling, Jr. "The Use of Electronic Ranking to Analyze Scientific Literature Used in Research at the University of Florida." **Collection Management** 18, nos. 3–4 (1994): 49–62.

Haas and Kisling explain how the Dialog "Rank" command can be used to list in rank order the journals of local importance to a specific academic institution. In this case, articles published by University of Florida faculty during 1991 and the journals cited in those articles, were identified by searching two databases. According to *SciSearch* (a "broad-based" database), the faculty produced 3,099 articles published in 1,036 journals, but 142 of these journals (14 percent), listed in an appendix, accounted for 50 percent of the articles. A total of 13,736 titles were cited by faculty in *SciSearch,* although the main analysis was limited to 836 identifiable journal titles cited in at least seven articles. The library subscribed to 93 percent of the 1,036 *SciSearch* titles in which faculty published, 99 percent of the 836 highly cited journal titles, and 91 percent of the 256 journals published in by faculty according to *Agricola,* an agricultural database. While noting a problem with the same journal being listed multiple times under variant title forms, the authors nevertheless decide the Rank command is a "powerful quantitative tool."

Youngen, Gregory K. "Using Current Awareness Search Results to Measure a Journal Collection's Relevancy." **Library Collections, Acquisitions, & Technical Services** 23 (summer 1999): 141–48.

Current awareness search subject profiles of 28 faculty and graduate students associated with the University of Illinois at Urbana-Champaign (UIUC)

Physics/Astronomy Library were run against the 1997 Institute for Scientific Information's (ISI's) *Current Contents* database, using Ovid as an interface, in order to generate 16,884 journal article citations used to evaluate the collection. More than 90 percent of the articles were held by the UIUC campus libraries, a figure that rose to 96 percent if recently cancelled titles were considered. More than 81 percent of the articles were concentrated in 16 percent of the 700 journals, of which all but 186 titles were held by the libraries. The author calculated a "relevancy factor," that is, the number of cited articles per title. While acknowledging some limitations, for example "retrieved citations are not necessarily relevant citations," Youngen contends retrieved citations represent potential uses and that "this study has helped identify the unique research interests" of library clientele.

CORE SERIAL LISTS

Adams, Barbara Kay. "Collection Assessment and Development of a Core List of Periodicals in Southern Culture." **Collection Management** 16, no. 1 (1992): 103–16.

This article describes a method for identifying core periodicals in the interdisciplinary area of Southern culture for use in collection evaluation by the University of Mississippi library. The annual bibliographies in the *Journal of Southern History,* 1986–90, and *Mississippi Quarterly,* 1985–89, were analyzed, resulting in 7,104 periodical citations from 661 journal titles. Titles that received thirty or more citations (averaging 6 per year) and coverage in at least one major index were defined as core. These 61 journals, listed in alphabetical order in an appendix, are described by the author as "diverse" and "of importance" to Southern culture and other subjects. The library held 87 percent of them. Adams comments that the experience gained from the year spent working on this project will assist in developing core periodical lists for other interdisciplinary fields at the University of Mississippi.

Black, Steven. "Using Citation Analysis to Pursue a Core Collection of Journals for Communication Disorders." **Library Resources & Technical Services** 45 (January 2001): 3–9.

Noting that neither *Magazines for Libraries* nor the *JCR* contain a section for communications disorders, the author uses citation analysis to propose a core list for that discipline. He analyzes every citation in the *Journal of Communication Disorders* during 1997, 1998, and 1999 and in the *Journal of Speech, Language, and Hearing Disorders* for 1997 and 1999. Of 11,704 citations, 66 percent were to journals, and 25 percent to books, while only two citations were to Web sites. An age breakdown of the journal citations found that "fully half" were at least 8 years old and 16 percent at least 20 years, while citation "peaks" at 5 years. Altogether 791 journals were cited, of which 13 percent provided 80 percent of the citations, 361 journals (45.6 percent) were cited only once.[1] The 103 journals (those cited twelve or more times) that provided 80 percent of the citations were considered the core and listed in an appendix. Black states that his methodology "suggests" but does not "define" the core, and that a cutoff of 12 citations is "arbitrary." This entry's analysis is trenchant.

Burnham, Judy F., Barbara S. Schearer, and James C. Wall. "Combining New Technologies for Effective Collection Development: A Bibliometric Study Using CD-ROM and a Database Management Program." **Bulletin of the Medical Library Association** 80 (April 1992): 150–56.

This entry explains how CD-ROM databases can be used in conjunction with a database management program to determine core journals and obtain additional information to support collection development. Articles dealing with "gait," that is, the study of human locomotion, were downloaded from the *MEDLINE* and *Cumulative Index to Nursing and Allied Health Literature (CINAHL)* CD-ROM databases covering January 1983 to June 1990 and analyzed with *Papyrus* software. The twenty-five journals—mostly in medicine—producing the most articles are listed in a table along with the percentage of their articles devoted to "gait" and their *JCR* impact factor. It is reported that 10 percent of the 232 *MEDLINE* journals published 50 percent of the articles and 10 percent of the 21 *CINAHL* journals produced 53 percent of its "gait" articles.[2] Only six authors in *MEDLINE* wrote 10 percent of the articles. Burnham, Schearer, and Wall correctly believe this approach can be used for other subjects besides "gait." Although not explicitly stated by the authors, their article illustrates how production of relevant articles can be used to identify core journals in obscure subjects.

Chung, Yeon-Kyoung. "Core International Journals of Classification Systems: An Application of Bradford's Law." **Knowledge Organization** 21, no. 2 (1994): 75–83.

Chung's stated objective is to determine the core international journals in the field of classification for the years 1981 to 1990. She initially identified, by checking the journal *International Classification's* bibliography section, 427 articles on classification distributed among 120 journals (termed the "level-one literature"). The thirteen most productive journals, of which three originate from the United States, are listed in a table. The 2,002 serial citations at level-one were then analyzed as the "level-two literature." A table lists in rank order the twenty-four most frequently cited journals: presumably the core although not explicitly stated. Eleven of these are U.S. titles with four other countries represented. The researcher found a Bradford distribution in both the level-one and level-two literatures. Chung concludes that her findings offer a "tool" to support journal selection.

Kushkowski, Jeffrey D., Kristin H. Gerhard, and Cynthia Dobson. "A Method for Building Core Journal Lists in Interdisciplinary Subject Areas." **Journal of Documentation** 54 (September 1998): 477–88.

The Simple Index Method (SIM), developed by the authors for identifying core journals in interdisciplinary fields, is introduced here. Terms appropriate to a field are entered into multiple electronic indexes, and the retrieved journal titles then ranked according to the number of articles produced. A test of the method in industrial relations, using five electronic indexes including *ABI/Inform* and *Econlit,* retrieved 2,753 articles published between 1991 and 1995 from 479 different journals. The 55 journals cited ten or more times (listed in a table) were defined as the core. Next, Graeme Hirst's "Discipline Impact Factor" (DIF), which manipulates *JCR* data to rank journals based on citation from their discipline only rather than the entire ISI database, was used to identify 49 core industrial relations journals.[3] Eight titles were common to both the DIF and SIM lists. While recognizing the SIM is quantitative, the researchers believe their technique can support journal selection and collection evaluation in other interdisciplinary fields and specialized areas by creating core lists. This is first-rate research.

McCain, Katherine W. "Biotechnology in Context: A Database-Filtering Approach to Identifying Core and Productive Non-Core Journals Supporting Multidisciplinary R & D." **Journal of the American Society for Information Science** 46 (May 1995): 306–17.

McCain uses a complicated but meticulously done research methodology to analyze the core and other important journals supporting the interdisciplinary field of biotechnology research and development. The following steps were taken:

1. The 1991 *SCI JCR* was used to identify a set of eighty-nine titles.

2. The *SciSearch* program covering the 1988–92 publication years was used to conduct a cocitation (when two journals are jointed cited in later publications) analysis for these eighty-nine titles.

3. A "subject heading profile analysis" of the titles was conducted in *Biotechnology Abstracts* for 1990–92.

4. "Productivity filtering" calculated the percentage of each journal's indexable items that were actually indexed in *Biotechnology Abstracts.*

Based on cocitation, the journals were organized into twelve subject-based clusters, including biotechnology, basic and applied microbiology, food science and technology, molecular genetics, and so on. Two complex maps illustrate these clusters and a table lists the titles in each. Of most practical application for journal evaluation is a lengthy table that lists twelve "core" titles (with 70 percent coverage or higher in *Biotechnology Abstracts*), fourteen "significant" titles (30 to 69 percent coverage), nineteen "titles of interest" (10 to 29 percent coverage), and twenty-three "marginal" journals (less than 10 percent coverage). This rigorous approach was later used by Zipp (see entry later in this chapter).

Sittig, Dean F. "Identifying a Core Set of Medical Informatics Serials: An Analysis Using the MEDLINE Database." **Bulletin of the Medical Library Association** 84 (April 1996): 200–204.

The author searched the *MEDLINE* CD-ROM database for 1990–94 under the term "medical informatics" and found 2,350 journals had published 19,895 articles "primarily concerned" with the topic. The fourteen journals (rank ordered in a table) that contained at least 100 pertinent articles, and for which 70 percent of their total articles were relevant to the subject, were identified as the core. Further analysis indicated that Bradford's Law "holds" for medical informatics and identified eighty-four "core" zone one journals.

The author believes it is "unrealistic" to expect a library to subscribe to that many core medical informatics journals and notes that only 23.4 percent of the articles were topically pertinent in the journal ranked eighty-fourth. He thus implies his methodology is preferable to Bradford's and asserts that it offers "another tool" for librarians.

Wilder, Stanley J. "A Simple Method for Producing Core Scientific and Technical Journal Title Lists." **Library Resources & Technical Services** 44 (April 2000): 92–96.

Wilder introduces a new citation measure termed Estimated Annual Citation Rate (EACR), which is calculated by manipulating data readily obtainable from the *JCR*. The EACR uses half-life data and is similar to impact factor, except it does not normalize for journal size as the author contends size is related to journal value. For illustrative purposes, the EACR was calculated for the sets of physics and chemistry journals in the 1997 *JCR*. In physics, 22 percent of the titles produce 78 percent of the total EACR, while 20 percent of the chemistry titles account for 82 percent of EACR. The titles with average or above EACRs (55 of 263 physics and 71 of 306 chemistry journals) were defined as the core. A table displays data on core and noncore journals for eight physics and six chemistry subject categories, although specific titles are not named. Comparison of EACR scores with current subscription price found that core titles are more expensive "but many times more cost-effective than non-core titles." This intriguing study utilizes price to a much greater extent than other core journal studies.

Zipp, Louise S. "Core Serial Titles in an Interdisciplinary Field: The Case of Environmental Geology." **Library Resources & Technical Services** 43 (January 1999): 28–36.

Zipp partially replicates the method used by McCain for biotechnology journals to identify core journals in the interdisciplinary field of environmental geology. A survey of geoscience librarians at eight major universities (each was asked to name the field's five "best" journals) resulted in a list of seventeen titles that served as the study's starting point. Twenty core journals—listed alphabetically in a table—were determined through cocitation analysis using 1995 *JCR* data. These titles fell into three clusters: "Engineering/Materials" (six titles), "Geochemistry" (three titles), and "Water/Soil" (eleven titles). It is noteworthy that only five titles appeared on both the initial list of seventeen and the final core list. Most of the core titles were from other disciplines, leading Zipp to conclude that "established, older" journals in such areas as hydrology, agronomy, and civil engineering are actually supporting environmental geology. Further analysis indicates that environmental geology is generally not displaying the characteristics of a maturing discipline.

SERIALS CANCELLATION/DESELECTION

Brown, Linda A. "Balancing Information Needs with Serials Value and Cost." **Against the Grain** 9 (April 1997): 22, 24, 26, 28.

Brown recounts a two-phase serials cancellation project at the Bowling Green State University (BGSU) library. In 1996, 184 titles (net) were cancelled because they had no recorded uses in 1991–92 and 1994–95 reshelving studies. During the second phase in 1997, such factors as use, cost, faculty input, and availability through UnCover and OhioLINK were used to prioritize titles, and the science departments recommended 20 percent of serials expenditures for cancellation. Modeled on Louisiana State University's experience, BGSU adopted alternate strategies for providing access to cancelled titles, including commercial document delivery. A pilot project with UnCover (conducted for six departments from March through Fall 1996) found that 25 percent of faculty requests were from journals subscribed to by the BGSU library and that the average cost per article was $13.25. Four cancellation project goals are outlined (staying within the budget, providing basic student and faculty information needs, starting some new subscriptions, and saving money for monographs) and the degree to which they were achieved is discussed. The article is based on the author's presentation at the 1996 Charleston Conference.

Chrzastowski, Tina E., and Karen A. Schmidt. "Collections at Risk: Revisiting Serial Cancellations in Academic Libraries." **College & Research Libraries** 57 (July 1996): 351–64.

This follow-up to the authors' 1993 study (see the following entry) analyzes serial cancellations at the Illinois, Iowa, Michigan State, Ohio State, and Wisconsin university libraries during the 1991 and 1992 fiscal years. The authors discovered that 7.2 percent of the 6,518 cancelled titles overlapped among libraries, that is, were cancelled by more than one. Moreover, 80.5 percent of cancelled titles were in English, 55.4 percent were published outside the United States, 45.6 percent were in science, technology, or medicine, and the average price was $193.43 compared to an average list price of $165 for all serials. A breakdown of the 5,643 new serial subscriptions ordered during the same two fiscal years by four of these institutions (ordering data was not available from Wisconsin) found that 88.4 percent were in English, 60.2 percent were published in the United States, 25.1 percent and 20.0 percent were in the sciences and social sciences respectively, and the average cost was $107.73.[4] Chrzastowski and Schmidt correctly observe that high-priced titles were cancelled, whereas low-priced ones were ordered. Eighty-one CD-ROMs were ordered, while only eight were cancelled, thus testifying to that format's importance in the early 1990s. Numerous statistical comparisons are offered between ordered and cancelled titles as well as between cancellations in 1991–92 and 1988–90. This intriguing study essentially confirms the findings of its 1993 predecessor.

Chrzastowski, Tina E. and Karen A. Schmidt. "Surveying the Damage: Academic Library Serial Cancellations, 1987–88 through 1989–90." **College & Research Libraries** 54 (March 1993): 93–102.

This entry investigates the serials that were cancelled during three years at five ARL university libraries: Illinois, Iowa, Michigan State, Ohio State, and Wisconsin. Based on lists provided by the institutions, a total of 6,503 titles, costing $690,225.64 were cancelled. Only 4 percent of these titles (281) overlapped among two or more libraries. Titles costing over $200 had a disproportionately high cancellation rate. Almost 40 percent of the cancelled titles feel into four LC class numbers: Q (science), T (technology), R (medicine), and S (agriculture). A country-of-publication breakdown found the following: United States, 47 percent; United Kingdom, 9 percent; West Germany, 9 percent; and the Netherlands, 4 percent. Moreover, 74 percent were English language and 26 percent were non-English. The authors conclude that the serial most at-risk for cancellation is "a high-cost English-language title in a science subject area." Although a valuable study, this research may have underestimated the number of overlapping subscriptions actually cancelled because the analysis is restricted to a three-year period.

Dadashzadeh, Mohammad, Kathryn Payne, and John H. Williams. "The Development and Implementation of the Periodicals Analysis Database." **Serials Review** 22, no. 4 (1996): 13–25.

The Periodicals Analysis Database (PAD), developed during the 1990s at the Wichita State University to support cancellation and other functions, is described here. In-house use data, recorded by bar code scanners, along with additional information was placed into a *Paradox* database. Numerous tables and figures illustrate the various reports tabulating use (both in-house and circulation), cost, cost per use, and price projections that can be produced on demand for LC class ranges, departments, or librarians responsible for a set of serials. In a final assessment, the authors state PAD was successfully used in three cancellation projects to identify high-cost, low-use titles (the average cost of a canceled title was $760 in the most recent round), predicted serials expenditures within one or two percentage points, and provided quality data partially responsible for the library obtaining more than $200,000 in supplemental funds from the university administration over three fiscal years.

Dole, Wanda V., and Sherry S. Chang. "Survey and Analysis of Demand for Journals at the State University of New York at Stony Brook." **Library Acquisitions: Practice & Theory** 20 (spring 1996): 23–38.

Dole and Chang write in considerable detail about a major serials cancellation project carried out by the SUNY at Stony Brook library during the early 1990s. From September 1991 to September 1992, an unobtrusive reshelving study (using hatch marks on attached labels) gathered data for 16,199 bound volumes plus 5,827 current issues. In April 1993 faculty were asked to rate journals in their discipline on a 1 ("essential") to 4 ("not important") scale. Note that 33 percent of 900 responded. Librarians reviewed ranked lists based on the average ratings as well as usage, price, and other data during the fall of 1993 and made cancellation recommendations. After negotiation with department chairs and deans, 1,969 titles costing $562,013 (26.5 percent of the subscription list's value) had been cancelled by December 1993. A section of the article describes four citation studies conducted by SUNY at Stony Brook science librarians between 1986 and 1993. The authors comment this project represents an attempt to use "statistical and objective criteria" in serials cancellation.

Francq, Carole. "Bottoming out the Bottomless Pit with the Journal Usage/Cost Relational Index." **Technical Services Quarterly** 11, no. 4 (1994): 13–26.

The Usage/Cost Relational Index (UCRI), developed at the Indiana University Medical Library in Indianapolis in 1992 to assist in serials cancellation, is described in this entry. A journal's UCRI Index Number is calculated by dividing its current subscription cost by the number of uses during a time period defined by the library. Two figures illustrate the calculation. Index Numbers allow comparison of journals according to cost-effectiveness but are not cost per use figures per se because they are not based on total usage and subscription costs. Francq stresses the method's flexibility as the library staff can decide the study's time length (she recommends one year) and the type of usage data to be included, that is, circulation, in-house, and/or ILL. Francq notes that during 1992–93, the UCRI method identified 96 titles for cancellation out of 1,830 subscriptions, saving $31,780 in subscription fees for a $2,205 data gathering cost. The author emphasizes that use studies are time-consuming but the cost can be covered through cancellations.

Harrington, Sue Anne, and Ila M. Grice. "Serials Cancellation: A Continuing Saga." **Serials Librarian** 23, nos. 1–2 (1992): 99–112.

This entry provides a historical review of serials cancellations at the University of Oklahoma libraries over fifteen years. A survey of Big Ten and Big Eight institutions in the fall of 1990 found that only four of fourteen respondents were not planning future serials cancellations. Following the cancellation of 1,314 periodicals and standing orders in 1977 (in which academic departments identified 25 percent of their serials costs for cancellation), the Oklahoma library instigated a two-year moratorium on new titles. Due to continuing serials price increases and the desire to maintain a 60:40 serials/monographs expenditures ratio, it was necessary in 1985 to cancel 804 titles after faculty rated 10 percent of their subscription lists "cancel" and 5 percent "marginal." Another round of cancellations for the 1991–92 academic year was avoided when the university administration agreed to a $1 per credit hour student library fee. The authors conclude that access and electronic publishing "may be the answer" to the serials problem. This item is useful for its detailed account of the cancellation processes.

Hasslöw, Rolf, and Annika Sverrung. "Deselection of Serials: The Chalmers University of Technology Library Method." **Collection Management** 19, nos. 3–4 (1995): 151–70.

A sudden decline in the kroner's value in 1992 necessitated a major serials cancellation project at the Chalmers University of Technology library, in Gotëborg, Sweden, because 96 percent of its serials were published outside the country. In the introductory section, the authors facetiously mention three collection development strategies "Just-in-Case, Just-in-Time, or the famous Swedish model, Somewhere-in-Between." The following use measures was gathered for 3,000 journals from the fall of 1989 through the spring of 1990:

1. The Institutional Cost Ratio—developed at the Lawrence Livermore National Laboratory Biomedical Library by Richard K. Hunt, considers six factors: annual use, annual subscription cost, size of bound collection, cost of an ILL, annual subscription cost, and shelving and storage cost.[5]

2. Cost per Use—developed by Dorothy Milne and Bill Tiffany at Memorial University of Newfoundland library, estimates the cost for each use.[6]

3. The Chalmers Library Model—journals were assigned to academic departments and placed in descending order by use. Journals in the lowest quartile were cancelled.

The story had a semi-happy ending as the library received an unexpected 20 percent budget increase and only had to cancel $100,000 rather than $250,000 worth of journals.

Lambert, Jill, and Sue Taylor. "Evaluating a Journals Collection in an Academic Library." **Serials: The Journal of the United Kingdom Serials Group** 9 (November 1996): 317–21.

This entry reports use of the "voting" method to assist journal cancellations at the Staffordshire University School of Engineering in the United Kingdom. Teaching staff and research students (color coding of the forms distinguished the two groups) were given separate lists of current subscriptions and newly proposed titles and asked to distribute 100 votes among each list. "Virtually everyone" responded after telephone and e-mail reminders. A table tabulates the results received and the number of voters for each title. Fourteen titles receiving no votes from the teaching staff were cancelled. Because the budget situation was worse than originally anticipated additional titles were cancelled and only two new tiles were recommended for subscription. Lambert and Taylor observe "the cancellations have been made in as systematic a way as possible."

Metz, Paul. "Thirteen Steps to Avoiding Bad Luck in a Serials Cancellation Project." **Journal of Academic Librarianship** 18 (May 1992): 76–82.

Drawing upon lessons from the "ordeal" of canceling more than 1,250 subscriptions costing over $300,000 at the Virginia Tech Libraries in the early 1990s, a well-known collection development authority explains, in sequential order, thirteen steps "to help ensure a successful serials cancellation project." Among the most important steps, one should mention the following:

*   "Measure use"

*   "Put one person in charge"

*   "Honesty is the best policy"

- "Use a variety of criteria in making decisions"

- "Publicize what you have done"

In other steps, Metz advocates starting early, flexibility, and judicious use of quotas. This frequently cited article offers valuable practical advice concerning the serials cancellation process.

Parrish, Marilyn McKinley. "Deselection of Inactive Serials or What to Do When It's Already Dead." **Serials Review** 22 (fall 1996): 49–59.

Inactive serials, that is, titles that have been cancelled or ceased publication, have received relatively little attention in the evaluation literature. Parrish depicts a one-semester project in which she developed a process to review inactive titles for possible weeding at the Millersville University of Pennsylvania library before entering them into their new Dynix periodicals module—to save the expense of data entry for unneeded titles. Information was gathered through a literature review, posting on the *SERIALST* listserv, and review of previous serials department decisions. Evaluative criteria were indexing, physical condition, curricular support, and length plus age of the run. Generally runs of six or fewer years were withdrawn from the collection and liaison librarians were consulted in doubtful cases. Advice offered by Parrish includes appointing a project head, setting a time frame, contacting librarians at neighboring institutions, and keeping a sense of humor. During the spring semester of 1995, 575 inactive titles were reviewed and 275 (47.8 percent) were withdrawn.[7] The article is illustrated with a number of worksheets and decision-making charts.

Richards, Daniel T., and Antonija Prelec. "Serials Cancellation Projects: Necessary Evil or Collection Assessment Opportunity?" **Journal of Library Administration** 17, no. 2 (1992): 31–45.

This entry begins by explaining that collection assessment is an "integral part" of collection development and linked to most other library functions. Fourteen reasons for assessment are outlined in bullet format. Then, the results of a survey of 125 North American medical school libraries (75 percent responded) concerning their serials cancellations from 1986 to 1990 are analyzed. Among the findings, 66 percent of the responding libraries reported annual cancellations; 69 percent reported "low use" and 49 percent "subscription cost" as cancellation criteria; and 3,341 unique titles were cancelled in the five-year period. The most frequently cancelled serials were indexing and abstracting services as well as foreign language, nonmedical, or interdisciplinary titles. Finally, revising a methodology submitted by the Columbia University Health Sciences Library, the authors outline five steps for a generic serials review plan:

1. A project goals statement

2. General guidelines (e.g., who will carry out the project)

3. Determination of criteria to be used

4. Development of methodology

5. Outcome statement

Schoch, Natalie, and Eileen G. Abels. "Using a Valuative Instrument for Decision Making in the Cancellation of Science Journals in a University Setting." In **The Economics of Information; The 1994 ASIS Annual Meeting: Proceedings of the 57th ASIS Annual Meeting; Alexandria, VA, October 17–20, 1994,** edited by Bruce Maxian, 41–50. Medford, NJ: published for the American Society for Information Science by Information Today, 1994. ISBN 0-938734-93-8.

Schoch and Abels' research sought to identity cost-effective factors to be used in canceling science journals in the Life Sciences and Agricultural Library at the University of Maryland at College Park. Initially nineteen factors were identified in three categories: journal attributes, citation factors, and availability. Four "key faculty liaisons" were surveyed concerning each factor's "utility" and alternate data-gathering methods were tested on samples of titles. These tests revealed, among other things, that checking a title on the shelf provided more information than searching *Ulrich's* but took an average of 12 minutes contrasted to 2.5 minutes for checking *Ulrich's*. Finally, seven factors were identified as the most cost-effective means of obtaining the data for serials cancellation. In category 1, cost per year can be obtained from the local accounting system whereas cost per issue, the publisher, and language can be calculated from *Ulrichs*. For category 2, impact factor is available from ISI and local departmental citations from *SciSearch* through Dialog. In category 3, availability elsewhere on the University of Maryland campus or at the National Agricultural Library is ascertainable through OPAC searches.

Tucker, Betty E. "The Journal Deselection Project: The LSUMC-S Experience." **Library Acquisitions: Practice & Theory** 19 (fall 1995): 313–20.

A serials cancellation project at the Louisiana State University Medical Center at Shreveport (LSUMC-S) is described by Tucker. The two major criteria were usage statistics, compiled from reshelving counts for the seven months from October 1, 1992, to April 30, 1993, and faculty input, based on rating a list of their subject specialty's journals using a 1 (not important) to 5 (very important) scale. A chart for each journal tabulated these findings along with its cost, impact factor in the *JCR,* and indexing coverage as indicated by EBSCO Scientific Subscriptions. A small group of high-ranking library staff reviewed the charts and sent a list of proposed cancellations to department heads. The project, termed "very successful" by Tucker, resulted in 20 percent of the subscriptions, accounting for 12 percent of expenditures, being cancelled. Of 266 cancelled titles, 89 percent were not deemed "very important" by even a single faculty member and 88 percent had been used six or fewer times. This entry provides a detailed description of gathering and tabulating the data used in the decision-making process.

Widdicombe, Richard P. "Eliminating All Journal Subscriptions Has Freed Our Customers to Seek the Information They Really Want and Need: The Result— More Access, Not Less." **Science & Technology Libraries** 14, no. 1 (1993): 3–13.

This entry describes the ultimate journal cancellation project—eliminating all journal subscriptions! The essay outlines serials collection management at the Stevens Institute of Technology from the early 1970s, when the library subscribed to 1,500 journals, to the decision in the early 1990s to cancel all subscriptions. ISI citation data, a database of titles cited by faculty, and hiding titles (to see if anyone noticed they were gone) were used for serials evaluation during this period. The author explains the library decided to rely exclusively on access to articles because it could no longer afford subscriptions to the core titles wanted by faculty. He notes several "safety nets" including the major research libraries in nearby New York City and the recent relocation of a commercial document delivery service to the Stephens campus. Writing six months after the cancellations, Widdicombe concludes "we are encountering for the first time in many years an almost unanimously positive faculty." Data supporting this assertion is not provided.

SERIALS DECISION MODELS

Barooah, P.K., and B.R. Bhuyan. "An Approach for Selection of Journals in Libraries of R & D Institutions." **Annals of Library Science & Documentation** 40 (September 1993): 115–24.

The authors describe a model used at the library of the Regional Research Laboratory in Jorhat, India, during a seventeen-month period from February 1, 1990, to August 31, 1991, to make retention decisions for 166 foreign periodicals. Weights of 1, 2, 4, and 8 were applied to four variables, covering the number of times journals were browsed (based on patron signatures on attached slips) when on a display table, borrowed on overnight loan, cited in any of 111 staff publications during the study period, and published in by a staff member. The model is then applied to journals in organic chemistry, inorganic chemistry, biochemistry, and geosciences. Although developed on the Asian subcontinent, this methodology could be used by libraries elsewhere.

Deurenberg, Rikie. "Journal Deselection in a Medical University Library by Ranking Periodicals Based on Multiple Factors." **Bulletin of the Medical Library Association** 81 (July 1993): 316–19.

Deurenberg explains a journal deselection methodology developed and used at the Faculty of Medicine of the University of Nijmegen in the Netherlands. Titles in the top quartile in their subject category's impact factor ranking in the 1988 *JCR* were deemed core journals and not cancelled. A formula combining impact factor and cited half-life was used to identify candidates for cancellation among journals in the lower three quartiles. Then, the following scoring system was applied to titles not covered in the *JCR* and those in the *JCR* initially identified for cancellation:

- One point if covered by *Index Medicus*

- One point if covered in *JCR*

- One point for high use, two for "very high" use

- One point if in English by a "well-known publisher"

- One point if among the 1,000 titles most frequently requested on ILL in the Netherlands during nine months of 1990.

Titles with a score lower than 5 were cancelled. Based on this multistage method, 514 of 1,582 subscriptions were cancelled and 31 new titles ordered. This approach is noteworthy for its use of *JCR* cited half-life, but some modifications would probably be required for use by non-Dutch libraries.

Hughes, Janet. "Use of Faculty Publication Lists and ISI Citation Data to Identify a Core List of Journals with Local Importance." **Library Acquisitions: Practice & Theory** 19 (winter 1995): 403–13.
    During three weeks in the spring of 1993, Hughes weighted and combined four variables to create a ranked core list of fifty molecular and cellular biology titles to be protected during an anticipated serials cancellation project at the Pennsylvania State University (PSU) at University Park's Life Sciences Library. The following scale was developed:

- 5 points for each publication in the journal between 1989 and 1992 by a PSU Molecular and Cellular Biology Department faculty member—gathered primarily from departmental faculty bibliographies

- 1 point for each faculty citation to the journal in 1992—identified by searching *SciSearch* through Dialog

- 1 to 10 points based on the journal's 1989 *JCR* total citations ranking— titles in the top ten received 10 points, in the next ten, 9 points, and so on

- 1 to 10 points for the journal's 1989 *JCR* impact factor ranking—using the above method

Hughes regrets her data sets came from different time periods. A table lists in order the fifty titles receiving the most points. That one of them was not subscribed to by the Pennsylvania State University Libraries was an "unexpected" finding. This method for combining national and local data can, as stressed by the author, be used in other departments and at other universities.

Metz, Paul, and John Cosgriff. "Building a Comprehensive Serials Decision Database at Virginia Tech." **College & Research Libraries** 61 (July 2000): 324–34.
    Metz and Cosgriff describe an effort at Virginia Polytechnic Institute and State University to identify core journals to be protected from future cancellation. A database was created incorporating a variety of data, including votes for more than 4,000 serials submitted by faculty through a Web site in the spring of 1999, a current periodical reshelving count ongoing since June 1998, ILL requests, the number of faculty

who profiled the title in the CARL (Colorado Association of Research Libraries) Reveal table of contents service, and the ISI's *Local Journal Utilization Report* data on journals published in or cited by Virginia Tech faculty during 1994–98. The 4,563 titles (with an estimated $3,588,000 annual subscription cost) meeting one or more of the following six criteria were defined as core for Virginia Tech:

- Received at least one individual or departmental vote

- Profiled on CARL Reveal by at least five individuals

- Requested at least twenty times on ILL

- Contained at least ten articles written by Virginia Tech faculty

- Cited at least fifty times by Virginia Tech faculty

- Reshelved at least fifty times

In summary, the process displayed a major characteristic of a serials decision model because disparate data is combined to support retention and cancellation decision making.

Murphy, Penelope. *Determining Measures of the Quality and Impact of Journals: Abridged Report Prepared for the Australian Research Council.* (Commissioned Report, no. 49). Canberra, Australian Capital Territory: National Board of Employment, Education, and Training, 1996. 210p. ISBN 0-644-47235-9.

This lengthy study, commissioned by the Australian Research Council and written by a University of Wollongong School of Education faculty member, investigates quality assurance in research journals. Data were gathered through questionnaires answered by 453 journal editors (out of a 1,151 initial sample) during the latter part of 1995. The survey instrument design was "informed" by in-depth interviews with twenty-one Australian journal editors. The findings were separately analyzed for ISI and non-ISI journals, that is, whether or not ISI covers the journal, and titles in different subject areas. The report concludes with nine recommendations including the following: the definition of a peer-reviewed journal (all articles are reviewed by at least one external reviewer), use of ISI citation measures (not for comparing journals in different subfields nor distributing research funding to Australian universities), and outlines of two four-level options for classifying journals by quality. Option 1 is as follows:

1. All ISI journals

2. Non-ISI journals with comparable quality assurance through peer review

3. Peer-reviewed, non-ISI journals without comparable quality insurance

4. Non-peer reviewed, non-ISI journals

Option 2 is as follows:

1. All ISI journals

2. Non-ISI journals defined as academic or academic/professional

3. Non-ISI journals defined as professional

4. All other non-ISI journals

The massive amount of data, frequently comparing ISI with non-ISI journals, contained in the twenty-four appendices do not lend themselves well to summarization. Although not literally a decision model, this large scale study represents an ambitious effort to create hierarchical levels for measuring journal quality.

Rhine, Leonard. "The Development of a Journal Evaluation Database Using *Microsoft Access.*" **Serials Review** 22 (winter 1996): 27–34.

A journal evaluation model developed at the University of Florida Health Sciences Center Library is depicted in this article. The Worth of Journal (WJ) score is calculated by assigning a 1 (high) to 5 (low) value to five factors and averaging the score:

- In-house use

- Whether the journal is indexed

- ILL requests

- *Journal Citation Reports* ranking

- Faculty input

Note that in-house use and faculty input are assigned twice the weight of the other three variables. The WJ is then multiplied by the Cost per Journal Article (CJA), based on the current annual subscription price, to derive a Benefit Ratio of Journal (BRJ), which is used to rank journals by subject. Rhine reports on his library's use of the model to select titles for cancellation but observes that the twenty-eight-field database developed to support the system can be used for a variety of other functions, including budgeting and general serials evaluation.

Robb, David J., and Angela McCormick. "Decision Support for Serials Deselection and Acquisition: A Case Study." **Journal of the American Society for Information Science** 48 (March 1997): 270–73.

Robb and McCormick illustrate a model, developed and used at the University of Calgary's Management Resource Centre, for calculating journal "worth."

The model incorporates three components, "usage," "relevance," and "availability elsewhere," originally proposed by Barbara Rush, Sam Steinberg, and Donald H. Kraft.[8] Usage was assessed through a survey of 100 faculty, e-mail and ILL article requests from a two-month period, and reshelving data for one week. A journal's relevance was determined by its coverage in six indexing/abstracting services and the number of faculty publications it contained during a four-year period. Finally, an adjustment was made if the title was not available at other Calgary "public institutions" or the University of Alberta. After ascertaining journal worth, a cost/benefit ratio was calculated. Then, 206 of about 670 subscriptions, accounting for $35,800 of the $78,000 total 1993 subscription costs, were cancelled.

Sittig, Dean F. "Use of Fuzzy Set Theory to Extend Dhawan's Journal Selection Model: Ranking the Biomedical Informatics Serials." **Bulletin of the Medical Library Association** 87 (January 1999): 43–49.

Dhawan's journal selection model, which incorporates citation, abstract, and use data, is applied to biomedical informatics journals using fuzzy set theory.[9] Rather than referring to teddy bears, this theory, according to Sittig, "allows representation of imprecise and qualitative information in an exact manner." An initial set of thirty-four journals were ranked according to ten criteria, including *JCR* impact factor, immediacy index, half-life, and total citations as well as ILL requests to the NLM and whether the title is indexed in *MEDLINE*. A number of methods (including both classical and fuzzy set theory) were used to combine the ten rankings, resulting in a final ranking of the top twelve bioinformatics journals. The interested reader can consult the article itself for a number of technical and statistical details. This entry is remarkable because it reports a follow-up application of a previously published journal decision model.

Triolo, Victor A., and Dachun Bao. "A Decision Model for Technical Journal Deselection with an Experiment in Biomedical Communications." **Journal of the American Society for Information Science** 44 (April 1993): 148–60.

The two researchers propose a journal decision making model based on utility and cost-effectiveness. A Bradford distribution is used to rank journals according to the number of articles produced. Then a Cost Savings Benefit, which considers subscription, shelving, and ILL costs, is calculated. In essence, the method identifies low productivity, non-cost-effective titles as cancellation candidates. To illustrate the procedure for "pediatrics," a search under that term in *Index Medicus* for 1985 through 1989 retrieved 1,315 articles from 359 journals. A table lists the 49 titles in the first two Bradford zones. A language breakdown revealed 71.86 percent of the articles were in English followed by 7.68 percent in Russian. Triolo and Bao estimate subscriptions to the top seventeen journals producing 50 percent of coverage would cost $1,530 while the additional 50 percent of coverage would cost $30,780. Integrating previously published research, Triolo and Bao provide an exceedingly sophisticated methodological and statistical analysis, which incorporates numerous technical points from previously published research.

NOTES

1. The percentage is Nisonger's calculation from Black's raw data.

2. These numbers tabulated from the authors' raw data by Nisonger.

3. Graeme Hirst, "Discipline Impact Factors: A Method for Determining Core Journal Lists," *Journal of the American Society for Information Science* 29 (July 1978): 171–72.

4. The percentages are Nisonger's calculation from the authors' raw data.

5. Richard K. Hunt, "Journal Deselection in a Biomedical Research Library: A Mediated Mathematical Approach," *Bulletin of the Medical Library Association* 78 (January 1990): 45–48.

6. Dorothy Milne and Bill Tiffany, "A Survey of the Cost-Effectiveness of Serials: A Cost-Per-Use Method and Its Results," *Serials Librarian* 19 nos. 3–4 (1991): 137–49.

7. The percentage is Nisonger's calculation.

8. Barbara Rush, Sam Steinberg, and Donald H. Kraft, "Journal Disposition Decision Policies," *Journal of the American Society for Information Science* 25 (July/August 1974): 213–17.

9. S.M. Dhawan, S.K. Phull, and S.P. Jain, "Selection of Scientific Journals: A Model, *Journal of Documentation* 36 (March 1980): 24–32.

8

Evaluation of Use

The first of S. R. Ranganathan's Five Laws of Library Science stipulates "books are for use."[1] The evaluation of the use of traditional library resources was a major concern for the library profession throughout the twentieth century. Stanley J. Slote reveals that as far back as 1902, Harvard President Charles William Eliot penned a *Library Journal* article advocating use studies to support weeding.[2] Herman H. Fussler's and Julian L. Simon's classic investigation at the University of Chicago library, *Patterns in the Use of Books in Large Research Libraries,* published in 1969, found, among numerous conclusions, that past use is the best predictor of future use.[3] Probably the best-known examination of library use patterns, the Pittsburgh Study, revealed that nearly half the books acquired by the University of Pittsburgh's main library during a single year did not circulate once during the seven years following their acquisition.[4] While some have said the controversy generated by this inquiry caused use studies in general to fall into disfavor, these studies continue to appear in the literature.[5] During the 1960s the industrial engineer Richard W. Trueswell discovered that in most types of libraries, approximately 20 percent of the books accounted for about 80 percent of the circulation.[6] This finding has entered library lore as the famous 80/20 Rule. Since then numerous (but not all) studies have found a permutation on this fundamental pattern in the circulation, in-house use, electronic access, and citation of various types of library materials.

The distinction between "use" and "user" studies should be noted. The former focuses on the information resources being used, whereas the latter addresses who is using the information resources and why. In actuality, many investigations combine use and user studies. This book's primary focus is on use studies, but user studies are covered when they address a particular format, such as electronic journals. Also, the emphasis is on use of information sources per se, rather than information finding tools, such as OPACs or Web search engines. Information seeking behavior, about which a voluminous amount has been published, is beyond this literature review's scope. However, some annotations may include data pertinent to information seeking if the entry otherwise falls within this book's parameters.

Studies of traditional library material usage investigate circulation (items checked out), in-house use (consulted by patrons without being checked out), or both. Automated library systems can usually provide circulation data. The most frequently employed in-house measurement technique counts items while reshelving them and is variously termed the table count, sweep, or reshelving method. Other techniques include direct observation, the check-off method (in which patrons make checkmarks on attached tags), and user surveys or interviews. Use studies have most frequently been conducted in order to identify high-use titles, low-use or non-cost-effective items (to support cancellation/deselection), and general usage patterns as well as to support the budgeting process. The literature has focused on such topics as the following:

- The various methods for measuring use, their validity, and comparison of results obtained from different methods

- Overall usage patterns addressing concentration and scatter in use, the 80/20 Rule, the percentage of unused item, and so on

- Relative use by age, subject, and format

Chapter 8 covers the use of traditional resources. The use of reference materials is covered in chapter 4 and of electronic resources in chapter 11 in order to consolidate entries dealing with these two formats. Entries comparing use of the print and electronic formats and investigating the impact of electronic resources on print usage are included in chapter 11. This chapter is organized into four sections covering methodological issues, use of periodicals, use of books, and other use studies.

METHODOLOGICAL ISSUES

Bustion, Marifran, John Eltinge, and John Harer. "On the Merits of Direct Observation of Periodical Usage: An Empirical Study." **College & Research Libraries** 53 (November 1992): 537–50.

This entry addresses methodological issues concerning the direct observation technique for measuring periodical use. The analysis is based on student observations in the Current Periodicals Department of Texas A & M University's main library at randomly selected times during the week of April 15 to April 22, 1990. Furthermore, the project investigators observed the students to assess their accuracy. It was found that the data reported by students "contain a substantial component of observational error," tentatively attributed to inadequate training and boredom. Causal uses, requiring the observer's judgment whether it was a use or not, were more likely to result in measurement error than a careful use, which is "relatively straightforward." The authors, in conclusion, give this methodology "mixed reviews." Its allows librarians to define use however they wish but is subject to observational errors and can be costly. Although the authors' extensive statistical analysis may intimidate nonstatistically inclined readers, this item makes an important methodological contribution.

Day, Linda, and Linda Graburn. **Conducting an In-House Periodical Use Study: A Checklist.** Guelph, ON: Canadian Library Association, Canadian Association of College and University Libraries, 1998. 28p.

This publication by the Canadian Association of College and University Libraries (CACUL) offers a step-by-step guide to conducting an in-house periodical use study. The authors emphasize factors to be considered in planning the study and stress that six months should be dedicated to the planning process. If possible, they state a pilot study should be conducted. The pamphlet is organized as follows:

1. Purpose

2. Scope, including length of study, titles to be surveyed, and sampling method

3. Methodology—collection-centered or user-centered

4. Data tabulation, including database entry points plus use, cost, and user fields

5. Publicity

6. Staffing

7. Costs

About two-thirds of the item is devoted to a checklist of planning options, organized in outline format under the seven headings mentioned above. For example, under 2D "sampling," the choices are a simple random sample, a stratified random sample, a systematic sample, time sampling, or "other." An "extensive," but not "exhaustive" bibliography of approximately fifty items follows the checklist. This pamphlet should be helpful for large academic libraries contemplating an in-house periodicals use study.

Everhart, Nancy. "Usage." In **Evaluating the School Library Media Center: Analysis Techniques and Research Practices,** 209–33. Englewood, CO: Libraries Unlimited, 1998. ISBN 1-56308-085-0.

Everhart's chapter offers an overview of methods for measuring use in school library media centers. She presents model questionnaires for surveying students and faculty concerning their use and satisfaction with the media center. Formulas illustrate the calculation of the "relative use factor" (an area's circulation compared to its holdings), circulation per student, circulation per hour, and turnover rate. Step-by-step instructions are given for calculating the "title, subject, author," browsing fill rates, and analyzing the citations in student paper bibliographies. Separate sections deal with in-house use, library attendance, interlibrary loan, and theft of materials (a type of use most librarians could do without). It is observed that yearly usage totals can be estimated from data gathered during a typical week or month. The chapter ends with previously published lists of the most frequently used magazines in high schools, junior high or middle, and elementary schools and an unannotated bibliography of about twenty items. This entry, synthesizing tools from several sources and taking a broad conceptualization of use, should be of practical value for school librarians.

Garland, Kathleen. "Circulation Sampling As a Technique for Library Media Program Management." **School Library Media Quarterly** 20 (winter 1992): 73–78.

The author begins by explaining random ("each date has an equal chance of being drawn") and purposive (typical dates are chosen on purpose) methods in selecting days for sampling circulation in school libraries. Then the results of four purposive samples analyzing the subject distribution of nonfiction book circulation were compared to year-end data in an unidentified elementary school library media center. The four correlations ranged from 0.81 to 0.94. Consequently, she recommends a week-long sample in a "typical week" during each grading period or, as a second choice, during a typical week at mid-year. The researcher stresses that circulation data can demonstrate use of curricular-related materials and thus support of the school's educational mission. The data can also be used in conjunction with collection mapping. In summary, Garland puts forward a persuasive argument in favor of purposive sampling of circulation patterns in school libraries.

Herzog, Kate, Harry Armistead, and Marla Edelman. "Designing Effective Journal Use Studies." **Serials Librarian** 24, nos. 3–4 (1994): 189–92.

This North American Serials Interest Group (NASIG) presentation discusses methodological issues in conducting a journal use study, drawing upon Herzog's experience at SUNY at Buffalo and Armistead's at Thomas Jefferson University. Herzog stressed the importance of planning the study and explained that, at best, one can expect relative rather than absolute use data (i.e., identification of high- and low-use titles). She warned that patron-supplied information may not be "dependable" as they might "fix" the data to exaggerate usage. Armistead described the use of a bar code scanner to gather in-house use data and upload it into an automated system but acknowledged several limitations to this approach (i.e., the automated system "lost" data when an item was sent for binding). Edelman wrote the report.

Lancaster, F. W. "In-House Use." In **If You Want to Evaluate Your Library…**, 76–86. 2d ed. Champaign, IL: University of Illinois, Graduate School of Library and Information Science, 1993. ISBN 0-87845-091-2.

Synthesizing from numerous published sources, this chapter addresses methodological approaches for measurement of in-house use. Lancaster comments that different methods produce divergent results. While the table count method is "easiest," it underestimates total use due to patron reshelving (although high-use titles are still identified). If a total count is required, direct observation can be used to estimate the number of items being reshelved by patrons. W. M. Shaw Jr's "dotting method," whereby dots are attached to spines while reshelving to distinguish used from unused volumes, is described.[7] Surveys or patron interviews are suggested if information is needed about users. A brief final section devoted to reference collections speculates that a "great majority" of the volumes will not be used during a five-year period and recommends Shaw's method for evaluation of reference use. Lancaster maintains that in-house use, while undercounting total usage, correlates with circulation, although he acknowledges some studies dispute this point.

Moore, Matthew S. "Measuring and Managing Circulation Activity Using Circulation Rates." **Collection Management** 17, nos. 1–2 (1992): 193–216.

Moore argues that "circulation rate," the number of items circulated per unit of time such as days or hours, is a more accurate measure than total circulation statistics. Also, it is easier to visualize as yearly circulation figures may be perceived as a "big pile" of books. Formulas are used to explain the calculation of a library's circulation rate and a "system rate" for libraries with branches open different numbers of days or hours. It is explained that circulation rates can be compared among branches and types of material as well as longitudinally to support collection development and other types of decision-making. The author frequently uses illustrative data from the Clearwater Public Library in Florida, noting that January through March 1990 trendlines showed decreasing circulation rates even though gross circulation was increasing. Applying his method to previously published findings from the Pittsburgh Study, Moore calculated circulation rates at University of Pittsburgh branch libraries ranged from 0.6 to 5.4 items per hour. Although methodologically valid, this measure does not appear to have been widely adopted by other libraries.

Nisonger, Thomas E. "Study of Periodical Use." In **Management of Serials in Libraries,** 157–87. Englewood, CO: Libraries Unlimited, 1998. ISBN 1-56308-213-6.

Nisonger begins this chapter by listing six purposes of periodical use studies (including identification of high- and low-use titles plus calculation of cost per use) and five drawbacks, such as counting all uses equally and ignoring non-users. Eleven specific methods are described along with their advantages and disadvantages: circulation data, table count, the slip method, surveys, direct observation, call slip analysis, photocopy request analysis, ILL/document delivery requests, adhesive labels, the check-off method, and subjective impression. Six steps in a periodical use study, synthesized from other sources, are explained and outlined: problem definition, design of the study (including determination of the methods plus the study's length and timing), implementation, data tabulation, interpretation of the findings, and recommendations for action. Other sections of this chapter cover the role of automation, cost per use, and a summary of previously published periodical use studies. An appended "Further Readings" section lists without annotation sixty items.

Ralston, Rick. "Use of a Relational Database to Manage an Automated Periodical Use Study." **Serials Review** 24, nos. 3–4 (1998): 21–32.

Ralston explains the methodology employed to gather serials use data for the Usage/Cost Relational Index (UCRI) developed at the Indiana University Ruth Lilly Medical Library in Indianapolis (see Francq entry in chapter 7). In January

1994 the library began using two Intermec model 9445 Trakker Scanners to record serials reshelving data (by reading bar codes) to be entered into a relational database management system (DBMS) based on *Paradox for Windows v. 4.5.* A major segment of this article is devoted to explaining the five tables comprising the DBMS:

- Title—which contains fields for title, International Standard Serial Number (ISSN), and the NOTIS (Northwestern Online Total Integrated System) Library Management System record number

- Scan—where raw use data is uploaded from the scanners

- Use—which tabulates raw data for specified time periods

- Price—which contains price, ISSN, publisher, subject heading, and country of origin fields

- Combosub—which combines data for titles purchased as a package

Three types of usage reports generated by the system are illustrated. Ralston contends that a relational database, compared to a spreadsheet, offers more efficient data manipulation (data from one table can be used in other tables) and a greater ability to illustrate complex relationships. Many articles have been published about relational databases, but this entry is significant because it addresses their application to serials usage data.

Ralston, Rick, Deborah Broadwater, and Karen Cargille. "Automating Journal Use Studies: A Tale of Two Libraries." **Serials Librarian** 28, nos. 3–4 (1996): 349–53.

This NASIG conference workshop describes two methodologies for automated journal use studies. Ralston depicted the use of portable bar code scanners at the Indiana University Medical Library (for details see the preceding entry). Broadwater recounted an ongoing project at Vanderbilt University's Biomedical Library in which data from portable bar code readers was downloaded on a regular basis into the NOTIS system. More significantly, she also discussed the Chisnell-Dunn-Sittig Method (CDS Method) developed by three Vanderbilt librarians. In the CDS Method, the library's Ovid technology analyzes searching by defined user groups in such online databases as *MEDLINE*. This approach offers the benefit of focusing on specific patron categories and is described as "patron centric, automatic, and quantitative." Of the top 330 journals identified by this technique, 90 percent were owned locally. The CDS Method has apparently never been discussed elsewhere in the literature.

Riley, Julie D. "Measuring Journal Use: A Mini-Review at the Elizabeth Gaskell Library." **Managing Information** 4, no. 3 (1996): 20–22.

This short piece addresses methods for measuring periodical use and recounts those used at the Manchester Metropolitan University (MMU) library in the United Kingdom. Four general methods are briefly described:

- "Sweep," counting titles left on tables

- "Survey slip," attaching tags that users tick when using the journal, some-times called "check-off"

- "Survey sweep," patrons are asked not to reshelve selected titles so staff can count how often they are reshelved

- "Relevance" methods, including citation analysis, production of articles in CD-ROM databases, and "value judgements" solicited through patron surveys

She stresses that use data can be related to other variables such as time on the shelf, shelf-space occupied, cost, or the number of users. Three methods used at MMU are the survey slip, the sweep method during "sample weeks," and surveys sent to academic staff. Specific data concerning findings are not given.

PERIODICAL USE

Multimethod Studies

Blecic, Deborah D. "Measurements of Journal Use: An Analysis of the Correlations Between Three Methods." **Bulletin of the Medical Library Association** 87 (January 1999): 20–25.

Blecic investigates the correlation between three journal use measurements at the University of Illinois at Chicago's Library of Health Sciences. In-house use data was gathered for 5,370 titles utilizing reshelving counts on fifty-nine days between October 1992 and January 1994. Circulation data from 1992 through 1994 was obtained for 4,165 titles from the library's automated system. The ISI's *Local Journal Utilization Reports* provided data on 2,261 journals cited by faculty between 1992 and 1994, which were broken down into separate categories for all faculty and faculty at one of the two Chicago campuses. High, statistically significant correlations were found using both Spearman (ranging from 0.640 to 0.852 for five data sets) and Pearson (ranging from 0.591 to 0.857). Blecic contends, based on her literature review, the correlations were much higher than in previous studies because of the large sample size (83,283 in-house uses, 67,285 circulations, and 58,064 citations). Accordingly, she implies a library can rely on one type of use data.

Chrzastowski, Tina E., and Brian M. Olesko. "Chemistry Journal Use and Cost: Results of a Longitudinal Study." **Library Resources & Technical Services** 41 (April 1997): 101–11.

The results of three journal use studies carried out at the University of Illinois at Urbana-Champaign Chemistry Library are analyzed by Chrzastowski and Olesko. The studies were conducted during the first six months of 1988 and the first three months of both 1993 and 1996. Four types of use were investigated: in-house use based on reshelving, two-hour circulation, ILL lending, and ILL borrowing. Among this detailed study's numerous findings, one should note:

- The amount spent on serials increased 66.9 percent from 1988 to 1996, the percentage of the budget devoted to serials increased 9.2 percent, and total use rose 34.2 percent.

- Use of the top 100 titles increased 41 percent and their cost 137 percent, while use of the top 10 rose 60 percent with a 159 percent cost increase.

- In 1996 84 percent of the use was produced by approximately 20 percent of the titles and 40 percent of use by 2 percent of the titles, leading to a "40/2" equation to supplement the "80/20" Rule.

- Twenty-three point four percent of the 1996 IIL requests to borrow articles were from journals currently or previously in the collection.

- A reshelving study may underestimate use because a 1996 survey of the student reshelvers found they tallied use only 84 percent of the time.

For conducting a journal use study, the authors recommend bar coding the collection, explaining the study's purpose to the staff conducting it, and collecting data on every measurable type of use. This well-done research effort, offering the benefits of longitudinal comparison, is noteworthy for showing an accelerating concentration of use and cost in heavily used titles.

Dess, Howard M. "Gauging Faculty Utilization of Science Journals: A Defensive Strategy for a Lean Budget Era." **Science & Technology Libraries** 16, nos. 3–4 (1997): 171–90.

This entry explores four different measures of faculty journal use at the Chemistry Library on the Rutgers University Busch Campus in Piscataway, New Jersey:

1. In the spring of 1991, a faculty survey asked them to indicate their use of each library serial subscription as "frequent," "occasional," or not used (twenty-two responded representing a 50 percent rate).

2. A reshelving study was conducted during the fourteen weeks from March 11 through June 16, 1991.

3. 1,239 serials published in by faculty during 1994 through mid-1996 were identified through *SciSearch.*

4. 21,328 sources cited by faculty during the same time period were also identified through *SciSearch.*

Separate tables list and tabulate the results for the top twenty-five serials according to each method. More statistics are presented than can be summarized in an appropriate length annotation. Note that of 206 titles subscribed to by the library, faculty published in "about 30 percent" and cited 62 percent, but they neither published in nor cited 29 percent of the titles.[8] That there was overlap in the high-ranking serials among the four methods but not among the low-ranking titles was a noteworthy finding. Dess stresses each method has "limitations" and "any given measuring technique . . . may not reflect more subtle nuances" of use.

Joswick, Kathleen E. and Jeanne Koekkoek Stierman. "The Core List Mirage: A Comparison of the Journals Frequently Consulted by Faculty and Students." **College & Research Libraries** 58 (January 1997): 48–55.
     Joswick and Stierman compare the results of five different periodical use measures at Western Illinois University:

- 1,195 titles downloaded from the *Expanded Academic Index* on InfoTrac from March 23, 1993, through January 3, 1994, and assumed to measure student use

- 89 periodicals cited more than once in 204 Freshman composition papers from the 1991 spring semester

- 221 journals, identified through a Dialog search, in which faculty published between 1988 and 1992

- 338 journals cited more than once by faculty in the above publications, again identified through Dialog

- The 50 most frequently cited journals in the *Science Citation Index (SCI)* and *SSCI JCR* from 1988 to 1992

Comparison of top twenty title lists (actually twenty-four through twenty-seven because of tied positions) by each method found that 60 percent of the top titles were on only one list and only two titles appeared on as many as three lists. Thus, the authors decided that "a single measurement of journal usage is not effective," an "ultimate" core list "remains illusionary," and local opposed to national citation data is important. However, one wonders if there would have been greater congruence between the lists had they limited their comparisons to journals in the same subject areas.

Joswick, Kathleen E., and Jeanne Koekkoek Stierman. "Perceptions vs. Use: Comparing Faculty Evaluations of Journal Titles with Faculty and Student Usage." **Journal of Academic Librarianship** 21 (November 1995): 454–58.
     As advertised in the title, this entry compares faculty journal ratings with four measures of use at Western Illinois University (WIU):

1. 221 journals published in by faculty between 1988 and 1992, identified through a Dialog search of the *Arts & Humanities Citation Index,* the *Science Citation Index,* and the *Social Sciences Citation Index*

2. 467 titles cited in 1988–92 faculty publications, also identified through the same databases

3. The number of times articles from the 1,400 journals in the *Expanded Academic Index* were downloaded at library work stations between March 23, 1993, and January 3, 1994.

4. The journals (the number is not stated) cited in 204 freshman papers written during the spring semester of 1991

In 1991 the faculty rated research journals, but not core undergraduate titles on a four-level scale (A = essential, B = important, C = supplemental, and D = marginal). Because faculty gave high ratings to frequently used journals by all four measures, the authors conclude "faculty should definitely continue to be consulted in deselection decisions." However, based on WIU's experience, Joswick and Stierman advocate faculty evaluation of specialized research journals but librarian control of general periodicals supporting undergraduate teaching.

Millson-Martula, Christopher, and MaryFrances Watson. "Evaluating Students' Serials Needs: Effective Methodologies for College Libraries." **College & Undergraduate Libraries** 3, no. 2 (1996): 75–89.

This entry begins with a general discussion of methods for assessing student serial needs. Millson-Martula and Watson distinguish between "met" need through subscription, licensing, or document delivery and "unmet" need, which does not result in actual use. Then four methods used at St. Xavier College in Chicago during September through May of an unnamed academic year are described and the results revealed:

- Reshelving—7,449 assumed uses by students for academic purposes of an undisclosed number of serials

- ILL—466 uses of 286 titles, of which 18 percent were owned by the library

- Bibliography method—analysis of citations in 1,025 student papers. There were 3,423 citations to 731 serials, of which the library owned 59 percent

- Survey method—1,550 forms were completed. The library owned 47 percent of the 502 identified titles.

The authors conclude that reshelving and ILL combined are best for assessing the need for titles held in the collection, whereas the bibliography method is preferable for identifying titles for subscription and the "most valid indicator" for need in general, both met and unmet. Unfortunately, their conclusions are not demonstrated by the data presented.

Naylor, Maiken. "Comparative Results of Two Current Periodical Use Studies." **Library Resources & Technical Services** 38 (October 1994): 373–88.

Based on 1987–88 and 1991–92 year-long journal use studies at the SUNY at Buffalo Science and Engineering Library and its branches, the author compares the sweep, that is, reshelving count, and check-off (user self-reporting on attached label) methods for measuring use. In the four-year interval, use statistics for ninety-two "high-use" journals declined approximately 40 percent and for the 828 total journals in the study, approximately 18 percent. Naylor concludes the check-off method is "relatively low in cost," but "open to manipulation" by users and "might provide results where a considerable portion of use goes unrecorded." This study's data is meticulously analyzed in a variety of ways, yet the author fails to fully come to grips with the possibility that the declining usage statistics might reflect longitudinal changes in user behavior rather than the difference between the sweep and check-off methods.

Naylor, Maiken. "A Comparison of Two Methodologies for Counting Current Periodical Use." **Serials Review** 19 (spring 1993): 27–34, 62.

This preliminary report contains some data not included in the final version, annotated above. Tables present comparative statistics concerning the number of users and open days and hours during the 1987–88 and 1991–92 studies. Usage analysis of ninety "high-use" journal current issues during 148-day periods in 1987–88 by the sweep method and in 1991–92 by the check-off technique led to the conclusion "the check-off method yields lower use than the sweep method." It is noted that in 1987–88, 6.1 percent of the titles produced 36 percent of total use, and 38.3 percent accounted for 80 percent of use. Naylor stresses the sweep and check-off methods were applied to the identical titles in the same library for an equivalent number of days at approximately the same time of the academic year, but observes, "[u]nfortunately it is economically unfeasible to use the two methods simultaneously."

Noga, Michael Mark, Charlotte R. M. Derksen, and Barbara E. Haner. "Characteristics of Geoscience Serial Use by Faculty and Students." In **Finding and Communicating Geoscience Information: Proceedings of the Twenty-Eighth Meeting of the Geoscience Information Society, October 25–28, 1993, Boston, Massachusetts,** vol. 24, edited by Connie Wick, 61–97. Alexandria, VA: Geoscience Information Society, 1994. ISBN 0-934485-22-4.

Serials use methodologies are compared by analyzing five methods employed at the UCLA geology/geophysics library (in-house use, circulation, theses citations, faculty citations, and faculty publications) and six at Stanford's earth sciences library (the same five plus ISI data on serials cited by all Stanford faculty during a five-year period). Most of the data was gathered during twelve- and eighteen-month periods in the early 1990s. About 90 percent of the article is devoted to eleven appendices, which extensively analyze usage by the various methods at the two libraries. The authors conclude that data from one library can not predict use at another library and that neither circulation nor in-house use predict each other. Furthermore, a "substantial amount" of total usage comes from low-use titles. Asserting "each methodology gives a different result and indicates another aspect of serial use," they imply that in-house use is the most important measurement, followed by circulation and then thesis citation data, but an "effective use study" should include all three. Zipp (see entry in the first section of chapter 9) synthesizes this study's findings with those in other libraries.

Schmidt, Diane, Elisabeth B. Davis, and Ruby Jahr. "Biology Journal Use at an Academic Library: A Comparison of Use Studies." **Serials Review** 20 (summer 1994): 45–64.

Incorporating data from the University of Illinois at Urbana-Champaign Biology Library, the authors compare the results of four serial evaluation methods:

1. Library use based on circulation and a reshelving count during the six weeks from October 1 to November 15, 1990, during which more than 1,000 titles were used with 20 percent producing 73 percent of use transactions

2. A ranked list of 951 journals cited in faculty publications during 1990, generated by the Cited Work field in *SciSearch:* 29 percent of these journals accounted for 80 percent of approximately 3,500 citations to journals

3. Impact factor ranking in the *JCR*

4. A core list of 207 titles subjectively selected from faculty input during a previous cancellation project

Several tables list the top-ranked journals by various approaches. It is noteworthy that 41 percent of the 951 journals cited by faculty were not held by the Biology Library and 11 percent were not held by any UIUC library. Weak but statistically significant correlations were found between library use and faculty citations (0.354), library use and impact factor (0.225), plus faculty citation and impact factor (0.208). The authors conclude that the *JCR* impact factor is a weaker indicator of a journal's local importance than are library use and citation in faculty publications. This is a meticulously detailed investigation that attempts to place its findings in the context of earlier research.

Other Case Studies

Altmann, Klaus G., and Gary E. Gorman. "Anatomy of a Serials Collection and Its Usage: Case Study of an Australian Academic Library." **Library Collections, Acquisitions, & Technical Services** 23 (summer 1999): 149–61.

Altmann and Gorman analyze the use during an academic year of serials in the Dewey 500s, 600s, and 900s (science, technology, and history) at an unidentified Australian academic library. A total of 36,451 uses were tabulated based on marking adhesive labels on volumes' spines while reshelving. They found that

44.58 percent of 4,459 titles were active, whereas 55.42 percent were closed, that is, cancelled or ceased publication; only 40.86 percent of all titles were actually used; 12.86 percent of total use was for closed titles; 90.34 percent of the shelf space was occupied; and that 36.01 percent of the occupied space was devoted to closed titles. Further analysis indicated that if all unused titles were relegated to remote storage, occupied shelf space would be reduced to 64.91 percent and uses per meter of shelf would increase from 8.433 to 11.737, thus increasing efficiency. Ten tables tabulate the findings for thirty divisions of the DDC, while another table lists sixteen closed titles that had been used fifty or more times. The authors discuss the implications for weeding. This top-notch investigation differs from most other serials use studies by virtue of its emphasis on shelf-space utilization plus the comparison of data for closed and open titles.

Blecic, Deborah D., and Ann E. Robinson. "Use of Print Journals in an Intracampus Exchange Program: Implications for Service and Electronic Journal Subscriptions." **Bulletin of the Medical Library Association 88** (January 2000): 75–77.

Rather than purchasing duplicate subscriptions, the Library of the Health Sciences and the Science Library at the University of Illinois at Chicago began an exchange program in 1988 whereby newly received journals were routed to the other library for a week then returned. Use of the titles in the exchange library was studied in October-November 1998 by means of user self-reports and a shelving count. A follow-up survey queried user preference for the print or electronic version. The study revealed the following: 90 percent of the titles from Science were used at the Health Sciences Library, but only 25 percent of the Health Sciences titles were used at the Science Library; $186,000 was saved in 1999 by not purchasing duplicate print subscriptions; and five of eight responding faculty expressing a preference were willing to use electronic journals, but three of the faculty wanted the print version retained. This entry is noteworthy because use studies of exchange journals are seldom found in the literature.

Butkovich, Nancy J. "Reshelving Study of Review Literature in the Physical Sciences." **Library Resources & Technical Services** 40 (April 1996): 139–44.

A use study of the review literature (250 monographic series or annual reviews and 50 periodicals) at the Physical Sciences Library of the Pennsylvania State University's University Park Campus is reported in this article. A reshelving count was taken during October 1991 to October 1992. A total of 1,337 uses were recorded, of which 826 were monographic series or annuals and 511 periodicals.[9] Approximately 51 percent of all the titles, 44 percent of the series or annuals, and 82 percent of the periodicals were used at least once. Several tables present the findings by LC classification number and publication date. Butkovich acknowledges limitations to the study; for example patrons may have reshelved items, and, in any case, the nature of their use is unknown. Unfortunately, this not especially well-done article is difficult to summarize because the tables do not contain total figures.

Chrzastowski, Tina E., and David Stern. "Duplicate Serial Subscriptions: Can Use Justify the Cost of Duplication?" **Serials Librarian** 25, nos. 1–2 (1994): 187–200.

The use of 14 periodicals, subscribed to by two different branch libraries at the University of Illinois at Urbana-Champaign, was compared during January through March 1993 in order to analyze the cost-effectiveness of duplicate subscriptions. The researchers found that in the Chemistry Library the duplicate subscriptions generated 11.5 percent of 23,412 uses and cost 6.26 percent of the serials budget. In the Physics/Astronomy Library duplicates accounted for 39.0 percent of 7,636 uses and represented 11.3 percent of the serials expenditures. The average cost per use for duplicate subscriptions was $6.31 in chemistry and $2.86 in physics/astronomy while the respective figures were $3.35 and $15.50 for all titles. Consultation of the *Science Citation Index* indicated that duplicate titles display "high citation frequency." Chrzastowski and Stern conclude that duplicate subscriptions for high-use journals are more cost-effective than relying on external access. This is the book's only entry addressing the usage of duplicate journal titles.

Cooper, Michael D., and George F. McGregor. "Using Article Photocopy Data in Bibliographic Models for Journal Collection Management." **Library Quarterly** 64 (October 1994): 386–413.

The two authors analyze over 48,000 journal article photocopy requests at the Cetus Corporation information center in Emeryville, California during 1987, 1988, and 1989. Of 1,673 requested journals, "very few" were frequently used (the top journal accounted for 5.6 percent of photocopy requests) and "a very large number" used infrequently. The ten most frequently requested titles are listed in a table along with those from previous studies at the Lawrence Livermore National Laboratory, Washington University, and Temple University.[10] Interestingly, there was a negative correlation between use and *JCR* impact factor for the nineteen most used journals. Forty-two percent of the requests were for articles from the current year's issue, and the average requested article's age was "just over one year." Only three hundred titles had a cost per use below $35. The authors calculate that 78 percent of the journal article demand could be met with a $100,000 subscription budget and 85 percent with a $200,000 budget. In short, this is a thorough study.

Dee, Cheryl R., Jocelyn A. Rankin, and Carol A. Burns. "Using Scientific Evidence to Improve Hospital Library Services: Southern Chapter/Medical Library Association Journal Usage Study." **Bulletin of the Medical Library Association** 86 (July 1998): 301–06.

This entry reports journal use data at an aggregate level from thirty-six hospital libraries that were members of the Southern Chapter/Medical Library Association. All journal uses (bound volume, unbound issues, and microform reshelving plus circulation, ILL, routing, and photocopying) were compiled from January through December 1995, whereas pilot projects had been carried out in 1992 and 1993. The results, usually presented as the low, high, and average value for the thirty-six hospitals, are summarized below:

- Average use per journal title: 8.3 to 54.7 with an average of 30.4

- Average 1995 subscription price per use (based on used titles only): $2.71 to $19.19 with a $6.76 average

- Average 1995 subscription cost per use (based on both used and unused titles): no ranges given, the average was $7.74

- Average subscription cost of non-used titles: $0.00 to $459.93 with a $147.26 average

- The percentage of titles that were unused: 0 percent to 28 percent with a 7 percent average

- The percentage of titles required to meet 80 percent of need: 21 percent to 50 percent with an average of 38 percent

- The number of subscriptions per library: 53 to 578, no average given but 1,442 different titles in total

Because only three titles ranked among the top 20 percent in use in all thirty-six libraries, the authors assert that unique collections tailored to local library needs are important. Dee, Rankin, and Burns quite correctly maintain their study provides benchmark journal use data for hospital libraries.

Duran, Nancy, Chad E. Buckley, and Manwa L. Ng. "A Use Study of Speech Pathology and Audiology Periodicals at Illinois State University." **Bulletin of the Medical Library Association** 85 (October 1997): 373–77.

The authors recount a study of speech pathology and audiology journal use at the Illinois State University library, conducted in anticipation of a cancellation project. A reshelving count from May 1995 though May 1996 was supplemented with data on ILL requests during the same one-year period and the number of times titles were "straightened" on the shelf during weekdays from July 1995 through May 1996. A table rank orders the thirty-three most frequently reshelved titles while indicating the number of times each was straightened. The authors observe that the reshelving and straightening data "do not appear to be correlated." Other tables list in alphabetical order fifteen titles that were unused and the sixty-two tiles requested on ILL, only five of which were requested five or more times. Further research showed that "most" of the journals in this study are covered by *Index Medicus* and UnCover and that the library owned "most" of the titles in *Abridged Index Medicus.* This use study is noteworthy because it incorporates data on both reshelving and straightening on the shelf.

French, Carol, and Eleanor Pollard. "Serials Usage Study in a Public Library." **Public Library Quarterly** 16, no. 4, (1997): 45–53.

A periodical usage study, conducted during 1995 and 1996 at the Broward County Main Library in Fort Lauderdale, Florida, is written about in this entry. Volunteers and community service workers tallied requests by patrons for print periodicals (they were housed in closed stacks), and library clerks did reshelving counts of microfilm. LOTUS 1–2–3 generated monthly and quarterly reports. Through September 1996, 147,074 periodicals were requested, 82,623 rolls of microfilm reshelved, and 11,500 articles faxed to branch libraries.[11] As a result of the investigation, 200 unused titles were identified and $10,000 worth of subscriptions were cancelled in the first year. French and Pollard emphasize that public library periodical studies are "rare" in the literature and wonder if this is because they are not being conducted or not being published.

Gammon, Julia A., and Phyllis O'Connor. "An Analysis of the Results of Two Periodical Use Studies: How Usage in the 1990s Compares to Usage in the 1970s." **Serials Review** 22 (winter 1996): 35–53.

Periodical use data, gathered from reshelving counts at the University of Akron library from 1988 to 1992, are compared with 1975–77 data based on application of adhesive labels to determine whether a volume was used or not. In the 1990s study, the top 10 percent of the titles averaged 408 uses and accounted for 73 percent of total usage while the bottom 20 percent were not used at all. In the 1970s, 99.9 percent of the volumes among the top 10 percent of titles were used, and the bottom 20 percent of titles were unused. Subject breakdowns show that humanities and social science journals were the most heavily used in the 1970s whereas science and technology titles were most frequently used in the 1990s. Heavy-use titles from the 1970s were still heavily used in the 1990s, and (a "surprising finding") many low-use titles from the 1970s were regularly used in the 1990s. The authors thus conclude that use patterns change over time and question the maxim "past use predicts future use."

Gardner, W. Jeanne. "Evaluating the Periodicals Collection." In **Community College Reference Services: A Working Guide for and by Librarians,** edited by Bill Katz, 344–51. Metuchen, NJ: Scarecrow Press, 1992. ISBN 0-8108-2615-1.

Here periodical use is analyzed, based on call slip analysis of a two-year period (1988–89 and 1989–90) in an unnamed community college Learning Resource Center (LRC) in Colorado. Gardner found that "for the most part" indexed titles were used more than unindexed ones while 34 percent of the collection accounted for 80 percent of use and 43 percent accounted for all use. Although this is not an especially good contribution, published reports of periodical use studies in community college libraries are scarce.

Green, Paul Robert. "Monitoring the Usage of Science and Engineering Journals at the Edward Boyle Library, University of Leeds." **Serials Librarian** 25, nos. 1–2 (1994): 169–80.

The "usage index," developed at the Science and Engineering Library at the University of Leeds in the United Kingdom, is described by Green. A journal's usage index is calculated by dividing the number of uses by the number of months on the shelf, that is, the index represents the average number of uses per month for each part of the title. The data was tabulated in November 1992 based on readers signing survey slips attached to current issues for varying periods of time during 1991–92. Three tables illustrate the calculation of the usage index for approximately ninety titles. Titles with an index below 0.1 were considered candidates for cancellation and eleven were actually cancelled. Green concedes this approach is "not as sophisticated" as other techniques but is "easy to administer." This index is noteworthy because it relates use to the amount of time spent on the shelf.

Hill, J. B., Cherie Madarash-Hill, and Nancy Hayes. "Monitoring Serials Use in a Science and Technology Library: Results of a Ten Year Study." **Science & Technology Libraries** 18, no. 1 (1999): 89–103.

The three authors reflect upon a space and budgetary constraint inspired periodical use study at the University of Akron Science and Technology Library, ongoing since 1988. The use of student assistants to mark bound and unbound items while reshelving them is explained. They found that 24 percent of the titles accounted for 80 percent of the use (the raw data is not given). Analysis by discipline demonstrated that polymer science/engineering and nursing/allied health periodicals accounted for a much higher percentage of usage than of expenditures, whereas physics, geology, and mathematics received a higher proportion of expenditures than of use. More than 500 low-use titles have been cancelled, and 75,000 serial volumes moved to remote storage during this use study. The writers state in conclusion that the cost of monitoring use is "minor" compared to the expense of serial subscriptions. This item is somewhat remarkable because ten-year periodical use studies are seldom conducted.

Hill, J. B., Cherie Madarash-Hill, and Nancy Hayes. "Remote Storage of Serials: Its Impact on Use." **Serials Librarian** 39, no. 1 (2000): 29–39.

The impact on use of transferring more than 50,000 serial volumes from the University of Akron Science and Technology Library to the Northeastern Ohio Cooperative Library Depository in Rootstown, Ohio during 1995 is reported here. The remote storage location was indicated in the catalog and patrons had to request delivery, with a mean turnaround of three days. For the two years prior to transfer (1993 and 1994), the stored volumes were used an average of 2,651 times per year, but in the three years after transfer (1996 through 1998) their average annual total use was 536. Hill, Madarash-Hill, and Hayes conclude "storage can be a significant disincentive to patrons' use of serials" and predict that in their library post-storage use will be less than 30 percent of pre-storage use. The authors are undoubtedly correct that placement in storage diminishes use and acknowledge that "some" of the reduced usage might result from the "aging process," but they do not adequately investigate the relative proportions of the observed decline in use due to aging or storage.

Kachel, Debra E. "Improving Access to Periodicals: A Cooperative Collection Management Project." **School Library Media Quarterly** 24 (winter 1996): 93–103.

Kachel's large-scale periodical use study analyzes data from fifteen members (fourteen school libraries from middle through senior high plus one public library) of the Lancaster-Lebanon Intermediate Unit 13 Library Consortium in Pennsylvania. Data on magazines requested by patrons (all were placed in closed stack areas) and articles received on ILL were gathered for the 1991–92 and 1992–93 school years. A total of 542 titles were used, of which 70.8 percent were owned within the consortium.[12] For school libraries, titles producing 75 percent of the uses (45 periodicals for high schools, 27 for junior-senior schools, 15 for junior high or middle schools) were considered "core." Four separate tables list the most frequently used magazines in the four types of libraries in the consortium. A breakdown by age demonstrates that 83.9 percent of 138,724 uses were from the most recent five years. Interestingly, about one-third of the articles requested in school libraries had been owned but were unavailable due to discarding backfiles or mutilation/theft. Kachel outlines seven factors for consideration in access versus ownership decisions: use data, cost, indexing coverage, appropriateness for users, authority and quality, local availability, and outside availability. This entry is noteworthy because use data from multitype library consortia dominated by school libraries are not often available.

Lent, Robin. "Women's Studies Journals: Getting the Collection Right!" **Serials Librarian** 35, nos. 1–2 (1998): 45–58.

In this entry, Lent analyzes the results in women's studies (80 percent of 20 faculty members responded) from a survey of all University of New Hampshire (UNH) faculty concerning the journals they read. (For more details about this survey and the findings in animal and nutrition science see the next entry). She discovered that 70.3 percent of the 37 titles read by faculty were subscribed to by the library and that the faculty read 61.9 percent of the library's 42 women's studies subscriptions.[13] After analyzing the women's studies journals covered by *Women Studies Abstracts, Expanded Academic Index,* and four major Wilson indexes, Lent found that during the 1995–96 academic year, there were only 16 ILL requests for articles from journals included in these indexes but not subscribed to by the UNH library nor read by faculty. Predicated on the assumption that journals indexed in major services are sometimes defined as the core, Lent concludes that "there is no such thing as a core list in any field" echoing Joswick and Stierman (see entry by Joswick and Stierman, "The Core List Mirage: A Comparison of the Journals Frequently Consulted by Faculty and Students," earlier in this chapter). Lent concedes, however, that collecting only what the faculty wants will not serve the students' needs.

Lent, Robin, Louise A. Buckley, and David Lane. "Money Talks but Can It Listen?: How We Found Out What Our Faculty Really Read." **Against the Grain** 9 (April 1997): 1, 16, 18, 20, 34.

Written in an informal, first-person style, this adaptation of a presentation from the 1996 Charleston conference recounts a survey concerning faculty journal use conducted at the University of New Hampshire library. By July 15, 1996, 51 percent of the 600 total faculty members had responded to a questionnaire sent on March 8 in which they were asked to list the journals they read and answer other questions. Of 2,098 listed titles, 75.9 percent were subscribed to by the library, 16.6 percent were not subscribed to, and 7.4 percent were unverifiable or illegible.[14] On average, the faculty indicated 63 percent of their journal needs were met by the library, although the responses ranged from 0 percent to 100 percent. A detailed examination of the Animal and Nutrition Sciences Department found that the library subscribed to 86 percent of 132 listed titles and that 31 percent of these were read by more than one faculty member. Other issues addressed here include interdisciplinary use and faculty attitudes toward electronic journals, table of contents services, and so on. The authors question the core concept because each faculty member and department has an "idiosyncratic" core.

Maxfield, Margaret W., Rebecca DiCarlo, and Michael A. DiCarlo. "Decreasing Use of Monthly Serials After Publication Date." **Serials Librarian** 27, no. 4 (1995): 71–77.

Decline in serial use with age is analyzed at the Northeast Louisiana University library. The investigation was based on 692 checkout records for monthly serial issues during March, April, and June 1993 (unbound journals for the last ten years had to be obtained from a controlled access area). An exponential curve was fitted to the cumulative frequency data in order to estimate how many months would be required to account for 50 percent, 75 percent, 90 percent, and 95 percent of use. An appended "technical note" explains the mathematics. The authors decided that use "peaks three months after publication;" 50 percent of use has occurred after eighteen months (when they recommend binding); and 90 percent of use has taken place after approximately five years (when they suggest titles may be placed in remote storage). Detailed inspection of five subjects revealed that 90 percent of observed use takes place after 45 months in biology, 46 to 47 months in economics, 68 to 84 months in education, 52 to 58 months in business, and 41 to 43 months in pharmacy. Unfortunately, this study does not fully consider differences among subjects as no humanities area was examined.

Price, Anna L., and Kjestine R. Carey. "Serials Use Study Raises Questions About Cooperative Ventures." **Serials Review** 19, no. 3 (1993): 79–84.

This article examines the use of eighty-four science titles at the Montana State University library that were ordered under the guidelines of a cooperative collection development grant rather than in response to local need. Circulation, ILL, and in-house use data, based on reshelving counts, were gathered for the nine-month period April through January 1991. The authors found that 36 percent of the titles were not used and 19 percent were used only once, although one was used seventy-eight times. Only nine of the eighty-four were requested on ILL. Seventy percent of the eighty-four titles and 72 percent (thirty-three) of the forty-six titles used one or fewer times were available through the UnCover2 document delivery service. The annual subscriptions fees for these thirty-three titles were $11,523 compared to $5,000 for the "UnCover campuswide account cost." Price and Carey conclude by noting "the limitations in cooperative serial purchasing."

Scigliano, Marisa. "Serial Use in a Small Academic Library: Determining Cost-Effectiveness." **Serials Review** 26, no. 1 (2000): 43–52.

Scigliano describes a reshelving study of bound and microformat serials at the Trent University library in Peterborough, Ontario from October 1997 to April 1998. The analysis concentrates on 1,827 current titles (accounting for 37,892 uses) assigned to twenty-four academic departments. A table tabulating usage data by department showed an average cost per use of $7.80, ranging from $2.75 to $1,002.96 among the twenty-four departments. The overall average use per student enrolled in a full-year course was 1.59, varying from 0.04 to 6.43 among departments. Additional tables reveal the average cost per use for humanities journals was $8.56 and the use per student 1.10, while the corresponding figures for the social sciences were $12.45 and 1.25, and $6.54 and 2.42 for the sciences.

Titles with no recorded use or with a cost per use exceeding $100 were presented to faculty as cancellation candidates after which 180 titles were actually cancelled. This case study is quite thorough.

Sennyey, Pongracz, Gillian D. Ellern, and Nancy Newsome. "Collection Development and a Long-Term Periodical Use Study: Methodology and Implications." **Serials Review** 28, no. 1 (2002): 38–44.

This item recapitulates 1998 to 2000 data from an ongoing study of periodical use, employing a reshelving count, at the Western Carolina University library. The methodology and the building of a relational database, using *Microsoft Access,* are discussed at some length. Among the numerous reported data on findings, the most significant, in the annotator's opinion, are outlined below:

- Fifteen percent of 4,734 titles received 80 percent of 68, 684 uses during the three years.

- Use of specific titles was "intermittent," (e.g., 112 titles had no use for two consecutive semesters prior to a semester of six or more uses).

- More than 70 percent of the collection was used fewer than five times raising the possibility that ILL would be more cost-effective for them (it is unclear whether this figure represented a single year or the three-year total).

- The overall use of periodicals declined 21.6 percent from 1998 to 1999 and 24.3 percent between 1999 and 2000.

The authors attribute this decline to the impact of electronic versions of print journals (for which usage data was not available), but concede other factors may have been involved.

Sutton, Ellen D., and Karen Havill Bingham. "Psychology Serials Usage: A Faculty Survey Revisited." **Behavioral & Social Sciences Librarian** 11, no. 2 (1992): 59–89.

A survey of psychology and educational psychology faculty at the University of Illinois at Urbana-Champaign concerning their serials usage is reported in this entry. Modeled upon a 1977 survey of all UIUC social science faculty by Ruth B. McBride and Patricia Stenstrom, the authors sent a questionnaire to the 113 faculty from the two departments in 1988 and received a 65 percent response rate.[15] Extensive statistical findings are presented throughout the article. Among the most interesting, 97 percent of the psychology faculty used serials in research, 93 percent regularly read journals, and 45 percent read more than ten journals. The corresponding figures for educational psychology faculty were: 100 percent, 90 percent, and 21 percent. Further analysis demonstrated that faculty tended to use current articles written in English. Respondents listed thirty-four titles they were unable to find in the libraries, but fourteen were currently being received! Altogether 227 titles were read by faculty, of which the eighteen read by at least 10 percent of the respondents were deemed the core. Sutton and Bingham found that 78 percent of these core titles had 1988 *JCR* impact factors over 1.000 and all but five had been cited more than 1,000 times that year, leading to the conclusion that UIUC faculty "reflect use by the psychology research community at large."

Walter, Pat L. "A Journal Use Study: Checkouts and In-House Use." **Bulletin of the Medical Library Association** 84 (October 1996): 461–67.

A major periodical use study conducted at the University of California at Los Angeles (UCLA) Biomedical Library is reported by Walter. In addition to circulation and ILL statistics, in-house use was calculated by taking a reshelving count one week per month and multiplying the twelve-week total by 4.3 to generate a yearly estimate. Total usage between September 1993 and September 1994 for the 1990 or later volumes of 2,552 titles stood at the following: circulation, 34,887; in-house use, 197,953; and ILL requests, 4,734. It was also found that 385 titles that never circulated were used in-house 4,184 times while only 147 titles were neither checked out nor used in-house. All types of use were higher for more frequently published journals. Analysis by ten subject areas found that the ratio of in-house use to circulation ranged from 5.59:1 in dentistry to 12.90:1 in biology. However, the authors conclude there is no universal formula (i.e., "each checkout equals x in-house uses") to express the ratio between these two types of use because of variation by subject and publication frequency. This entry is notable for addressing the relationship between circulation and in-house use of periodicals as well as between periodical use and frequency of publication.

Young, Ian R. "The Use of a General Periodicals Bibliographic Database Transaction Log As a Serials Collection Management Tool." **Serials Review** 18 (winter 1992): 49–60.

Citations printed from EBSCO's CD-ROM *Magazine Articles Summary (MAS)* from August 1990 to July 1991 are compared with actual journal usage, based on reshelving counts during ninety-nine "scattered" days from May 1990 to April 1991, at the University College of Cape Breton library in Nova Scotia, Canada. The extensive data presented here is analyzed in a variety of ways. The fifty-nine titles selected for study were used 3,402 times (extrapolated to 11,400 yearly uses) and 2,624 citations to them were printed from the *MAS* database. Young found a "moderate positive correlation" (0.3595) between printed citations and actual use, especially retrospective use. Patrons, by a factor of 3.07, were more likely to print citations if the journal was held by the library. Investigation of the 80/20 Rule revealed that 16.4 percent of the indexed journals accounted for 80.0 percent of the printed citations and 17.2 percent of the currently received journals produced 80.1 percent of actual use. This sophisticated investigation incorporates a creative utilization of database transaction logs for serials usage evaluation.

USE OF BOOKS

Blecic, Deborah D. "Monograph Use at an Academic Health Sciences Library: The First Three Years of Shelf Life." **Bulletin of the Medical Library Association** 88 (April 2000): 145–51.

Blecic's topnotch study examines the circulation of books during their first three years on the shelf at the University of Illinois at Chicago health sciences library. Due date stamps were read exactly three years after new books acquired between mid-August 1994 and mid-August 1995 were shelved. Of 1,674 titles with complete records, 60.45 percent circulated during their first year on the shelf and 81.48 percent during the three years. Of 7,659 circulations, 38.69 percent were in the first year, 32.37 percent the second, and 28.95 percent the third. The data "did not conform" to the 80/20 Rule because 38 percent of the books accounted for 80 percent of circulation, but supported Joseph M. Juran's "vital few" principle (see entry by Eldredge) as 2.21 percent of the books provided 21.84 percent of the circulation.[16] A subject breakdown showed that the history of medicine, ophthalmology, geriatrics, and chronic disease had the highest percentages of unused books. The author observes that her findings contrast with those of Fenske (see entry later in this chapter) in a different branch of the same library, but support the theory that the percentage of books used increases with a lower book-to-user ratio.

Britten, William A., and Judith D. Webster. "Comparing Characteristics of Highly Circulated Titles for Demand-Driven Collection Development." **College & Research Libraries** 53 (May 1992): 239–48.

The University of Tennessee at Knoxville library used its Geac automated system to identify the 400 most frequently circulated books during 1982 through 1990 in twenty LC classes. These 8,000 titles circulated more than twenty-six times each, contrasted to an average of 2.65 for the entire collection. A breakdown of the highly used books' age showed they "were well used for many years" following publication. Detailed analysis by language demonstrated low use for non-English titles, that is, German titles accounted for 80 percent of LC class PT (German language and literature) but only 16 percent of the top 400 titles. Finally, keyword searches of "popular" subject headings were conducted in the OPACs of the Iowa, Minnesota, and Michigan State Universities libraries to identify additional relevant titles to be used for evaluation and selection. This method, which the authors say can be used by other libraries with automated systems, is noteworthy for its focus on high circulation books and utilization of the data for collection building.

Day, Mike, and Don Revill. "Towards the Active Collection: The Use of Circulation Analyses in Collection Evaluation." **Journal of Librarianship & Information Science** 27 (September 1995): 149–57.

Modeled on Adrian N. Peasgood's study at the University of Sussex using the Geac system, Day and Revill used circulation data from the Dynix library automation system for collection evaluation at Liverpool John Moores University in the United Kingdom.[17] The investigation's major objective was to determine for forty-two subject areas:

1. The percentage of books that circulated during the first year after acquisition

2. The mean number of annual circulations per item

The authors decided that subjects in which these measures exceeded 80 percent and 4 were "high performing," while areas falling below 40 percent and 1 were considered "low performing." In most subject areas, the proportion of items circulating in the first year fell between 60 to 70 percent and the mean number of uses for reported subjects ranged from 0.83 to 7.10. A few limitations, some relating to technical aspects of Dynix plus the fact that in-house use was not considered, are acknowledged. The authors assert that they plan to use their data to reallocate the budget from low-performing to high-performing subjects. This article offers an intriguing permutation of the user-centered approach to collection evaluation.

De Jager, Karin. "Obsolescence and Stress: A Study of the Use of Books on Open Shelves at a University Library." **Journal of Librarianship & Information Science** 26 (June 1994): 71–82.

This methodologically rigorous but verbosely written article reports the results from two book circulation measurements at the University of Cape Town library in South Africa. A diachronous study, based on a 2,654 title random sample from the shelf and using the last circulation date stamped in the book, was conducted between December 11 to 17, 1992. It was found that 20.7 percent of the sample accounted for all 1992 circulation, 54 percent had circulated in the past six years, and 16 percent had never circulated. Analysis by age indicated "fairly significant use" of "old" books in all subjects including science and engineering. De Jager notes a "strange phenomenon:" after the purchase of new books began declining in 1986, the use of "older books" acquired before 1970 began increasing. To address possible "shelf bias" (i.e., the best books are checked out rather than on the shelf), a random sample of 1,023 books on loan on December 15, 1992, was taken (a synchronous study). However, the findings were "not very different." De Jager points out that many of her results do not correspond with those of the well-known Pittsburgh Study. For example, she found that use peaked three years after acquisition rather than in the first year.

Eldredge, Jonathan D. "The Vital Few Meet the Trivial Many: Unexpected Use Patterns in a Monographs Collection." **Bulletin of the Medical Library Association** 86 (October 1998): 496–503.

The author investigates the use through November 1997 of the 1,306 monographs acquired by the University of New Mexico health sciences library during 1993. Eldredge asserts Juran's principle that a "vital few" have a large influence is demonstrated because 5 percent of the books produced 26 percent of the circulation.[18] However, Trueswell's 80/20 Rule is questioned as 20 percent of the monographs in this study accounted for 58 percent of the use and 36 percent produced 80 percent of total circulation. The fact that 84 percent of the books circulated and total usage rose to 90.7 percent with the inclusion of in-house use contrasts with the earlier findings of the Pittsburgh Study, Larry L. Hardesty, and Ruth E. Fenske (see entry later in this chapter), that a large proportion of newly acquired books are not used.[19] The 213 items that never circulated tended to be highly technical and narrowly focused. Eldredge states his results may deviate from the standard pattern because of a lower monographs acquired/customer ratio in his library and the recent introduction of a problem-based learning curriculum that might have increased library usage. This first-rate article is valuable for its review and analysis of previous research regarding book use patterns.

Ettelt, Harold. "Accountability in Book Acquisition and Weeding." **Reference Librarian** 38 (1992): 257–59.

Incorporating an informal question and answer format, this short piece reports book use statistics from the Columbia Green Community College in Hudson, New York. Since 1977, manual surveys requiring about 200 staff hours per year sampled use for about 10 percent of the circulating collection. The author reports that 83 percent of the entire collection had been used since 1977 as had 91 percent of the books acquired since that date. Moreover, 82 percent of the titles obtained in 1990 had been used by June 1991. Ettelt reveals that about 25 percent of the collection is used each year, but "it is never the same 25 percent" from year to year. Taking a contrarian view, he maintains the 80/20 Rule "does not hold here." The author then offers a rather self-evident defense of acquiring new books and of weeding, but the entry's main contribution is the data on book use in a community college library.

Fenske, Ruth E. "Evaluation of Monograph Selection in a Health Sciences Library." **Bulletin of the Medical Library Association** 82 (July 1994): 265–70.

This entry depicts a circulation study of books at the University of Illinois at Chicago's Library of the Health Science at Urbana. In the fall of 1989, total circulation was ascertained by reviewing the due-date slips (described as "very time consuming") for the 2,625 books acquired by the library between July 1987 and September 1989. The author discovered that "nearly 60 percent" of these had no (41.7 percent) or one (17.6 percent) use. Breaking usage down according to sixty-one subjects revealed that immunology, occupational medicine, and clinical pathology are low-use areas, whereas Alzheimer's disease, AIDS, and alcoholism are high use. Fenske admits that books obtained in 1989 did not have enough shelf time to adequately determine use. Nevertheless, she decides that comprehensive collections are "not needed" in health science libraries because access can be provided to low-use books.

Lancaster, F. W. "Evaluation of the Collection: Analysis of Use." In **If You Want to Evaluate Your Library...**, 51–75. 2d ed. Champaign, IL: University of Illinois, Graduate School of Library and Information Science, 1993. ISBN 0-87845-091-2.

This chapter's primary focus is on book circulation patterns and methods for measuring them. Prior to automation, sampling techniques included a "collection sample" (studying the selected books' complete circulation history) and a "check-out sample" (analyzing what circulated during a specific time period). Considerable attention is given to the "relative use" concept for identifying "overused" (the proportion of use is greater than the proportion of holdings) and "underused" (circulation is proportionately smaller than holdings) subject areas. "Shelf bias" is also explained, that is, only titles no one wanted remain on the shelves. The Pittsburgh Study, the 80/20 rule, the "circulation/inventory ratio," and the "last circulation date" method (which calculates the time lapse between a current check-out and the last previous check-out) are also discussed. Final sections cover the role of ILL statistics in evaluation and collection/curriculum matching techniques. Lancaster closes with the perceptive observation that use studies focus on success (the user found something he or she wanted), but ignore failures (nothing worth using was found).

Saunders, E. Stewart. "The Effect of Quality on Circulation in an Aging Collection." **Collection Management** 20, nos. 3–4 (1996): 149–56.

Saunders investigates the intriguing question of whether the "relationship between book review evaluations and library circulation will become stronger as the book becomes older." This entry is a sequel to a 1983 study by John P. Schmidt and Saunders which found for a 310 book sample a "modest" correlation between the quality of review in *Choice* and circulation in the Purdue University library in 1981.[20] Note that each review was rated on a 1 (not recommended) to 5 (highly recommended) scale. Subsequently, the circulation for 293 of these books (some had to be eliminated because they were on reserve) was analyzed for the years 1981 to 1991. Stewart discovered the increase in correlation between book review quality and circulation was so small (0.121 compared to 0.094 in the 1983 study) that one can not have "faith in the notion" that the circulation of better books relative to lesser quality titles increases over time. While the assumption is plausible, it is not supported by this research project.

Schmidt, Cynthia M., and Nancy L. Eckerman. "Circulation of Core Collection Monographs in an Academic Medical Library." **Bulletin of the Medical Library Association** 89 (April 2001): 165–69.

This entry investigates whether books on core medical lists actually have higher circulation rates in academic medical libraries than unlisted titles. The study is based upon two years and three months of circulation records at the Indiana University School of Medicine Library for hematology books published between 1990 and 1996. The authors found that 30.3 percent of 109 books were included on at least one of four core lists, such as the famous Brandon-Hill list.[21] The circulation ratio of core to noncore titles stood at 3 to 1 during the last three months of 1997, 2.7 to 1 in 1998, and 2.3 to 1 in 1999. The 22 books that did not circulate at all were not included on any of the core lists. Schmidt and Eckerman conclude that "this heavy-use pattern" justifies use of core lists as selection tools by academic medical librarians. Note that the first author has outstanding credentials, holding both the M.D. and M.L.S. degrees.

Selth, Jeff, Nancy Koller, and Peter Briscoe. "The Use of Books Within the Library." **College & Research Libraries** 53 (May 1992): 197–205.

In a well-done preliminary literature review, the authors contest the generally accepted assumption from both Fussler and Simon's classic book and the Pittsburgh Study that circulation and in-house use are highly correlated with each other.[22] Selth, Koller, and Briscoe analyze the circulation and in-house use of 13,029 book and serial volumes (sampled from a million volume collection) during seven years at the University of California at Riverside library. They found that from 25 percent to 30 percent of the sample received one type of use but not the other while noting "striking differences" by subject. Moreover, the authors calculate that if a million volume collection were weeded based on noncirculation, at least 112,000 volumes would be moved that were actually used in-house. The article ends with a bibliography, chronologically arranged, of twenty-six items relating to in-house use published between 1956 and 1988. This entry is important because it challenges the conventional wisdom on a long debated issue.

OTHER USE STUDIES

Lee, Tamara P., and Lawrence J. Myers. "Document Delivery at a Veterinary Medical Library: A One-Year Study of Use Patterns." **Collection Management** 16, no. 2 (1992): 75–92.

The authors analyze the items requested on ILL and for courier delivery (from the main library) at Auburn University's Veterinary Medical Library between October 1989 through September 1990. The study's three hypotheses were confirmed:

1. The majority of requested items would be serials—92 percent of 2,376 requests were for serials, with the remaining 8 percent for monographs

2. Most serial requests would be for nonveterinary journals—73 percent of 1,608 serial requests were for nonveterinary titles

3. The number of items requested per month would be unequal—wide month-to-month variation was found.

Among other findings, note the following: 76 percent of ninety-six serials on a core list were held by the library and 89 percent by the library system, 64 of 127 disciplines listed in the *Science Citation Index* were requested on document delivery, and the "numerous requests" for pre-1971 volumes (the exact percentage is not stated).[23] A table names in rank order the forty-seven journal titles requested ten or more times by courier, while another table lists the seven titles requested at least five times on ILL. This article is unusual in its focus on the items requested for document delivery in a veterinary library and, as noted by Lee and Myers, complements Robert J. Veenstra's earlier study of in-house journal use in the identical library.[24]

Pohjanvalta, Terhikki. "Surveying the Use of Quality in Espoo City Library." **Scandinavian Public Library Quarterly** 26, no. 4 (1993): 24–27.

The use and users of "quality" material in the public library of Espoo City (Finland's second largest metropolis bordering on Helsinki) is reported here. Detailed definitions of "quality" and "entertainment" materials are given, although the author admits the classification is "extremely subjective." Based on samples of 2,305 loan transactions during 1991's spring and summer, 33.7 percent of all loans were quality material, while the corresponding percentages for books were 32.9; music, 39.4;

and video, 44.6. Furthermore, 50.5 percent of users borrowed entertainment materials only, 20.1 percent (termed "the elite") borrowed only quality items, and 29.4 percent borrowed both. Several bar graphs provide additional data regarding the proportion of quality items circulating in the collection and on the shelves for fiction versus nonfiction, as well as for the main library and two branches. This investigation's results were used in developing a Coping Strategy "for surviving on a meagre budget" and Choice Principles for selection. "Quality versus entertainment" is identical to the familiar "quality versus demand" debate in American public library collection development, although North American sources are not cited.

NOTES

1. S. R. Ranganathan, *The Five Laws of Library Science,* 2d ed. (Bombay: Asia Publishing House, 1957).

2. Stanley J. Slote, *Weeding Library Collections: Library Weeding Methods,* 4th ed. (Englewood, CO: Libraries Unlimited, 1997), 53; Charles William Eliot, "The Division of a Library into Books in Use and Books Not in Use, with Different Storage Methods for the Two Classes of Books, *Library Journal* 27 (July 1902): 51–56.

3. Herman H. Fussler and Julian L. Simon, *Patterns in the Use of Books in Large Research Libraries.* (Chicago: University of Chicago Press, 1969).

4. Allen Kent et al., *Use of Library Materials: The University of Pittsburgh Study* (New York: Marcel Dekker, 1979).

5. Sheila S. Intner, "Objectifying Subjectivity," *Technicalities* 21 (January/February 2001): 3–7.

6. Richard W. Trueswell, "Some Behavioral Patterns of Library Users: The 80/20 Rule," *Wilson Library Bulletin* 43 (January 1969): 458–61.

7. W. M. Shaw, Jr., "A Practical Journal Usage Technique," *College & Research Libraries* 39 (November 1978): 479–84; Shaw, "A Journal Resource Sharing Strategy, *Library Research* 1 (Spring 1979): 19–29.

8. Nisonger's calculation from Dess's figures.

9. These figures are Nisonger's calculation from Butkovich's raw data.

10. Richard K. Hunt, "Journal Deselection in a Biomedical Research Library: A Mediated Mathematical Approach," *Bulletin of the Medical Library Association* 78 (January 1990): 45–48; Loretta Stucki, "Annual Review of Current Journals to Identify Titles for Cancellation," *Newsletter: Washington University School of Medicine Library and Biomedical Communications Center* 31 (summer 1991): 2–4; Katherine W. McCain and James E. Bobick, "Patterns of Journal Use in a Department Library: A Citation Analysis," *Journal of the American Society for Information Science* 32 (July 1981): 257–67.

11. The figures in this sentence are Nisonger's calculation from French and Pollard's raw data.

12. Nisonger's calculation from Kachel's raw data.

13. The percentages in this sentence are Nisonger's calculations from Lent's data.

14. The percentages, Nisonger's calculations from the authors' raw data, do not add to 100 due to rounding.

15. Ruth B. McBride and Patricia Stenstrom, "Psychology Journal Usage," *Behavioral & Social Sciences Librarian* 2 (Fall 1980/81): 1–12.

16. Joseph M. Juran, "Universals in Management Planning and Controlling," *Management Review* 43 (November 1954): 748–61.

17. Adrian N. Peasgood, "Towards Demand-Led Book Acquisitions: Experiences in the University of Sussex Library," *Journal of Librarianship* 18 (October 1986): 242–56.

18. Juran, "Universals in Management Planning and Controlling."

19. Larry Hardesty, "Use of Library Materials at a Small Liberal Arts College," *Library Research* 3 (Fall 1981): 261–82.

20. John P. Schmidt and Stewart E. Saunders, "An Assessment of *Choice* as a Tool for Selection," *College & Research Libraries* 44 (September 1983): 375–80.

21. Nisonger's calculation from Schmidt and Eckerman's raw data.

22. Fussler and Simon, *Patterns in the Use of Books in Large Research Libraries.*

23. C. Trenton Boyd, "Basic List of Veterinary Medical Serials, 2d edition, 1981, with revisions to April 1, 1986," *Serials Librarian* 11 (October 1986): 5–39.

24. Robert J. Veenstra, "A One-Year Journal Use Study in a Veterinary Medical Library," *Journal of the American Veterinary Medical Association* 190 (March 15, 1987): 623–26.

9

Use of Citation Analysis in Evaluation

What is citation analysis? Citation analysis is generally considered a subset of bibliometrics. One should explain a variety of terms ending in "metrics" or "metry"—the application of statistical methods to a particular subject—that have developed over the years and sometimes been discarded. At an Association of Special Libraries and Information Bureaux (ASLIB) Conference at Leamington Spa, the United Kingdom, in September 1948, the great library science theoretician S.R. Ranganathan coined the term "librametry," which he defined as the application of "statistical calculus" to such library operations as staffing, classification, cataloging, book selection, and so on.[1] However, this term was never adopted or widely used in North America or Europe. The term "bibliometrices" was widely used after being introduced in 1969 through a letter to the editor of *Journal of Documentation* by the British librarian Alan Pritchard.[2] He defined bibliometrics as "the application of mathematics and statistical methods to books and other media of communication."[3] The International Society for Scientometrics and Informetrics, founded in 1995, dropped the word "bibliometrics" on the assumption that scientometrics and infometrics are broader terms that encompass bibliometrics, although the latter term is still used in other contexts. Recent years have witnessed the emergence of the terms "cybermetrics" or "webliometrics," which imply the application of quantitative methods to cyberspace, such as analysis of hits on a Web page or links between Web sites. The reader is referred to Dorothy H. Hertzel for a detailed discussion concerning the development of the term "bibliometrics."[4]

The *Journal Citation Reports,* published annually since the 1970s by the Institute for Scientific Information in Philadelphia, offers citation data for thousands of journals. Four major types of citation data are provided for each title each year. "Total Citations" states the aggregate number of citations received by all issues of a journal during the year. "Impact Factor," arguably the most important for evaluation purposes because it normalizes for a journal's age and size, represents the ratio of citations received to articles published, in other words, the number of times an average article has been cited. "Cited Half-Life" indicates the median age of the articles cited from a particular journal. "Immediacy Index" reveals how quickly a journal's articles are cited. For further details about the *Journal Citation Reports* and the calculation of these citation measures, see Nisonger.[5]

Citation analysis is controversial and subject to numerous criticisms: it is unclear what a citation actually indicates; most citation studies count all citations (positive, negative, and neutral) equally; a resource might have been cited simply because it was readily available to the researcher; and an item could be cited without actually having been used. The literature contains considerable discussion of technical issues beyond this book's scope concerning the *Journal Citations Reports* or what various citation measures actually mean. For an example of the latter, see Harter and Nisonger.[6] However, only studies with practical relevance to use of the *JCR* or citation data by librarians are included in this chapter.

In a library context, citation analysis is based on the assumption that if a researcher has cited an information resource in a bibliography, footnote, endnote, or text, he or she must have somehow used the item in the research process. Accordingly, citation analysis will provide clues that help librarians develop strategies for meeting the information needs of researchers. Clearly, citation data is most relevant to university and research libraries, although occasionally studies are published concerning the application of citation analysis for other types of libraries. Citation data can or has been used for the following: journal subscription, cancellation, weeding, relegation to remote storage, and filling-in-gap decisions; budgeting; a checklist for collection evaluation; defining the core; collection development planning concerning the age, language, or formats collected; and comparing scholarly communication patterns among different disciplines.

In addition to these objectives, topics such as the following have been investigated in the LIS literature:

- The effective utilization of the *Journal Citation Reports*

- The development of new citations measures as alternatives to impact factor

- The relationship between citation data and in-library usage data

- Patterns of concentration and scatter in cited documents (such as Bradford's Law where a few journals are highly cited and many infrequently cited)

- The relationship between national and local citation data

Chapter 9 is organized into five sections: general and miscellaneous issues, citation data in serials management, citation data in collection evaluation, structures of disciplines and subjects, and other citation studies. Note that citation studies concerning Web pages or electronic journals are included in chapter 11.

GENERAL AND MISCELLANEOUS ISSUES

Altmann, Klaus G., and Gary E. Gorman. "The Usefulness of Impact Factors in Serial Selection: A Rank and Mean Analysis Using Ecology Journals." **Library Acquisitions: Practice & Theory** 22 (summer 1998): 147–59.

Predicated on the assumption that impact factors should be relatively consistent from year to year if used in journal collection management decisions, the authors investigate the stability of ecology journal *JCR* impact factors from 1991 through 1995. They found the median year-to-year variation in impact factor for the seventy-three listed titles was 21.97 percent. A table summarizing the yearly change in rank among the fifty-five titles listed all five years indicates changes between years up to twenty-nine positions. Altmann and Gorman calculate there is a 24.57 percent chance that the ratio of journal subscription cost to impact factor will vary 48.77 percent. (One wonders if the local bookie gives you better odds!) Accordingly, they propose that one should not conclude journal A is preferable to journal B unless the cost/impact factor ratio between them exceeds 3.0. The authors also suggest that cost per citation rather than cost per impact factor should be considered by journal managers. Quite clearly, this research has important practical implications for librarians using impact factor.

Bandyopadhyay, Amit Kumar. "Bradford's Law in Different Disciplines." **Annals of Library Science & Documentation** 46 (December 1999): 133–38.

This study is based on the 6,844 journal citations in ninety-two doctoral dissertations submitted to the University of Burdwan in India from 1981 to 1990. Following a brief explanation of Bradford's Law and a short literature review, the author explains his objective is to investigate the applicability of Bradford's Law to various disciplines and subareas. A lengthy table presents the number of journals and citations in each of three Bradfordian zones for five disciplines (mathematics, physics, mechanical engineering, philosophy, and political science) plus thirteen subareas such as pure mathematics and optics. The article would have been strengthened if percentages had been presented rather than limiting the findings to raw data. It was found that Bradford's Law fit some areas "well," such as pure mathematics and philosophy as a whole discipline; others "moderately," that is, mathematics as a discipline and optics; and some, such as political science, "it does not fit well." This entry's major contribution is the author's conclusion that Bradford's Law should be applied to specific subject areas rather than large disciplines.

Burdick, Amrita J., Anne Butler, and Marilyn G. Sullivan. "Citation Patterns in the Health Sciences: Implications for Serials/Monographic Fund Allocation." **Bulletin of the Medical Library Association** 81 (January 1993): 44–47.

Although budgeting per se is beyond this book's scope, Burdick, Butler, and Sullivan's article is included as an example of the use of citation data for guidance in budgeting. More than 21,000 citations in fifty randomly selected articles from each of ten high-ranking general internal medicine journals in the 1989 *SCI* and in fifty randomly selected chapters from seven textbooks were tabulated. A table, summarizing the results for each journal and monograph, indicates that the proportion of citations to serials was 91 percent in the journals, 79 percent in the textbooks, and 88.3 percent overall. Furthermore, a study of 124 items consulted by eleven teaching physicians on hospital rounds during a two-week period found that 89.5 percent were serials. Yet the so-called "Houston statistics" for the years 1980–81, 1985–86, and 1989–90 revealed an average budget expenditure by U.S. and Canadian medical libraries of 79 percent for serials and 21 percent for monographs.[7] The authors assert, based on their citation data, that an 88:12 serials/monographic budgetary allocation would be more appropriate. For a subsequent study that questions whether the recommended ratio is applicable to all areas of the health sciences, see Wehmeyer and Wehmeyer.

Dilevko, Juris, and Esther Atkinson. "Evaluating Academic Journals Without Impact Factors for Collection Management Decisions." **College & Research Libraries** 63 (November 2002): 562–77.

Dilevko and Atkinson introduce a rather complex method for gathering citation data to evaluate journals which are not covered in the *Journal Citation Reports.* They outline a seven-step procedure:

1. Locate a "comparator" journal covered by the *JCR* similar to the nonranked journal one is evaluating

2. Select a type of article to focus on (research articles are recommended)

3. Select a range of years—they recommend a five-year period ending at least three years earlier than the current year

4. Identify citations to the selected article type in the nonranked and comparator journal through the *Web of Science*

5. Calculate an adjusted impact factor (based on research articles only) and other citation measures for the two journals

6. Compare the JCR impact factors of the journals which cite the nonranked and comparator journals

7. Analyze the "citation context" for the two journals (i.e., are the citations positive or negative)

They use *Annals of the Royal College of Physicians and Surgeons* (the nonranked title) and *Canadian Family Physician* (the comparator) for illustrative purposes. The approach is theoretically sophisticated, yet the authors' concluding comment, "Not every collection development department will want to devote the extensive person-hours to an exercise of this kind," is an understatement.

Funkhouser, Edward Truman. "The Evaluative Use of Citation Analysis for Communications Journals." **Human Communications Research** 22 (June 1996): 563–74.

This entry explores the impact the ISI citation indexes' incomplete coverage of scholarly journals has on citation data in the field of communications and, as a dual objective, introduces a new citation indicator, which is claimed to measure a journal's impact on its discipline better than does the *JCR* impact factor. The investigation is based on the 4,587 items cited in 1990 in twenty-seven communications journals: thirteen covered in *SSCI* or *AHCI* (Arts and Humanities Citation

Index) and fourteen not covered. It was found that 26 percent of all citations to authors and 25 percent of citations to journals were from non-ISI journals. The fifty most cited authors (listed in a table) "lost" from 0 to 70 percent of their citations, that is, the citations were from journals not included in the ISI database. The newly proposed Journal Impact Rating is calculated by multiplying a journal's citations times its "exoteric ratio" (the percentage of citations received from other journals rather than self-citations) times its "citation ratio" (the proportion of journal titles in the database that cite it). A table rank orders the study's twenty-seven source journals according to this method. The author concludes "we must have more complete data" than offered by ISI citation indexes to accurately measure the scholarly impact of journals, authors, or academic departments.

Karanjai, A., U. M. Munshi, and B. K. Sen. "Are the *JCR* Impact Factors of Indian S & T Journals Reliable?" **Annals of Library Science & Documentation** 39 (March 1992): 26–29.

The reliability of *JCR* impact factor scores for Indian journals is addressed here. While the number of Indian journals covered in the ISI database varies from year to year, the authors note that only forty were covered in recent years and eleven in 1988. Using data for Indian and non-Indian journals in agriculture, chemistry, medicine, and physics, the authors demonstrate that the inclusion of more Indian journals in the database would increase the impact factors for Indian journals (because the citations received from the country's other journals would then be counted in the impact factor calculation).Thus, the *JCR* impact factor "is not the true reflection of the quality of Indian journals." This entry supports the frequently voiced contention that *JCR* citation data disadvantages journals published outside North America and Europe

Nisonger, Thomas E. "Journal Self-Citedness in *Journal Citation Reports* Library and Information Science and Genetics Journal Rankings." In **ASIS '98: Proceedings of the 61st ASIS Annual Meeting, Pittsburgh, PA, October 24–29, 1998; Information Access in the Global Information Economy,** vol. 35, edited by Cecilia M. Preston, 267–78. Medford, NJ: published for the American Society for Information Science by Information Today, 1998. ISBN 1-57387-066-8.

Nisonger, Thomas E. "Use of the *Journal Citation Reports* for Serials Management in Research Libraries: An Investigation of the Effect of Self-Citation on Journal Rankings in Library and Information Science and Genetics." **College & Research Libraries** 61 (May 2000): 263–75.

These two entries, one a preliminary report, the other the final version, examine the effect of journal self-citations on *JCR* rankings in two disciplines: library and information science and genetics. Nisonger explains that because the validity of self-citations have been questioned, it is necessary to investigate their influence on *JCR* rankings. The 1994 *JCR* impact factor and total citation rankings in these two subjects were reconstructed with journal self-citations eliminated and then the reconstructed rankings compared with the original ones. Three comparison methods (Pearson Product Moment correlation, mean journal movement in ranking position, and overlap among the top five and ten titles before and after correction for journal self-citation) found that except for a small number of titles, self-citations are having a negligible impact on the rankings. The author concludes that librarians can use *JCR* citation data for serials decision-making purposes without correcting for journal self-citation.

Nisonger, Thomas E. "A Methodological Issue Concerning the Use of *Social Sciences Citation Index Journal Citation Reports* Impact Factor Data for Journal Ranking." **Library Acquisitions: Practice & Theory** 18 (winter 1994): 447–58.

After reviewing the use of *JCR* impact factor for journal ranking and a number of previous rankings based on average impact factor for a range of adjacent years, Nisonger explains that averaging impact factors contains a subtle methodological flaw. If the 1989 and 1988 impact factors are averaged, 1987 data will be counted twice, but 1988 and 1986 data only once, because the 1989 impact factor is based on data from 1988 and 1987, while the 1988 impact factor is calculated from 1987 and 1986 data. To correct this bias, the author proposes an "adjusted impact factor." Rankings by traditional averaging methods and "adjusted impact factor" for 1987, 1988, and 1989 for a set of 64 political science journals from an earlier study (see entry by Nisonger, "A Ranking of Political Science Journals Based on Citation Data," in chapter 10) are then compared with each other. Some journals display a "striking" difference in ranking position, thus indicating the methodological flaw does have an actual influence. This item addresses a technical issue that should be brought to the attention of scholars and librarians using the *JCR*.

Nisonger, Thomas E. "The Stability of *Social Sciences Citation Index Journal Citation Reports* Data for Journal Rankings in Three Disciplines." **JISSI: The International Journal of Scientometrics & Informetrics** 1 (June 1995): 139–49.

This item investigates the stability, that is, year-to-year consistency, of *JCR* impact factor and total citation rankings for library and information science, geography, and economics journals for the years 1980 through 1990. Three methods of analysis were used: the Pearson Product Moment correlation, mean movement in ranking position (for all journals in the discipline), and overlap among the topmost ten and top twenty journals. The major findings were impact factor rankings are less stable than those based on total citations received, the average movement in rank is higher in disciplines with more journals, and high-ranking journals are more stable than middle- or low-ranking journals. The author concludes that one should not rely on a single year's *JCR* data for journal decision-making purposes.

Peritz, Bluma C. "On the Association Between Journal Circulation and Impact Factor." **Journal of Information Science** 21, no. 1 (1995): 63–67.

This interesting "brief communication" addresses the relationship between *JCR* impact factor (a proxy for "status") and a journal's circulation, as indicated in *Ulrich's International Periodicals Directory,* used as a proxy for "visibility." Note that "circulation" refers to the number of subscribers, not check-out in a library. For seven of ten social science disciplines and seven of eleven science disciplines, the correlation between impact factor and circulation fell between 0.25

and 0.50. In all but one discipline (water resources), the correlation was positive. It is asserted that the correlation between impact factor and circulation is "fairly high" in research disciplines, but "lower" in disciplines comprised of both researchers and practitioners, such as LIS, because practitioners may use high-circulation low-impact journals. Peritz conjectures that high-circulation journals attract quality papers thus increasing their impact factor. Although not stated by the author, this research implies that circulation can be validly used as a criterion in library journal evaluation.

Shapiro, Fred R. "The Most-Cited Legal Books Published Since 1978." **Journal of Legal Studies** 29 (January 2000): 397–407.

The researcher uses ISI data in combination with online searches in the West-law service to identify the most highly cited legal books published since 1978. A table lists the fifty most frequently cited American scholarly law monographs. It is interesting that half were published by Harvard University Press. Other tables lists the twenty most highly cited student-oriented texts or practitioner-oriented treatises and the ten British legal books most cited in American scholarship. Note that these three rankings are constructed from citations in both legal and social science literature. In contrast, a final table names the twenty nonlegal books most cited in legal periodicals. Shapiro observes the subjects addressed in these non-legal titles are "all over the map." Citation studies of books, like those for jour-nals, can be used in selection and collection evaluation.

Stegmann, Johannes. "Building a List of Journals with Constructed Impact Fac-tors." **Journal of Documentation** 55 (June 1999): 310–24.

This entry illustrates a method for creating impact factors for ranking and evaluating journals not covered in the *JCR*. Termed the Constructed Impact Fac-tor (CIF), the measure is analogous to the *JCR's* impact factor because it repre-sents the ratio of citations received to articles published, except that journal self-citations are excluded. Five steps are outlined for creating the CIF, while detailed attention is given to technical issues and online searching strategies that are not a major concern for this book's purpose. The method was tested for bio-medical journals by online searching of the three ISI databases (*SciSearch, Social SciSearch,* and *Arts & Humanities Search*), which nevertheless cover journals not included in the *JCR*. CIFs for the year 1996 were constructed for 338 titles, of which the leading 100 are rank ordered in an appendix with the CIF calculation demonstrated. Stegmann's work can potentially help overcome the *JCR's* limited journal coverage, but the downside is that many librarians might find it difficult to implement his technique.

Wehmeyer, Jeffrey M., and Susan Wehmeyer. "The Comparative Importance of Books: Clinical Psychology in the Health Sciences Library." **Bulletin of the Medical Library Association** 87 (April 1999): 187–91.

This entry investigates whether the 88:12 serials to monographs budgeting ratio for health sciences libraries recommended by Burdick and others (see earlier entry in this chapter) is appropriate for clinical psychology, based on the number of books cited in theses and dissertations. More than 18,000 citations in ninety clinical psychology dissertations, ninety-one nursing master's theses, and ninety biomedical science dissertations or theses completed at Wright State University between 1986 and 1996 serve as the study's source. Approximately 35 percent of the clinical psychology citations were to books or book chapters compared to 25 percent in nursing and 8 percent in the biomedical sciences—a statistically significant difference. The authors believe their results are "comparable" with the findings of previous citation studies. In an unusual type of analysis, the Wehmeyers found the ratio of journal citations to book citations was 2.61 to 1 in clinical psychology, 3.88 to 1 in nursing, and 33.27 to 1 in biomedical sciences. The authors conclude that the Wright State clinical psychology program is more similar to the social sciences than the biomedical sciences, and thus the 88:12 budgeting ratio recommended for health sciences is "likely to be inappropriate" for all segments of the collection.

Wilson, T. D. "A Local Study of Journal Use." **Journal of Information Science** 20, no. 6 (1994): 444–50.

Completed fifteen years prior to its publication, this study analyzed the articles abstracted in the first twenty issues of *Social Work Information Bulletin* and then requested for photocopying by members of an unnamed United Kingdom consortium. In total, 1,707 articles from 196 journals were abstracted (11 titles produced 50 percent of the abstracts) and 9,171 photocopies were requested. Forty-one high-demand items (requested twenty or more times) were from 27 journals, whereas 191 "zero-demand" items were from 45 journals. Three separate tables rank order the top 20 journals based on the average number of abstracts per issue, the number of requested items, and the "use ratio" (requested items normalized for the number of abstracts), which include a number of titles from the field's "fringe" areas. Correlating the use ratio ranking with *JCR* impact factor (0.634) for the twelve journals common to both lead to the conclusion one "should be wary" of using citation data for selecting "materials for practitioners in a field such as social work."

Zipp, Louise S. "Thesis and Dissertation Citations As Indicators of Faculty Research Use of University Library Journal Collections." **Library Resources & Technical Services** 40 (October 1996): 335–42.

The extent to which the journals most cited by graduate students in theses and dissertations correspond to those cited in faculty publications is rigorously investigated based on four data sets: geology citations at Iowa State University compiled by the author; geology citations at UCLA and at Stanford previously published by Noga, Derksen, and Haner (see entry in chapter 8); and biology citations at Temple University from a previous study by Katherine W. McCain and James E. Bobick.[8] In each case, the forty journals most cited in theses/dissertations and faculty publications were compared with each other and then compiled into single lists of fifty-two titles at Iowa State (named in a table), fifty-two at Stanford, fifty-six at UCLA, and sixty at Temple. In all four cases approximately 70 percent of the faculty's top forty journals were among the forty titles most cited by graduate students. Following sophisticated statistical analysis using Kendall's tau, Zipp asserts that the correspondence between the journals cited by graduate students and faculty is closer "than had been previously assumed." Although not stated by the author, her research suggests that a library with data on the most frequently cited journals in one of these two sources (theses/dissertations or faculty publications) might not need to gather data from the other.

CITATION DATA IN SERIALS MANAGEMENT

Altmann, Klaus G., and Gary E. Gorman. "Can Impact Factors Substitute for the Results of Local Use Studies? Findings from an Australian Case Study." **Collection Building** 18, no. 2 (1999): 90–94.

Journal use (measured by marking spine labels when reshelving throughout an academic year) in ten scientific subject areas at an unidentified Australian university library was correlated with *Journal Citation Reports* impact factors. Regression analysis and plotting the data revealed a "very low" correlation between the two variables. The authors therefore conclude "impact factors are no substitute for local use studies" in journal collection management decisions. Moreover, the correlations were even lower for Australian journals, suggesting that *JCR* data is less useful for non-North American/European titles (a point that could have been emphasized to a greater extent). Altmann and Gorman offer a rigorous investigation of a significant issue.

Altmann, Klaus G., and Gary E. Gorman. "The Relevance of 'Cited by Leading Journal' to Serials Management in Australian University Libraries." **Australian Library Journal** 48 (May 1999): 101–15.

Altmann and Gorman test the Cited by Leading Journal Approach's (CBLJ's) (see Stankus and Mills) applicability to serials selection/deselection in Australian libraries by comparing the journals cited in *Ecology* (determined to be the leading ecology journal by examining five years of *JCR* rankings) with those used (based on a reshelving count) in an anonymous university library. Their analysis revealed that the CBLJ approach would be "inappropriate" for Australian libraries because many highly used Australian titles would be cancelled due to low citation scores. An examination of additional data from the *JCR* showed that a number of Australian journals are highly cited by other Australian journals but not by foreign journals. Accordingly, the authors outline a four-step process for modifying the CBLJ approach by giving more weight to citations from Australian journals, thus assuring that both mainstream and locally relevant titles are selected. They term this revised process the Cited by Leading Australian Journal strategy and state it might be useful in other countries as a Cited by Leading National Journal Strategy.

Aziagba, Philip C. "Scientific Journal Selection Based on the Study of a Local Journal." **Information Processing & Management** 29 (January/February 1993): 83–93.

This study investigates the citations in the *Nigerian Journal of Microbiology's* 1982 through 1986 volumes. A table indicated that 70.13 percent of 1,688 citations were to periodicals and 17.61 percent to books. A total of 308 different periodicals were cited, but only 56, rank ordered in a table, were cited five or more times. A graph shows that the "highest number" of citations were published between 1971 and 1975 and a few predated 1940 (deemed a "warning" when weeding). Data is also presented on co-authorship as well as the authors' geographical location and departmental affiliation. Since a Nigerian journal was used as a source, Aziagba believes his study should assist journal selection decisions by Nigerian librarians and suggests the fourteen most cited journals should meet the needs of "most" of the county's microbiology researchers.

Brown, Kincaid C. "How Many Copies Are Enough? Using Citation Studies to Limit Journal Holdings." **Law Library Journal** 94 (Spring 2002): 301–14.

Facing a space crunch, the University of Michigan Law Library used citation data to develop a multiple copy policy for law review journals. Five categories were established, ranging from retaining three paper copies plus a microfilm copy if available (number 1) to no paper copies, but one microfilm copy when available (number 5). The average ranking in eighteen law journal citation studies published between 1930 and 2000 was calculated for 105 journals (the data is presented in a lengthy appendix) and used to assign journals to categories. For example, five historically top-ranked journals were considered category 1, and eighteen journals that consistently ranked in the top thirty were placed in category 2. Approximately 800 linear feet of shelf space were freed up as a result of this policy. This article illustrates use of citation data for serials management decisions beyond such basic functions as subscription, cancellation, and weeding.

Byrd, Gary D. "Medical Faculty Use of the Journal Literature, Publishing Productivity, and the Size of Health Sciences Library Journal Collections." **Bulletin of the Medical Library Association** 87 (July 1999): 312–21.

This rigorous research paper investigates whether the size of an academic medical library's journal collection correlates with the number of articles published by its faculty and the number of journals cited in faculty publications. Data on the 1990–91 publications of 622 faculty in medical school departments of biochemistry and medicine were gathered by searching ISI's *SciSearch* database, while information on their 104 medical school health science libraries was obtained in the *Annual Statistics of Medical School Libraries in the United States & Canada*. Two regression models were employed for twenty-eight variables relating to characteristics of the faculty member, the article itself, the faculty member's institution, and the institution's health sciences library. Byrd discovered that neither the number of publications produced nor the number of journals cited in the publications correlated significantly with the size of the health science library journal collection. Rather, the numbers of publications and journals cited were associated primarily with gender, academic rank, and previous publishing experience. Assistant professors cited 29.77 journals per paper published, associate professors 35.23, and full professors 38.44. Byrd's research suggests that spending more on journal collections does not inevitably result in greater faculty productivity.

Dykeman, Amy. "Faculty Citations: An Approach to Assessing the Impact of Diminishing Resources on Scientific Research." **Library Acquisitions: Practice & Theory** 18 (summer 1994): 137–46.

The use of faculty citations for collection evaluation at the Georgia Institute of Technology library is described by Dykeman. Items cited by faculty in 1989 were located through the Information Services in Physics, Electronics, and Computers (INSPEC) database, covering such fields as electrical engineering, physics, and computer science, and ISI's *Science Citation Index.* A breakdown of 13,982 citations (from 711 articles) found that 64 percent were periodicals, 15 percent were monographs, and 12 percent proceedings. The library owned 91.2 percent of the periodical citations (despite the cancellation of about 25 percent of Georgia Tech's serials between 1976 and 1991) and 82.3 percent of all the cited resources.[9] Further analysis showed that 1,309 different periodicals were cited, of which 573 were cited only once and 143 ten or more times. The top twenty-five titles—listed in a table—accounted for 31 percent of the periodical citations. The author discusses the collection development implications of these findings as well as the results for six other formats, including proceedings and technical reports. Dykeman judges it "may be partially true" that "this study only reinforces the notion that the faculty primarily cite only what the library owns."

Gluibizzi, Amanda. "Citation Analysis in the Decorative Arts: A Tool for Shaping a Collection Development Policy for Serials." **Art Documentation** 21 (spring 2002): 23–26.

The author analyzed the 1,792 citations to serials in the fifty-four master's theses completed at the Bard Graduate Center for the Study of Decorative Arts, Design, and Culture through the spring of 2001. She found that 582 serials were cited, of which 370 were cited once while 28 were cited ten or more times. The ten most cited journal titles are listed in the appendix, which also lists the ten most frequently cited material types (headed by metal), the ten most highly cited categories (topped by fashion design) and the top ten material types in combination with a category (textile materials in fashion design ranked highest). Moreover, 47 percent of the total citations were to the decorative arts, and the most frequently cited publication date range was 1920 through 1940. Gluibizzi believes her study justifies the institution's serials collection development policy. Certainly it fills a niche in the literature.

Gooden, Angela M. "Citation Analysis of Chemistry Doctoral Dissertations: An Ohio State University Case Study." **Issues in Science & Technology Librarianship** 32 (fall 2001). [Electronic Journal.] Available: http://www.istl.org/istl/01-fall/refereed.html (accessed August 28, 2003).

Gooden, Angela M. "Regarding: Citation Analysis of Chemistry Doctoral Dissertations: An Ohio State University Case Study." **Issues in Science & Technology Librarianship** 33 (winter 2002). [Electronic Journal.] Available: http://www.istl.org/02-winter/letters.html#gooden (accessed August 28, 2003).

In order to assist in chemistry collection development, the author analyzed the citations in thirty randomly selected chemistry Ph.D. dissertations completed at Ohio State University between 1996 and 2000. Not unexpectedly, 85.8 percent of the 3,704 total citations were to journal articles and 8.4 percent to monographs. Gooden found that 12 of the 441 cited journals produced 50 percent of the citations to journals and the top 20, rank ordered in a table, accounted for 61 percent. The citation publication dates ranged from 1817 to 1999. Finally, 97.7 percent of the 441 journals and 86.2 percent of the 312 monographs were held by Ohio State Science and Engineering Library, while most of the unheld items were available elsewhere on campus or through OhioLINK.[10] In a subsequent communication (the second entry preceding this annotation) responding to a letter to the journal editor, Gooden presented histograms depicting the distribution of citations by date for the twenty most highly cited journals.

Greene, Robert J. "Computer Analysis of Local Citation Information in Collection Management." **Collection Management** 17, no. 4 (1993): 11–24.

A local citation study for the Emory University Physics Department is reported by Greene. A Dialog search of *SciSeach* covering 1988 through August 1991 retrieved 101 articles written by Emory physics faculty. They contained 2,617 citations, of which 83.4 percent were serials and 7.2 percent books. The serial articles' publication dates ranged from 1906 to 1991, and about half of them were produced by 11 of 276 titles. The researcher found that 96.8 percent of all the citations were owned by an Emory University library. Subject analysis of the serial citations showed that 49.06 percent fell in the physics segment of the LC classification, whereas about 43 percent were in chemistry, biology, or medicine. As 40 percent were housed in the Health Sciences or Chemistry libraries, Greene observes that use by physicists should by considered when canceling chemistry or biology journals—an important but sometimes unappreciated point in serials collection management.

Klassen, Timothy W. "Measuring Serials Usage Using Faculty Cited Journals Data." **Bottom Line** 14, no. 1 (2001): 37–43.

The use of faculty citation data in a major serials review project during the late 1990s at the Wesleyan University library is recounted here. Data from a reshelving study were supplemented with data on journals cited by the Wesleyan faculty, gathered from the ISI's three citation indexes: *SCI, SSCI,* and the *Arts and Humanities Citation Index.* A table indicates that 29 percent of 2,747 journals were cited by faculty, 57 percent were used in the library, 64 percent were either cited or used, 6 percent were cited but not used, and 36 percent were neither cited nor used. Almost 100 titles were cancelled, but 71 journals cited by faculty but not reshelved in the library were spared from cancellation because it "might have elicited controversy." A discussion of methodological issues acknowledges limitations to use of citations by faculty, that is, monographs and proceedings are missed and "the data can be expensive."

Lascar, Claudia, and Loren D. Mendelsohn. "An Analysis of Journal Use by Structural Biologists with Applications for Journal Collection Development Decisions." **College & Research Libraries** 62 (September 2001): 422–33.

This citation study was conducted to support journal selection at the Center for Structural Biology, established by a consortium of New York state research institutions on City University of New York's (CUNY's) City College campus in December 1998. A large section of the article explains the historical evolution of structural biology, defining it as studying the "relationship between molecular structure and function in the living cell." One hundred and six articles, identified through the *Web of Science* as published between 1995 and 1999 by ten affiliated researchers, serve as the study's source. Not surprisingly, 95.10 percent of 4,283 total citations were to journals (with 386 different titles cited) and only 4.09 percent to monographs. Two tables present, both in rank order, the 43 journals in which the researchers published and the 58 cited six or more times. Note that eight of the top ten titles on the two lists are the same. As a result of this exercise, six new journals were proposed for subscription. The authors state that a citation study provided helpful data because "the user group was unresponsive to both telephone and e-mail requests."

Loughner, William. "Scientific Journal Usage in a Large University Library: A Local Citation Analysis." **Serials Librarian** 29, nos. 3–4 (1996): 79–88.

Loughner explains the use of the *Science Citation Index CD-ROM* product to generate local citation data as a usage measure. The 1994 version identified 35,035 citations in 1,335 articles written by University of Georgia science faculty. Six steps are outlined for producing alphabetical and ranked journal lists:

1. Locate all articles in *SCI* by local faculty

2. Download all the identified citations to a computer file

3. Edit the citations to remove nonpertinent data

4. Sort into alphabetical order and combine identical titles

5. Edit the list to combine items cited differently into a single entry

6. Sort hierarchically to create a second (ranked) list

Altogether, 7,084 "publications," (the author states most "publications" were journals) were cited, of which 4,364 (61.6 percent) were cited once.[11] The top fifty produced 29 percent of all citations. A table rank orders the ten most frequently cited titles. While acknowledging limitations (student needs are not considered), Loughner contends this is a "practical way" to measure journal use. This paper is most valuable for its description of the methodology.

McCain, Katherine W. "Bibliometric Tools for Serials Collection Management in Academic Libraries." In **Advances in Serials Management,** vol. 6, edited by Cindy Hepfer, Teresa Malinowski, and Julia Gammon, 105–46. Greenwich, CT: JAI Press, 1997. ISBN 0-7623-0101-5.

An excellent overview of citation data's practical application to journal selection, cancellation, evaluation, and weeding is provided in this book chapter. The use of the Dialog Rank command to identify highly productive journals and to rank the journals published in or cited by a university's faculty members is explained. A thorough discussion of the *Journal Citation Reports* covers impact factor, alternate or modified forms of impact factor, immediacy index, and cited half-life. Other topics include the use of citation networks and cocitation analysis to identify core journals and various bibliometric measures of cost-effectiveness. McCain successfully integrates into her analysis a review of the appropriate literature published between 1985 and 1995, citing studies that illustrate the use of specific citation measures or discuss fundamental issues. Note that there are 110 footnotes. In short, this detailed contribution takes a well-grounded approach while also addressing theoretical issues.

Nisonger, Thomas E. "The Application of Citation Analysis to Serials Collection Management." In **Management of Serials in Libraries,** 121–56. Englewood, CO: Libraries Unlimited, 1998. ISBN 1-56308-213-6.

This chapter offers an overview of citation analysis and its role in serials management. Considerable attention is devoted to the *Journal Citation Reports,* explaining the types of data it contains (including total citations received and impact factor), as well as potential benefits and limitations, while offering practical tips on use of the *JCR.* Then Bradfordian distribution is illustrated with specific examples and possible applications suggested, such as identifying core journals, setting priorities among journal titles, and demonstrating the law of diminishing returns in serials management. Other chapter sections discuss local citation studies, the structure of disciplines as indicated by citation patterns, citation data's role in budgeting, and pertinent research regarding citation analysis. The author concludes that citation analysis, although traditionally used for the print format, is also applicable to electronic journals. An unannotated bibliography of twenty-five items follows the chapter.

Ovens, Cora S. H. "Citation Patterns of University of the Orange Free State Scientists." **South African Journal of Library & Information Science** 63 (June 1995): 47–55.

After science department faculty complaints about a sudden 10 percent serials budget cut, a local citation study was conducted at the University of the Orange Free State in South Africa. The final analysis was based on 132 articles by faculty from five departments containing 2,844 citations, downloaded from the *Science Citation Index* CD-ROM covering January 1993–May 1994, and a questionnaire surveying fifty-two faculty (78.7 percent responded) concerning the source of information about their citations and how the items were obtained. Tables list the ten journals most frequently cited by each department and the twenty-five highest cited by all five departments. The library owned 76 percent of fifty different titles (there was overlap among the lists).[12] The questionnaire found that 36.26 percent of the citations were identified through the "invisible college," that is, a network of colleagues, and 35.16 percent through "seeing the citation in a published article." Moreover, 50.55 percent of the cited items were obtained through the library (34.62 percent via subscription and 15.93 percent ILL), while 43.41 percent were procured from colleagues. The especially detailed description of the methodology acknowledges drawing, in part, upon the work of Dykeman (see entry earlier in this chapter).

Shontz, David. "The Serial/Monograph Ratio in Psychology: Application at the Local Level." **Behavioral & Social Sciences Librarian** 11, no. 2 (1992): 91–105.

Articles, identified in the *PsycINFO* and *PsychLIT* databases as published in 1989 by University of Florida faculty, served as this study's source. A breakdown by format demonstrated that 76 percent of 3,326 citations were to journals, 13 percent to monographs, and 11 percent to edited monographic volumes. Shontz found 65 percent of the citations were to the last ten years with 1986 being "the peak year." Moreover, the serial/monograph citation ratio was essentially the same for items published before and after 1979. Tables analyze the citations by department of the author and subareas of psychology, although these findings are not emphasized in the text. Based on this local citation study and journal price data, the author concludes that psychology, for library budgeting purposes, should be treated as a science rather than a social science, where only 30 percent to 50 percent of the citations are normally to journals.

Stankus, Tony, and Carolyn V. Mills. "Which Life Science Journals Will Constitute the Locally Sustainable Core Collection of the 1990s and Which Will Become 'Fax-Access' Only? Predictions Based on Citation and Price Patterns 1979–1989." **Science & Technology Libraries** 13 (fall 1992): 73–114.

After discussing the benefits of fax access as an alternative to subscription, Stankus and Mills propose the Cited By Leading Journal method for developing a local core collection. They outline a three-step procedure: identify the leading journal by examining ten years of *JCR* rankings, identify through the *JCR's* Citing Journal Package several other titles cited by the impact factor leader, and reach selection/deselection decisions by comparing citation data with cost. Most of the article is devoted to describing the method's application in ten life sciences specialty areas including biochemistry, molecular biology, general cell biology, and developmental biology. This essay concludes with a table organizing fifty-six life sciences journals into four categories: "subscriptions highly secure," "subscriptions somewhat secure," "some fax migration," and "frequent fax migration." See the earlier entry by Altmann and Gorman concerning the CBLJ approach's applicability to Australian libraries.

Tsay, Ming-yueh. "The Relationship Between Journal Use in a Medical Library and Citation Use." **Bulletin of the Medical Library Association** 86 (January 1998): 31–39.

This investigation, based on the author's doctoral dissertation, examines the relationship between journal use (as measured by a reshelving count) in the Veterans General Hospital Library in Taiwan and total citation and impact factor scores in the 1997 *Journal Citation Reports*. The author found that frequently published journals displayed higher use and citation rates. A table lists the fifty most highly used journals. Analysis of the 835 titles used between November 1994 and April 1995 found statistically significant correlations between use and both total citations and impact factor, but the former was more strongly associated with use. Twenty-four of the top fifty titles by use and total citations were identical, whereas seventeen of the top fifty by use and impact factor were the same. Thus, Tsay suggests that total citation data predict actual usage better than do impact factor data.

Walcott, Rosalind. "Local Citation Studies: A Shortcut to Local Knowledge." **Science & Technology Libraries** 14, no. 3 (1994): 1–14.

In order to obtain, in face of budget cuts, "local knowledge" about use of the Biology Library at SUNY at Stony Brook, Walcott sampled 2,030 of 13,100 citations in the eighty theses and dissertations written by Division of Biological Sciences graduate students between 1989 and 1992. The author found that 91.8 percent of the citations were to serials and 8.2 percent to books, thus reaffirming "the importance placed on serials by biologists." Two hundred ninety-five of the 700 journals the library subscribes to were cited, with 22 providing 50 percent of the citations and 45 two-thirds of them. A table displays the top 45 journals while other tables list the leading journals in several biology subareas. By language, 99.7 percent of the citations were in English, 0.2 percent in French, and 0.1 percent in German. Although one citation was 189 years old, the median age was 5 years and the last ten years accounted for 80 percent of the citations. It is noteworthy that a higher proportion of books (19.3 percent) was cited in ecology and evolution than in other biology subareas.

Walcott, Rosalind. "Serials Cited by Marine Sciences Research Center Faculty, University at Stony Brook, 1986–1991." **Science & Technology Libraries** 14, no. 3 (1994): 15–33.

Updating a study of faculty serials use by Doris Williams published in 1989, Walcott examined the citations in 130 of the 285 books, book chapters, and articles published between 1986 and 1991 by faculty associated with SUNY at Stony Brook's Marine Science Research Center.[13] She found that 78.8 percent of the citations were to serials and 21.2 percent to "monographic works." Ten of the 415 cited serial titles accounted for 41.9 percent of the serial citations, and 52 covered 79.4 percent of the citations. These 52 are rank ordered in a table, and another table lists all 415 titles in alphabetical order along with their number of citations (perhaps more information than the reader wants). Ironically, even though this investigation's primary emphasis is on serials, the author concludes that books, dissertations, and theses are also important to marine science.

Zipp, Louise S. "Identifying Core Geologic Research Journals: A Model for Interlibrary Cooperative Collection Development." In **Changing Gateways; The Impact of Technology on Geoscience Information Exchange: Proceedings of the Twenty-Ninth Meeting of the Geoscience Information Society, October 24–27, 1994, Seattle, Washington,** vol. 25, edited by Barbara E. Haner and Jim O'Donnell, 59–65. Alexandria, VA: Geoscience Information Society, 1995. ISBN 0-934485-23-2.

This study focuses on citations to serials in publications and grant applications written by geosciences faculty at the University of Iowa (UI), Iowa State University, and the University of Northern Iowa during 1991 to 1993. A table lists in rank order the thirty-eight serial titles, costing $21,399, most frequently cited by faculty from the three institutions combined. Zipp calls these titles "the Regents' Collection" because the three universities are governed by the State Board of Regents. Four other tables list the most highly cited titles by each institution's faculty and in grant applications with the three universities combined. Twenty-four of the twenty-six (92.3 percent) titles on the UI list were held by that library, and all twenty-nine on the list of titles cited in grant applications were held by at least one of the three libraries. Five uncited titles costing greater than $500 annually were identified as candidates for cancellation. Stressing the project's labor-intensive nature, Zipp candidly comments "there were several instances when I gave ambiguous instructions and work had to be redone." This entry is notable because it reports a state-wide citation study.

CITATION DATA IN COLLECTION EVALUATION

Barooah, P. K., D. Begum, and N. N. Sharma. "Bibliometric Study of Doctoral Dissertations in Organic Chemistry Submitted by S & T Workers of RRL, Jorhat to Evaluate the Utility Factor of the Library." **Annals of Library Science & Documentation** 46 (March 1999): 1–8.

This entry is based on analysis of 4,253 citations in nineteen organic chemistry doctoral dissertations, completed between 1977 and 1997, from various unnamed universities presumably on the Indian subcontinent. The half-life of the cited items was a surprisingly high twenty-seven years. A breakdown by format reveals 85.42 percent of the citations were to journals and 8.30 percent to books. The thirty most frequently cited journals (only two of which were Indian) accounted for 85 percent of the serial citations and are listed in rank order. The Regional Research Laboratory Library, in the city of Jorhat (Assam state of India) owned twenty-two of these thirty journals and could supply 86.40 percent of the journal citations from its collection. This article suggests that Indian organic chemists heavily rely on non-Indian journals.

Ching, Joanna Tan Yeok, and K. R. Chennupati. "Collection Evaluation Through Citation Analysis Techniques: A Case Study of the Ministry of Education, Singapore." **Library Review** 51, no. 8 (2002): 398–405.

This entry discusses a citation-based evaluation of the Singapore Ministry of Education library collection. A breakdown of 2,089 citations compiled from thirty-five teachers' guides in eight secondary school subject area found that 96.89 percent were to books and only 1.48 percent to journals. Further analysis of the book citations showed that 69 percent were published between 1980 and 1994 with less than 20 percent published prior to 1980. Then, checking the 1,528 unique titles against the library's holdings revealed that 19.1 percent were in the collection. A table presents comparative results from checking other education libraries: the National Institute of Education library held 56.4 percent, the Institute of Southeast Asia held 16.2 percent, and the Regional Language Centre held 1.4 percent. Thus, it is no surprise that a supplemental study of 221 ILL transactions between July 1995 and July 1999 revealed that 70.13 percent of the requests had been sent to the National Institute of Education library.

Crotteau, Mark. "Support for Biological Research by an Academic Library: A Journal Citation Study." **Science & Technology Libraries** 17, no. 1 (1997): 67–86.

Crotteau constructed his evaluation on the 4,231 unique journal citations in 140 of the faculty and student publications (those available in the library) listed in the University of North Carolina at Chapel Hill Biology Department 1989–90 annual report. Of the 708 cited journals, the campus libraries had complete holdings for 65 percent, partial holdings for 23 percent, and no holdings for 12 percent. Completely held journals accounted for 81 percent of the citations, whereas fewer than 3 percent of citations were to journals not held at all. A survey of faculty who cited unheld items indicated 40 percent had obtained a reprint, 26 percent visited another library, and 16 percent owned personal subscriptions. An appendix lists the 101 most frequently cited titles and their rank by *JCR* data. A comparison of the two rankings found a 0.527 correlation, which increased to 0.622 when interdisciplinary journals were eliminated. Findings from earlier research are integrated into the thoughtful conclusion. This is a complex and well-done study.

Edwards, Sherri. "Citation Analysis As a Collection Development Tool: A Bibliometric Study of Polymer Science Theses and Dissertations." **Serials Review** 25, no. 1 (1999): 11–20.

The study is based upon 5,874 citations in thirty-two dissertations and thirty-two theses (a 25 percent sample) completed in polymer science and polymer engineering at the University of Akron between 1990 and 1996. A breakdown by format showed that 72.8 percent of the citations were to journals, 15.4 percent to monographs, and 4.6 percent to patents. Four of the 405 cited journal titles accounted for 25 percent of the citations, while forty titles produced 75 percent. A table lists the forty most frequently cited journal titles. The University of Akron libraries subscribed to thirty-six of these, whereas two had ceased publication and two had previously been cancelled. The ten least cost-effective journals are also listed. A comparison of the citation data with the results of an ongoing reshelving count revealed that several low-citation journals had high reshelving counts. Thus, Edwards stresses that both citation data and shelving counts are necessary for "a complete picture of journal use."

Heidenwolf, Terese. "Evaluating an Interdisciplinary Research Collection." **Collection Management** 18, nos. 3–4 (1994): 33–48.

In this project, a 623 citation sample (selected from each 1991 article in five epidemiological journals, including the *American Journal of Epidemiology*) was used as a checklist to evaluate the epidemiology collection of the University of Michigan library system and its public health branch. Heidenwolf found that 89.57 percent of the citations were held by the University of Michigan libraries and 57.30 percent by the public health branch, but only 23.76 percent were unique to the latter. The library system held 94.94 percent of the cited serials, 74.67 percent of the books, and 91.57 percent of the English language citations contrasted to 22.22 percent of those in other languages. However, there was no statistically significant difference in the percentage of items held by decade of publication. Analysis of the sample to explore characteristics of the epidemiological literature revealed, among other things, that 82.50 percent were serials and 12.04 percent monographs. Heidenwolf's article is especially interesting to this book's author because she cites earlier work by Nisonger as the source of her methodology for selecting citations.[14]

Iya, Jameela Abba. "A Citation Study of Education Dissertations at the University of Maiduguri, Nigeria." **African Journal of Library, Archives, & Information Science** 6 (October 1996): 129–32.

Iya investigated the references in fifty-six of the sixty dissertations submitted to the Department of Education for the M. Ed. degree at the University of Maiduguri between 1983 and 1991. Analysis by format demonstrated that 40.3 percent of 2,377 citations were to monographs, 22.4 percent to journals, and 14.3 percent to conference proceedings. A table lists the ten most frequently cited journals. Seven of these, but not the titles ranked first and third, were held by the library. The author claims her study could assist selection of education journals in Nigerian University libraries.

Johnson, William T. "Citation Analysis of the Texas Tech University's Statistics Faculty: A Study Applied to Collection Development at the University Library." **LIBRES: Library & Information Science Research** 6 (September 1996). [Electronic Journal.] Available: http://libres.curtin.edu.au/libre6n3/johnson.htm (accessed August 29, 2003).

This electronic journal article reports a local citation study conducted at the Texas Tech University (TTU) library. The investigation is based on citations in fourteen articles published during 1993 and the first half of 1994 by the seven faculty in the Mathematics Department's statistics program. The study focuses on the 122 titles that were cited rather than the 394 citations they contained: 46.7 percent of the titles were journals and 36.9 percent monographs. The TTU library owned 68.4 percent of the journals and 60 percent of the books. When the analysis is restricted to titles cited three or more times (presumably the most important) 46.7 percent were journals and 36.9 percent monographs. Furthermore, TTU held 81 percent of the former and 75 percent of the latter. Johnson found that if three monographs and two journal subscriptions were added, the library would hold 90 percent of the heavily cited titles. The average age of all cited titles was 12.3 years, compared to 11.2 years for those cited three or more times. This entry demonstrates the practical use of a local citation study. See the next entry for a similar study by the same author.

Johnson, William T. "Environmental Impact: A Preliminary Citation Analysis of Local Faculty in a New Academic Program in Environmental and Human Health Applied to Collection Development at Texas Tech University Library." **LIBRES: Library & Information Science Research** 9 (March 31, 1999). [Electronic Journal.] Available: http://libres.curtin.edu.au/libre9n1/toxcite.htm (accessed August 29, 2003); "Environmental Impact: A Preliminary Citation Analysis of Local Faculty in a New Academic Program in Environmental and Human Health Applied to Collection Development in an Academic Library." *Library Philosophy & Practice* 2 (spring 2000). [Electronic Journal.] Available: http://www.uidaho.edu/~mbolin/johnson.html (accessed August 29, 2003).

As acknowledged by Johnson, this article appears in two different electronic journals. Modeled upon his earlier work, this citation study was conducted at Texas Tech University's Institute of Environmental and Human Health. The source was 950 references in twenty-four papers published by nine Institute faculty during 1996 and 1997. It was found that 67 percent of the references were to journals and 17 percent to books. The average citation age was 9.4 years for books and 10.5 to journals, contrary to the more typical finding that cited books are older than cited journals. The TTU library owned 58 percent of the cited books and 66 percent of the journals. As a result of Johnson's study, eight books were acquired, twelve journals reviewed for possible subscription, and more than fifty keyword/subject terms identified to aid book selection. Tables in the appendix rank order the thirty-three most frequently cited journals and the fifty-two most highly cited books. Also appended is an internal Texas Tech University library document containing data on collection expenditures, holdings, and ILL performance. Although somewhat carelessly written, this article is more detailed and sophisticated than the author's other study.

Ruddy, Margaret. "Using Citation Analysis to Identify and Monitor Journal Usage by Off-Campus Graduate Students. " In **Eight Off-Campus Library Services Conference Proceedings: Providence, Rhode Island, April 22–24, 1998,** edited by Thomas P. Steven and Maryhelen Jones, 239–43. Mount Pleasant, MI: Central Michigan University, 1998.

The 100 master's theses submitted in 1996 for the Programs in Management for Adults at Cardinal Stritch University, located in Milwaukee, serve as Ruddy's source. The findings are presented separately for theses from region one, on campus, and region two, the remainder of Wisconsin, and as raw numbers (all percentages in this annotation are Nisonger's calculations). Of 1,208 citations in region one theses, 60.6 percent were to serials and 30.9 percent to books, while the breakdown of 923 region two citations was 64.5 percent serials and 24.9 percent books. The library held 57.5 percent of the 280 different serials titles cited in region one and 57.2 percent of the 285 cited by region two theses. Because only thirteen serials (a combined total from the two regions) were cited ten or more times, the author decides that development of a core journal list "is almost impossible." While not a topnotch study, evaluations of collections serving adult education programs (an increasingly important trend) are always welcome.

Soehner, Catherine B., S. Tanner Wray, and Daniel T. Richards. "The Landmark Citation Method: Analysis of a Citation Pattern As a Collection Assessment Method." **Bulletin of the Medical Library Association** 80 (October 1992): 361–66.

The "landmark citation method," which uses citations to a highly cited article as a checklist for collection evaluation, is introduced here. The technique was developed at the National Library of Medicine for assessing its collection's comprehensiveness in the newly emerging field of biotechnology. A 10 percent sample was taken from the more than 11,000 citations to an article by two-time Nobel Prize winner Frederick Sanger and two co-authors.[15] This resulted in an "initial assessment bibliography" of 135 different journal titles and 2 books, although 8 journals were eliminated as out-of-scope according to the NLM collection development policy. The library owned 99.2 percent of the final list of 127 journals, but there were not enough books for meaningful analysis. The entry concludes by describing this method's advantages, such as it is useful for emerging disciplines, it "eliminates bibliography bias," and so on, as well as disadvantages, such as it is restricted to the cited literature, expensive, and does not consider the user.

Sylvia, Margaret J. "Citation Analysis As an Unobtrusive Method for Journal Collection Evaluation Using Psychology Student Research Bibliographies." **Collection Building** 17, no. 1 (1998): 20–28.

Following a review of the citation analysis literature's application to psychology journals, this entry reports an evaluation at St. Mary's University library in San Antonio, Texas, based on citations in 157 Psychology Department graduate and undergraduate student papers during the three consecutive semesters from fall 1994 to fall 1995. When unverified titles and citations were deleted, 1,289 citations to 383 journals remained, of which 197 titles were cited only once. The top 23 percent of the journals accounted for 66 percent of the citations. A checklist evaluation determined 70 percent of the citations as well as 13 of the 14 most frequently cited journals and 15 of the 16 most cost-effective titles (calculated according to cost per citation) were held by the library. Analysis by date revealed that 60 percent of the citations were to the 1990s and only 2 percent predated the 1970s. See the next entry for a similar study in the same library.

Sylvia, Margaret J., and Marcella Lesher. "What Journals Do Psychology Graduate Students Need? A Citation Analysis of Thesis References." **College & Research Libraries** 56 (July 1995): 313–18.

Three techniques were used to evaluate the psychology serials at the St. Mary's University library: citation counts, cost per citation, and reshelving counts. Citations were counted in dissertations and theses written by psychology and counseling students during a six-year period (possibly 1989 through 1994 although this fact is not made explicit). Twenty percent of the 376 cited journal titles accounted for 62 percent of the 1,732 citations. A table lists the 28 titles cited ten or more times. Twenty-one of these 28 (75 percent) and 58 of the top 75 (77.3 percent) were held by the library.[16] Analysis of cost per use, that is, per citation, found that 30 titles had a cost per use of less than $100. A brief analysis of 1991–92 reshelving counts showed that several highly used titles had low citation counts. Accordingly, Sylvia and Lesher conclude, "Each technique complements the other." The authors could have done a better job of presenting their data.

Thomas, Joy. "Graduate Student Use of Journals: A Bibliometric Study of Psychology Theses." **Behavioral & Social Sciences Librarian** 12, no. 1 (1993): 1–7.

To gather data to assist with a serials cancellation project, the California State University at Long Beach (CSULB) library analyzed the citations in 342 psychology theses written at the university from 1981 through 1990. The theses contained 7,797 citations to 1,050 journals, of which 14.2 percent were cited ten or more times and 47.6 percent only once. Illustrating the importance of interdisciplinarity to scholarship, only 37.4 percent of the citations were to psychology journals, while 16.0 percent were to sociology journals, 10.5 percent to management journals, and 8.8 percent to nursing. The CSULB library owned 66.6 percent of the cited journals and 91.9 percent of the cited articles. Of the 140 psychology journals subscribed to by CSULB, 75 percent were cited at least once, whereas the other 25 percent became candidates for cancellation. The twenty most frequently cited journals are listed in a table. Only 7 of these appeared among the top twenty on lists similarly compiled at Indiana University and DePauw University in an earlier study by Larry Hardesty and Gail Oltmanns, which was the "inspiration" for this investigation.[17]

Thomas, Joy. "Never Enough: Graduate Student Use of Journals—Citation Analysis of Social Work Theses." **Behavioral & Social Sciences Librarian** 19, no. 1 (2000): 1–16.

The source for this citation study of journals is the 22,183 citations in approximately 1,000 Master of Social Work (MSW) theses written at California State University at Long Beach between 1987 and 1996. Because 0.78 percent of the citations were unconfirmed, Thomas states her findings can assume to be no more than 99.22 percent accurate. In total 1,964 journals were cited: 19.1 percent were cited ten or more times and 40.5 percent were cited just once. Three journals produced 10 percent of the citations, and 10 journals produced 20 percent. Thomas observed a "logarithmical" pattern in which the number of journals approximately doubles with each additional 10 percent of citations. Additional findings were the following:

1. Sixteen point four percent of the titles produced 80.01 percent of the citations.

2. The average citation age was 4.94 years in all journals, but 8.05 years in the top 100.

3. The subject distribution was highly interdisciplinary as 23.72 percent of the citations came from social work, 14.56 percent from health and medicine, and 7.32 percent from sociology.

4. Ninety-one point six percent of the citations were held by the library system.

A table names in rank order the fifty most frequently cited journals along with the average citation age for each. This is a thoughtful and well-done study.

STRUCTURES OF DISCIPLINES AND SUBJECTS

Social Sciences

Ashman, Allen B. "A Bibliometric Look at Four Regional Library Publications." **Kentucky Libraries** 64 (spring 2000): 3–8.

Ashman's bibliometric investigation analyzes citations in articles from *Indiana Libraries, Kentucky Libraries, Illinois Libraries,* and *Tennessee Librarian* during the years 1994 through 1997. Data is presented separately for each journal, but of the 865 total citations in all four, 56.5 percent were to serials, 24.7 percent to books, 4.8 percent to primary legal material, 3.6 percent to Web sites, and 2.0 percent to interviews. A total of 181 different serial titles were cited, of which 61 percent were cited only once and 75.7 percent in only one journal. The six most frequently cited serials are listed collectively and for each journal, while the number "outside of librarianship" is deemed surprising. The author also addresses other topics beyond this book's scope such as the average number of references per article and author publication history. This item is noteworthy because of its focus on regional library science journals.

Berman, Yitzhak, and A. Solomon Eaglstein. "The Knowledge Base of Social Work: A Citation Analysis." **Aslib Proceedings** 46 (September 1994): 225–30.

The 1992 volumes of three U.S. social work journals, including the *Journal of Social Service Research,* and two United Kingdom journals, including the *British Journal of Social Work,* were used as sources for this citation study. Books accounted for 34.3 percent of the 5,129 citations, followed by nonsocial work journals, 29.5 percent; gray documents, 19.3 percent; and social work journals, 16.8 percent. U.S. journals were more likely than their British counterparts to cite both social work journals and those from other disciplines, whereas United Kingdom journals cited books and gray literature with greater frequency. Because less than one-fifth of the citations were to social work journals, the authors question previous social work city studies based exclusively on the field's journals.

Bliss, Nonie Janet. "International Librarianship: A Bibliometric Analysis of the Field." **International Information & Library Review** 25 (June 1993): 93–107.

This investigation is based on citations in the 605 articles and books indexed under the term "international librarianship" in *Library Literature* from 1958 through 1990. The study uses a 10 percent sample (935 of 9,252 citations). Bliss found that 86.98 percent of the citations were from library and information science. The other leading disciplines were education, 4.68 percent, political science, 1.26 percent, and law, 1.26 percent. A breakdown by place of publication suggested a "dominance by the more industrialized countries," as 40.00 percent were published in the United States, 15.50 percent in Great Britain, and 6.41 percent in the former West Germany. Not surprisingly, 85.03 percent were in English followed by 7.70 percent in German. A table lists in rank order the ten most frequently cited journals. Price's Index, which calculates the percentage of citations to the five most recent years, stood at 66.21 percent, qualifying the field as a "hard science."[18] Data is also presented on authorship patterns, the number of citations per document, and distribution of the source documents by publication data. Bliss decides that international librarianship is both "self-sufficient" and "extremely insular."

Buchanan, Anne L., and Jean-Pierre V. M. Hérubel. "Interdisciplinarity: The Case of Historical Geography Through Citation Analysis." **Collection Building** 14, no. 1 (1994): 15–21.

To examine the interdisciplinary make-up of historical geography (which a diagram depicts as the intersection of human geography, physical geography, and history) this research project analyzed the citations to journals in every third issue of the *Journal of Historical Geography* during the years 1975 through 1993. Among the 1,019 total citations, 20.90 percent were to geography and 15.57 percent to history. The respective percentages rise to 35.32 and 26.69 when limited to the 603 citations in titles cited twice and to 42.83 and 24.54 when restricted to the 383 citations from the thirty-four journals cited five or more times. These thirty-four titles, listed in a table, indicate, according to the authors, the influence of economic history, "the official organs of historical societies," interdisciplinary journals, and "top geography journals" on the field. Price's Index ranged from 13.79 percent in 1976 to 56.68 percent in 1984 with an overall average of 31.18 percent. Buchanan and Hérubel conclude that historical geography "is indeed complex and heavily social science dependent." As indicated by the authors, their research demonstrates that citation analysis can be applied to subdisciplines as well as entire disciplines.

Buttlar, Lois. "Information Sources in Library and Information Science Doctoral Research." **Library & Information Science Research** 21, no. 2 (1999): 227–45.

Buttlar's study is structured on 7,980 citations in sixty-one Ph.D. dissertations (forty-seven in library science and fourteen in information science) completed at ALA accredited LIS programs between July 1994 and March 1997, representing a 47 percent sample size. The author offers a lengthy and thorough review of earlier library and information science citation studies. Analysis by format revealed that 46.15 percent of the citations were to journal articles, 31.88 percent to books, and 7.32 percent to book chapters. Less than half the citations (49.54 percent) were to library and information science (11.45 percent were to education and 5.72 percent to computer science) contradicting previous research by James K. Bracken and John Mack Tucker, Bluma C. Peritz, and Jeffrey N. Gaten that found much lower levels of interdisciplinary research in LIS.[19] Altogether 815 different journals were cited. A ranked list of the twenty-five most frequently cited titles shows that *College and Research Libraries* and *Journal of the American Society for Information Science* are in a tie for first place. Distribution by country of publication found 83.08 percent were from the United States, 8.38 percent from England, and 1.93 percent from Canada. By publication date, 2.93 percent were less then two years old, 24.05 percent less than five years old, and 55.67 percent less than ten years old.[20] Buttlar rejects the contention that information science corresponds to a "hard science" more than does library science because the citation patterns by format and publication date are quite similar for the two fields. This exceedingly well-done and interesting citation study also contains data on authorship patterns and gender, the distribution of dissertations by university, and the topics and types of libraries covered.

Goedeken, Edward A. "Diplomatic History As Interdisciplinary History: A Citation Study of the Journal Literature." **Society for Historians of American Foreign Relations Newsletter** 23 (December 1992): 1–7.

Scholarly journals cited in *Diplomatic History* from 1977 to 1991 form the basis of this study. It was found that 39.1 percent of the 434 cited titles were interdisciplinary, 27.4 percent were in history, and 17.1 percent in political science, while 57.2 percent of the 2,034 citations were in history, 23.1 percent in political science, and 13.7 percent were interdisciplinary. Only 8.2 percent of the titles and 3.9 percent of the citations were in "foreign," that is, non-English, languages. The most frequent languages for these titles were, respectively, German, French, and Italian, and for citations, Italian, French, and German. Tables rank order the leading seventeen history journals (the text refers to "twenty" so there may be an editorial error in the table), the twenty most cited in political science as well as the top ten interdisciplinary titles. The most frequently cited articles are also listed. Goedeken concludes that diplomatic history is "an interdisciplinary field, dominated by English language sources."

Goedeken, Edward A., and Jean-Pierre V. M. Hérubel. "Periodical Dispersion in American History: Observations on Article Bibliographies from the **Journal of American History.**" **Serials Librarian** 27, no. 1 (1995): 59–74.

This essay about research trends in American history is based on analysis of the bibliographies of current research articles in each quarterly issue of *Journal of American History* during 1980, 1985, and 1990. The articles were widely dispersed among thirty-six subareas. Careful examination of a table reveals that the largest subarea, "intellectual" history, provided only 6.5 percent of 6,906 articles followed by religion at 6.2 percent.[21] The 504 cited journal titles fell into fourteen subject categories, headed by history (48.6 percent), interdisciplinary (21.3 percent), general (7.3 percent), and political science (5.8 percent). An exceedingly lengthy table presents the number of articles in thirty-five subject areas published by each of the top 20 journals. The authors conclude that their research shows "a heightened profile of transdisciplinary and interdisciplinary activity" in American history. This item takes a somewhat atypical approach because it is based on bibliographies and thus measures the number of articles contributed to the discipline rather than citations received from other journals.

Jaffe, Eugene D. "International Marketing Textbooks: A Citation Analysis As an Indicator of the Discipline's Boundaries." **International Marketing Review** 14, no. 1 (1997): 9–19.

Jaffe's investigation uses as sources the fifteen international marketing textbooks, published between 1988 and 1995, that are, according to the author's survey, most frequently used in U.S. and European business schools. Of 6,166 citations, 50.3 percent were to marketing and 16 percent were to economics and international business. The final tabulation of data regarding cited journals was limited to those titles cited in ten of the fifteen textbooks, resulting in a list of fifty-five. A table rank orders the top fifteen based on the percentage of total journal citations they received—a somewhat unusual approach. About 25 percent of the journal citations were to marketing titles. Another table lists the most cited authors and their impact is analyzed. This is an interesting but not especially outstanding piece of research.

Joswick, Kathleen E. "A Profile of Police Administration Resources: Using Text-book Citations to Determine Collecting Parameters." **Library Collections, Acquisitions, & Technical Services** 25 (summer 2001): 159–69.

Joswick's citation study of police administration, a field of criminal justice, uses as sources the 1997 or 1998 editions of four "heavily used" undergraduate textbooks. A breakdown of the 3,098 citations by format revealed 39 percent were to books or book chapters and 24 percent were to serials, whereas there was only one citation to a Web site. Altogether 229 journals were cited, of which 12 were cited ten or more times and 160 were cited only once. The top five produced about 80 percent of the journal citations. A table lists the twenty most frequently cited titles in rank order without presenting the actual citation data. Analysis by LC classification number showed that 47 percent of the citations were to criminal justice administration, 12.45 percent to business/labor, and 8.44 percent to law. The median publication date was 1977 for books and book chapters, 1985 for serials, and 1980 overall. Note that highly cited authors as well as professional organizations and associations are also listed. These findings, as stressed by the author, can be applied to collection development in support of the teaching function because the investigation is based on textbooks.

Metoyer-Duran, Cheryl. "The American Indian Culture and Research Journal and the American Indian Quarterly: A Citation Analysis." **American Indian Culture & Research Journal** 17, no. 4 (1993): 25–54.

Metoyer-Duran investigated scholarly communications patterns in American Indian studies using the 4,212 citations in 198 randomly selected articles from the *American Indian Culture and Research Journal,* 1971–90, and the *American Indian Quarterly,* 1974–90. Her findings may be summarized as follows:

- About 99 percent of the citations were in English, while no American Indian language was cited.

- Fourteen percent of the citations were to primary sources and 86 percent to secondary sources.

- Ninety-two point one percent of the citations were to the print medium and 1.4 percent to microformat.

- Forty-eight point eight percent of the citations were to books, followed by journals (21.3 percent) and government documents (8.7 percent).

- Fifty-seven subjects were cited, headed by anthropology (33.5 percent) and U.S. history (10.9 percent).

- Forty-six point six percent of the cited items were published from 1970 to 1990, while 11.1 percent predated 1900.

A table lists the nineteen most cited journals, of which only one is in the field of American Indian studies. In addition, she compared citation patterns in books and journals plus citation patterns between the two source journals, analyzed the characteristics of the citing documents, and identified the leading citing and cited authors. This is an especially detailed and well-done investigation.

Metoyer-Duran, Cheryl, and Peter Hernon. "Economic Development on American Indian Reservations: A Citation Analysis." **Library & Information Science Research** 17 (winter 1995): 49–67.

"Gaming" and "natural resources and the environment" in the context of American Indian reservations are analyzed in this citation study. Fifty-seven works, all published since 1975 and identified through a variety of sources, were used as the source. The most frequently cited authors are listed and multiple authorship patterns examined. Metoyer-Duran and Hernon found that 48.1 percent of 2,799 citations were to government publications.[22] Among these, 88.4 percent were to the U.S. national government, 5.5 percent to state governments, 3.5 percent to tribal governments, and 2.4 percent to international organizations. Tables show that for both topics, the most frequently cited government publications were court cases and statutes, and court reporters were the highest cited nongovernment publication. Another table lists the most frequently cited governmental and nongovernmental titles. The median publication date of the citations was 1983 in gaming, 1979 in natural resources, and 1980 when the two are combined. This follow-up to Metoyer-Duran's earlier investigation (see previous entry) demonstrates the importance of government documents in the study of contemporary American Indian affairs.

Mohanta, Rabindra Nath. "Information Use Pattern of Indian Library and Information Scientists." **Herald of Library Science** 31 (July/October 1992): 217–24.

Citations in the 1985 through 1989 volumes of five Indian library and information science journals serve as this investigation's source. The author found that 47.31 percent of the 4,022 total citations were to periodicals and 35.28 percent to books. The fifteen most frequently cited periodicals (listed in rank order in a table along with their country of origin) accounted for 45.83 percent of the periodical citations. The text states that five of these fifteen titles were published in India, but the table itself indicated that six were. The table also indicated that five are U.S. journals. Analysis by age revealed a 7.7 year half-life for periodicals and 10.3 years for books. Journal self-citation data is also reported. This is not an outstanding study, but it provides data about LIS communications patterns in India.

Sciences

Arora, Jagdish, and Sharan Pal Kaur. "Bibliometric Analysis of Core Journals on Immunology: A Study Based on the **Annual Review of Immunology**." **Annals of Library Science & Documentation** 41 (September 1994): 81–94.

Arguing the benefits of using review articles as a source for citation studies, Arora and Kaur analyze the citations in 87 articles published in the *Annual Review of Immunology* between 1983 and 1986. Of 10,830 citations, 92.558 percent were to journals and 4.432 percent to books. The 66 most cited journals, out of 425 titles, were considered the core and listed in rank order in a table with, in an unusual twist, impact factor being used to break tied positions. The journal citations were highly concentrated with the top two titles accounting for 29.679 percent of that format's citations and the top four 47.955 percent. The half-life of the journal citations was less than six years, while the oldest citation dated to 1874. Further investigation of the 66 core journals showed that 33.33 percent were in the medical sciences and 31.82 percent in immunology, while 65.151 percent were published in the United States and 18.181 percent in the United Kingdom. Bradford's Law is applied to the journal citations, and additional data is provided about core journals in the biomedical sciences. Although published in India, this entry does not display a pro-Indian bias because it uses a U.S. title as the source.

Butkovich, Nancy J., Joni Gomez, and Vicki Baker. "Formats of Cited References in Geological Journal Literature, 1965–1985." **Collection Management** 16, no. 2 (1992): 61–73.

The references in articles from five leading geology journals (*Journal of Petrology, American Journal of Science, Journal of Geology, Bulletin of the Geological Society of America,* and *American Mineralogist*) were analyzed at ten-year intervals: 1965, 1975, and 1985. The 5,374 total citations were broken down into twelve formats, distributed as follows: journals, 64.7 percent; monographs and monographic series, 14.0 percent; U.S. documents, 4.6 percent; conference papers, 4.6 percent; and foreign documents, 2.9 percent. All other categories were 2.1 percent or less. The high rate of monographic citations was an "unexpected finding." The authors observe "the distribution of formats remained stable" over the twenty years. The "just under 5%" increase in the proportion of journals fell within the sampling error margin. The results are compared with those of earlier citation studies in geology and other scientific disciplines. This item differs from most similar studies by focusing on a single variable (format) and offering a longitudinal comparison.

Darko-Ampem, K.O. "An Analysis of the Literature of Crop Science in Ghana, 1977–1992." **Quarterly Bulletin of the International Association of Agricultural Information Specialists** 38, no. 4 (1993): 191–96.

Darko-Ampem analyzes the citations in thirteen master's and doctoral theses submitted to the Department of Crop Science at the University of Science and Technology in Kumasi, Ghana, between 1977 and 1992. Of 1,357 references, 66.1 percent were journals and 12.6 percent monographs. A language breakdown indicated that 96.6 percent were in English, 1.9 percent in French, and 1.3 percent in Spanish. Unexpectedly, 42.8 percent of the references were more than twenty-five years old, a finding attributed to the "depressing picture" in Ghanian librarians that forced researchers to cite older material because current items were unavailable. Collaboration among authors, authorship productivity patterns (in a highly unusual twist, Bradford's Law is applied to authors), and the most highly cited core authors are also studied. This entry illustrates how local conditions, that is, poor library collections in Ghana, can influence the results of citation studies, that is, a disproportionate number of older citations.

Fuseler, Elizabeth A., and Virginia Allen. "Riding the Waves of Publication: A Citation Analysis of the **Proceedings of IAMSLIC, 1984–1994.**" In **Information Across the Waves: The World As a Multimedia Experience: Proceedings of the 21st Annual Conference of the International Association of Aquatic and Marine Science Libraries and Information Centers; 21st Annual Conference of IAMSLIC held 8–12 October, 1995 at Southampton, England,** edited by James W. Markham and Andrea L. Duda, 219–25. Fort Pierce, FL: IAMSLIC, 1996. ISSN 8755-6332.

This entry offers a citation analysis of the first eleven published volumes of the *IAMSLIC Proceedings,* covering 1984 to 1994. They found that 43 percent of 292 papers contained no references. Of 1,513 citations, 41.4 percent were to journals and 33.4 percent to books. Interestingly, 3.4 percent were citations to the *IAMSLIC Proceedings.* The oldest citation dated to 1725, although the chronological age of the citations is not analyzed. A table lists in alphabetical order the ten LIS journals cited at least ten times, but raw data is not given. A topical breakdown revealed that papers dealing with library methods were more likely to contain citations than papers on other topics, that is, library methods accounted for 33.6 percent of the papers but produced 41.8 percent of the total citations. Additional data is given about co-authorship patterns as well as the authors' institutional affiliations and geographical origins. This item is worth noting because it describes scholarly communication patterns in a specialized area of library and information science.

Goodrum, Abby A., et al. "Scholarly Publishing in the Internet Age: A Citation Analysis of Computer Science Literature." **Information Processing & Management** 37 (September 2001): 661–75.

This article compares computer science scholarly communication patterns in Web documents and in traditional print resources. Analysis of the 488 most highly cited documents in CiteSeer, an autonomous citation indexing (ACI) tool that indexes freely available Portable Document Format (PDF) and Postscript Web documents, found that 37 percent were journal articles, 42 percent books or book chapters, and 15 percent conference proceedings, while 42 percent dated from the 1990s and another 42 percent from the 1980s. A similar breakdown of the 515 most frequently cited documents in *SciSearch,* an ISI index of print items, revealed that 39 percent were journal articles, 56 percent books/book chapters, and 3 percent conference proceedings, while 5 percent dated from the 1990s and 42 percent from the 1980s. (In contrast to most citation studies, this analysis is based on the most cited items rather than those cited during a synchronous time period.) Goodrum and her co-authors conclude the Web cites a greater proportion of conference proceedings and more recent material. The authors also discuss CiteSeer, the make-up of source documents, and the role played by conference proceedings in scholarly communication. It is asserted "it may be premature to ring the death knell for traditional publishing." This research is noteworthy for its innovative approach to citation analysis.

Hurd, Julie M., Deborah D. Blecic, and Rama Vishwanatham. "Information Use by Molecular Biologists: Implications for Library Collections and Services." **College & Research Libraries** 60 (January 1999): 31–43.

This entry reports a local citation study done at the University of Illinois at Chicago based on publications by faculty located in the Molecular Biology Research Building. Forty-four articles, from a stratified sample of sixty identified through *Current Contents,* published during a three-year period by twenty faculty, served as a source. Not surprisingly, 91.3 percent of 1,683 citations were to journals and only 4.0 percent to books. Of 267 cited journals, the top 16 (listed in a table) accounted for 55.3 percent of the citations. Analysis by five major subject classes from *Ulrich's* revealed 59.4 percent were to biology, 18.2 percent to science in general, and 17.7 percent to medicine. Also, 58 percent of the citations were no more than five years old. The authors hypothesize that electronic resources will become more important to molecular biologists in the future (although none was cited) because, as of their writing, five of the ten most cited journals were available electronically. This is a notable example of a citation study in an interdisciplinary field.

Lifshin, Arthur. "Citation Analysis of **Geochimica et Cosmochimica Acta,** 1951–1960." **Journal of the American Society for Information Society** 44 (July 1993): 322–26.

The structure of geochemistry was studied by analyzing every citation during 1951 through 1960 in *Geochimica et Cosmochimica Acta,* the field's first English language journal. Tables present year-by-year and mean percentages for the citations' language, format, and subject. The ten-year citation totals reveal the following: 78.3 percent were to journals and 11.3 percent to books; 69.0 percent were in English, 16.0 percent in German, and 3.1 percent in Latin; and 52.1 percent were to geology, 13.9 percent to chemistry, and 10.7 percent to physics. Longitudinal trends showed an increasing proportion of citations in English and to the discipline of geology. The mode for citation age was one to two years prior to the volume's publication date. Taking a unique approach, forty-seven journals are ranked according to the number of years they were cited ten or more times. The five journals, four of which were geology titles, cited ten times all 10 years were labeled "a core group." The focus on the 1950s limits this investigation's usefulness for collection management decisions.

Madkey, V.D. , and D. Rajyalakshmi. "Citation Analysis of Ph.D. Thesis [Sic] in Environmental Science and Engineering Used by NEERI Scientists During 1977–1991." **Annals of Library Science & Documentation** 41 (June 1994): 63–75.

Madkey and Rajyalakshmi study the 5,466 citations in 31 engineering and environmental science Ph.D. dissertations, competed from 1977 to 1991, held in the National Environmental Engineering Research Institute (NEERI) and Nagpur University libraries in India. They discovered that 67.00 percent of the citations were to journals and 18.51 percent to books, 92.78 percent of the authors were foreign and 7.22 percent Indian, and the half-life was 17 years for journals opposed to 18 for books. Of the 146 cited journals, 52.05 percent were published in the United States, 18.49 percent in the United Kingdom, and 8.90 percent in India. The sixty-seven journals cited ten or more times are rank ordered in a table.

This entry somewhat differs from similar studies because it is based on dissertations held in libraries rather than submitted to Ph.D. programs.

Majid, Shaheen. "Trends in Publishing Agricultural Research Literature in Pakistan." **Science & Technology Libraries** 15, no. 3 (1995): 55–75.

Majid used the 1988 and 1989 volumes of the *Pakistan Journal of Agricultural Research* as the source for this bibliometric study. Of exactly 2,500 total citations, 66.8 percent were to journals and 33.2 percent to nonserial literature. The author found 25.55 percent of the journal citations were to Pakistani and Indian journals. Altogether 559 journals were cited, of which 64.2 percent were cited only once and 5.0 percent ten or more times. The twenty most frequently cited journals, listed in a table, contained ten U.S., five Pakistani, and two Indian titles. The distribution of citations among journals did not conform to Bradford's Law except for the core zone. The half-life for all the citations was 11.5 years, with 18.7 percent to the last five years and 15.3 percent exceeding twenty-five years. Further analysis regarding authorship patterns and the source articles found, among other things, that 36 percent of the authors cited themselves. Majid offers a thoughtful analysis in this well-done study concerning a country whose importance is receiving increasing appreciation in the United States.

Mubeen, M. A. "Citation Analysis of Doctoral Dissertations in Chemistry." **Annals of Library Science & Documentation** 43 (June 1996): 48–58.

Mubeen analyzed the 5,012 citations in the twenty-two chemistry dissertations submitted to Mangalore University, in India, between 1980 and 1993. Among her major findings are the following: 73.00 percent of the citations were to journals, 11.48 percent to books; the cited items were published in twenty-seven countries, with 30.20 percent originating in the United States and 20.01 percent in India; and 79.4 percent were in English. A total of 418 journals were cited, with the 58 cited ten or more times accounting for 74.45 percent of the journal citations. These 58 are rank ordered in a table. The article concludes with a detailed statistical application of Bradford's Law to the journal data and the division of the journals into three Bradford zones.

Musser, Linda R., and Thomas W. Conkling. "Characteristics of Engineering Citations." **Science & Technology Libraries** 15, no. 4 (1996): 41–49.

The 4,780 citations from scholarly articles in the first 1994 issue of sixteen U.S. society-published engineering journals, chosen to cover the full range of engineering subdisciplines, serve as this investigation's source. Musser and Conkling expected 80 percent of the citations would be to journals, but actually found that only 53 percent were journals, with 19 percent to conference papers, 12 percent to monographs, and 9 percent to technical reports. Approximately 99 percent of the citations were in English, followed "in decreasing order" by French, German, and Japanese. The citations ranged from 0 to 121 years in age with the median eight years. Age analysis by format showed that monographs maintain their value longer, that is, older books are cited, than other formats and that ten to fifteen years of journal backruns "would satisfy the majority of user requests."

The authors' assertion that this is the first citation analysis for engineering in more than twenty years is probably correct if one disregards studies published in India.

Tiew, W. S., and K. Kaur. "Citation Analysis of **Journal of Natural Rubber Research,** 1988–1997." **Malaysian Journal of Library & Information Science** 5 (December 2000): 45–56.
   The source for this citation study is stated in the title. A table shows that 71.80 percent of 4,181 citations were to journals or serials (elsewhere in the text the figure is given as 72.40 percent) and 13.11 percent to monographs. A total of 893 journals or serials were cited, of which the top thirty—listed in rank order in a table—accounted for 43.37 percent of the citations. A decade-by-decade breakdown found that 55.97 percent of the citations were published during the last two decades (1978–97) whereas 4.46 percent were published prior to 1948.[23] The article also addresses the number of citations per article and per volume. The authors are correct in their assertion, "Bibliometric studies on rubber literature are quite lacking."

Walcott, Rosalind. "Characteristics of Citations in 1993 Volumes of **Auk, Condor, Ibis,** and **Wilson Bulletin.**" **Science & Technology Libraries** 15, no. 4 (1996): 29–39.
   Walcott's investigation is derived from all the citations in the 1993 volumes of *Auk, Condor, Ibis,* and *Wilson Bulletin,* the four most frequently cited ornithology journals in the ISI's *SciSearch* database. Of 10,447 citations, 75.0 percent were to serials, 22.5 percent to books, and 2.5 percent to theses or dissertations, leading Walcott to conclude books are more important in ornithology than other biological areas. Overall, 96.73 percent of the citations were in English, although the figure exceeded 98 percent for the three journals published in the United States. It is noteworthy that only 93.33 percent of the citations were English in the source journal published in Europe, *Ibis.* A table indicated eleven languages were cited in the four journals. A total of 755 serials were cited, of which 16 accounted for 50 percent of the journal citations and 69 (rank ordered in a table) covered 75 percent of the citations. Because the median citation age was ten years and it took thirty-three years to cover 90 percent of the citations, Walcott advises librarians to "keep long backfiles of serials." The author states this is the only published citation analysis for ornithology.

Humanities

Barkett, Gina R. "Conducting a Citation Study." In **Library Evaluation: A Casebook and Can-Do Guide**, edited by Danny P. Wallace and Connie Van Fleet, 155–64. Englewood, CO: Libraries Unlimited, 2001. ISBN 1-56308-862-2 (paper).
   This case study from a library evaluation textbook seeks to illustrate the purpose, procedures, and findings of a citation study. The field of art history is analyzed based on 1,140 citations in *Art Bulletin* during the years 1994 through 1998. Tables tabulate the data concerning the six variables under investigation. They

reveal the following: 84.7 percent of the authors were from the United States; 18.6 percent of the citations were to 1990–98 and 26.1 percent to 1980–89; 51.1 percent were to art and 23.4 percent to history; 52.5 percent were monographs and 14.3 percent journals; 58.2 percent were in English, 13.7 percent in Italian and 12.9 percent in French; and 41.7 percent were published in the United States, 14.6 percent in Italy, and 13.0 percent in England. The author indicates the findings can not be used for journal selection because fewer than ten journal titles were cited more than once. Barkett stresses the interdisciplinary nature of art history. This entry successfully achieves its objective of demonstrating a well-done citation study.

Buchanan, Anne L., and Jean-Pierre V. M. Hérubel. "Comparing Materials Used in Philosophy and Political Science Dissertations: A Technical Note." **Behavioral & Social Sciences Librarian** 12, no. 2 (1993): 63–70.

The citation patterns in five Purdue University philosophy and five political science dissertations (the most recently accepted at the time the research was conducted) are analyzed here. Of 391 citations in the philosophy dissertations, 81.329 percent were to monographs and 13.299 percent to journals, while the corresponding percentages were 75.456 and 21.111 for the 876 political science dissertation citations. An age breakdown revealed that 52.83 percent of the philosophy and 28.29 percent of the political science monographic citations predate 1970. For journals, 23.66 percent of the philosophy and 10.75 percent of the political science citations were prior to 1970. This study reaffirms the well-known pattern whereby the humanities cite more monographs and older materials than the social sciences, but Buchanan and Hérubel observe an "unexpected finding" of a trend toward citing current material in philosophy as 51.16 percent of the philosophy journal citations were to the last five years compared to 55.11 percent for political science. Unlike this chapter's other entries, this investigation compares two disciplines. It has been assigned to the section for the discipline named first in the title.

Cullars, John M. "Citation Characteristics of French and German Fine Arts Monographs." **Library Quarterly** 66 (April 1996): 138–60.

In a follow-up to the research described in the next entry, Cullars analyzes citation patterns in French and German language fine arts monographs. Three hundred ninety citations were randomly selected from 155 single-author books at least seventy-five pages in length, published between 1982 and 1990, and indexed in *Répetoire international de la littérature de l'art (RILA)*. As noted by Cullars, his work differs from most other citation studies because monographs rather than journals are the source. Results are given for French monographs, the German ones, and both combined. In French books, 64.2 percent of the citations were to books, 17.2 percent to articles, and 8.9 percent to articles in books, whereas the corresponding figures for German monographs were 62.1 percent, 9.4 percent, and 10.9 percent. Not surprisingly, the French books cited French sources (68.7 percent French, 10.5 percent English, and 8.2 percent German) while German books cited German sources, (69.9 percent German, 10.9 percent French, and 6.3 percent English). Analysis by age showed that 11.9 percent of the citations in French books and 15.2 percent in German books dated from 1980 while 23.1 percent of the former and 16.4 percent of the latter predated 1890. When French and German are combined, 6.7 percent of the citations were positive, 4.6 percent negative, and 88.7 percent "value-free." After extensive comparisons, Cullars concludes that his findings "for the most part" agree with other fine arts citation studies.

Cullars, John M. "Citation Characteristics of Monographs in the Fine Arts." **Library Quarterly** 62 (July 1992): 325–42.

Following a discussion of scholarly trends in fine arts, 581 randomly selected citations from 158 English language, *RILA*-indexed monographs, published in 1985 or 1986, are used to analyze fine arts. Cullars discovered that 40.8 percent of the citations were to primary sources and 59.2 percent to secondary sources, although he questions these figures' reliability and validity due to problems distinguishing between primary and secondary sources in fine arts. A breakdown by format revealed that the proportion of monographs (60.6 percent) was lower, but of manuscripts higher (14.8 percent) than in other humanities studies. Among the other findings are the following:

- Seventy point two percent of the citations were in English (an additional 6.0 percent were translated into English from other languages) and 11.9 percent in French.

- Sixty point seven percent were from fine arts, 8.4 percent literature, and 7.9 percent history.

- Forty-seven point three percent dated from 1960 or later and 18.6 percent predated 1890.

- Four point zero percent were positive, 2.2 percent negative, and 93.8 percent neutral.

Cullars concludes that "for the most part" his findings agree with other investigations based on journals. Written earlier, this work is quite similar in methodology, style, and scope to the preceding entry.

Deo, V.N., S.M. Mohal, and S.S. Survey. "Bibliometric Study of Doctoral Dissertations on English Language and Literature." **Annals of Library Science & Documentation** 42 (September 1995): 81–95.

This citation study is constructed from 4,066 citations in twenty-six doctoral dissertations in English language and literature accepted by Dr. Babasaheb Ambedkar Marathwada University, in India, through the end of 1992. The authors discovered the following: 64.01 percent of the citations were to books and 29.92 percent to periodicals, 99.09 percent were in English with the remaining in Marathi and Sanskrit, 66.52 percent of periodical citations were to U.S. journals and 22.60 percent to U.K. titles, 46.87 percent of the book citations originated in the United Kingdom and 37.84 percent in the United States, the half-life of the journal citations was 27.5 years, and 32 of the 221 cited journals account for 58 percent of the periodical citations. These 32 journals are listed in a table, while other tables rank order the most cited books and the most cited authors. Deo, Mohal, and Survey conclude the journal citations do not conform to a Bradford distribution. Among the fairly numerous analyses of Indian doctoral dissertations, this is one of the most thorough.

Dowell, Erika. "Interdisciplinarity and New Methodologies in Art History: A Citation Analysis." **Art Documentation** 18 (spring 1999): 14–19.

In order to test whether art history is becoming more interdisciplinary due to the influence of semiotic, feminist, and Marxist theories, this entry compares the subject dispersion of citations in *Art Bulletin* and *Burlington Magazine* during 1987, 1989, 1991, 1993, and 1995 with 1948 through 1957 data for these two journals from Wesley Clark Simonton's dissertation.[24] Dowell used a sample of 978 citations: 100 from each journal for every year studied minus 22 whose subject classification could not be determined. She found that with the passage of forty years, the percentage of citations to fine arts had declined from 68.3 percent to 64.4 percent and to history from 14.8 percent to 11 percent, whereas religion and theology increased from 3.3 percent to 5.9 percent and language and literature from 3.3 percent to 5.8 percent. Thus, the author detects a "small but definite trend" toward greater interdisciplinarity. Separate data for the two journals from both Dowell's and Simonton's studies, including dispersion in ten broad subject areas, are tabulated in four appended tables. Dowell cautions that her findings should not be used in collection development decisions. This is a notable example of a citation analysis of a single parameter: subject dispersion.

OTHER CITATION STUDIES

Joswick, Kathleen E. "Library Materials Use by College Freshman: A Citation Analysis of Composition Papers." **College & Undergraduate Libraries** 1, no. 1 (1994): 43–66.

Two hundred four Western Illinois University freshman composition papers supplied to the investigator in the spring of 1991 serve as this study's source. Of 1,224 citations, 46.4 percent were to books and 43.5 percent to periodicals. Joswick notes the unusually high proportion of books, based on her review of earlier studies. The publication dates of cited sources ranged from 1906 to 1991, while 31.8 percent predated 1980. It was found that 86.4 percent of the cited publications were available in the library, and 96 percent of the remaining items were "readily available" on ILL because they were held by another Illinois library. The article is illustrated with numerous graphs and tables. Commenting that freshman cite "a remarkably high percentage" of songs, television programs, films, and personal interviews, the author advocates bibliographic instruction to teach them to evaluate sources. This entry's focus on freshman composition differentiates it from the other citation studies of undergraduate papers.

Kreider, Janice. "The Correlation of Local Citation Data with Citation Data from **Journal Citation Reports.**" **Library Resources & Technical Services** 43 (April 1999): 67–77.

The relationship between the *JCR's* "global" citation data and local citations by the University of British Columbia faculty is explored in this interesting article. For journals in twenty science and social science subject areas, the total citations in the 1994 *JCR* were correlated with the total citations by local faculty during the 12.5 years from January 1981 to June 1993 as indicated by the ISI's Local Journal Utilization Report. The author explains technical difficulties, such as errors and inconsistencies, with the raw ISI data and how they were resolved. The correlations were "moderate to moderately high" for all subjects with only five areas displaying figures below 0.7. Kreider cautions that journals with low global citation counts may nevertheless be highly cited locally and concedes the overall correlations may not have been as high if less than 12.5 years of local citation data were used. She concludes that "with certain cautions" university libraries "could considering substituting" global citation data for local data in journal evaluation.

Kuyper-Rushing, Lois. "Identifying Uniform Core Journal Titles for Music Libraries: A Dissertation Citation Study." **College & Research Libraries** 60 (March 1999): 153–63.

In order to conduct a national citation level study, Kuyper-Rushing analyzed the citations in 118 dissertations for music Ph.D's. awarded in 1993 by Carnegie I research institutions. A breakdown by format of the 13,111 citations found that 41 percent were books and 29 percent serials, while it was "surprising" that only 4 percent were scores and sound recordings. Among the 939 total journals, the top 5.5 percent produced 50 percent of the journal citations. Tables list in rank order the fifty-three most frequently cited journal titles as well as the top forty-nine in musicology, the leading nine in music theory, the most cited fourteen in music education, and the top thirty-three in applied music. Comparison of the results with Richard Griscom's 1983 study of music dissertations at Indiana University revealed that only nineteen titles were on the top-ranked lists in both studies.[25] Accordingly, the author asserts that citation data from a single institution may not be applicable to other institutions or on a national level.

Marinko, Rita A. "Citations to Women's Studies Journals in Dissertations, 1989 and 1994." **Serials Librarian** 35, nos. 1–2 (1998): 29–44.

Marinko examines citations to core women's studies journals in 57 women's studies dissertations completed in 1989 and 103 in 1994 at U.S. academic institutions. The journals listed under the "women's studies" category in the *SSCI JCR* (seven in 1989 and twelve in 1994) were deemed the core. She found that 65 percent of the 1989 dissertations cited a core journal, but only 58 percent of the 1994 dissertations did so. In the 1989 dissertations, the core women's studies titles accounted for only 0.57 percent of the 3,324 citations to twentieth-century journals, whereas in the 1994 dissertations they provided 0.69 percent of 4,419 citations. Moreover, 80 percent of the 494 total citations to core journals were to four titles: *Signs, Feminist Studies, Psychology of Women Quarterly,* and *Sex Roles.* By limiting itself to core titles, this not especially rigorous entry takes a different approach than most other journal citation studies.

Oppenheim, Charles, and Richard Smith. "Student Citation Practices in an Information Science Department." **Education for Information** 19 (December 2001): 299–323.

In this interesting study Oppenheim and Smith analyzed the 2,095 citations in sixty undergraduate "final year projects" (twenty each from 1997, 1998, and 1999) at the Loughborough University Department of Information Science (in the United Kingdom). Overall, 40.2 percent of the citations were to books, 29.5 percent to journals, and 9.3 percent to Internet resources, that is, URLs on the Web. However, the latter had increased from 1.9 percent of the citations in 1997 to 17.2 percent in 1999. There were 399 citations to sixty-three LIS journals (listed in rank order in an appendix), but the distribution did not conform to Bradford's Law. All cited journals were held by the Loughborough library, but thirty-seven journals held by the library were not cited. The mean age of all citations was 7.3 years, but 9.5 years for books, 5.3 years for journals, and 0.4 years for Internet resources. A supplementary survey of second- and third-year students sent in November 1999 (42.6 percent of 136 questionnaires were returned) found that "nearly 40%" cited a larger number of sources in order to enhance their grade and 6.9 percent cited the person grading the paper. Because of a negative correlation (-0.151) between the ranking of LIS journals in this study and in the 1998 *JCR,* the authors conclude that student citing behavior differs from LIS professionals.

St. Clair, Gloriana and Rose Mary Magrill. "Undergraduate Use of Four Library Collections: Format and Age of Materials." **Collection Building** 11, no. 4 (1992): 2–15.

One of an ongoing series of articles, this piece analyzes the format and age of cited material in thirteen disciplines from 1,775 student papers, mostly completed between 1986 and 1988, at four academic institutions: East Texas Baptist University, Oregon State University, Texas A & M, and Westmar College.[26] In composite (the tables present separate data for each discipline) 53 percent of the citations were to books, 35 percent to journals, and 12 percent "other," which included government documents, newspapers, and encyclopedias. To analyze age, the mean and median of the newest and oldest citation in each paper was calculated. For all citations, the mean oldest was 1957.5 and the mean newest 1982.6, while the respective figures for books were 1955.6 and 1979.9 and, for journals, 1975.0 and 1980.7. St. Clair and Magrill state "the use of older material was more extensive than expected." The humanities disciplines tended to cite more books and older material than the sciences and social sciences, although a few exceptions were observed. The entry contains a lengthy, unannotated bibliography of more than 120 items. These research findings are significant because they suggest the basic bibliometric patterns found in books, journals, and dissertations also generally apply to undergraduate papers.

NOTES

1. S. R. Ranganathan, "Librametry and Its Scope," *JISSI: The International Journal of Scientometrics and Informetrics* 1 (March 1995): 15–21.

2. Alan Pritchard, "Statistical Bibliography or Bibliometrics," *Journal of Documentation* 25 (December 1969): 348–49.

3. Ibid.

4. Dorothy H. Hertzel, "Bibliometrics, History of the Development of Ideas," *Encyclopedia of Library and Information Science* 42, supplement 7 (1987): 144–219.

5. Thomas E. Nisonger, *Management of Serials in Libraries* (Englewood, CO: Libraries Unlimited, 1998), 124–30.

6. Stephen P. Harter and Thomas E. Nisonger, "ISI's Impact Factor as Misnomer: A Proposed New Measure to Assess Journal Impact," *Journal of the American Society for Information Science* 48 (December 1997): 1146–48.

7. *Annual Statistics of Medical School Libraries in the United States and Canada, 1980–1981,*4th ed. (Houston: Association of Academic Health Sciences Library Directors, 1981); *Annual Statistics of Medical School Libraries, 1985–1986,* 9th ed. (Houston: Association of Academic Health Sciences Library Directors, 1986); *Annual Statistics of Medical School Libraries, 1989–1990,*13th ed. (Houston: Association of Academic Health Sciences Library Directors, 1991).

8. Katherine W. McCain and James E. Bobick, "Patterns of Journal Use in a Departmental Library: A Citation Analysis," *Journal of the American Society for Information Science* 32 (July 1981): 257–67.

9. Nisonger's calculation from data presented in a table.

10. The percentages are Nisonger's calculation from Gooden's raw data.

11. The percentage is Nisonger's calculation from Loughner's data.

12. Nisonger's calculation from Ovens' raw data.

13. Doris Williams, "Using Core Journals to Justify Subscriptions and Services," in *IAMSLIC at a Crossroads; Proceedings of the 15th Annual Conference,* edited by Robert W. Burkhart and Joyce C. Burkhart (n.p.: International Association of Marine Science Libraries and Information Centers, 1990), 123–34.

14. Thomas E. Nisonger, "A Test of Two Citation Checking Techniques for Evaluating Political Science Collections in University Libraries," *Library Resources & Technical Services* 27 (April/June 1983): 163–76.

15. Frederick Sanger, S. Nicklen, and A. R. Coulson, "DNA Sequencing with Chain-Terminating Inhibitors," *Proceedings of the National Academy of Sciences* 74 (December 1977): 5463–67.

16. The percentages are Nisonger's calculations.

17. Larry Hardesty and Gail Oltmanns, "How Many Psychology Journals Are Enough?: A Study of the Use of Psychology Journals by Undergraduates," *Serials Librarian* 16, nos. 1–2 (1989): 133–53.

18. Derek de Solla Price, "Citation Measures of Hard Science, Soft Science, Technology, and Non-Science," in *Communication Among Scientists and Engineers,* edited by Carnot E. Nelson and Donald K. Pollack (Lexington, MA: Heath Lexington Books, 1970), 3–22.

19. James K. Bracken and John Mack Tucker, "Characteristics of the Journal Literature of Bibliographic Instruction," *College & Research Libraries* 50 (November 1989):

665–73; Bluma C. Peritz, "Citation Characteristics in Library Science: Some Further Results from a Bibliometric Study," *Library Research* 3 (spring 1981): 55–65; Jeffrey N. Gaten, "Paradigm Restrictions on Interdisciplinary Research into Librarianship," *College & Research Libraries* (November 1991): 575–84.

20. Nisonger's tabulation of separate percentages presented by Buttlar.

21. All percentages in this article are Nisonger's calculation from the raw data of Goedeken and Hérubel.

22. Nisonger's calculation from Metoyer-Duran and Hernon's raw data.

23. Nisonger's calculation from Tiew's data.

24. Wesley Clark Simonton, "Characteristics of the Research Literature in Fine Arts During the Period 1948–1957" (Ph.D. diss., University of Illinois at Urbana-Champaign, 1960).

25. Richard Griscom, "Periodical Use in a University Music Library: A Citation Study of Theses and Dissertations Submitted to the Indiana University School of Music from 1975–1980," *Serials Librarian* 7, no. 3 (1983): 35–52.

26. Rose Mary Magrill and Gloriana St. Clair, "Undergraduate Term Paper Citations," *College & Research Libraries News* 51 (January 1990): 25–28; Magrill and St. Clair, "Incomplete Citations in Undergraduate Term Papers from Four Campuses," *RQ* 30 (fall 1990): 75–81; Magrill and St. Clair, "Undergraduate Term Paper Citation Patterns by Discipline and Level of Course," *Collection Management* 12, nos. 3–4 (1990): 25–56.

10

Journal Ranking Studies

What is a journal ranking and why are journal rankings important? A journal ranking places a set of journals representing a discipline or subject area in hierarchical order, usually using a single criterion for estimating journal worth. Most journal rankings have been based on citation data (typically impact factor or total citations received) or the subjective judgments of experts in a field, although other criteria are occasionally employed. Closely related to a journal ranking is a journal rating, which assigns a score or numerical evaluation to each journal in a set but lists them in alphabetical rather than hierarchical order. Because a ranking can be constructed from the scores, a rating may be viewed as an implicit ranking. In contrast to a ranking or rating, a core list identifies a subject area's most important journal titles but generally lists them alphabetically rather than hierarchically and without numerical rating scores. Admittedly some ambiguity exists between the two concepts as core lists sometimes rank order their journals and a few ranked lists purportedly represent the core. While a ranking is usually based on a single dimension, a serials decision model is an algorithm that incorporates and weighs numerous variables in order to construct a ranking for a set of journals.

Journal rankings have obvious application to serials evaluation and journal collection management decisions in academic libraries. One presumably would wish to subscribe to high-ranking titles while serials at or near the bottom might be candidates for cancellation, weeding, or relegation to remote storage. A journal ranking can be used as a weighted checklist for evaluation of the serials collection with higher ranking journals counting more than lower ranking ones. Furthermore, journal rankings can be used for a variety of purposes apart from a library setting, including the following:

- Assisting scholars with manuscript submission decisions

- Evaluating faculty performance for purpose of promotion and tenure as well as annual pay raises

- Helping editors assess their journal's stature and progress

- Indicating the relative status of a discipline's journals to new doctoral students and scholars from other areas

Besides rating journals, ranking studies have addressed such issues as the following:

- The correspondence between two or more different ranking methods (i.e., objective versus subjective)

- Comparisons with earlier rankings in the same discipline or subject

- Comparisons of rankings by different categories of raters, such as academic deans and library administrators

A citation-based ranking of chemistry journals, published in 1927 by P.L.K. Gross and E. M. Gross, is generally acknowledged as the first journal ranking.[1] During the 1930s and 1940s, rankings using citation data were published in a variety of scientific and technical fields. Since then, rankings using various citation measures or the subjective perceptions of experts have been published in many science and social science subject areas. Unlike the vast majority of this book's entries, numerous journal ranking studies have been published by scholars from fields other than library and information science.

This chapter annotates works that have a primary focus on journal ranking. The reader is advised that many journal rankings that constitute minor parts of broader studies, often of a bibliometric nature, are not included in this book. Also excluded are law journal rankings based exclusively on citations in judicial opinions, such as by the U.S. Supreme Court, because such rankings do not indicate scholarly prestige.[2] Note, however, that some of the entries in chapter 9 contain journal rankings and that a few of the core journal lists covered in chapter 7 are presented in rank order. This chapter is organized into sections covering general and theoretical studies, rankings in library and information science (an area where reader interest is assumed), social science journal rankings, science journal rankings, and rankings in allied health.

GENERAL AND THEORETICAL STUDIES

Cooper, Randolph B., David Blair, and Miranda Pao. "Communicating MIS Research: A Citation Study of Journal Influence." **Information Processing & Management** 29 (January/February 1993): 113–27.

The three authors employ a complex but eloquent methodological approach to answer the question: is there a stable core of Management Information Systems (MIS) journals? First, the citations in 146 articles from a previous MIS literature review were analyzed, resulting in 2,272 citations to 294 journals.[3] A table lists the top fifteen journals in each of four ranking methods:

1. Total citations including journal self-citations

2. Total citations excluding journal self-citations

3. Normalized citation scores (the ratio of citations received to articles published) including journal self-citations

4. Normalized citation scores excluding journal self-citations

The fourteen titles that appeared in the top ten in at least one of these rankings are listed alphabetically as "the most influential core MIS journals." To test cohesiveness, an investigation of citation patterns among these journals found two were strongly connected to the core and seven weakly connected. After reviewing previously published MIS journal rankings, Cooper, Blair, and Pao conclude there is a stable core consisting of one "very influential" title, two "influential," titles, and two "less influential" ones. In short, this article addresses a number of important methodological issues regarding journal ranking and core titles.

Furr, L. Allen. "The Relative Influence of Social Work Journals: Impact Factor vs. Core Influence." **Journal of Social Work Education** 31 (winter 1995): 38–45.

In this ranking, Allen's Core Influence (CI) citation measure (the ratio of citations received to articles published based on a discipline's core journals rather than the entire ISI database) is applied in modified form to social work journals.[4] Furr, unlike Allen, eliminated journal self-citations because they do not indicate "influence" on other titles. Twenty-two core social work journals, identified through coverage in the *SSCI* and *Social Work Research and Abstracts* for four of the five years between 1988 and 1992, serve as the study's source. Four separate rankings of social work journals are presented using 1991 data: the twenty journals in the *SSCI* *JCR* impact factor ranking, the top twenty-two by total citations in core journals, the top twenty-two by total citations in core journals with self-citations removed, and the top twenty-two according to Furr's modified CI. The author found "clear differences" between the impact factor and CI rankings as three of the top five journals were different. This article illustrates a noteworthy methodological consideration—that interdisciplinary citations in the *JCR* can influence journal rankings.

Holsapple, Clyde W., et al. "Business Computing Research Journals: A Normalized Citation Analysis." **Journal of Management Information Systems** 11 (summer 1994): 131–40.

This is "an extension" of the authors' previous ranking (see entry later in this chapter) of business computing journals based on total citations. Because such an approach unfairly advantages older journals with longer backruns (i.e., they have more opportunities to be cited), Holsapple and colleagues normalize for journal longevity by dividing the total citations received by the number of years between when a journal began publication and 1990. Acknowledging this tactic might disadvantage older journals since most citations tend to be to recent years, the researchers also normalize using the year 1977 and then the year 1967 as starting points. A table presents the initial and the three normalized rankings for the forty-one titles initially receiving fifty or more citations. A detailed discussion of the observed differences among the four notes that a number of journals make "'large' moves" in ranking position. Holsapple and his co-authors make a commendable effort to deal with issues relating to journal age, but do not address journal size as measured by the number of articles published because, among several reasons, of what they term "article counting ambiguity."

Lancaster, F. W. "Evaluation of Periodicals." In **If You Want to Evaluate Your Library…**, 87–108. 2d ed. Champaign, IL: University of Illinois, Graduate School of Library and Information Science, 1993. ISBN 0-87845-091-2.

The author's primary focus is on evaluation for serials cancellation purposes. He suggests prioritization of periodicals through ranking, noting that low-ranking titles could be deselected with the "least disturbance to library users." Seven ranking criteria are outlined:

- Usage in the library compiling the ranking

- Usage from another library

- Opinion

- Number of citations received

- Impact factor

- Cost-effectiveness

- Articles contributed to a subject

After reviewing previous studies, Lancaster finds inconsistencies in the results among different ranking methods, especially in bottom-ranking journals that would be cancellation candidates. He also critiques models for combining several criteria in deselection decision-making. Lancaster concludes that cancellation should be based primarily on ranking journals by cost-effectiveness. That a book chapter ostensibly about periodical evaluation concentrates on their ranking demonstrates the relevance of journal ranking to library serials management.

Nisonger, Thomas E. "Journal Ranking Studies." In **Management of Serials in Libraries,** 189–213. Englewood, CO: Libraries Unlimited, 1998. ISBN 1-56308-213-6.

An overview of the journal ranking concept is provided in this chapter. Eight dimensions for classifying journal rankings are outlined, including the ranking method, whether its compiled locally or by national/international data, the degree of subject specificity, and purpose. The differences among a journal ranking, a core list, and a serials decision model are explained. Specific rankings based on citation data and the subjective perception of experts are examined in detail. After the pros and cons of citation versus subjective rankings are reviewed, the author concludes that a "perfect" method does not exist. Chapter sections are devoted to the potential uses of rankings in collection management and outside libraries. While acknowledging that some question the utility of journal rankings, Nisonger contends they are central to serials collection management because they provide a context for assessing how a journal compares to its peers. An unannotated listing of eighty ranking studies follows the chapter.

JOURNAL RANKINGS IN LIBRARY AND INFORMATION SCIENCE

Altuna Esteibar, Belen, and F. W. Lancaster. "Ranking of Journals in Library and Information Science by Research and Teaching Relatedness." **Serials Librarian** 23, nos. 1–2 (1992): 1–10.
    LIS journals are ranked by five methods:

1. The number of times they appeared on 131 course reading lists between the spring 1989 semester and the fall 1990 semester at the University of Illinois at Urbana-Champaign School of Library and Information Science (to measure "teaching-relatedness")

2. Citations in forty-one University of Illinois SLIS doctoral dissertations between 1981 and 1990

3. Citations in 114 SLIS faculty publications from 1986 to 1990 (both 2 and 3 to measure "research-relatedness")

4. An unweighted total of the first three rankings

5. A weighted total of the three, using a 1–5–10 scale

The top twenty journals in each ranking are listed. Analysis revealed "considerable differences" between teaching and research-related rankings. This is a praiseworthy example of LIS journal ranking based on local citation data.

Blake, Virgil L. P. "The Perceived Prestige of Professional Journals, 1995: A Replication of the Kohl-Davis Study." **Education for Information** 14 (October 1996): 157–79.
    In perhaps the best-known ranking of LIS journals, published in 1985 by David F. Kohl and Charles H. Davis, library school deans and ARL library directors were asked to rate a list of journals on a 1 (low) to 5 (high) scale and then separately name the field's "top five" titles.[5] Blake replicated their study in 1992 by surveying library school deans (forty-four responded for a 75.8 percent response rate) and ARL library directors (receiving fifty-nine useable responses for a 59 percent rate). Numerous tables display the following:

*   The fifty-seven listed titles rank ordered according to the deans' average ratings

*   The same titles rank ordered by the directors' ratings

- Thirty-four listed among the top five by deans

- Twenty-seven listed by directors

- Twenty-eight additional titles (not originally listed) suggested by deans

- Twelve additional ones suggested by directors

The author points out that the "hierarchy of perceived prestigious journals" is "distinctly different" between deans and directors. Specifically, there was a statistically significant difference between the two groups' ratings for 27 of the 57 titles, and only 4 additional titles were suggested in common by both deans and directors. Also, there was limited "internal consensus" (in which 50 percent of the respondents agreed on their ratings) on the part of both groups. Blake suggests a future study comparing citation and subjective rankings of LIS journals would be a useful investigation.

Deshpande, Meera, and D. Rajyalakshmi. "Citation Study of Dissertations in Library and Information Science." **Annals of Library Science & Documentation** 44 (June 1997): 41–53.

The major contribution of this entry is a journal ranking structured on the citations received in sixty-five LIS dissertations submitted to Nagpur University, in India, in the 1990–94 period. A lengthy table presents in rank order the 134 titles cited four or more times, while noting that 33 titles were cited three times, 55 twice, and 310 once. The authors also found, among other things, that 68.74 percent of the 3,109 total citations in the dissertations were to journals compared with 16.47 percent to books, and the cited half-life for journals was eleven years. Although some might question this entry's relevance to a North American audience, one can observe that four of the top ten journals are published in the United States and two others in the United Kingdom.

Hérubel, Jean-Pierre V.M., and Edward A. Goedeken. "Journals Publishing American Library History: A Research Note." **Libraries & Culture** 29 (spring 1994): 205–09.

Journals contributing to American library history are ranked by the number of citations received in essays in *Journal of Library History* (retitled *Libraries & Culture* in 1988) between 1968 and 1990. A total of 203 journals were included among 1,030 citations. A table lists in rank order the twenty most cited journals. Analysis by disciplinary affiliation (based on 202 titles) revealed that 41.6 percent were from library and information science and 18.3 percent were state history organs.[6] Hérubel and Goedeken provide the only known journal ranking in this relatively narrow field.

Nisonger, Thomas E. "Impact Factor-Based Ranking of Library and Information Science Journals in the *Social Sciences Citation Index Journal Citation Reports,* 1980 to 1992." In **Fifth International Conference of the International Society for Scientometrics and Informetrics: Proceedings—1995, June 7–10, 1995,** edited by Michael E. D. Koenig and Abraham Bookstein, 393–402. Medford, NJ: Learned Information, 1995. ISBN 1-57387-010-2.

Following a literature review of twenty-four LIS journal ranking studies published from 1952 through 1994, a table rank orders fifty-five LIS journals based on their mean impact factor in the *SSCI JCR* for the thirteen-year period 1980–92. Only journals covered in the *JCR* for seven of the thirteen years were included in the analysis. Another table displays the top ten journals' positions in previous rankings by Kohl and Davis and by Altuna Esteibar and Lancaster (see entry at the beginning of this section).[7] To investigate year-to-year consistency in *JCR* rankings, the mean yearly change in ranking position between 1980 and 1992 was examined for the fifty-five journals in the study. Because twenty-eight of them changed, on average, more than eight ranking position each year, the author recommends that librarians not rely upon a single year's *JCR* data for serial decision-making purposes.

Nkereuwem, E. E. "Accrediting Knowledge: The Ranking of Library and Information Science Journals." **Library Review** 46, nos. 1–2 (1997): 99–104 and **Asian Libraries** 6, nos. 1–2 (1997): 71–76.

For this subjective ranking, 200 Nigerian university librarians were sent a list of LIS journals (with a response rate of 81.5 percent) and asked to rate those titles they were familiar with on a 0 (poor) to 10 (outstanding) scale. Twenty-six journals are rank ordered in a table according to "journal impact," which is calculated by the following formula for combining the mean rating ("evaluation" in the formula) with the percentage of respondents familiar enough with the journal to rate it ("familiarity" in the formula):

$$\text{Impact} = \text{evaluation} + (\text{evaluation} \times \text{familiarity})$$

While taking a Nigerian perspective, this entry is noteworthy because it applies to LIS a ranking method ("journal impact" as explained above) developed for political science journals by James P. Lester.[8]

Tjoumas, Renee, and Virgil L. P. Blake. "Faculty Perceptions of the Professional Journal Literature: Quo Vadis?" **Journal of Education for Library & Information Science** 33 (summer 1992): 173–94.

The authors used the Kohl-Davis methodology to rank journals based on the perceptions of LIS faculty in two specialized areas identified through a 1986–87 directory of ALA accredited programs. Usable survey responses were received from thirty-five faculty specializing in school librarianship (a 52.2 percent response rate) and thirty public library faculty (a 60 percent rate). Two tables rank order the fifty-five surveyed titles according to their mean 1–5 rating by each group. Other tables name the twenty-five journals listed among the top five by school library faculty and the twenty-eight by public library faculty. Twelve additional titles suggested by school library faculty and four by school faculty are also indicated. Detailed analysis showed variation in the rankings by the two groups and with the earlier ranking by deans in the original Kohl-Davis study. Moreover, neither group displayed "strong internal consensus" in their ratings. Surprisingly, deans had "a somewhat higher opinion of the professional literature than their teaching colleagues." Although not stated by the authors, the divergence of opinion within a discipline complicates serials collection management for librarians.

JOURNAL RANKINGS IN THE SOCIAL SCIENCES

Alexander, John C., Jr., and Rodney H. Mabry. "Relative Significance of Journals, Authors, and Articles Cited in Financial Research." **Journal of Finance** 49 (June 1994): 697–712.

The authors rank finance journals using as their source the "over 17,000" citations in four "top-level" journals (*Journal of Finance, Journal of Financial Economics, Journal of Financial and Quantitative Analysis,* and *Review of Financial Studies*) from January 1987 through March 1991. They created three rankings based on total citations, "article effectiveness" (i.e., citations per articles published), and "impact efficiency" calculated as citations per 10,000 words published. A table rank orders the fifty most cited journals and "other media" defined as the total citations to a particular format such as books, dissertations, and so on. Economics journals predominate in the table, while working papers were ranked number three and books number four. Another table ranks the leading forty-one titles by impact efficiency and article effectiveness. Comparison of the two tables shows "a significant shift in the relative rankings" with some journals changing as many as ten positions. The fifty most cited authors and the fifty most cited articles are identified in other tables. Analysis by date revealed that citations to an article "reach a peak" two years after its publication and about 50 percent are received within five years.

Brinn, Tony, Michael John Jones, and Maurice Pendlebury. "U.K. Accountants' Perceptions of Research Journal Quality." **Accounting & Business Research** 26 (summer 1996): 265–78.

Brinn, Jones, and Pendlebury ranked accounting and finance journals by surveying in 1993 260 "active researchers" at British and Irish universities, generating a 33.8 percent usable response rate. Respondents indicated their familiarity with forty-nine "academic journals" according to a 1 ("not at all familiar") to 5 (very familiar) scale. Then, using the "magnitude estimated method of attitude measurement" they rated each journal's quality from 0 to no upper limit with *Accounting and Business Research* serving as a benchmark at 100. A table rank orders forty-four titles based on their overall familiarity rating, while five journals were eliminated because fewer than 11 respondents were familiar with them. The geometric mean (a computation that reduces the effect of extreme scores) of the quality ratings was used to rank separately thirty-nine "established journals" and five "recently established" titles based on perceived quality. Another table summarizes five earlier perception studies of accounting journals and makes comparisons with this study's findings. The authors found it "particularly striking" that U.K. academics ranked American journals higher than British journals.

Brown, Lawrence D., and Ronald J. Huefner. "The Familiarity with and Perceived Quality of Accounting Journals: Views of Senior Accounting Faculty in Leading U.S. MBA Programs." **Contemporary Accounting Research** 11 (summer 1994): 223–50.

Brown and Huefner offer a series of perception-based rankings of accounting journals. Senior (associate and full professors) accounting faculty at *Business Week's* forty best MBA programs were surveyed in March 1992 (49.3 percent of 367 responded) asking them to rate a list of forty-four journals on a 1 ("most prestigious") to 4 ("insignificant") scale or NF, not familiar. The journals are ranked according to the following: familiarity, that is, the percentage of respondents familiar with each title; the percentage who rated the title a 1; the composite score (the sum of each journal's rating time the percentage choosing that rating); and the percentage rating each title a 1 or 2. They found "relatively few" high quality journals and "substantial agreement" among faculty in the areas of financial, managerial, auditing, and tax accounting. After methodological analysis, the researchers do not believe response bias (respondents differ from nonrespondents), representation bias (their sample frame was not representative of all accounting faculty), or position bias (reflecting the journals order on the survey) "seriously" affected their findings.

Buchanan, Anne L., and Jean-Pierre V. M. Hérubel. "Profiling Ph.D. Dissertation Bibliographies: Serials and Collection Development in Political Science." **Behavioral & Social Sciences Librarian** 13, no. 1 (1994): 1–10.

This article ranks political science journals according to the number of times they were cited in the thirty-two dissertations accepted for the Ph.D. by Purdue University's Department of Political Science from 1970 to 1989. The authors found 327 journals were cited 1,351 times. A table lists in rank order the 98 titles cited twice or more. Analysis of all cited material by format indicated that 46.66 percent of the 3,673 total citations were to monographs and 43.9 percent to serials and periodicals. The Purdue University Libraries held all but 43 (13.14 percent) of the cited journal titles. This entry is significant because it was the only identified ranking of political science journals based on local citation data.

Cnaan, Ram A., Richard K. Caputo, and Yochi Shmuely. "Senior Faculty Perceptions of Social Work Journals." **Journal of Social Work Education** 30 (spring/ summer 1994): 185–99.

The authors offer a subjective ranking of social work journals. In February 1990, 421 senior U.S. social work faculty were mailed a list of 40 journals (42 percent responded) asking them to rate those titles with which they were familiar on a 1 (not acceptable) to 7 (outstanding) Likert scale. Actually 120 journals were involved in the study, but to save respondents' time, each survey form listed only 40 titles: 20 core titles and 20 other titles unique to that questionnaire. (There were five sets of questionnaires so each noncore title had equal coverage). The analysis was limited to the 97 titles with which at least 10 percent of the respondents were familiar. These are listed in rank order in a lengthy table according to what the authors term "prestige"—calculated by the following formula:

Prestige = Square root of proportion of familiarity $\times$
Mean overall quality rating.

This is an interesting study because of its methodology.

Cullen, Colleen M., and S. Randall Kalberg. "Chicago-Kent Law Review Faculty Scholarship Survey." **Chicago-Kent Law Review** 70, no. 3 (1995): 1445–60.

This item represents the third (earlier versions appeared in 1989 plus 1990) and evidently most recent "Faculty Scholarship Survey" by the *Chicago-Kent Law* Review. A table lists the leading forty law reviews according to the number of citations received in *Shepard's,* apparently from 1987 through 1993, although the authors' explanation on this point is inconsistent. Another table ranks the leading forty law reviews using a combination of *SSCI* data, with the total 1991 citations received counting half and the average of the 1988 and 1991 impact factors constituting the remaining half. Finally, a rather complex method is used to combine the initial two rankings to derive a final table listing the top twenty law review journals. Cullen and Kalberg admit their methodology employs "arbitrary weighing of factors." Also included are several rankings of law schools based on various types of faculty publication activity in the top twenty journals.

Goh, C. H., et al. "An Empirical Assessment of Influences on POM Research." **Omega** 24 (June 1996): 337–45.

This entry offers a citation-based ranking of journals in the rather specialized business field of production and operations management (POM). The 1989 to 1993 issues of five POM journals serve as the study's source. Of 30,944 citations, 64.4 percent were to journals, with 1,296 different ones cited, and 26.3 percent to books. A large table lists the top-ranking fifty journals according to a normalized total citation measure in which each base journal was weighted equally despite the number of citations it contained. The table also indicates each journal ranking based on unnormalized total citations and in an earlier subjective ranking by Barman and others.[9] Fifteen of the twenty journals covered in the subjective study ranked in the top twenty here. Another table presented the leading fifty journals based on an age-adjusted ranking using 1975 as a threshold. The top five journals remained the same, but eight journals moved up at least twenty ranking positions. While some might dispute the authors' claim to "a wholly objective methodology," this is a solid study.

Holsapple, Clyde W., et al. "A Citation Analysis of Business Computing Research Journals." **Information & Management** 25 (November 1993): 231–44.

In this entry, journals are ranked in the somewhat amorphous area of "business computing" based on the total citations received in five source journals during 1987 to 1991. A breakdown of the 27,543 citations revealed that 53.7 percent were to journals and 34.8 percent to books. In total, 1,366 journals were cited of which the top eighty-three (those receiving twenty-five or more citations) are listed in rank order in a table. The top twenty-five journals in each of the five source journals (listed in a table) displayed "statistically significant variations" in their rankings. In contrast, there was no statistically significant difference among the rankings of the leading twenty-five journals during each year from 1987 to 1991. Another table compares this ranking to six previously published ones. Analysis of these seven rankings was used to identify nineteen "first tier" journals (placing in the upper 25 percent in at least half the rankings) and twenty-five "second tier" titles (placing in the top 25 percent in over a quarter of them). The titles in both tiers are listed in alphabetical order. See entry earlier in this chapter for a follow-up study.

Laband, David N., and Michael J. Piette. "The Relative Impacts of Economics Journals: 1970–1990." **Journal of Economic Literature** 32 (June 1994): 640–66.

This study builds upon an important ranking of economics journals published in 1984 by Stanley J. Liebowitz and John P. Palmer.[10] Applying the latter's technique, ISI data was used to calculate for 130 journals the average number of citations received in 1990 per article published during 1985–89. A lengthy table rank orders these 130 titles plus 108 titles based on 1980 citations to 1975–79 articles and 50 titles using 1970 citations to 1965–69 articles. A second table ranks the same 1970, 1980, and 1990 journal sets using a weighted method, termed "adjusted citation per article," giving more influence to citations received from high-ranking journals. An appendix provides 1970, 1980, and 1990 rankings based on average citations per character and adjusted citations per character to normalize for varying article publishing policies among journals. Further analysis showed that the number of published pages of scholarly economics literature more than doubled between 1970 and 1990 and the citation rate rose 484 percent, but the concentration of citations to top-ranked journals decreased. The authors conclude that top general interest economics journals "more-or-less maintained their prominence," from 1970 to 1990 but second-tier general interest titles lost influence due to the rise of specialty journals. In this thoughtful study, Laband and Piette observe that "citations are the scientific community's version of dollar voting by consumers."

Nisonger, Thomas E. "A Ranking of Political Science Journals Based on Citation Data." **Serials Review** 19 (winter 1993): 7–14.

In order to provide a citation-based political science journal ranking as an alternative to earlier subjective rankings by Giles, Mizell, and Patterson as well as by Garand, Nisonger ranked the 65 journals from the former study for which data is available in the *SSCI JCR*.[11] The ranking was based on each journal's "adjusted" average *JCR* impact factor for 1987, 1988, and 1989. For a discussion of adjusted impact factor see entry by Nisonger, "A Methodological Issue Concerning the Use of *Social Sciences Citation Index Journal Citation Reports* Impact Factor Data for Journal Ranking," in chapter 9. He found a 0.71 correlation between his ranking and Giles, Mizell, and Patterson's and a 0.59 correlation with Garand's. A table lists the sixty-five journals in rank order along with their scores and positions in the two other rankings mentioned above, while another table identifies six consistently high-ranking political science journals from several studies. The author concludes the various rankings are neither "right" nor "wrong," but they measure "different nuances of value."

Ramsay, Ian, and G. P. Stapledon. "A Citation Analysis of Australian Law Journals." **Melbourne University Law Review** 21 (November 1997): 676–92.

This entry begins with an introduction to citation analysis and an extensive review of citation studies in the field of law. Three "limitations" to the Warren ranking, based on Australian law journals (see entry later in this section), are pointed out: a bias toward older journals with longer backruns, a bias toward titles publishing more pages, and the inclusion of journal self-citations. Ramsay and Stapledon analyzed the 1994 and 1995 years of fourteen Australian law journals (thirteen, such as the *University of Tasmania Law Review,* published at law schools plus the *Australian Law Journal)* focusing on journal citations, with self-citations excluded, published from 1990 to 1993 to normalize for titles with longer backruns. Of 1,596 citations, 21 percent were to the fourteen source journals, 25 percent to other Australian law journals, 48 percent to overseas law journals, and 6 percent to nonlaw journals. One hundred forty-four titles were cited with ten accounting for 26 percent of the total citations. A table lists the twenty most cited titles and an adjusted ranking structured on citations normalized to 1,000 pages of text (nine of the top ten and thirteen of the leading twenty are the same in both rankings). Although a methodologically meticulous study is offered here, more explicit analysis of this ranking compared to Warren's would have been welcome.

Shapiro, Fred R. "The Most-Cited Law Reviews." **Journal of Legal Studies** 29 (January 2000): 389–96.

Shapiro uses a "powerful database," provided to him by the West Group, containing 1981 to 1997 *SSCI* data for legal periodicals to construct four citation-based rankings of law journals:

- The top thirty general law reviews according to total citations received from 1987 to 1997

- The top thirty general law reviews according to average 1987 through 1997 impact factor

- The top thirty specialized legal periodicals based on total citations from 1987 to 1997

- The top thirty specialized legal periodicals based on average 1987 to 1997 impact factor

Four separate tables list the journals in each ranking. That *Yale Law Journal* placed first in the two general review rankings is termed "the most notable result" as a table summarizing eight previous citation-based law review rankings published between 1969 and 1995 showed *Harvard Law Review* was first in each.

Smyth, Russell. "A Citation Analysis of Australian Economic Journals." **Australian Academic & Research Libraries** 30 (June 1999): 119–33.

After reviewing rankings of economics journals published outside of Australia, variously using authors' institutional affiliation, the Delphi method, and citation data, Smyth conducted his own investigation structured on the 1993 to 1997 volumes of five Australian journals including *Australian Economic Papers* and the *Australian Economic Review.* Limiting his study to journal citations published between 1980 and 1996, he counted total citations and calculated his own "impact factor," (i.e., the number of citations per 1,000 pages of text). Altogether 514 titles were cited, of which 4 percent were Australian economics or econometrics periodicals, 47 percent were overseas periodicals in those fields, and 49 percent were from other disciplines (without distinction between Australian and non-Australian titles). A table rank orders the top thirty journals by both total citations and impact factor. The top five by citation count produced 23 percent of the 3,975 citations and the top ten 35 percent. Two of the top ten in Liebowitz and Palmer's study and three in Laband and Piette's (see entry earlier in this section) top ten ranked among the ten highest by impact factor in Smyth's ranking.[12] The author of this methodologically well-done study concludes "there is a core of important journals, which Australian economists use," but it differs from the core in non-Australian rankings.

Verma, Maya. "Citation Analysis of Some Selected Indian Journals in Economics." **Annals of Library Science & Documentation** 41 (March 1994): 33–39.
 Economics journals are ranked according to the number of citations received in three Indian economics journals (*Indian Economic Journal, Indian Economic Review,* and *Indian Journal of Economics*) between 1986 and 1990. Of the total citations, 46.91 percent were to journals and 33.80 percent to books, while their median age was between 13 and 14 years. A table presents in rank order the top 54 journal titles of the 324 cited 2,599 times. This entry is listed under journal rankings because it contains considerably less information than most other citation studies published in India.

Walstrom, Kent A. "A Review of the Relative Prestige of Business Research Journals." **Serials Librarian** 41, no. 2 (2001): 85–99.
 Fourteen business journal rankings published between 1987 and 1997 in seven business areas, such as finance, accounting, management and marketing, are combined in this investigation. Altogether 326 journals were included in these rankings, but Walstrom's analysis is limited to the thirty-four titles ranked in more than one discipline. A formula, combining a journal's rank with the number of titles in the ranking, was used to rate each title on a 1 to 100 scale. A table listing the titles in alphabetical order, presents each of the thirty-four journal's ratings in the seven business areas along with an overall average. The author then identifies 10 "high quality" journals rated at 50 or more in at least three business areas. Walstrom found "agreement" between his study and earlier rankings by Elaine Hobbs Fry, C. Glenn Walters, and Lawrence E. Scheuermann in 1985 and Laurence J. Moore and Bernard W. Taylor, III in 1980.[13] This study is notable because it uses meta-analysis of rankings in specific business subdisciplines to create a general business ranking and rating.

Warren, Dennis. "Australian Law Journals: An Analysis of Citation Patterns." **Australian Academic & Research Libraries** 27 (December 1996): 261–69.
 Warren's study uses as a source the journal citations from the 547 articles in the 1995 issues of thirty-two Australian law journals covered in *Index to Legal*

Periodicals and Books. A total of 999 journal articles were cited. The 100 most frequently cited journals (cited ten or more times) are rank ordered in a table. The top fourteen journals produced 25 percent of the 4,705 total citations and the leading sixty accounted for 50 percent. Furthermore, 42 percent of the citations were from Australia, 33 percent the United States, and 17 percent the United Kingdom. Sixty-four percent of the citations published in 1995 were to Australian journals contrasted to 30 percent of citations published a decade earlier: a pattern attributed to growth in Australian legal scholarship. A comparison with James Leonard's 1990 ranking based on citations in U.S. law journals found that eight of the top ten journals were the same in both studies.[14] See also Ramsay and Stapledon for a later ranking also structured on Australian law journals.

Wicks, Andrew C., and Robbin Derry. "An Evaluation of Journal Quality: The Perspective of Business Ethics Researchers." **Business Ethics Quarterly** 6 (July 1996): 359–72.
A subjective or, using the authors' words, "opinion-based" ranking of business ethics journals is provided in this piece. One hundred fifty members of the Society for Business Ethics were surveyed with a 25.5 percent response rate. The respondents rated a list of fourteen business ethics and management journals using a 1 (poor) to 5 (excellent) scale according to five criteria:

1. "Overall journal quality"

2. "Quality of business ethics articles"

3. "Centrality of ethics articles to 'the dialogue'"

4. "Selectivity," (i.e., the respondents perception of the journal's acceptance rate)

5. "Overall rating"

Three tables rank order the journals by criteria 5, criteria 2 and 3 in combination with each other, and a combination of criteria 1 and 4. Business ethics journals rated highly on criteria 2 and 3 and management journals on 1 and 4, indicating "a strong division" between journals in the two areas. This is, according to the authors, the first ranking of business ethics journals.

JOURNAL RANKINGS IN THE SCIENCES

Bandyopadhyay, Amit Kumar. "Citation Analysis of Doctoral Dissertations in Mathematics Using dBase III." **Annals of Library Science & Documentation** 43 (September 1996): 81–107.
This entry, based on citations in twenty-seven doctoral dissertations submitted between 1981 and 1990 to the University of Burdwan (West Bengal, India) contains numerous rankings of mathematics journals. Bandyopadhyay found that 80.01 percent of the 2,261 citations were to journals and 14.86 percent to books.

A total of 384 journals were cited with 32 accounting for 50 percent of the citations. Tables list in rank order abbreviations for the 41 titles cited eleven or more times, the 46 most frequently cited journals in pure mathematics, the top 42 in applied mathematics, and the leading 30 in statistics. There are several other rankings based on narrow technical criteria that would not be especially useful to this book's readers. Appendices explain the use of *dBase III* for compiling the data.

Barooah, P. K. "Pattern of Information Use by Indian Entomologists." **Annals of Library Science & Documentation** 40 (September 1993): 104–114.

This ranking of entomology journals is based on citations in the *Indian Journal of Entomology's* 1989 volume. Barooah found that 73.2 percent of the 981 citations were to journals whereas 7.95 percent were to books, and 41.1 percent were from Indian sources compared to 23.05 percent from the United States. Of the 214 cited journals, 27.1 percent originate in India. A table rank orders the 82 journals cited at least twice, while another table lists the 21 most frequently cited Indian journals. The half-life of all cited literature ranged between 18 and 19 years. The author asserts the distribution of journal citations "is in accordance with Bradford's Law."

Biradar, B. S., and T. Vijayalaxmi. "Pattern of Information Use by Indian Neurological Scientists: A Bibliometric Study." **Annals of Library Science & Documentation** 44 (December 1997): 143–51.

The authors rank neurology journals according to the number of citations received in thirty-nine dissertations submitted to the Department of Neurology, the National Institute of Mental Health and Neuro Sciences, at Deemed University, Bangalore, India from 1979 to 1996. Of 3,635 citations, 80.20 percent were to journals and 17.36 percent to books. The seventy-five journals cited at least six times are listed in a table. The top twenty-five journals account for 70 percent of the 2,915 journal citations. Further analysis of the journal citations found that 49.61 percent ranged in age from 0 to 10 years with the oldest at 111 years.

Dame, Mark A., and Fredric D. Wolinsky. "Rating Journals in Health Care Administration: The Use of Bibliometric Measures." **Medical Care** 31, no. 6 (1993): 520–24.

This investigation offers citation-based alternatives to a 1991 ranking of health care administration journals by Charles H. Brooks, Lawrence R. Walker, and Richard Szorady using the perceptions of department chairs.[15] Three citation rankings (1989 impact factor, average 1981–89 impact factor, and "discounted average impact factor," giving greater weight to more recent years) were created for twenty-six of the fifty-three journals from the later study covered in the *JCR*. Dame and Wolinsky discovered that the three citations rankings were highly correlated with each other (none less than 0.928) but only moderately (ranging from 0.461 to 0.551) with the perception-based ranking. Further comparison of the citation and perception approaches showed that four of the top five journals were different and seven titles differed by at least ten ranking positions. This entry is noteworthy for exploring the relationship between citation and subjective rankings in a narrow field.

Lal, Arjun. "Literature Contribution in Indian Journal of Genetics and Plant Breeding: A Citation Analysis." **Annals of Library Science & Documentation** 40 (June 1993): 64–76.

Lal states, "The main objective of this study is to prepare a rank list of journals...in the field of genetics and plant breeding." The study is based on 4,136 citations in the *Indian Journal of Genetics and Plant Breeding* from 1985 to 1989. Lal found 78.72 percent of these citations were to periodicals and 21.28 percent to nonperiodical items. In total, 574 periodicals were cited. The top 60, cited eight or more times and accounting for 66.86 percent of periodical citations, are separately listed in a table. A table analyzing the leading 60 periodicals indicates that 21 accounting for 21.50 percent of the periodical citations originated in the United States, whereas 16 accounting for 22.60 percent of the citations were published in India. Other tables provide additional data, such as that concerning Indian theses and authorship patterns, which are not of concern for this book's objectives. The word "periodical" rather than "journal" is used in this annotation because Lal confuses the traditional distinction between the two terms.

Lal, Arjun, and K. C. Panda. "Research in Plant Patholoy: A Bibliometric Analysis." **Library Science with a Slant to Documentation** 33 (September 1996): 135–47.

This journal ranking and citation study of plant pathology uses as its source the twenty Ph.D. dissertations submitted to the Department of Plant Pathology of Rajendra Agricultural University in Bihar, India from 1980 to 1993. They counted 3,685 citations of which 82.04 percent were periodicals and 66.11 percent journals. Altogether 631 periodicals were cited with the 10 most frequently cited titles producing 38.93 percent of the total citations and the top 20 producing 50.31 percent while 352 titles were cited only once. A four-page table, listing the top 100 periodicals according to the number of total citations received, also indicates their language, year of establishment, and county of publication. The authors note the "high status" of multidisciplinary science journals. Similarities and differences with three earlier rankings of plant pathology journals are pointed out. Lal and Panda could have strengthened the article by tabulating their data about the top 100 titles' language and country of origin, although a cursory examinations reveals that 6 of the leading 20 were published in the United States or Canada.

Moorbath, Paul. "A Study of Journals Needed to Support the Project 2000 Nursing Course with an Evaluation of Citation Counting as a Method of Journal Selection." **Aslib Proceedings** 45 (February 1993): 39–46.

This complex inquiry, conducted in support of a U.K. nursing education program termed Project 2000, contains eight different rankings of nursing journals. The first ranking, deemed a citation ranking, identifies the most frequently listed titles in the *International Nursing Index,* 1990, issue 3's "Citation Index." Unfortunately, coverage in an index is not a genuine citation whereby one journal cites another. (Technically, an index-coverage ranking is based on production.) There are four actual citation rankings structured on total citations during one-year periods (1989 or 1990) in the journals *Paediatric Nursing, Journal of Advanced Nursing, British Journal of Mental Subnormality,* and *Journal of Psychosocial*

Nursing. Two other rankings were constructed from student use, that is, photo-copying and citations in their papers, and the mean subjective judgment of tutors using a four-point scale from "not necessary" to "essential." Finally, these seven rankings are combined (by adding ranking positions) to create a composite rank-ing of twenty-eight nursing journals. The author concludes that citation rankings are not "suitable" for journal selection because the "Citation Index" ranking dis-played weak, nonstatistically significant correlations with the student use ranking (0.2535) and the tudor's subjective ranking (0.3631). This is an interesting but flawed study.

Sittig, Dean. F., and J. Kaalass-Sittig. "A Quantitative Ranking of the Biomedical Informatics Serials." **Methods of Information in Medicine** 34 (September 1995): 397–410.

Arguing that rankings based on citation data, use, expert opinion, or size/pro-ductivity all have limitations, the authors offer a ranking of biomedical informat-ics serials that incorporates fourteen variables, including the following: coverage by *Index Medicus,* subscription cost, the percentage of major biomedical libraries holding the title, total circulation, year first published, subjective assessment by American College of Medical Informatics members, and impact factor, immedi-acy index, and cited half-life from the *Journal Citation Reports.* Thirty-four titles were ranked on each variables and the final ranking (presented in a table) was based on the average of these fourteen scores. Recalculation of the final ranking with each factor removed revealed that expert opinion had the largest impact on the final ranking and coverage by *Index Medicus* the least. Regression analysis on the variables found, among other things, that older journals were held by more libraries, but there was "little relationship" between the cost per article and library holdings. The authors admit that counting each of the fourteen variables equally and the fact that *JCR* citation data was available for only thirteen titles represent limitations to their study. Nevertheless, this is a rigorous and meticulously done ranking in a subject that is assuming increasing importance to society.

Slater, Barbara M., and Mark A. Slater. "Determining Core Journals in Behavioral Medicine." **Bulletin of the Medical Library Association** 82, no. 1 (1994): 70–72.

Slater offers two journal rankings in the multidisciplinary field of behavioral medicine. The first ranking was based on counting journals whose articles were abstracted in *Behavioral Medicine Abstracts* during 1990–91. A table rank orders the forty-seven titles whose articles were abstracted 13 or more time. These titles represented 38 percent of the 122 total titles and accounted for 77 percent of the 1,566 published abstracts. The second ranking was constructed from the journals cited in the articles abstracted by *Behavioral Medicine Abstracts* in 1991. Table 2 rank orders the 77 titles (which represent 4 percent of the 1,820 cited titles and produce 77 percent of the 17,649 journal citations) cited more than fifty times. Combination of the two lists results in a single listing of 91 journals, which Slater states she will supply the reader upon request. Further analysis showed that 30.7 percent of the 91 titles were covered by both the Brandon Hill list and *Abridged Index Medicus.*[16] The authors observe that "very few" of the ranked titles are specific to behavioral medicine, concluding that ILL and document delivery services are necessary to meet professional needs.

Udofia, Udofia Iton. "Selecting Veterinary Medical Periodicals Through Citation Analysis." **Library Review** 46, no. 2 (1997): 105–12.

This ranking is constructed from journal citations in 105 veterinary medicine journals for the five-year period 1982–86. Udofia found 119 journals were cited more than 1,500 times. The top forty-nine journals are listed in rank order. Eight journals, accounting for 66.2 percent of the total citations, were labeled the core while second and third Bradford zones were also identified. Because the ranking seems somewhat skewed toward African titles (the author is a Nigerian librarian), one wishes the selection criteria for the 105 source journals had been explained.

JOURNAL RANKINGS IN ALLIED HEALTH

Burnham, Judy F. "Mapping the Literature of Radiologic Technology." **Bulletin of the Medical Library Association** 85 (July 1997): 289–92.

(Note that this article is part of the Project for Mapping the Literature of Allied Health. For details about the project, see the entry by Barbara F. Schloman, "Mapping the Literature of Allied Health: Project Overview" later in this section.) The 1991 through 1993 volumes of *Applied Radiology, Canadian Journal of Medical Radiology,* and *Radiologic Technology* were used as the source for this study. The investigator discovered that 81.4 percent of the 5,269 citations were to journals and 14.0 percent to books. In regard to years cited, 22.5 percent of the journal citations were to 1990–93 and 61.6 percent to 1980–89, whereas the corresponding figures for books were 18.6 percent and 61.2 percent. Organization of cited journals into Bradford zones revealed 4 journals in zone 1, 51 in zone 2, and 604 in zone 3, respectively producing 34.3 percent, 32.5 percent, and 33.2 percent of the citations. Burnham notes that 376 titles were cited only once. *MEDLINE* and *EMBASE* "provided the best indexing coverage."

Burnham, Judy F. "Mapping the Literature of Respiratory Therapy." **Bulletin of the Medical Library Association** 85 (July 1997): 293–96.

Burnham analyzed all the citations in *Respiratory Care* and *RRT: The Canadian Journal of Respiratory Therapy* for the years 1991 through 1993 and every tenth citation in *Chest* during those years. She found that 90.5 percent of 16,159 citations were to journal articles, while 7.5 percent were to books. Analysis by age indicated that 18.0 percent of the journal citations were to 1990–93 and 60.2 percent to 1980–89, while the respective figures were 25.3 percent and 53.7 percent for citations to books. The Bradford analysis showed 5 journals accounting for 32.2 percent of the citations in zone 1, 32 accounting for 33.5 percent in zone 2, and 1,191 in zone 3 producing 34.3 percent of the citations. Moreover, 609 zone 3 journals received only one citation. A table lists the journals in zones 1 and 2. Analysis of indexing found *MEDLINE* offered the best coverage, while *EMBASE* was "adequate." The top 55 journals are rank ordered in a table.

Haaland, Ardis. "Mapping the Literature of Dental Hygiene." **Bulletin of the Medical Library Association** 87 (July 1999): 283–86.

This study is constructed from citations in all the 1993 through 1995 articles in three journals: *Journal of Dental Hygiene, Journal of Practical Hygiene,* and *Probe.* Analysis by format showed that 69.5 percent of the 2,632 citations were to journals, 18.1 percent to books, and 5.0 percent to government documents. Haaland found that 36.4 percent of the citations were to 1990–95 and 35.0 percent to 1985–89. Government documents were deemed the "most current" format as 81.1 percent of their citations date to 1985–95, whereas books, with only 66.5 percent of their citations to those years, were termed "the oldest material." Organization of the cited journal titles in three Bradford zones found 5, 42, and 342 titles accounting for 34.5 percent, 34.5 percent, and 31.0 percent of the citations. The 47 journals in the first two zones are named in a table. *MEDLINE* "had the best indexing coverage."

Hall, Ellen F. "Mapping the Literature of Perfusion." **Bulletin of the Medical Library Association** 87 (July 1999): 305–11.

Hall explains that perfusion concerns maintaining machines that support patient's circulatory or respiratory functions and that the Cleveland Clinic started the first organized training for perfusionists in 1963. The years 1993–95 of the journals *Perfusion* and *Journal of Extra-Corporeal Technology* served as this investigation's source. Of 5,051 citations, 88.2 percent were to journals and 10.8 percent to books. Analysis by publication date demonstrated that 36.2 percent of the journal citations were to 1990–95 and 27.1 percent to 1985–89, while the corresponding figures for books were 36.1 percent and 29.1 percent. Data for three Bradford zones were as follows: zone 1, 6 journals, 34.1 percent of the citations; zone 2, 37 journals, 33.1 percent; and zone 3, 506 journals, 32.8 percent. Three hundred ninety-four journals were cited only once. A table lists the 43 journals from the first two Bradford zones. The best indexing was provided by *MEDLINE*.

Hook, Sara Anne, and Crystal F. Wagner. "Mapping the Literature of Dental Assisting." **Bulletin of the Medical Library Association** 87 (July 1999): 277–82.

The 1995–97 years of *Dental Assistant* and *Journal of the CDAA* plus the 1995–96 volumes of *Dental Teamwork* were used as this investigation's source journals. Of 528 total citations, 73.7 percent were to journals, 14.9 percent to books, 3.8 percent to government documents, 1.9 percent to laws, and 0.8 percent to Web sites. Analysis by publication date shows that 13.6 percent of all the citations were to the years 1995–97, 45.3 percent to 1990–94, and 16.9 percent to 1985–89. Three zone 1 journals—*Journal of the American Dental Association, MMWR: Morbidity Mortality Weekly Report,* and *Journal of Periodontology*—produced 32.9 percent of the citations, while 16 zone 2 titles accounted for 30.6 percent, and 108 in the third zone produced 36.5 percent. *MEDLINE* "appeared to be the database of choice." The top 19 journals, comprising the first two zones, are listed.

Reed, Kathlyn L. "Mapping the Literature of Occupational Therapy." **Bulletin of the Medical Library Association** 87 (July 1999): 298–304.

The 8,068 citations from 1995 and 1996 articles in *American Journal of Occupational Therapy, Occupational Therapy Journal of Research,* and *Occupational Therapy in Health Care* served as this investigation's source. Analysis by format revealed that 61.2 percent of the citations were to journals and 26.1 percent to books. Exactly 35.0 percent of the citations were to 1990–96 and 47.0 percent to 1980–89. It is not possible to provide data for books or journals because Reed tabulated the age data differently than the other authors in this series. *American Journal of Occupational Therapy, Archives of Physical Medicine and Rehabilitation,* and *Occupational Therapy Journal of Research* (two of which were source journals), producing 35.0 percent of the citations, comprised the first Bradford zone. There were 117 journals in zone 2 and 657 in zone 3, accounting, respectively, for 31.7 percent and 33.3 percent of the citations. The author observes that twelve different disciplines are represented in the second zone. The top 120 journals from the first two zones are listed. *MEDLINE* provided the best overall coverage but *Cumulative Index to Nursing and Allied Health Literature* was the only index covering the top three journals.

Roberts, Dave. "The Journal Literature of Occupational Therapy: A Comparison of Coverage by Four Bibliographic Information Services." **British Journal of Occupational Therapy** 55 (April 1992): 143–47.
   This study provides a citation-based ranking of occupational therapy journals and investigates their coverage in four indexing services: *Index Medicus, Excerpta Medica, CINAHL,* and *Occupational Therapy Index.* Seven journals, including the *American Journal of Occupational Therapy,* the *British Journal of Occupational Therapy,* and *Australian Occupational Therapy Journal* were used as the citation source. Roberts tabulated 2,791 citations to 622 different journals. A table lists in rank order the thirty-five titles cited twelve or more times. An analysis of indexing for the 35 ranked titles found that no index offered comprehensive coverage, but *Occupational Therapy Index's* was the most complete. This entry is quite similar in scope to those in the Project for Mapping the Literature of Allied Health series, except Bradford analysis is not used.

Schloman, Barbara F. "Mapping the Literature of Allied Health: Project Overview." **Bulletin of the Medical Library Association** 85 (July 1997): 271–77.
   This item describes the Project for Mapping the Literature of Allied Health's background and methodology. Note that most of this section's entries are byproducts of the Project, which dates to 1993 when the Medical Library Association's (MLA's) Nursing and Allied Health Resources Section appointed a task force to identify core journals in allied health fields and assess their coverage by indexing and abstracting services. Allied health is defined as all "health-related disciplines with the exception of nursing . . . medicine, osteopathy, dentistry, veterinary medicine, optometry, pharmacy, and podiatry."
   Explaining the Project's methodology, Schloman states the initial step is to identify source journals appropriate to the field. The citations in each source journal article during a three-year period (initially 1991 through 1993) serve as the basis of the study. These citations are then broken down by age and format (i.e., book, journal, and miscellaneous). To examine concentration and scatter of the

journal literature, the cited journal titles are organized into three Bradford zones, each zone accounting for approximately one-third the journal citations. The small number of titles in zone 1 are considered the nucleus or core. Although of lesser concern for this book's purpose, indexing coverage is analyzed for zone 1 and 2 journals. Chi-square tests are used to assess the statistical significance of the findings on age, format, and journal dispersion.

Finally, Schloman summaries the results from five studies in the Project's first phase: health education by herself, physical therapy by Wakiji, radiologic technology and respiratory therapy both by Burnham, and speech-language pathology by Slater (see entries in this section). Composite data from the five studies revealed that 18.4 percent of the 73,099 citations were to books and 75.1 percent to journals, while 16.2 percent of 72,987 citations were to the years 1990–93, 59.4 percent to 1980–89, and 7.8 percent predated 1970. There were a total of 39 zone 1 journals, 296 in zone 2, and 5,705 in the third zone. The "strongest" indexing coverage was offered by *MEDLINE* followed by *EMBASE*.

Schloman, Barbara F. "Mapping the Literature of Health Education." **Bulletin of the Medical Library Association** 85 (July 1997): 278–83.

Schloman's analysis was based on 1991 to 1993 citations in four source journals (in contrast to this series' usual three): *Health Education Quarterly, Journal of American College Health, Journal of Health Education,* and *Journal of School Health.* The results showed that 64.8 percent of the 11,054 citations were to journals, 18.9 percent to books, and 6.0 percent to government documents. The breakdown by date indicated 31.3 percent of the government document citations, 20.1 percent of the journal ones, and 16.4 percent of the book citations were published from 1990 to 1993, while the percentage between 1985 and 1989 was 43.6 for government documents, 47.9 for journals, and 34.6 for books. Bradford distribution by zone revealed 13 journals in zone 1, 80 in the second, and 1,041 in the third zone, with the three zones accounting for 33.5 percent, 32.8 percent, and 33.7 percent of the citations. "*MEDLINE* gives the best indexing coverage...followed by *EMBASE*...and *PsycINFO*." The 93 journal titles from the first two zones are displayed in a table.

Slater, Linda G. "Mapping the Literature of Speech-Language Pathology." **Bulletin of the Medical Library Association** 85 (July 1997): 297–302.

All the 1991 through 1993 citations in *American Journal of Speech-Language Pathology, Journal of Speech and Hearing Research, British Journal of Disorders of Communication/European Journal of Disorders of Communication,* and *Journal of Communication Disorders* served as the source for this investigation. Slater discovered that 63.1 percent of the 17,672 citations were to journals and 29.8 percent to monographs. In terms of age, 13.4 percent of the journal citations and 9.9 percent of the book citations fell between 1990 and 1993, while 56.0 percent of the journal and 56.6 percent of the monographic citations fell in the 1980–89 range. Three titles (*Journal of Speech and Hearing Research, Journal of Speech and Hearing Disorders,* and *Journal of the Acoustical Society of America*) comprised zone 1, while there were 38 journals in zone 2 and 840 in zone 3. Each zone received approximately one-third the citations, although the precise percentages are not reported. Examination of zone 1 and 2 journals, identified in a table, leads Slater to conclude "speech-language pathology authors draw very heavily from the literature of their own field." *Current Contents* and *MEDLINE* had the best indexing coverage.

Smith, Aida Marissa. "Mapping the Literature of Dietetics." **Bulletin of the Medical Library Association** 87 (July 1999): 292–97.

Citations in "all full-length feature articles" in the 1995 to 1997 issues of *Journal of the American Dietetic Association, Journal of Nutrition Education,* and *Nutrition Today* served as this investigation's source. Of 14,241 citations, 76.0 percent were to journals, 16.2 percent to books, 5.0 percent to government documents, and 0.1 percent to Internet resources. Smith found books were the "least current" as 47.2 percent of monographic citations were to the years 1990–98, whereas Internet resources were the "most current" because, not surprisingly, 100 percent of their citations were to those years. In total, 54.4 percent of all the citations were to 1990–98. Eight journals, producing 33.5 percent of the citations made up Bradford zone 1, while there were 78 journals with 33.2 percent of the citations in zone 2, and 1,280 with 33.1 percent in the third zone. The top 86 journals are identified in a table extending more than one page. The most complete indexing coverage was provided by *EMBASE/Excerpta Medica* closely followed by *MEDLINE*.

Stevens, Sheryl R. "Mapping the Literature of Cytotechnology." **Bulletin of the Medical Library Association** 88 (April 2000): 172–77.

The field of cytotechnology, that is, the application of medical laboratory techniques to cells, was mapped based on analysis of three journals: *Acta Cytologica* and *Diagnostic Cytopathology,* 1995 through 1997, and *Cancer Cytopathology,* for 1997 only. Stevens found that 89.2 percent of 21,021 cited references were to journals and 9.6 percent to books, and that 45.7 percent of the citations were to the years 1990 to 1997. The three journals in zone 1 (*Acta Cytologica, Cancer,* and *Diagnostic Cytopathology*) accounted for 36.8 percent of journal citations, whereas 26 zone 2 journals contained 30.1 percent of the citations, and the remaining 33.1 percent were scattered among 1,069 zone 3 journals. The zone 1 and 2 titles were checked for coverage in five databases. It is interesting that two of the three source journals were also in the first zone.

Wakiji, Eileen M. "Mapping the Literature of Physical Therapy." **Bulletin of the Medical Library Association** 85 (July 1997): 284–88.

Unlike most entries in the series, this study used only two source journals, *Physical Therapy* and *Archives of Physical Medicine and Rehabilitation,* analyzing the years 1991 through 1993 for both. Of the 22,945 total citations, 77.0 percent were to journal articles, 18.2 percent to books, and 0.7 percent to government documents. Wakiji observes that government documents were the most "current" as 26.3 percent of those citations were to 1990–93 and 55.1 percent to 1980–89. In contrast, 13.0 percent of the book citations were to 1990–93 and 62.8 percent to 1980–89, while the figures for journals were 12.9 percent and 58.6 percent. The Bradford distribution data were: zone 1, 14 journals, 33.7 percent of the citations;

zone 2, 95 journals, 33.2 percent; and zone 3, 1,694 journals, 33.0 percent. The zone 1 and 2 journals are listed.

Walcott, Barbara M. "Mapping the Literature of Diagnostic Medical Sonography." **Bulletin of the Medical Library Association** 87 (July 1999): 287–91.

Journals are ranked in diagnostic medical sonography (i.e., use of ultrasound imaging) based on 6,467 citations in *Journal of Diagnostic Medical Sonography, Journal of the American Society of Echocardiography,* and *Ultrasonic Imaging* during 1993 through 1995. A breakdown by format showed 90.2 percent of the citations were to journals and 8.5 percent to books. Furthermore, 42.5 percent of the book citations and 40.7 percent of the journal citations were to 1990–95, whereas 25.9 percent of book and 33.6 percent of journal citations dated to 1985–89. Moreover, 97 percent of all citations were published since 1970. The concentration of citations to a few journals was exceedingly high. Only two titles accounting for 33.6 percent of the citations *(Journal of the American College of Cardiology* and *Circulation*) made up the first Bradford zone, and there were only 12 journals producing 34.0 percent of the citations in zone 2. However, 461 zone 3 journals produced the remaining citations. As usual in this series, the 14 journals in zones 1 and 2 are listed in rank order. *MEDLINE* "does a little better" than *EMBASE/Excerpta Medica* in indexing coverage.

NOTES

1. P. L. K. Gross and E. M. Gross, "College Libraries and Chemical Education," *Science* 66 (October 28, 1927): 385–89.

2. Fred R. Shapiro, "The Most-Cited Law Reviews," *Journal of Legal Studies* 29 (January 2000): 390.

3. Randolph B. Cooper, "Review of Management Information Systems Research: A Management Support Emphasis," *Information Processing & Management* 24, no. 1 (1988): 73–102.

4. M. P. Allen, "The Quality of Journals in Sociology Reconsidered: Objective Measures of Journal Influence," *Footnotes* 18 (November 1990): 4–5. *Footnotes* is a journal published by the American Sociological Association.

5. David F. Kohl and Charles H. Davis, "Ratings of Journals by ARL Library Directors and Deans of Library and Information Science Schools," *College & Research Libraries* 46 (January 1985): 40–47.

6. The percentages are Nisonger's calculation from the original authors' raw data.

7. Kohl and Davis, "Ratings of Journals by ARL Library Directors and Deans of Library and Information Science Schools."

8. James P. Lester, "Evaluating the Evaluators: Accrediting Knowledge and the Ranking of Political Science Journals," *PS: Political Science & Politics* 23 (September 1990): 445–47.

9. Samir Barman, Richard J. Tersine, and M. Ronald Buckley, "An Empirical Assessment of the Perceived Relevance and Quality of POM-Related Journals by Academicians," *Journal of Operations Management* 10 (April 1991):194–212.

10. Stanley J. Liebowitz and John P. Palmer, "Assessing the Relative Impacts of Economics Journals," *Journal of Economic Literature* 22 (March 1984): 77–88.

11. Micheal W. Giles, Francie Mizell, and David Patterson, "Political Scientists' Journal Evaluations Revisited," *PS: Political Science & Politics* 22 (September 1989): 613–17; James C. Garand, "An Alternative Interpretation of Recent Political Science Journal Evaluations."

12. Liebowitz and Palmer, "Assessing the Relative Impacts of Economics Journals."

13. Elaine Hobbs Fry, C. Glenn Walters , and Lawrence E. Scheuermann, "Perceived Quality of Fifty Selected Journals: Academicians and Practitioners," *Journal of the Academy of Marketing Science* 13 (spring 1985): 352–61; Laurence J. Moore and Bernard W. Taylor, III, "A Study of Institutional Publications in Business-Related Academic Journals, 1972–1978," *Quarterly Review of Economics and Business* 20 (spring 1980): 87–97.

14. James Leonard, "Seein' the Cites: A Guided Tour of Citation Patterns in Recent American Law Review Articles," *Saint Louis University Law Journal* 34 (winter 1990): 181–239.

15. Charles H. Brooks, Lawrence R. Walker, and Richard Szorady, "Rating Journals in Health Care Administration: The Perceptions of Program Chairpersons," *Medical Care* 29 (August 1991): 755–65.

16. Percentage is Nisonger's calculation from Slaters' raw data; Alfred N. Brandon and Dorothy R. Hill, "Selected List of Books and Journals for the Small Medical Library," *Bulletin of the Medical Library Association* 81 (April 1993): 141–68.

11

Evaluation of Electronic Resources

Throughout the twentieth century, libraries integrated new formats into their collection management strategies, including microfilm in the 1930s, audio-visual materials in the post-World War II era, and CD-ROMs in the 1980s. During the last decade, electronic journals, electronic books, the World Wide Web, and full-text databases have emerged as important formats that present numerous challenges to librarians.

A voluminous amount has been published concerning electronic resources in recent years. A search of the *Library Literature and Information Science* database retrieved 1,026 items pertaining to electronic journals, published between 1992 and July 2002.[1] However, much of this literature is prescriptive or descriptive and does not relate to evaluation. A Boolean search combining "evaluation" with the previously mentioned search results reduced the number of recalled entries to 81. A major portion of the electronic resource evaluation literature relates to technological issues, including hardware and software, the user interface, navigation, searching features, screen display, and so on, that are obviously beyond this book's scope. Much of the nontechnical literature also addresses topics irrelevant to this volume, such as cataloging or technical services. Yet a significant portion addresses content issues, such as coverage and currency. Since electronic resource content may be viewed as part of a library's collection, evaluation of electronic resource content is a logical extension of collection evaluation. Indeed, the well-known content management expert Péter Jacsó notes that some of its evaluation criteria can be traced to those long-used for collection evaluation.[2] In addition to criteria, such traditional evaluation approaches as use studies and citation analysis can, with some modifications, be applied to electronic resources.

Accordingly, this chapter annotates items pertaining to the evaluation of electronic resources for collection management purposes and their use in a library context. The primary focus is on Web sites, full-text databases, electronic journals, and electronic books. Excluded are items that primarily deal with the following: technological issues, the evaluation of the Web collectively rather than specific Web sites, Web search engines, Web design, the use of electronic resources apart from a library context, the acceptance of electronic resources by scholars, and basic descriptions of vendor products or library implementation of e-resources without offering evaluation.

Electronic resource evaluation often takes place at the micro-level (evaluation of a specific resource) rather than the macro-level (evaluation of an entire collection of resources). Thus, the traditional collection development distinction between selection and evaluation sometimes blurs in regard to electronic resources, as they are frequently evaluated for selection purposes. As a caveat regarding electronic journal evaluation and use studies, note that this format has been inconsistently defined in the literature as exclusively electronic titles or as electronic versions of established print journals.[3] Also note that a number of the Web-based reviewing sites mentioned in this chapter, such as Infofilter, are no longer operating.

Perhaps inevitably, a large portion of chapter 11's entries concern evaluation criteria. As electronic resources are relatively new on the library scene, the identification of the criteria to be used is the logical initial step in confronting the challenges posed by evaluation of these resources. Because lists of evaluation criteria for Web and other electronic resources abound in the literature and are somewhat repetitive of each other, this chapter includes only representative examples in which a significant portion of the criteria relate to content issues. Numerous lists of evaluative criteria posted on the Web in unpublished form are not included.

Chapter 11 is organized into five sections devoted to evaluation of Web sites and Internet resources, evaluation of full-text databases, evaluation of electronic journals and other electronic resources, the application of citation analysis to electronic resources, and use of electronic resources.

Separate sets of issues pertinent to collection development/management of collection evaluation are outlined below for each section.

Web Sites:

- Identification of Web site evaluation criteria

- Comparison of different sets of criteria

- Addressing the applicability of traditional print evaluation criteria to the Web

- Identification of core Web sites

Content and Coverage of Full-Text Databases:

- The extent or completeness of full-text coverage

- Overlap in coverage among different databases

- The quality of the journals contained in the database

- Currency of database coverage compared to the print versions of the journals

- Suitability of a specific database for a particular library

Evaluation of Electronic Journals and Other Electronic Resources:

- Methods for counting electronic journal holdings

- Criteria for choice between the electronic and print formats

- Criteria, metrics, or performance measures for electronic journal evaluation and selection

- The applicability of traditional evaluation criteria to electronic resources

- The development of new metrics or measures for electronic resources

Note that these criteria usually address fundamental issues relating to electronic resource management and evaluation including archiving, cost, copyright, use, coverage, and so on. The full complexities of electronic journal management are beyond the scope of this literature review.

The Application of Citation Analysis to Electronic Resources:

- The extent to which print sources cite electronic resources

- The extent to which electronic resources contribute to scholarly communication

- The comparative citation rates of print and electronic journals

- The continuing accessibility of cited Web resources

- Use of citation data for evaluation of electronic resources

Use of Electronic Resources:

- Definition of what constitutes use of an electronic resource

- Identification of methods lending themselves to valid cross-library comparisons of use

- General usage patterns reported by libraries and/or vendors

- The comparative use of print and electronic resources

- The impact of electronic resources on the use of print materials

WEB SITE AND INTERNET RESOURCE EVALUATION

Brown, Jeanne M. "Core Sites and Categories: An Overlap Study of Architecture Resources on the Internet." **Art Documentation** 18 (fall 1999): 34–38.

The external links to architectural resources on the Web pages of 82 institutions accredited by the National Architectural Accrediting Board (NAAB) are analyzed here. Note that 28 percent of 112 NAAB accredited institutions did not have Web sites with external links to architecture. Brown found "surprising variety:" of 942 external sites, approximately 600 were linked to only once; 3.9 percent were linked to by ten or more libraries; and 8 percent were linked to by at least five libraries. The "most popular" sites tended to be in English and in existence for at least a year, while more than half were reference sites and 49 percent were from educational institutions. Analysis of the categories in which external sites were grouped found two to fifteen categories per library Web page with a total of forty-one different categories used altogether. The core categories were Web directories, organizations, images, e-journals, and libraries. An appendix lists the twenty-four most frequently linked to sites along with the number of links and linking libraries to each (a library may have more than one link to the same site). As observed by Brown, overlap among architectural links is low compared to the rate found among books in print collections.

Collins, Boyd R. "Beyond Cruising: Reviewing." **Library Journal** 121 (February 15, 1996): 122–24.

The founder of the Infofilter Project (for reviewing and selecting sources on the Web) argues that librarians should capitalize on the patron trust they have earned from their book recommendations and apply "well-developed and tested principles of reference reviewing" to Web resources. Collins criticizes Web-based reviewing tools, such as Magellan, as "mostly ingenious variations on the concept of 'cool.'" Six Web site evaluation standards are proposed:

- Content—uniqueness, usefulness, and accuracy are listed

- Authority—the credibility of those responsible for the site

- Currency—how often is it updated?

- Organization—the "three-click rule" (are more than three clicks necessary to find something useful?) is noted

- Search Engine—does it include Boolean and keyword searching plus relevance ranking?

- Accessibility—is it consistently available?

This article has received considerable attention on the Web itself.

Everhart, Nancy. "Web Page Evaluation." **Emergency Librarian** 25 (May/June 1998): 22.

Written by a LIS faculty member at St. John's University for an audience of school librarians, this short item offers a framework for rating Web sites. The evaluating librarian, using his or her judgment, assigns up to a predetermined number of points for eight major headings, with specific considerations outlined for each heading. For example 0–15 points are assigned for "content," considering such factors as usefulness, thoroughness, accuracy, good taste, and grammar plus spelling. Zero to 10 points are devoted to "treatment," considering bias, stereotyping, and age appropriateness for the intended audience. Other headings are currency (0–15 points), authority (0–10 points), navigation (0–10 points), experience (0–10 points), multimedia (0–10 points), access (0–5 points), and miscellaneous (0–15 points). After the points are totaled, a site scoring 90 or above is rated excellent, while 80–89 is good, 70–79 is average, 60–69 borderline acceptable, and below 60 unacceptable.

King, Angelynn. "Caveat Surfer: End-User Research on the Web." **Journal of Interlibrary Loan, Document Delivery, & Information Supply** 8, no. 1 (1997): 53–60.

Apparently drawing upon a course taught at the University of the Redlands, this entry addresses criteria end-users should employ for Web site evaluation. The paper is organized around five major "considerations," outlined below along with King's salient observations:

- Authority—ideally "an internationally known not-for-profit organization or expert."

- Agenda—is the sponsor selling something or advocating an "idea or philosophy?"

- Scope—historical, cultural plus geographical coverage and limitations, as well as whether "unauthorized abridgement" is used.

- Currency—the date the site was last updated does not indicate the extent of the changes.

- Accuracy—are there "glaring" factual errors or obvious bias? King implies that complete objectivity may be impossible.

Examples of specific Web sites illustrating these concepts are discussed. Appended is a checklist of issues pertaining to each criteria. The author emphasizes that end-users must be educated to undertake their own evaluation of Web resources because, unlike material in the collection, there has been no preliminary evaluation by a librarian.

Lilly, Erica B. "Evaluating the Virtual Library Collection." In **Library Evaluation: A Casebook and Can-Do Guide,** edited by Danny P. Wallace and Connie

Van Fleet, 165–84. Englewood, CO: Libraries Unlimited, 2001. ISBN 1-56308-862-2 (paper).

The primary focus of this textbook chapter falls on criteria for evaluation of electronic resources. A chart lists criteria for CD-ROM evaluation under three categories: administrative, content, and technical. Beginning with a section entitled "on the Internet, nobody knows you're a dog" most of this item is devoted to the Web. Lilly defines three "levels of evaluation:"

- Intellectual Access: Web page content and design

- Physical Access: responsiveness to the needs of the disabled and use of universal design principles

- Technological Access: the technological infrastructure

A chart outlines key issues, and separate headings discuss each of twelve criteria for evaluation of intellectual access: authority, sponsoring organization, accuracy, objectivity, currency, coverage, scope, access, design, ease of use, general content, and external validation (i.e., adherence to accepted design standards). Short paragraphs are devoted to network connections, computer workstations, Web browser software, Hyper Text Markup Language (HTML) standards, Web server logs, and Internet filters for evaluation of technological access. However, specific criteria for physical access, such as space and a comfortable working area, are only briefly mentioned.

Pratt, Gregory F., Patrick Flannery, and Cassandra L. D. Perkins. "Guidelines for Internet Resource Selection." **College & Research Libraries News** 57 (March 1996): 134–35.

These guidelines for evaluation and selection of Internet resources were developed at the Houston Academy of Medicine-Texas Medical Center Library to be used as an addendum to their collection development policy. Six general criteria, with supporting points under each, are outlined: quality and content, relevancy, ease of use, reliability and stability, cost and copyright, and hardware and software. The most developed criterion, "quality and content," lists four sub-headings:

- Credibility through peer review, indexing, or electronic archiving.

- Importance as indicated by availability through multiple Internet sites or in multiple formats.

- Content is comprehensive or unique.

- The Internet version's content is complete or meets client needs.

Relevancy is indicated by a relationship to medicine, a recommendation by a staff member or client, major health science libraries providing access, or usage data. The authors assert that basic evaluation criteria are "still issues," but they "must be viewed in new ways."

Rettig, James. "Beyond 'Cool': Analog Models for Reviewing Digital Resources." **Online** 20 (September/October 1996): 52–64.

Because the Web contains "the good, the bad, and the ugly," Rettig begins by stressing the importance of Web site evaluation. Brief summaries of seven online services for rating Web sites (Excite, GNN Select, Magellan, CyberHound, iGuide, Yahoo! Internet Life, and Point) reveal the generally descriptive rather than evaluative nature of these services. The author believes that four services provided by librarians (*College & Research Libraries News'* "Internet Reviews," *Library Journal's* "WebWatch," his own "Rettig on Reference," and the Infofilter project—the later two on the Web) offer more in-depth evaluations "rooted in the long-established criteria of print reviewing traditions." This article's most useful feature is a table listing eighteen criteria for reference books and assessing their applicability to Web sites. Familiar criteria applicable to Web evaluation include accuracy, authority, completeness, illustrations, and reliability. Only one of these criteria, "durability," which relates to quality of paper and binding, is judged "moot" for the Web. A search engine for a Web site is considered the equivalent of indexing for a book.

Rettig, James, and Cheryl LaGuardia. "Beyond 'Beyond Cool:' Reviewing Web Resources." **Online** 23 (July/August 1999): 51–55.

Two well-known librarian Web experts offer what they term "the Rettig/LaGuardia Review Canon" for Web resources. They synthesize from Smith (see the next entry in this section) and eight different lists of criteria posted on the Web by librarians. A chart tabulates which of sixteen possible criteria are included in each of eight librarians' lists. The two authors' final eight criteria are as follows:

- Parentage and provenance

- Authority

- Audience

- Content

- Creation and currency

- Design

- Usability

- Medium

They assert these represent "significant touchstones" rather than "endless, detailed checklists" and have "universal applicability" to Web resources. Their canon is illustrated by applying its criteria to the *Britannica Online's* D-Day entry. Emphasizing their composite list's role in selection, the authors direct a final thought toward Web producers, "If they build it right, *then* we will buy."

Smith, Alastair G. "Testing the Surf: Criteria for Evaluating Internet Information Resources." **Public-Access Computer Systems Review** 8, no. 3 (1997). [Electronic Journal.] Available: http://info.lib.uh.edu/pr/v8/n3/smit8n3.html (accessed August 29, 2003).

Smith proposes a set of criteria for evaluating Internet information resources. Following a well-done literature review, the author offers a "toolbox of criteria" organized in outline format under seven headings:

1. Scope, further subdivided into breadth, depth, time, and format

2. Content, organized into accuracy, authority, currency, uniqueness, links to other resources, and writing quality

3. Graphic and multimedia design

4. Purpose and audience

5. Reviews

6. Workability, which includes user friendliness, required hardware and software, searching capability, browsability and organization, interactivity, as well as connectivity

7. Cost, for both connecting to the resource and use of the intellectual property

A list of twenty-six specific criteria were distilled from this "toolbox" and checked against the criteria used by ten Internet evaluation sites, including the Argus Clearinghouse, the Internet Public Library, and the Magellan Internet Guide and the results presented in two tables. Graphic and multimedia design were used by all ten sites, browsability and organization plus currency by eight, content by seven, and authority by five. An appendix offers short descriptive annotations for the ten Internet evaluation sites. This entry is more systematic and thorough than most items that address Internet evaluation criteria.

Sweetland, James H. "Reviewing the World Wide Web—Theory Versus Reality." **Library Trends** 48 (spring 2000): 748–68.

Sweetland investigates whether a consensus actually exists among library and information professionals regarding Web evaluation criteria. The evaluation criteria used in a systematic random sample of forty-eight Web site reviews from the 1998 *Choice* magazine were compared with the criteria in three "consensus lists": the 1990 Southern California Online Users Group (SCOUG) 1990 criteria (obviously predating the Web), the University of Georgia Criteria (see Wilkinson, Bennett, and Oliver entry), and Rettig and LaGuardia (see earlier entry). The criteria in each of these three sources are listed and their coverage in the *Choice* reviews analyzed. Because few of the listed criteria appear in the reviews, the author perceives a "lack of consensus." Moreover, the reviews tend to emphasize ease of access and aesthetics rather than traditional quality measures such as authority, reliability, and content. Thus, the author questions the future importance of "old-fashioned" criteria. This research makes a significant contribution by comparing theoretical criteria with those that are actually used.

Symons, Ann K. "Sizing Up Sites: How to Judge What You Find on the Web." **School Library Journal** 43 (April 1997): 22–25.

Written for a school library audience by an author who is now a former ALA president, this entry describes, in alphabetical order, twenty-two Web site evaluation criteria. A majority of these are traditional collection evaluation/selection criteria, such as accuracy, attention from reviewers, audience, authority, clarity/readability, content, cost, currency, curriculum support, depth/breadth, diversity of viewpoint, duplication, purpose, and uniqueness. Other criteria include design, navigation, performance, and searchability. For illustration, the twenty-two criteria are applied to the Diego Rivera Web Museum site. Symons briefly discusses how to find Web sites through reviews and viewing library Web pages and appends a short bibliography on Web evaluation.

Wilkinson, Gene L., Lisa T. Bennett, and Kevin M. Oliver. "Evaluation Criteria and Indicators of Quality for Internet Resources." **Educational Technology** 37 (May/June 1997): 52–59.

This entry's criteria result from an ongoing University of Georgia project to establish criteria for evaluation of Internet resources. An initial set of 509 possible quality indicators were identified through an e-mail survey of Internet resource guide compilers, as well as through reviewing Internet rating systems, the library science literature on reference and other topics, and the Web design literature. After editing, the indicators were reduced to 125 criteria organized under eleven categories:

- Site access and usability

- Documentation and resource identification

- Author identification

- Author's authority

- Information structure and design

- Content relevance and scope

- Validity of content

- Content balance and accuracy

- Navigation

- Link quality

- Aesthetic aspects

Five to eighteen indicators are listed under each heading. For example, the six points under relevance and scope consider user need, provision of new information, and obvious omissions, while the nine criteria under content validity include peer review, bibliographies and footnotes, and statistics to support conclusions. In summary, this work is noteworthy for its systematic approach to the development of Web evaluation criteria.

Wolfe, Paula. "Evaluating Internet Resources: Criteria for Evaluation as a Collection Development Extension." In **Information Across the Waves: The World As a Multimedia Experience: Proceedings of the 21st Annual Conference of the International Association of Aquatic and Marine Science Libraries and Information Centers; 21st Annual Conference of IAMSLIC held 8–12 October, 1995 at Southampton, England,** edited by James W. Markham and Andrea L. Duda, 213–17. Fort Pierce, FL: IAMSLIC, 1996. ISSN 8755-6332.

Arguing that traditional materials selection criteria are a "starting point" for evaluation of electronic resources, a University of Wyoming librarian discusses twelve criteria for evaluation of Internet resources. Perhaps the most noteworthy is "collection value," defined as "ease of use and additional information beyond what a print source can provide." About half are fairly commonplace, such as content and coverage, currency, availability, stability, required user knowledge/ease of use, and cost. Other noteworthy criteria include the producer; whether the source of information and a contact person is given; the site's formats, that is, graphics, documents, databases, and so on; and whether the source is available in alternative formats. Wolfe notes that her library is "slowly adding" Internet resources to collection development duties.

EVALUATION OF FULL-TEXT DATABASE COVERAGE

Black, Steven. "An Assessment of Social Sciences Coverage by Four Prominent Full-Text Online Aggregated Journal Packages." **Library Collections, Acquisitions, & Technical Services** 23 (winter 1999): 411–19.

This interesting article investigates the quality and cost-effectiveness of the journals contained in four full-text aggregated packages: *EBSCOhost Academic Search FullTEXT,* University Microfilms International (UMI) *ProQuest Direct Periodicals Research II,* IAC's *Expanded Academic ASAP,* and H. W. Wilson's *OmniFile.* Impact factor in the 1996 *SSCI JCR* was considered an indicator of journal quality while subscription prices were obtained from EBSCO's 1997–98 *Librarian's Handbook.* The number of the 1,513 *JCR* journals contained in any of the four databases ranged from 108 to 234. In total, only 27 percent of the

JCR journals were available in any of the four databases, whereas 35 percent of the top quartile by impact factor were available. Black asserts that "to some degree" the aggregators offer "less expensive" journals. The average subscription price of all *SSCI JCR* journals was $230.80, while the average price of the *JCR* journals contained in the four aggregators ranged from $107.41 to $146.20. Moreover, the average price of the 36 *JCR* journals contained in all four databases (listed in a table) was $68.61. The average impact factor of the *JCR* journals was 0.758 and 1.586 for the top quartile, while the average in the four packages varied from 0.697 to 0.9353. This item suggests that the four aggregators offer limited coverage of top-ranked social science journals, but Black acknowledges "the packages offer substantial potential savings over purchasing individual subscriptions."

Brier, David J., and Vickery Kaye Lebbin. "Evaluating Title Coverage of Full-Text Periodical Databases." **Journal of Academic Librarianship** 25 (November 1999): 473–78.

A method for evaluating full-text database periodical content, developed in 1997 and pretested by the University of Hawaii at Manoa library, is explained by Brier and Lebbin. Three measurements were created:

- Full-Text Value—the number of titles in the database not subscribed to by the library but listed in *Magazines for Libraries*

- Abstract Value—for titles abstract in the database, the number in the collection in proportion to the number of titles not in the collection

- Interlibrary Loan Value—for abstracted titles not in the collection, the number in *Magazines for Libraries* in proportion to the number not included

A pretest of three databases, based on 2,914 titles beginning with the letter A (12 percent of the library's subscriptions) found that *Periodical Abstract Research II* ranked highest in full-text value, *Expanded Academic Index* in abstract value, and *Expanded Academic Index* or *Periodical Abstract Research II* in interlibrary loan value. Note that *EBSCOhost Academic Search* was the third database evaluated. Citing the Principle of Least Effort, the authors argue that full-text databases are highly used due to their convenience: thus evaluation of their quality is "necessary."

Carr, Jo Ann, and Amy Wolfe. "Core Journal Titles in Full-Text Databases." In **Racing Toward Tomorrow: Proceedings of the Ninth National Conference of the Association of College and Research Libraries April 8–11, 1999,** edited by Hugh A. Thompson, 234–41. Chicago: Association of College and Research Libraries, 1999. ISBN 0-8389-8015-5.

This conference paper reports an investigation of database content conducted on behalf of the University of Wisconsin System Libraries. Core lists of 255 education and 335 biology journals were compiled from various sources and checked against four electronic databases *(EBSCOhost Academic Search Full Text,* IAC's

Expanded Academic ASAP, ProQuest Periodical Abstracts Research II Full Text, and *Wilson Select Full Text)* using data supplied by vendors during March and April 1998. Four tables summarize the findings on the number and percentage of core journals and peer-reviewed core journals that were indexed and contained in full-text for both biology and education. For example, from 23.9 to 78.4 percent of the core education titles and from 10.6 to 40.5 percent of the peer-reviewed core titles were indexed, while the corresponding figures for full-text holdings ranged from 9.4 to 24.3 percent and 5.0 to 13.0 percent, respectively. Carr and Wolfe stress these are preliminary findings representing "a snapshot in time" because "content changes on a monthly basis." Following their literature review, the authors claim this is the first study to use core journal lists for evaluation of database coverage.

Everett, David. "Full-Text Online Databases and Document Delivery in an Academic Library: Too Little, Too Late?" **Online** 17 (March 1993): 22–25.

Everett tested whether obtaining full-text articles through such services as Westlaw, Dialog, or BRS (Bibliographic Retrieval Service) would be a viable document delivery strategy. The full-text availability of 1,896 ILL articles requested by Stetson University faculty and students during a recent year was determined by consulting *Fulltext Sources Online.* Only 63 items, "less than 4 percent," were available in full-text while an additional 84 would have been available had there been longer coverage of backruns. Thus, the author decided the full-text option could not meet patron demands. Investigation of five Wilson periodical indexes found that full-text availability ranged from 0.3 percent for the *Humanities Index* to 62.3 percent for the *Business Periodicals Index.* As this article was published about a decade ago, Everett was examining full-text access through a third-party such as Dialog rather than within a database itself.

Glavash, Keith. "Full-Text Retrieval for Document Delivery—A Viable Option?" **Online** 18 (May 1994): 81–84.

Retrieval of newspaper and newsletter articles from online full-text databases (mainly Dialog, but also including *Dow Jones,* and *DataTimes*) was evaluated by the MIT library during a ten-month period beginning in September 1990. Results for the seventy requests in the study were as follows: a 91 percent fill rate, an average staff time of five minutes to retrieve and print the item, an online charge of $4.15 per request, and a 2.1 day turnaround time from receipt of request to shipment to user. In contrast, Glavash reports that at MIT, retrieval from hardcopy or microform for photocopying takes "ten minutes or more per request" and two to five days turnaround time. A survey of end-users (generating a 10 percent response rate) found that all respondents preferred full-text to a photocopy, but about one-third indicated full-text would not be acceptable unless it included graphics and photos. Because most of the requested items were owned by the MIT Libraries, this investigation addresses electronic full-text retrieval versus photocopying rather than "access versus ownership."

Grzeszkiewicz, Anna, and A. Craig Hawbaker. "Investigating a Full-Text Journal Database: A Case of Detection." **Database** 19 (December 1996): 59–62.

Written in a zippy style, this paper investigates the full-text availability of 130 journals, subscribed to by the University of the Pacific library, in Information Access Corporation's (IAC's) *Business Index ASAP.* At least three issues of each title were checked in the database between February and April 1996. Although the vendor claimed all these journals were full-text, sixteen, "over 12 percent," were simply abstracted. Of the remaining journals, "only a few" received "consistent" full-text coverage. The authors cite specific examples of such problems as missing articles, missing issues, incorrect citations, typographical errors, and inconsistent availability within titles and issues. In a sidebar, they suggest CARL UnCover as a source for articles missing from a full-text database, as 111 of the 130 studied titles are available on twenty-four-hour document delivery. In the final paragraph, Grzeszkiewicz and Hawbaker stress that end-users must be educated concerning these problems by quoting Sherlock Holmes: "elementary, my dear Watson, elementary."

Hawbaker, A. Craig, and Cynthia K. Wagner. "Periodical Ownership Versus Full-Text Online Access: A Cost-Benefit Analysis." **Journal of Academic Librarianship** 22 (March 1996): 105–9.

The cost-effectiveness of subscribing to a full-text periodical database (IAC's *Business ASAP)* was investigated at the University of the Pacific (UOP) libraries during 1995. The database contained 44 percent of the titles covered in *Business Index,* but these were less expensive titles representing only 20 percent of *Business Index's* total subscription value. The UOP libraries subscribed to about 33 percent of the 407 periodicals in *Business ASAP,* whereas 44.6 percent of the library's 242 current print business subscriptions were not in the database.[4] By subscribing to *Business ASAP* and canceling 134 print subscriptions to titles it contained (but maintaining subscriptions to the other 108 titles), it was calculated the library could provide access to more than twice the number of journals—513 rather than 242—for a 15 percent cost increase. As a consequence of this study, the UOP libraries ordered a one-year trial subscription to *Business ASAP* but maintained their print subscriptions.

Hill, J.B. "Aggregated Science: An Examination of Three Multi-Disciplinary Databases." **Issues in Science & Technology Librarianship** no. 30 (spring 2001). [Electronic Journal]. Available: http://www.library.ucsb.edu/istl/01-spring/article4.html (accessed August 29, 2003).

Hill reports an evaluation of the science and technology coverage of Bell and Howell's *Research Library,* EBSCO's *Academic Search Elite* and Gale's *Expanded Academic ASAP,* undertaken on behalf of the Louisiana Academic Library Information Network Consortium (LALINC). Twelve evaluation factors used by LALINC (including number of full-text titles, number of peer-reviewed journals, and retrospective coverage) are listed. The study itself is based on title lists downloaded from the Web in February 2001. Numerous tables offer comparative data on the three products' indexing and full-text coverage of science and technology journals overall as well as in fourteen different scientific subject areas, such as general science, chemistry/chemical engineering, and physics. Altogether 884 different science and technology titles are contained in the three databases, of which 59.5 percent are full-text in at least one. Also, 9.7 percent of the full-text titles are in all three databases, 20 percent in two databases, and 70.3 percent in only one. An investigation of the publishers found "very little" full-text content from professional associations or major science publishers. Hill decides that *Expanded Academic* is best for indexing, *Academic Elite* for full-text, and *Research Library* is the least expensive, concluding that the "most appropriate database" depends on each institution's needs.

Jacsó, Péter. "Evaluating the Journal Base of Databases Using the Impact Factor of the ISI Journal Citation Reports." In **National Online Meeting Proceedings 2000: Proceedings of the 21st National Online Meeting, New York, May 16–18, 2000,** edited by Martha E. Williams, 169–72. Medford, NJ: Information Today, 2000. ISBN 1-57387-102-8.

This entry explains the use of the *Journal Citation Reports* for evaluating the periodical coverage of abstracting and indexing or full-text databases. In his description of the *JCR,* the author comments that the two most important figures for this purpose are a journal's impact factor and the number of articles it published. For illustration, the seventy-seven active titles listed under Psychiatry in the 1997 *JCR* were checked against two comparable databases. *PsycINFO* indexed or abstracted seventy-five of these titles and covered 702 articles whereas *Mental Health Abstracts* abstracted or indexed seventeen titles and covered 537 articles. Moreover, the latter database did not cover any of the ten journals with the highest impact factors and only two of the highest twenty. Jacsó asserts that one can add or subtract titles to those included in the *JCR,* expand the investigation to more than a single year, and that the "next stage of development" is to use the combined impact factors of the covered journals for database comparison.

Karp, Rashelle. "Comparing Three Full-Text Journal Services." **Booklist** 94 (May 15, 1998): 1646–1650.

This entry evaluates three full-text services: *InfoTrac Search Bank, EBSCOhost,* and *ProQuest Direct.* Based on examination of the vendor Web pages on February 23, 1998, it was found that the number of unique titles, that is, those contained in one service but not the other two, ranged from approximately 400 to 650. Approximately 500 titles were covered in two services, a "core" of 300 were contained in all three, and the total coverage exceeded 2,400 journals. Karp warns, however, that journal coverage "can change on an almost daily basis" and be customized to a specific library's need. Keyword searches under the term "global warming" were conducted in the three databases on February 8, 1998, for the months of October 1997 and January 1998 to determine the number of articles retrieved and assess how quickly items were entered into the databases. The author found that *ProQuest Direct* loads articles about when they appear in print, whereas the other two services take four to eight weeks. Indexing, search features, connectivity, output formats, statistical and administrative information are also evaluated. Karp concludes that *ProQuest Direct* is best in terms of article coverage and currency.

Orenstein, Ruth M. "'How Full Is Full' Revisited: A Status Report on Searching Full-Text Periodicals." **Database** 16 (October 1993): 14–23.

As the title reveals, this entry follows up Ruth Pagell's 1987 article (apparently one of the first on the topic) concerning the completeness and currency of full-text coverage.[5] Orenstein makes an important distinction between database producers, such as McGraw-Hill, who put the data into electronic form, and vendors or databanks, such as Dialog, who market online services to libraries. On February 3 and February 8, 1993, she found that the number of articles from the January 4, 1993, *Forbes* magazine in eight databases, including Mead *Nexis* and *ABI* on Dialog, ranged from 0 to 134. Comparison of the print and electronic versions indicated that divergent approaches to counting sidebars and tables as separate entries or parts of articles accounted for much of the variation among vendors. A table demonstrates that the mean "lag time" for adding articles to *Financial World* in 1993 varied from 0 to 28 days in six databases, contrasted to 0 to 127 days found by Pagell in 1987. A two-page table summarizes how eleven "features," such as articles, photographs, political cartoons, and so on, are covered by ten different producers. Orenstein observes that "'cover-to-cover' in the online world is not to be taken literally."

Preston, Laurie A., Corinne M. Ebbs, and Judy Luther. "'Full Text' Access Evaluation: Are We Getting the Real Thing?" **Serials Librarian** 34, nos. 3–4 (1998): 301–5.

The authors describe an evaluation of IAC's *Expanded Academic Index ASAP* conducted by the James Madison University Libraries. For seventy-five journal titles, equally distributed among the sciences, social sciences, and humanities, page-by-page comparisons of two print issues (including the most recent) were made with the content of the full-text database. Only nine of the seventy-five print titles (12 percent) were completely covered by the electronic database.[6] The authors stress that illustrations are often missing, lacking color, or of lower quality. Other missing items included feature articles, columns, letters, editorials, reviews, advertisements, and sidebars. The authors suggest each library create its own "Profile of Expectations," such as addition of new titles, replacement of current subscriptions, or expanded subject coverage, for full-text databases. This piece concludes with a provocative question "is full-text what you need or is it only a lot of information?"

Richter, Carole J., and Threasa L. Wesley. " IAC and UMI Go Head-to-Head on Full-Text: A Comparison of **Expanded Academic Index** via SearchBank and **Periodical Abstracts Research II** with PowerPages." **Database** 19 (August/September 1996): 62–71.

The authors offer a detailed comparison of two electronic indexing and full-text databases: IAC's *Expanded Academic Index,* accessed through the Internet, and UMI's *Periodical Abstracts Research II,* accessed locally via CD-ROM-based PowerPages. About half the article is devoted to such issues as system configuration, searching features, navigation and layout, cost, and technical support and the other half to content related issues. Examination of lists supplied by the two vendors in early 1996 revealed that UMI indexed 11 percent more periodical titles, but UMI included 15 percent more full-text titles. As further analysis showed the IAC product contained more social sciences and humanities journals while UMI contained hobby magazines, the authors decide the former would be "particularly valuable for undergraduate libraries." UMI provided more "depth" by including backruns dating to 1988 contrasted to 1992 by IAC. Richter and Wesley found that IAC added indexing entries five to ten days after the item's publication and full-text in three to six weeks, whereas the CD-ROM-based UMI product "can't compete" in terms of currency. The article concludes "there is no clear 'winner' in the full-text contest."

Salisbury, Lutishoor, Bryan Davidson, and Alberta Bailey. "Undergraduate Full Text Databases: **Bell and Howell Medical Complete** and **InfoTrac Health Reference Center—Academic.**" **Journal of Southern Academic and Special Librarianship** 2 (fall 2000). [Electronic Journal.] Available: http://southernlibrarianship. icaap.org/content/v02n01/salisbury_101.html (accessed August 29, 2003).

The authors compare the suitability of two full-text databases (*Bell and Howell Medical Complete (ProQuest)* and *Info Trac Health Reference Center—Academic*) to support the undergraduate nursing education program at the University of Arkansas, Fayetteville. Analysis of the databases coverage as of April 1999 revealed that 84 percent of *ProQuest's* titles were full-text, of which 57 percent were peer-reviewed and 68.97 percent were classified as academic by *Ulrich's*. The corresponding figures for *Info Trac* were 65 percent, 39 percent, and 52 percent. Moreover, ProQuest provided full-text for 10.72 percent of the titles indexed in the *Cumulative Index to Nursing and Allied Health Literature,* while *Info Trac* provided 6.40 percent. Salisbury, Davidson, and Bailey decided that neither full-text databases' content would "enhance" the nursing program, even though some libraries might like the searching features of both. A six-page appendix offers a detailed comparison of the search and help features of the two systems.

Sprague, Nancy, and Mary Beth Chambers. "Full-Text Databases and the Journal Cancellation Process: A Case Study." **Serials Review** 26, no. 3 (2000): 19–31.

Sprague and Chambers investigate the availability in five databases (*ABI/Inform, Periodical Abstracts, WilsonSelect, Expanded Academic Index ASAP,* and *General Business ASAP*) of 130 journals targeted for cancellation at the University of Colorado at Colorado Springs library. The article begins with an especially well-done literature review of earlier full-text database evaluations before investigating four criteria:

- Currency. For 55 percent of the titles the most current print issue was contained in at least one database, while 36 percent of the full-text titles were behind by one issue, and 9 percent two or more issues.

- Coverage. The percentage of the 130 journals with full-text coverage ranged from 62 to 89 with a mean of 83.

- Graphics. Although objective measures are "difficult," the researchers found "wide variation" among the databases and that important graphics were often omitted.

- Stability. Comparison of the total coverage of the five databases (not just the 130 study journals) revealed that between December 1998, when the study began, and May 1999, 490 titles were added and 140 dropped.

Further analysis indicated that 45 titles (57 percent) were covered in only one database, while only 2 (2.5 percent) were in all five. Because the database best in currency was worst in coverage and vice versa, the researchers observe that database selection depends upon what a library values.

Stebelman, Scott. "Analysis of Retrieval Performance in Four Cross-Disciplinary Databases: Article 1st, Faxon Finder, UnCover, and a Locally Mounted Database." **College & Research Libraries** 55 (November 1994): 562–67.

Stebelman evaluates the retrieval performance of the three databases mentioned in the title plus GENL, a locally mounted database (at the George Washington University library) composed of six Wilson databases, including the *Readers Guide to Periodical Literature* and the *Social Science Index.* The number of items published between 1990 and 1993 retrieved in searches, conducted in January 1994, of thirty subject areas form the basis of the study. While the number of journals indexed in the four databases ranged from 2,200 to 14,000, the number of retrieved articles ranged from 219 to 724 and the number of different periodical titles from 189 to 467. Twelve subject specialists at the George Washington University library judged whether each retrieved citation in their area was germane to the search topic. The relevancy ratio for the four databases varied from 45 percent to 62 percent. GENL, which produced the most citations, had the lowest relevance ratio. The author notes that when selecting databases libraries should also consider user-friendliness, cost, and document delivery features. Although the focus falls on performance retrieval, this entry has considerable relevance for database evaluation.

Still, Julie M., and Vibiana Kassabian. "Selecting Full-Text Undergraduate Periodicals Databases." **EContent** 22 (December 1999): 57–65.

This entry, using *ProQuest Direct, Periodical Abstracts,* and *EBSCOhost* for illustration, addresses the evaluation of full-text databases in order to assist selection for an undergraduate audience. For coverage comparison, the authors found that *EBSCOhost* retrieved 32 articles from the April 1999 issue of *Working Woman* and 43 from the May issue, whereas *ProQuest Direct* retrieved 27 and 28 from the two respective issues. Similar data was not presented for the third database. Searches under the term "greenhouse effect" retrieved 25 full-text articles in *ProQuest Direct,* 450 in *Periodical Abstracts,* and 300 in *EBSCOhost.* Manipulation of results, ease of searching, and "quirks in the experience" are also discussed. A comparison chart of the three databases concludes the article. While not exceedingly rigorous, this item is written in an especially humorous style. For example, the authors say the traditional Wilson databases were "like Barbara Bush…a bit dowdy but beloved by all."

EVALUATION OF ELECTRONIC JOURNALS AND OTHER ELECTRONIC RESOURCES

Bandyopadhyay, Aditi, and Heting Chu. "Electronic Journals Versus Print Journals: An Evaluation Framework." In **National Online Meeting Proceedings— 1999: Proceedings of the 20th National Online Meeting, New York, May 18–20, 1999,** edited by Martha E. Williams, 17–30. Medford, NJ: Information Today, 1999. ISBN 1-57387-084-6.

As the title indicates, this conference paper presents an evaluative framework for comparing Web-based electronic journals with the print counterpart of the same title. Using an outline format, seven criteria are described:

1. Design and presentation, including search options and graphics

2. Ease of access

3. Coverage

4. Pricing

5. Archiving

6. Licensing terms

7. Other features, including usage statistics tools and trial access

The Web version of fourteen journal titles in science, the social sciences, the humanities, medicine, and art were accessed through OCLC's *Electronic Collections Online* or directly from the publisher. Then the seven criteria are discussed again, incorporating information concerning these journals. An appended table summarizes the major features of the titles compared to their print equivalents. The proposed criteria are familiar, but this entry offers a somewhat unusual perspective in applying them to the Web editions of fourteen specific journals.

Bane, Adele F. "Business Periodicals Ondisc: How Full-Text Availability Affects the Library." **Computers in Libraries** 15 (May 1995): 54–56.

An evaluation of the *Business Periodicals Ondisc (BPO)* full-text CD-ROM, subscribed to on a one-year trial basis at the Penn State Great Valley campus, is reported by Bane. A February 1994 survey—responded to by 144 users representing a 66 percent rate—found that a majority were graduate students who "overwhelmingly" considered the product "essential." Further, 42 percent obtained 50 to 75 percent of the articles they needed from the system, while 30 percent retrieved between 75 and 100 percent. The number of articles supplied by the library increased by 147 percent from 1992–93 to 1993–94 following *BPO's* introduction. The author surmises *BPO* is "arguably" cost-effective because, using the ARL/RLG figure of $30 per ILL transaction, the articles delivered by the system would have cost approximately $360,000 compared to about $20,000 in actual expenditures.[7] While interesting, this article is methodologically suspect. The author employs both borrowing and lending cost in calculating the $360,000 figure, but her library would only pay the borrowing cost.

Christie, Anne, and Laurel Kristick. "Developing an Online Science Journal Collection: A Quick Tool for Assigning Priorities." **Issues in Science & Technology Librarianship** no. 30 (spring 2001). [Electronic Journal]. Available: http://www. library.ucsb.edu/istl/01-spring/article2.html (accessed August 29, 2003).

The authors relate the approaches used for electronic journal evaluation and management at the Oregon State University library. In January 2001, faculty were asked in an informal e-mail poll to list the ten journals to which they would most like electronic access. The 204 responses listed 711 titles, which were entered into an *Excel* spreadsheet along with other information such as ISI citation data. Follow-up analysis showed that the library had print subscriptions to 78.8 percent of the journals and provided electronic access to 14.5 percent.[8] Also, 21 percent were issued by 2 (Elsevier and Academic Press) of 195 publishers. The twenty-one titles listed by ten or more faculty and the twenty-two requested titles that ranked first in their ISI subject categories are listed in separate tables. The Collection Development Department decided that after selection based on coverage and currency, the following hierarchy would be used for adding e-journals to the collection:

- "Print plus free online version"

- "Online only and free"

- "Print or online, either one paid"

- "Print plus paid online version"

Christie and Kristick conclude that other libraries might apply variations of their methods.

Degener, Christie T., and Marjory A. Waite. "Fools Rush In…Thoughts About, and a Model for, Measuring Electronic Journal Collections." **Serials Review** 26, no. 4 (2000): 3–11.

Degener and Waite observe that statistical counts on journal volumes held and titles received have been used as a collection evaluation technique "for many years." This thoughtful article discusses the complexities of compiling electronic journal statistics. The authors reviewed the literature, which "yielded very little" and two major surveys for gathering journal statistics: the ARL Academic Medical Library Statistics Questionnaire and the questionnaire for the *Annual Statistics of Medical School Libraries in the United States and Canada.* They assert that volume counts are not appropriate for e-journals but present the model developed by the Health Sciences Library of the University of North Carolina at Chapel Hill for counting the titles received. Total numbers are compiled for ten categories:

- Print subscriptions with free electronic subscription

- Print subscriptions with paid electronic subscription

- Electronic subscriptions only—free

- Electronic subscriptions only—paid

- Electronically accessed titles partially paid for

- Electronically accessed titles by another library's effort

- Electronic titles available to off-campus users

- Electronic journals with duplicate access arrangements

- Total number of electronic journals

- Total unique titles, electronic and print

The authors believe their model can be used by other libraries and that it allows meaningful comparisons among peer institutions. This item makes an important contribution to the e-journal evaluation literature.

Hahn, Karla L., and Lila A. Faulkner. "Evaluative Usage-Based Metrics for the Selection of E-Journals." **College & Research Libraries** 63 (May 2002): 215–27.
Three metrics for evaluation of licensed e-journal collections are introduced:

- "Average Cost per Access:" the subscription price divided by annual number of full-text accesses

- "Average Cost per Article:" the subscription price divided by the number of articles online

- "Content-Adjusted Usage:" the number of full-text accesses divided by number of articles online

However, only "cost per article" can be used for collections under consideration since access data are unknown. The authors thus recommend selecting an already licensed "peer" collection (on a similar topic) for benchmarking purposes and propose three additional metrics for evaluating the candidate collection:

- "Cost-Based Usage Benchmark:" the number of yearly full-text accesses required for the candidate collection to have the same cost per access as the peer collection

- "Content-Based Usage Benchmark:" the yearly number of full-text accesses needed to provide the same content-adjusted usage as the peer product

- "Cost per Access at the Content-Based Usage Benchmark:" the hypothetical cost per access if the candidate were to receive the same number of yearly accesses as the peer collection

The practical application of these six metrics is illustrated by using the *Science* online site as a peer for evaluation of the *Nature* site. Hahn and Faulkner acknowledge that interpretation of the data generated by the measures and possible inconsistencies in vendor-supplied statistics pose "questions." Nonetheless, the authors make a commendable attempt to address the challenging dilemmas associated with e-journal metrics.

Henebry, Carolyn, Ellen Safley, and Sarah E. George. "Before You Cancel the Paper, Beware; All Electronic Journals in 2001 Are Not Created Equal." **Serials Librarian** 42, nos. 3–4 (2002): 267–73.

This item describes an ongoing electronic journal evaluation project at the University of Texas at Dallas library with the objective of canceling the print subscription when the electronic version's quality is acceptable. Five criteria are used to assess the electronic version when compared with sample print issues and bound volumes:

- Print quality

- Graphics quality

- Color quality

- Content accuracy

- Advertisements

Print legibility creates "no problem," and findings were inconsistent concerning whether the print or electronic versions were more current. Numerous difficulties include missing graphics, articles, and even issues as well as incorrect chronological ordering of issues. Benefits of the electronic format, including sharper graphics and keyword searching, are noted. It is concluded that "many electronic journals differ significantly from their print counterparts." Between 300 to 400 titles were reviewed in the project's preliminary phase and approximately 70 were cancelled.

Hurd, Julie M., Deborah D. Blecic, and Ann E. Robinson. "Performance Measures for Electronic Journals: A User-Centered Approach." **Science & Technology Libraries** 20, nos. 2–3 (2001): 57–71.

This article reports a pilot study, conducted at the University of Illinois at Chicago, to development electronic journal performance measures. The study used a purposive sample of nineteen Science, Technology, and Medicine (STM) e-journals. Seven user-centered criteria were developed:

- Currency: for print versus electronic versions

- Comprehensiveness: research articles, letters to the editor, communications, errata, advertising, news, and columns

- Links: to author Web pages, databases, and so on

- Access to the journal's content: search engines and navigational features

- Full-text options: HTML, PDF, helper applications

- Documentation: help buttons, Frequently Asked Questions (FAQs)

- Personalization: e-mail notification, saved searches

Next, "click tests" (the mouse clicks required to reach a desired Web site) for browsing the latest issue, known-item searches, and author/subject searches resulted in scores ranging from 1 to 8. Finally, the Kano Model from Japanese management literature, which defines three levels of customer expectations, was applied to electronic journals:

- "Expected features" include full-text and currency

- "Normal features" include easy navigation and low click count

- "Exciting features" include direct links to nontextual information

This item is valuable for its methodological framework rather than reported results.

Nisonger, Thomas E., and Gloria Guzi. "Approaches, Techniques, and Criteria for Serials Evaluation in the Electronic Environment." **Serials Librarian** 40, nos. 3–4 (2001): 393–407.

This item addresses the evaluation of electronic serials at the macro (the entire collection) and the micro (individual titles) levels. The applicability of traditional serials macro evaluation methods to electronic serial collections, including holdings, the checklist method, the Conspectus, document delivery tests, citation analysis, and use studies, is reviewed. It is concluded that many traditional methods can be adapted for evaluation of electronic resources but that the development of new evaluation approaches is a major challenge facing the library profession. Moreover, client-centered methods focusing on accessibility and availability will increase in importance in the electronic environment, whereas collection-centered techniques will become less relevant. Most micro evaluation criteria used in selection (i.e., library collecting priorities, indexing, etc.) also apply to electronic journals, but additional criteria, such as licensing and archiving terms, are superimposed on top of them. Serials collection development increasingly involves choice of format rather than title. Appended is an unannotated bibliography of approximately 120 items pertinent to various aspects of serials evaluation.

Pavelsek, Mary Jean. "Guidelines for Evaluating E-Journal Providers with Applications to JSTOR and Project Muse." **Advances in Librarianship** 22 (1998): 39–58.

Eleven criteria (Pavelsek uses the term "guidelines") for evaluation of electronic journal products are explained at the beginning of this entry:

- Economics

- Ease of use

- Archival issues

- Future electronic availability

- Type of access

- Copyright and licensing restrictions

- Single-publisher or multiple-publisher provider?

- Completeness of the electronic version and whether the articles are refereed

- User support

- Are individual titles separately available?

- Possible future enhancements

Next, these criteria are then used to provide detailed point-by-point evaluations of JSTOR (Journal STORage) and then Project Muse (a bundle of Johns Hopkins University Press journals in electronic form). The author asserts that electronic journal evaluation guidelines are necessary because we do not know the format's full economic or academic implications. This item serves dual purposes: outlining e-journal evaluation guidelines and offering in-depth analysis of two major electronic products.

Pillow, Lisa. "Scholarly African American Studies Journals: An Evaluation of Electronic Indexing Service Coverage." **Serials Review** 25, no. 4 (1999): 21–28.

This entry's title precisely describes its topic. The coverage in 1997 of thirteen African American journals—selected by the author as scholarly—was checked in eleven electronic indexing and abstracting services, such as *Article First, Infotrac Expanded Academic Index,* and *Black Studies on Disc.* A table shows that coverage of the thirteen titles ranged from two (15.3 percent) to twelve (92.3 percent). Another table reveals that ten of the eleven databases had less than 100 percent coverage of the titles they indexed with the lowest at 28.6 percent and the average at 66.0 percent. Pillow cites numerous examples in which coverage varies widely among different journals in the same database. A brief literature review found similar problems in another interdisciplinary area, women's studies, and states no previous study of abstracting and indexing in African American studies was identified. The author concludes that indexing for African American studies is inadequate.

Publicker, Stephanie, and Kristin Stoklosa. "Reaching the Researcher: How the National Institutes of Health Library Selects and Provides E-Journals via the World Wide Web." **Serials Review** 25, no. 3 (1999): 13–23.

The e-journal evaluation and selection model developed by an electronic resources team at the National Institutes of Health library between 1996 and 1999 is described here. A large portion of the text explains the major criteria, including the following: research relevance, currency and update frequency, page layout and navigation, (all categorized as content); pricing and licensing issues; the existence of direct links from search results to full-text articles; and whether users are authorized by Internet Protocol (IP) address. The team's nine-point evaluation form (which also addresses use and subject coverage) is presented in an appendix. Other sections describe user expectations, education and outreach efforts, and the process for identifying additional electronic titles. A table lists the fifty most frequently used journals at the library, of which, according to Nisonger's count, twenty-three are available electronically. Publicker and Stoklosa comment that these principles, while "flexible," stress use and currency, among other variables. In summary, this entry offers an example of e-journal evaluation by a specific library.

Schwartz, Candy. "Evaluating CD-ROM Products: Yet Another Checklist." **CD-ROM Professional** 6 (January 1993): 87–91.

A LIS educator offers a lengthy list—termed a checklist—of criteria for evaluating CD-ROM products. Organized on a three-level hierarchy, there are nine main headings, including hardware/software requirements, ease of use, searching capabilities, and content evaluation. Under the last mentioned heading are seven subdivisions: audience, authority, scope, time lag, information in records, searchable text fields, and other searchable fields. The twelve third-level headings listed under "scope," include starting year, serial coverage, monograph coverage, and language/place of publication. In the brief introduction, Schwartz notes that this list, under development for years, began in a reference class at the McGill University library school. She also observes that her checklist does not include issues pertinent to a specific library, such as overlap with current holdings or the percentage of a library's journals included in the database.

THE APPLICATION OF CITATION ANALYSIS TO ELECTRONIC RESOURCES

Chapman, Karen. "An Examination of the Usefulness of JSTOR to Researchers in Finance." **Behavioral & Social Sciences Librarian** 19, no. 2 (2001): 39–47.

A citation evaluation of JSTOR in the field of finance is reported in this entry. Citations in the 1999 volumes of the *Journal of Finance, Journal of Financial Economics,* and *Review of Financial Studies* (all identified as high impact factor journals) served as the source. Seventy-five percent of 5,806 citations were to journal articles, while working papers and books each accounted for 9 percent. The median publication date was 1991. A table lists in rank order the eight journals cited at least 100 times, seven of which are covered by JSTOR. Significantly, 46 percent of 4,270 valid journal citations were available in JSTOR as of 2000, 42 percent as of 1999, and 37 percent as of 1998. Chapman explains JSTOR's coverage changes because the most recent two to five years, depending upon a journal's policy, are excluded. She concludes JSTOR performed "tolerably well" according to five criteria of utility for finance research:

- The discipline is covered in JSTOR.

- Its leading journals are included in JSTOR.

- Journals from related disciplines, such as economics and statistics, are included.

- Finance research "draws heavily" upon journal articles (note that JSTOR's coverage is limited to articles).

- Finance tends to use resources older than two to five years.

Darmoni, Stefan J., et al. "Reading Factor: A New Bibliometric Criterion for Managing Digital Libraries." **Journal of the Medical Library Association** 90 (July 2002): 323–27.

Darmoni and his four coauthors propose a new bibliometric measure for electronic journal collection evaluation called "Reading Factor." A formula illustrates its calculation: the number of times end users "click" on an article from the e-journal, normalized for the average number of clicks for all journals in the study set. This investigation is based upon the electronic use (primarily by clinical physicians) of forty-six biomedical journals in the Rouen [France] University Hospital's digital library during 1998. A table presents the 1997 *JCR* impact factor and the 1998 reading factor for these forty-six titles. When the top two journals (the *New England Journal of Medicine* and *Lancet*) are disregarded, a variety of statistical techniques showed no correlation between impact factor and reading factor. Darmoni and colleagues thus conclude that reading factor provides a different type of information than impact factor and could be a "more relevant marker of a given journal's influence." The authors believe theirs is the first study to compare electronic journal use and citation data.

Davis, Philip M. "The Effect of the Web on Undergraduate Citation Behavior: A 2000 Update." **College & Research Libraries** 63 (January 2002): 53–60.

Following up the study annotated below, Davis analyzed the citations in sixty-three term papers electronically submitted during 2000 for the Freshman level Introduction to Microeconomics class at Cornell University. The rise in the mean number of citations per paper from ten in 1996 to thirteen in 2000 was due to increasing use of nonscholarly resources, such as Web sites and newspapers. Citations to scholarly sources, defined as books and journals, actually decreased. By 2000, 22 percent of all citations were to Web sites. Six months after submission, 65 percent of Web citations in the papers written in 2000 pointed directly to the cited document, 13 percent of the cited documents were at a different URL, and 16 percent could not be found at all. Limiting the analysis to the papers from 2000, there was no statistically significant correlation between the grade and the total number of citations, Web citations, scholarly citations, and nonscholarly citations. Davis concludes with concern about a "possible crisis in undergraduate scholarship" due to the increasing number of nonscholarly citations.

Davis, Philip M. "Where to Spend Our E-Journal Money?: Defining a University Library's Core Collection Through Citation Analysis." **Portals** 2 (January 2002): 155–66.

This article's objective is to provide a "fast, low cost" technique for identifying "core" journals for electronic access. A search of *Biosis Previews,* a "comprehensive" Life Sciences serials index, for articles published by Cornell University faculty from 1996 to 2001 retrieved 5,292 publications from 841 different journals. Davis found that the top 10 titles (1.2 percent) produced 25 percent of the citations and the top 240 (29 percent) produced 80 percent, while graphs illustrate a Bradford distribution. Replicating the technique for University of Wisconsin at Madison faculty found that 5 percent of the titles accounted for 50 percent of the articles and 27 percent produced 80 percent. Price analysis indicated that journals from commercial publishers were "more expensive by a factor of ten" than those from societies or associations. The researcher points out that his method is "scalable" to other subjects and can help decide where to spend money for electronic resources. Note that this item analyzes print journals to assist electronic selection.

Davis, Philip M., and Suzanne A. Cohen. "The Effect of the Web on Undergraduate Citation Behavior, 1996–1999." **Journal of the American Society for Information Science & Technology** 52 (February 15, 2001): 309–14.

In a preliminary version of the above Davis study in College and Research Libraries, sixty-seven term papers submitted to the same Cornell University class in 1996 and sixty-nine in 1999 were analyzed, as of January 2000. A table summarizes the raw data concerning total citations as well as citations by format for the two years. The mean number of total citations rose slightly from 11.3 to 11.9 and the median increased from 10 to 12. Books declined from 30 percent of the citations in 1996 to 19 percent in 1999, whereas newspapers increased from 7 to

19 percent and Web sites from 9 to 21 percent. In the 1999 papers, 55 percent of Web citations led to the cited site, 19 percent had a different URL, and 16 percent could not be located, while the corresponding figures for papers submitted in 1996 were 18 percent, 26 percent, and 53 percent. The authors lament that grades were not available to them as they would have liked to investigate the relationship between grades and the number of citations.

Fosmire, Michael, and Song Yu. "Free Scholarly Electronic Journals: How Good Are They?" **Issues in Science & Technology Librarianship** no. 27 (summer 2000). [Electronic Journal]. Available: http://www.istl.org/00-summer/refereed.html (accessed August 30, 2003).

The two researchers report their citation study of eighty-two free, scholarly electronic journals in the science, technology, and medicine fields. The journals' 1999 impact factor and immediacy index were calculated from data available in the Web of Science and the number of articles published obtained from the journals' Web sites. They found forty-seven of the eighty-two titles were cited at least once. To provide an evaluative context and because most e-journals are not covered in the *JCR,* the data for these forty-seven were compared to the 1998 *JCR* data for journals (mostly print) in their fields. For example, 43 percent of the e-journals had high enough 1999 impact factors to rank in their field's top quarter in the 1998 *JCR,* whereas 38 percent would have fallen in the bottom quarter. Appendices list the study journals plus their URLs and the comparative citation data in seven fields, such as agriculture, biological sciences, and computer science. Some e-journals with high impact factors, such as *Cybermetrics,* had published only a few articles. Nevertheless, Fosmire and Yu conclude there are several "high quality" free scholarly e-journals publishing enough articles to have "significant impact" on their fields.

Harter, Stephen P. "The Impact of Electronic Journals on Scholarly Communication: A Citation Analysis." **Public-Access Computer Systems Review** 7, no. 5 (1996). [Electronic Journal.] Available: http://info.lib.uh.edu/pr/v7/n5/hart7n5.html (accessed August 30, 2003).

Harter, Stephen P. "Scholarly Communication and Electronic Journals: An Impact Study." **Journal of the American Society for Information Science** 49 (May 1, 1998): 507–16.

These two entries provide the preliminary and final report of the same research project. The author investigated the citation records of thirty-nine scholarly peer-reviewed electronic journals (twenty-eight "pure" electronic plus eleven mixed electronic/print) that began publication no later than 1993. One of these titles was covered by the *JCR,* while data for the remaining thirty-eight were compiled by searching three ISI databases, as of February 1996. Harter found that fifteen e-journals had never been cited, and thirteen had been cited from one to five times throughout their entire history. Only eight titles, listed in a table, were cited ten or more times. The seven most highly cited e-journal articles are listed. Comparison of the e-journal findings with *JCR* citation data for print journals in the same disciplines and detailed examination of three highly cited e-journals (*Online*

Journal of Current Clinical Trials, Psychology, and *Public-Access Computer Systems Review*) led Harter to conclude "most e-journals are having very little impact on formal scientific and scholarly communication." This is a meticulously done article by a top-ranking LIS researcher whose early retirement was a major loss to the field.

Herring, Susan Davis. "Use of Electronic Resources in Scholarly Electronic Journals: A Citation Analysis." **College & Research Libraries** 63 (July 2002): 334–40.

One hundred seventy-five peer-reviewed research articles, published between summer 1999 and spring 2000 in twelve free Web-based e-journals from a variety of disciplines, serve as the source for this exploratory citation study. The investigator found that 16 percent of 4,289 unique references were to electronic resources. A breakdown of the cited electronic resources shows that 24.7 percent were self-citations to the same e-journal, 17.8 percent to other e-journals (thus 45.2 percent were to e-journals), 20.1 percent reports, and 15.3 percent Web home pages. Other "non-traditional resources," such as press releases, seminar papers, and speeches, were cited. Moreover, 27 percent of the electronic citations were interdisciplinary. A comparative breakdown of the cited print items revealed 45.2 percent were books and 43.4 percent articles. It is also interesting that 18 percent of the cited Web resources were inaccessible. Herring speculates that the electronic format promotes interdisciplinarity and use of nontraditional resources and concludes, after reviewing previous studies, that online resources are "increasingly important" to scholars.

Neth, Marcy. "Citation Analysis and the Web." **Art Documentation** 17 (Spring 1998): 29–33.

The external links on twenty-five U.S. art library Web pages (twenty-three academic libraries plus one public and one museum library) are analyzed by Neth. There were links to 1,408 sites, of which 22.4 percent were museums and galleries.[9] After the elimination of duplicates, approximately 900 sites remained. More than 500 of these were linked to only once. The four sites that were linked to twenty-five or more times were considered the core Web sites for an art library. Each of the thirteen Webmasters who responded to an e-mail survey indicated that external sites were evaluated before a link was created. Three appendices list the libraries whose Web pages were studied, the major categories of Web pages linked to, and the top twenty individual links in rank order. While acknowledging a small core, the author concludes "libraries are creating unique Web resources comparable to physical library collections."

Rumsey, Mary. "Runaway Train: Problems of Permanence, Accessibility, and Stability in the Use of Web Sources in Law Review Citations." **Law Library Journal** 94 (winter 2002): 27–39.

The prevalence and stability of citations to the Web in law review journal articles are investigated by Rumsey. Citations, excluding ones not intended to support scholarly argumentation, in 100 scholarly articles selected from Westlaw's *Journals and Law Reviews* database each year from 1997 through 2001 serve as the study's source. The percentage of articles with at least one citation to the Web increased from 0.57 percent in 1995 (the source of the 1995 data is unclear) to 23 percent in 2000, while the average number of Web citations in those articles rose from 1.9 in 1995 to 10.45 in 2000. Rumsey decides that law review citations to the Web suffer from "severe link rot" as only 30.27 percent of the 1997 citations could be accessed during May-June 2001 and only 61.08 percent of 2001 citations were accessible. Moreover, even if the link is still accessible, she worries the site's content may have changed. The investigator discusses her findings implications for the law field and suggests some remedies, such as authors providing parallel print citations whenever possible.

Vreeland, Robert C. "Law Libraries in Hyperspace: A Citation Analysis of World Wide Web Sites." **Law Library Journal** 92 (winter 2000): 9–25.

Contending that usability and information architecture are "obsolete notions," Vreeland argues that citation analysis of links is "more effective" for evaluation of Web site quality. Conducted in 1999's fall semester, this project analyzed links on the law library Web pages of 156 American Bar Association (ABA) accredited institutions. Shareware was used to count 71,851 external links (on 15,484 separate hosts) assumed to measure "luminosity" because they shed light. Vreeland found a "Trueswell distribution," that is, the 80/20 pattern, with approximately 20 percent of the sites providing about 80 percent of the links. Then Alta Vista (although this search engine's unreliability is acknowledged) counted links (the total number is not stated in the text) to the 156 Web sites, deemed to measure a site's visibility. Separate tables rank the 156 sites by both luminosity and visibility, while scatter plots show "no clear correlation" between the two concepts. Other tables list the most frequently linked to external URLs and as well as the most frequently linked to Web servers. This entry serves as an interesting example of applying a citation analysis approach to the Web.

Youngen, Gregory K. "Citation Patterns to Electronic Preprints in the Astronomy and Astrophysics Literature." In **Library & Information Services in Astronomy III (LISA III): Proceedings of a Conference Held in Puerto de la Cruz, Tenerife, Spain, 21–24 April 1998,** edited by Uta Grothkopf and others, 136–44. San Francisco: Astronomical Society of the Pacific, 1998. ISBN 1-8867-3373-2. Electronic version, edited by Harry E. Payne, available: http://www.stsci.edu/stsci/meetings/lisa3/youngeng.html (accessed August 30, 2003).

This entry applies citation analysis to e-prints in physics by searching the *SciSearch* database through Dialog and the Stanford Linear Accelerator Stanford Public Information Retrieval System (SPIRES) database. (Youngen defines an *e-print* as an electronic version of an article that has not yet been published and states the best known e-print server was founded for physics at the Los Alamos National Laboratory in 1991 by Paul Ginsparg.) The researcher discovered that the number of astrophysics preprints doubled every year from 1992 to 1997 while citations to them increased at "an exponential rate." Results for general relativity/quantum cosmology e-prints showed a "slower rate" of growth. The author asserts e-prints "are becoming more accepted" and are being cited in "important and influential" print journals. Separate tables rank order the ten journals that most frequently cite astrophysics e-prints and the ten that most frequently cite general relativity/quantum cosmology e-prints. Five "areas of concern" regarding e-prints are discussed, including guidelines for revision/withdrawal and archiving issues. The article should have included more data but is of passable quality.

Zhang, Yin. "The Impact of Internet-Based Electronic Resources on Formal Scholarly Communication in the Area of Library and Information Science: A Citation Analysis." **Journal of Information Science** 24, no. 4 (1998): 241–54.

The author analyzed citations to electronic resources in fourteen scholarly, peer-reviewed LIS journals (ten print and four electronic) during 1994 to 1996. He discovered that 7.49 percent of the articles had at least one reference to an electronic resource and 8.94 percent had one or more e-resource "pointers," defined as a footnote or mentioning in the text. Altogether, only 1.13 percent of 29,397 citations were to electronic resources. As one might expect, electronic journals, beginning in 1995, cited a higher proportion of e-resources than did print journals. Further analysis found a slight yearly increase in the proportion of total citations from all fourteen journals to electronic resources, but it was not statistically significant. Zhang decides that the impact of electronic resources on LIS research, as measured by citations, "is small." This entry represents rigorous, well-done research.

USE OF ELECTRONIC RESOURCES

Methodological Issues

Bauer, Kathleen. "Indexes As Tools for Measuring Usage of Print and Electronic Resources." **College & Research Libraries** 62 (January 2001): 36–42.

Two indexes developed at the Yale University Medical Library (one for measuring the use of electronic resources, the other for print resources) are described here. The Electronic Usage Index counts each time an electronic text is accessed through the library's Web page and each time a session is begun in the Ovid electronic journal full-text database. The Print Usage Index combines data from book circulation and photocopying. With 1997–98 as a base of 100, use of electronic resources showed a "dramatic" increase to 237.2 in 1998–99 whereas use of print resources declined to 90.7. The author explains that these indexes, like the Consumer Price Index or Dow Jones Industrial Average, combine different data points into single figures that will provide benchmarks for measuring the relative use of print and electronic resources. Bauer acknowledges more research will be necessary to judge their validity and whether they exaggerate or undercount actual usage.

Bertot, John Carlo, Charles R. McClure, and Joe Ryan. **Statistics and Performance Measures for Public Library Networked Services**. Chicago: American Library Association, 2001. 103p. ISBN 0-8389-0796-2.

The introduction explains that this work's objective is to assist public libraries in measuring the use of online databases, Web sites, and online reference. The second chapter defines basic statistics and outlines procedures for collecting them. For example, database usage statistics include the number of sessions, the number of queries/searches, and the number of items examined. Chapter 3 illustrates potential use of these statistics to create performance measures. An example would be "total library materials use," which combines circulation, in-house use, ILL, and electronic use data. Other chapters address the use of surveys and focus groups for user assessment, data collection and analysis, issues in deciding which electronic measures to use, and extension of use statistics to a networked environment. Helpful appendices cover additional statistics for consideration, analysis of vendor statistics, and software for statistical collection. This book offers a practical, "how-to" approach, reminiscent of *Output Measures for Public Libraries.*

Blecic, Deborah D., Joan B. Fiscella, and Stephen E. Wiberley, Jr. "The Measurement of Use of Web-Based Information Resources: An Early Look at Vendor-Supplied Data." **College & Research Libraries** 62 (September 2001): 434–53.

This sophisticated article investigates methodological issues regarding use of Web-based resources at an unnamed U.S. research university. A fall 2000 survey of fifty-one vendors found that three supplied all elements in the International Coalition of Library Consortia (ICOLC) guidelines" (see next entry), twenty-nine offered some elements, and twenty provided none. Analysis of vendor-supplied use data for 1999 and the initial eight months of 2000 indicated, among many things, wide month-to-month variation. Tables display a variety of usage statistics for ICOLC elements and more than a dozen electronic resources. Examination of four e-journal collections found that the percentage of titles required to produce 80 percent of use was twenty-eight in the American Chemical Society, forty-four in Karger, forty-three in Ovid, and forty-eighty in Project Muse. The authors conclude with five specific recommendations for vendors, including "supply documentation" and give use data for each title in e-journal collections, and seven recommendations for libraries, such as, "examine data at least monthly and occasionally daily," be cognizant that reported hourly data may not be in local time, "calculate queries per session," and consider use in proportion to the user population's size. This entry is especially valuable for both the results and the methodological insights.

International Coalition of Library Consortia. "Guidelines for Statistical Measures of Usage of Web-Based Indexed, Abstracted, and Full-Text Resources." **Information Technology & Libraries** 18 (September 1999): 161–63. Also available: http://www.library.yale.edu/consortia/webstats.html (accessed August 30, 2003).

These guidelines are intended to apply to vendor-supplied Web sites and software. They list the "minimum requirements" for vendor-provided use statistics. Adopted in November 1998, the guidelines "draw heavily" upon those developed by the JSTOR Web Statistics Task Force. The following elements "must be provided:"

- Number of searches

- Number of menu selections

- Number of logins

- Number of turnaways (i.e., a desired item is inaccessible)

- Number of items examined ("viewed, marked or selected, downloaded, e-mailed, printed"), including citations, full-text, tables of contents, and abstracts

There should be a capacity to subdivide the data by specific database, an institutionally defined set of IP addresses, total consortium, subscriber account or ID number, and time period. It is stipulated that user, institutional, and consortial confidentiality must be protected, comparative statistics among consortial members made available, and that statistical reports be provided through an access-protected Web interface. Appended is a list of the thirty-six ICOLC members in the United States, Canada, Europe, and Australia with the proviso, "This statement does not necessarily represent the official views of each consortium." These guidelines represent a milestone in the effort to standardize measurement of electronic resource usage.

Liu, Weiling, and Fannie M. Cox. "Tracking the Use of E-Journals: A Technique Collaboratively Developed by the Cataloging Department and the Office of Libraries Technology at the University of Louisville." **OCLC Systems & Services** 18, no. 1 (2002): 32–39.
    A method developed at the University of Louisville for compiling and reporting electronic journal usage statistics is described. Liu and Cox begin by emphasizing the importance of usage statistics for e-journal collection management and that the library decided to development its own data-gathering system because vendor reports "are not comparable, reliable or consistent." In this system, the e-journal vendor's URL is entered into the Machine Readable Cataloging (MARC) bibliographical and holdings record, and a common gateway interface tracking program, adapted from a shareware application, appends to a log file every use of the journal through the library Web page or OPAC. A *Microsoft Access* database then generates final usage reports. Five technical steps in the process are listed and explained, but need not be summarized here. Eight figures include a flow chart and an example of a usage report. The authors seem satisfied this approach meets their stated requirements for efficiency, effectiveness, and flexibility.

Luther, Judy. **White Paper on Electronic Journal Usage Statistics.** Washington, DC: Council on Library and Information Resources, 2000. 25p. ISBN 1-88733-479-3. Reprinted in **Serials Librarian** 41, no. 2 (2001): 119–48. Available: http://www.clir.org/pubs/reports/pub94/contents.html (accessed August 30, 2003).
    Luther offers an excellent overview of the basic issues involved in measuring the use of electronic journals. The analysis is partially based on interviewing librarians at OhioLINK, the Los Alamos National Laboratories, and the Florida

Center for Library Automation. Among the issues of concern to both librarians and publishers are the lack of comparable data, lack of context for evaluating the data, incomplete data, and user privacy. Librarians are concerned with the impact of electronic journal usage statistics on budget justification and selection. Publishers are no longer so worried that librarians will react to use data with cancellations but are looking for their own internal application for use statistics. Luther outlines three steps for processing raw data from servers: data collection, analysis, and presentation. She perceives the need to measure what is being used, who is using it, and the type of use activity. It is noted that the burden of measuring use has shifted from libraries to publishers. The importance of a standard methodology to facilitate the gathering of comparable and reliable data is strongly emphasized. The implications of caching, log files, and software are briefly mentioned. The author does an outstanding job of focusing on the major issues without becoming bogged down in technical minutiae.

Mercer, Linda S. "Measuring the Use and Value of Electronic Journals and Books." **Issues in Science & Technology Librarianship** no. 25 (winter 2000). [Electronic Journal] Available: http://www.library.ucsb.edu/istl/00-winter/article1.html (accessed August 30, 2003).

Contending that usage is a key electronic resource performance measure, Mercer describes two "mechanisms" for reporting electronic use for evaluative purposes. Seven types of usage data provided by Highwire Press for electronic journals are outlined:

- Total use

- Use of various journal parts, such as the table of contents

- Format used (i.e., HTML or PDF)

- Number of searches

- Number of IP addresses hitting the title

- Number of articles used by journal section

- The ten most frequently used articles

Detailed tables illustrate these data for the *Journal of Biological Chemistry* during December 1999 at the Washington University School of Medicine Library. Next, the author outlines nine electronic journal use measures this library locally developed based on data extracted from Ovid Technologies log files. These measures include usage by department, database, department/database, and patron group as well as full-text use according to department, patron group, and journal title. Mercer stresses that vendor-supplied use data is "often incomplete" and calls for the establishment of minimum national standards for basic statistics regarding use of electronic resources.

Case Studies

Adams, Judith A., and Sharon C. Bonk. "Electronic Information Technologies and Resources: Use by University Faculty and Faculty Preferences for Related Library Services." **College & Research Libraries** 56 (March 1995): 119–31.

Adams and Bonk report the results from a September 1992 questionnaire survey of 3,713 faculty and staff (27 percent responded) at four SUNY campuses (Albany, Binghamton, Buffalo, and Stony Brook) concerning use of electronic information resources and technologies. They found that 32 percent of the respondents used electronic journals and newsletters, 19.5 percent full-text electronic databases, and 53.4 percent CD-ROM indexing/abstracting databases in the library. Responses to an open-ended question revealed that the most desired unavailable resources were *Lexis/Nexis* followed by *Current Contents.* Lack of knowledge about available databases, mentioned by 61.5 percent of the respondents, was the most frequently noted obstacle to use of electronic resources. Data is also presented on topics unrelated to resources, such as training. The researchers also found "inequities in access to use of electronic technologies among the disciplines." The authors state theirs was the first such survey to cover all disciplines and faculty from multiple campuses.

Davis, Allan. "Database Usage and Title Analysis on a CD-ROM Workstation." **Serials Review** 19 (fall 1993): 85–94.

The use of *ProQuest* at the University of Wisconsin at Whitewater library is analyzed based on 10,026 citations printed out by library users during January through May 1992. The collection "had" 68 percent of 1,153 retrieved titles and 83 percent of the cited items. The publication date distribution revealed that 86 percent of the citations were to 1989–92 and 14 percent to 1985–88, while 1991 was the "dominant" year. A table lists the seven most frequently retrieved titles, which were mostly newspapers. Proportional use among the four *ProQuest* databases was as follows: *Periodical Abstracts,* 56 percent; *ABI/INFORM,* 34 percent, *Newspaper Abstracts,* 8 percent, and *Business Dateline,* 2 percent. The data "closely followed" Bradford's Law with 38 "highly productive" journals, 160 "moderately productive" ones, and 955 "low productivity" titles each contributing approximately one-third the retrieved items. However, the distribution of retrieved items among journal titles was more scattered than postulated by the 80/20 Rule. This is an interesting application of CD-ROM usage data to academic library collection evaluation issues.

Davis, Philip M. "Patterns in Electronic Journal Usage: Challenging the Composition of Geographic Consortia." **College & Research Libraries** 63 (November 2002): 484–97.

The researcher analyzes use, defined as the number of articles downloaded, for over 200 electronic journals in the Academic Press IDEAL (International Digital Electronic Access Library) package by more than twenty academic library members of the NorthEast Research Library consortium during 2000 and 2001. Trueswell's 80/20 Rule was supported as 4.4 percent of the titles (the top ten) produced 44 percent of the downloads and 24.3 percent (the top fifty) accounted for

80 percent of the uses. Due to the skewed usage patterns, the median use per title was 511 whereas the "average use" (the value of which Davis questions) was 1,681. Other important findings were "each institution had a unique pattern of use," "no institution used every title," "some titles were used very infrequently...[but]...every title was used," and titles subscribed to in print were much more heavily used than nonsubscribed titles. Because cluster analysis found different usage patterns among three library categories (large research libraries, medical institutions, and smaller universities plus liberal arts colleges), Davis advocates consortia based on library type rather than geographic proximity.

Dillon, Dennis. "E-Books: The University of Texas Experience, Part 1." **Library Hi Tech** 19, no. 2 (2001): 113–24.

This well-done article analyzes preliminary usage statistics of netLibrary electronic books focusing on the global netLibrary collection, an 11,000 title Amigos collection, a 5,000 title Texshare collection, and a 5,300 title University of Texas (UT) system collection. Gathered from the netLibrary Extranet site, data is presented for all users of these collections and for UT-Austin users separately. A table reveals 77 percent of all netLibrary titles have been used by at least one library somewhere in the world, but only 32 percent of the UT system collection had been used by any of its nine member libraries. Tables list the ten most frequently used titles and the ten titles generating the most turnaways in the various collections. Economics, business, and computer science were the most heavily used subjects followed by health and medicine. The ability of libraries to access global netLibrary use data serves as a "bestseller list" that aids e-book collection development. No "obvious correlation" was found between e-book usage and ownership of the print title. Dillon concludes "e-books are to printed books as television is to radio and movies" and their future is "bright." This entry offers a complex and thoughtful analysis of numerous subtle nuances that do not lend themselves well to summary in a brief annotation.

Dillon, Dennis. "E-Books: The University of Texas Experience, Part 2." **Library Hi Tech** 19, no. 4 (2001): 350–62.

This follow-up to the preceding entry examines the impact that cataloging (entering MARC records into the OPAC in November 2000) had on the use of the Amigos netLibrary electronic book collection at the University of Texas at Austin. Dillon found that 24 percent of the collection had been used in the fourteen months prior to cataloging compared to 34 percent in the three months after cataloging. Average monthly use more than doubled from 1,029 to 2,103 after cataloging was introduced. Postcataloging usage was "more evenly spread across subject area" and computer science's share of the ten most frequently used books declined from nine to four. A breakdown of 3,800 e-books individually selected at the UT system libraries revealed that 33 percent were classified in H (social sciences) and 12 percent in P (literature). The UT at Austin print collection has a 50 percent yearly "usage rate," that is, the ratio of total uses to items held, whereas the rate for the Amigos netLibrary collection is 200 percent. This exceedingly well-written essay also explores the role of electronic books in the digital information environment.

Goodman, David. "One Years' Experience Without Print at Princeton." In **National Online 2001 Proceedings: New York, May 15–17, 2001,** edited by Martha E. Williams, 183–89. Medford, NJ: Information Today, 2001. ISBN 1-57387-123-0.

Goodman reports some usage data on the Academic Press IDEAL suite of electronic journals at Princeton University. Beginning in January 2000, IDEAL's journals were only available to Princeton users electronically as all but 9 of 112 print equivalents were cancelled for financial reasons. Although a formal user survey had not been conducted, Goodman reports "no complaints at all" after one year. Comparison of print and electronic usage patterns, as the author originally intended, was impossible due to relocation of the Biology Library. However, Goodman did find that the 60 percent of IDEAL's journals previously subscribed to by Princeton accounted for 93 percent of the articles used during the year 2000, while only 7 percent of the articles used electronically were from titles not previously held in print. In contrast, similar data from Ohio State University indicated that 28 percent of the articles read electronically were from journals not previously held. Other e-journal issues, including archiving and usability, are also discussed. This conference presentation makes a contribution to the controversy concerning the extent to which previously unowned print journals are used electronically.

Haar, John M. "Project PEAK: Vanderbilt's Experience with Articles on Demand." **Serials Librarian** 38, nos. 1–2 (2000): 91–99.

Haar writes about the Pricing Electronic Access to Knowledge (PEAK) Project at Vanderbilt University in which the use of 1,175 Elsevier journals through accessing electronic full-text articles was experimentally tested during the 1997–98 academic year. A year's participation in PEAK cost $43,600 compared to $700,000 in annual subscription costs for the 403 PEAK journals also held in print form. A total of 2,808 unique articles were used (about 2 percent of the total) with each article used an average of 2.7 times. The average cost per use in PEAK was $4.57 per article compared to $8.32 for print journals. The library subscribed to 45 percent of the 637 different titles that were used in PEAK and did not subscribe to 55 percent, while 28 percent of the 403 PEAK titles the library subscribed to in print were not used electronically. The author believes the traditional journal subscription model is "flawed" because "people do not read journals; they read articles."

Holmquist, Jane E. "Survey on the Use of Electronic Journals at Princeton, 1997." In **Library & Information Services in Astronomy III (LISA III): Proceedings of a Conference Held in Puerto de la Cruz, Tenerife, Spain 21–24 April 1998,** edited by Uta Grothkopf et al, 169–76. San Francisco, CA: Astronomical Society of the Pacific, 1998. ISBN 1-886733-73-2. Electronic version, edited by Harry E. Payne, available: http://www.stsci.edu/stsci/meetings/lisa3/holmquistj.html (accessed August 30, 2003).

This entry reports a survey of electronic journal usage carried out by the Electronic Journals Task Force at Princeton University. In April 1997, 1,800 questionnaires were sent to 300 randomly selected members of six patron categories, including undergraduate students, graduate students, and faculty. Note that by September, there was a 26 percent response rate. They found that 37 percent of the respondents had used an electronic journal or the electronic version of a print journal in contrast to 56 percent who had not done so. Among the latter, 60 percent stated they preferred print-on-paper to a computer screen and 32 percent lacked time to learn about electronic journals. Also, 27 percent of all respondents indicated their preferred journals were not available in electronic form. As concluded by Holmquist, this study offers a benchmark for comparing future electronic journal use with the spring 1997 level.

Hughes, Carol Ann, and Nancy L. Buchanan. "Use of Electronic Monographs in the Humanities and Social Sciences." **Library Hi Tech** 19, no. 4 (2001): 368–75.

Two collection management librarians at Questia (a service that offers end-users direct personal subscriptions to 35,000 humanities and social science electronic books) present "preliminary" and "exploratory" analysis of 578,358 searches during the three months from January through April 2001. They found that 48 percent of the 35,000 titles received over ten page views (i.e., one reader viewing ten pages, ten readers viewing one page, etc.). That 82 percent of the page views came from 20 percent of the books (based on those titles receiving more than ten page views) was deemed an "interesting variation" on the 80/20 Rule. The "most popular" topics were literature (American and English followed by Classical Greek drama), sociology (e.g., contemporary social issues), and history (especially Hitler and Nazism). Hughes and Buchanan note that 150 of the 200 most frequently used titles pertained to literature, and they list the ten most frequently accessed works of primary literature. Additional data is presented concerning use of search terms.

Lenares, Deborah. "Faculty Use of Electronic Journals at Research Institutions." In **Racing Toward Tomorrow: Proceedings of the Ninth National Conference of the Association of College and Research Libraries April, 8–11, 1999,** edited by Hugh A. Thompson, 234–41. Chicago: Association of College and Research Libraries, 1999. ISBN 0-8389-8015-5.

This conference paper reports an investigation of electronic journal use by faculty at ARL institutions. In 1998, 112 faculty (a 22 percent response rate), and in 1999, 120 (a 26 percent response rate), answered questionnaires using two-stage systematic sampling. The author found "growing acceptance" of electronic journals as the respondents using them increased from 46 percent in 1998 to 61 percent in 1999. Moreover, responding faculty using them "frequently" rose from 10 percent to 14 percent, whereas faculty frequently using print journals declined from 74 percent to 65 percent. Note that "frequent" is not defined. Analysis by discipline revealed the highest use of e-journals in the physical sciences and lowest in the arts and humanities. In a fascinating application of Everett M. Rogers' Diffusion of Innovation Theory, Lenares decides that faculty using e-journals are "incomplete adopters," whereas those who do not use them are "laggards."[10]

Morse, David. H., and William A. Clintworth. "Comparing Patterns of Print and Electronic Journal Use in an Academic Health Science Library." **Issues in Science**

& Technology Librarianship no. 28 (fall 2000). [Electronic Journal] Available: http://www.library.ucsb.edu/istl/00-fall/refereed.html (accessed August 30, 2003).

An investigation of the comparative print versus electronic use of 194 biomedical journals simultaneously available in both formats at the University of Southern California Medical Library is reported here. Data on use of the 1998 issues during January through June 1999 was gathered for the electronic format through Ovid transaction logs and for the print through bar code scanning while reshelving. The electronic versions were used 27,777 times contrasted to 1,814 for the print, but the extent to which new uses or migration from print to electronic account for the large electronic figure is unknown. Separate rankings of the thirty-nine most frequently used print and electronic titles demonstrated that twenty-five were common to both. Moreover, the top 20 percent of electronic titles accounted for 57 percent of uses, and the print top 20 percent produced 58 percent of total usage, while for both formats the lower 40 percent of the titles represented 9 percent of use. This nearly identical pattern surprised the authors who expected greater concentration among the print journals because the electronic format allows easier accessibility to less important titles. This is both an interesting and important study.

Murphy, Alison. "JSTOR Usage." **Ariadne** no. 24 (June 2000). [Electronic Journal] Available: http://www.ariadne.ac.uk/issue24/jstor/ (accessed August 30, 2003).

This relatively short piece reports collective usage data by all participating libraries of the U.K. JSTOR Mirror Service, launched in March 1998 and maintained by the Manchester Information and Associated Datasets. As of the time of writing, 41 U.K. and 7 Irish higher education institutes were using the system, with Oxford University and the London School of Economics the two heaviest users. A graph depicts monthly JSTOR usage from January 1999 through April 2000 according to the number of accesses, searches, and articles viewed. A pie chart analyzing usage by subject during January-March 2000 shows that 34.5 percent of the accesses were in economics, 10.0 percent finance, and 9.9 percent in political science. Moreover, 76,288 articles were printed in 1999 compared to 77,132 during the first four months of 2000. Due to the benefits of a Web-based electronic journal, the reader can directly link to a list of participating libraries and a list of journals covered by JSTOR.

Ramirez, Diana, and Suzanne D. Gyeszly. "netLibrary: A New Direction in Collection Development." **Collection Building** 20, no. 4 (2001): 154–64.

The use of netLibrary electronic books by two consortia and at Texas A & M University is examined by Ramirez and Gyeszly. The six usage reports generated by netLibrary's Extranet software are briefly explained. Roughly 19,000 e-books were used by the 92 Amigos libraries and approximately 700 Texshare libraries a total of 92,928 times (a figure deemed "considerably lower than anticipated") during the 270-day period from August 2000 through May 2001. The Activity by Subject report indicated that economics and business books accounted for 14.0 percent of these uses, computer science books 12.5 percent, and literature 11.1 percent. Another report revealed 1,703 "turnaways," that is, a desired book could not be assessed because it was already in use, during the 90 days between February and May 2001. Data for 193 e-books separately acquired by TAMU revealed 4,484 total uses during the same 270-day period and 231 turnaways during the 90-day period. Lengthy tables summarize the findings for 55 subject areas. This is a helpful preliminary report on e-book use.

Rogers, Sally A. "Electronic Journal Usage at Ohio State University." **College & Research Libraries** 62 (January 2001): 25–34.

After OhioLINK established its Electronic Journal Center in April 1998, the author submitted questions about e-journals to the OSU poll in 1998, 1999, and 2000. Note that approximately 300 faculty and graduate students were surveyed each year. The respondents' perceptions of the benefits and drawbacks of electronic journals are discussed. The 1999 poll found that 61.3 percent of faculty and 63.4 percent of graduate students considered it "important" or "very important" that the library replace print journal subscriptions with electronic versions. The percentage of faculty who used electronic journals at least monthly rose from 36.2 in 1998 to 53.9 in 2000 and graduate student use increased from 42.6 to 54.3. Corresponding use of print journals by faculty declined from 74.3 percent to 65.6 percent and by graduate students from 62.3 percent to 55.2 percent. The author observes the increased e-journal usage may to some extent reflect the fact that the number of electronic journals available at Ohio State increased from 200 in 1998 to 3,000 in 2000. As noted by Rogers, this investigation differs from most earlier electronic journal usage studies by reporting longitudinal data for a three-year period.

Sanville, Thomas J. "A Method out of the Madness: OhioLINK's Collaborative Response to the Serials Crisis Three Years Later: A Progress Report." **Serials Librarian** 40, nos. 1–2 (2001): 129–55.

The OhioLINK Executive Director presents collective usage data of its Electronic Journal Center by participating libraries. His data demonstrate the increasing use of journal articles in electronic form. "Virtually all" (97.4 percent) of 2,906 titles from seven major publishers were used between January 1 and June 11, 2000, and the pattern "continues," although the rate varies among the publishers.[11] More significantly, the majority of electronic usage (58 percent of downloaded articles) from June 1999-May 2000 came from journals not held in print by the downloading institution. Concentration of usage in a fraction of the titles was "broader" than the 80/20 Rule as 40 percent of the electronic titles accounted for 80 percent of the downloaded articles. It is interesting that thirteen of the state's large university libraries on average subscribed in print to only 24.1 percent of 4,106 e-journals Ohio academic libraries wished to license, with the percentages ranging from 8.9 to 53.2 percent among the thirteen. More than a dozen charts and tables provide a wide variety of other usage statistics. In this provocative but important article, Sanville strongly advocates a shift from the "print-based island mentality," in which each library separately buys print materials, to consortial licensing of electronic access.

Summerfield, Mary, and Carol A. Mandel with Paul B. Kantor, consultant. "On-Line Books at Columbia: Early Findings on Use, Satisfaction, and Effect." In

Technology and Scholarly Communication, edited by Richard Ekman and Richard E. Quandt, 282–308. Berkeley, CA: University of California Press, 1999. ISBN 0-520-21762-4.

This rigorous, in-depth book chapter reports findings from Columbia University's Online Books Evaluation Project conducted from January 1995 through the fall of 1997. The complex methodology incorporated online book use data from the university computing services, library circulation, and reserve records for print books, and a variety of user surveys and interviews. An analysis of thirty-two nonreference books found 120 online users and 673 hits for the electronic version between March 15 and May 31, 1997, compared to 75 circulations for the same books' print versions during January through June 1997, representing a 1.6 to 1 electronic user to circulation ratio. Of six references works available both electronically and in print, only one, the *Oxford English Dictionary,* received "sizable" print usage. Among numerous other findings, the researchers discovered that an e-book can "attract scholars who would not have seen it otherwise." The authors conclude that online books are "finding a place" in scholar's work. In summary, this is a first-rate study.

Effect of Electronic Resources on Use of Print Resources

Cassel, Rachel. "Do Online Indexes Always Increase Journal Circulation? Results of a Study at the State University of New York at Binghamton." **Serials Librarian** 23, nos. 1–2 (1992): 49–64.

The author compares journal circulation before and after the introduction of six CD-ROM indexes at the State University of New York at Binghamton's main and fine arts libraries during a three-year period. In 1989–90, prior to the introduction of the indexes, the titles they covered accounted for 27.3 percent of total circulation. In 1989–90, when *ERIC, ABI-INFORM,* and *Periodical Abstracts* were introduced, this figure rose to 38.1 percent. However, the percentage decreased to 31.8 in 1990–91 after the *Humanities Index, Social Sciences Index,* and *General Science Index* had been provided. The decline in 1990–91 after an initial increase the previous year "needs further investigating," according to Cassel. She speculates that, among other reasons, the novelty of the online indexes may have worn off. This entry provides empirical data, although somewhat crude, which supports the widely held assumption that online indexes increase journal use.

De Groote, Sandra L., and Josephine L. Dorsch. "Online Journals: Impact on Print Journal Usage." **Bulletin of the Medical Library Association** 89 (October 2001): 372–78.

This article studies the impact of online journals on print journal usage at the Library of the Health Sciences at Peoria, a regional location of the University of Illinois at Chicago. The analysis is based on 1995 through 1999 use data (combining in-house reshelving counts with circulation statistics) for 149 journals. A comparison of relative total uses for 1995–99 issues among the five years found a statistically significant decline from 1998 to 1999 that the authors attribute to the introduction of 104 online journals in January of that year. The 86 titles available in print format only displayed a larger usage decline than the 63 titles available both in print and online, although the authors admit that heavily used titles were selected for dual print/online subscriptions. The use of pre-1995 issues for the 149 titles decreased every year from 1995 through 1999, but De Groote and Dorsch acknowledge this may reflect the normal journal aging process. This research is somewhat lacking in rigor.

Morris, Ruth C. "Online Tables of Contents for Books: Effect on Usage." **Bulletin of the Medical Library Association** 89 (January 2001): 29–36.

The effect that entering a book's table of contents (TOC) in the OPAC has on its use is investigated here. Morris compared the use of two randomly selected stratified samples (1,979 with their TOC in the InnoPac catalog and 1,978 without) at the University of New Mexico Health Sciences Center Library during a fourteen-month period beginning April 1, 1997. She discovered a statistically significant difference in the use of the two samples: 73 percent of the titles with their TOC in the catalog were used, compared to 66 percent of the other sample, and 69 percent of the 3,957 total titles were used. Moreover, she concludes that OPAC display of a book's TOC increased circulation 33 percent, in-house use 43 percent, and total use 45 percent, although the mathematical calculations are not explained. Further analysis showed that TOC inclusion in the OPAC produced a greater usage increase for current titles and those with a history of high use. This project's ostensible objective was to analyze the impact of enhanced bibliographical information in OPACs, but the findings certainly have relevance to the study of book use in libraries.

NOTES

1. Truncation was used to retrieve records with both the singular and plural form.

2. Péter Jacsó, *Content Evaluation of Textual CD-ROM and Web Databases* (Englewood, CO: Libraries Unlimited, 2001), 12.

3. I acknowledge the late Professor Rob Kling, Indiana University, School of Library and Information Science, for bringing this issue to my attention.

4. Percentage calculated by Nisonger from Hawbaker and Wagner's data.

5. Ruth Pagell, "Searching Full-Text Periodicals: How Full Is Full," *Database* 10 (October 1987): 33–36.

6. Nisonger calculated the percentage.

7. Marilyn M. Roche, *ARL/RLG Interlibrary Loan Cost Study* (Washington, DC: Association of Research Libraries, 1993).

8. The percentages are Nisonger's calculation from the two authors raw data.

9. Nisonger's calculation from Neth's raw data.

10. Everett M. Rogers, *Communication of Innovations: A Cross-Cultural Approach,* 2d ed. (New York: Free Press, 1971).

11. Nisonger's calculation from Sanville's data.

12

Evaluation of Access

Throughout most of their history, libraries met patron information needs through items they owned and housed. Hence the importance of collection evaluation. Thomas L. Kilpatrick's history of interlibrary loan, the source for the information in the remainder of this paragraph, traces the sharing of materials among libraries to a 1634 proposal by the French humanist Nicolas Claude Fabri de Peiresc.[1] Peiresc spent a year negotiating the loan of an item from the Royal Library in Paris to the Barberini Library in Rome. Individually negotiated loans among libraries served as a model for approximately two and a half centuries. In 1849, Charles Coffin Jewett found that only fourteen of more than 900 surveyed U.S. libraries reported a "regulation by which books may be lent by courtesy to persons at a distance." The first code for interlibrary loan was adopted by the American Library Association in 1916. The introduction and widespread adoption of photocopying technology in the 1960s facilitated the sharing of journal articles because libraries had previously been reluctant to lend bound journal volumes.

During the 1980s, commercial document delivery vendors began to compete with traditional ILL and became major players on the library scene. Well-known commercial document suppliers have included—some are now out of business—Faxon Finder, The Genuine Article (TGA), EBSCOdoc, and UnCover (variously called CARL, CARL UnCover, or UnCover2 during its historical evolution). This chapter's annotations use the vendor name employed by the author's of the original item. Many document delivery vendors, such as UnCover and Faxon Finder, also offer supplementary "table-of-contents services"—variously termed "current alerting services"—that index the content of current journal issues. These services—which may be viewed as a modern version of Selective Dissemination of Information (SDI)—complement document delivery because they inform end-users about recently published articles so they can order those of interest to them. Throughout the 1990s, the slogans "access versus ownership" and "just-in-time versus just-in-case" were heard so frequently they almost seem trite.

The terms "interlibrary loan" and "document delivery" have been used somewhat inconsistently in the literature. In many usages, the two terms are near synonyms for each other. Alternatively, interlibrary loan means borrowing among libraries whereas document delivery implies the use of commercial vendors. In actual practice, the same unit—frequently termed Interlibrary Loan or Access Services—may be responsible for obtaining documents from both other libraries and commercial vendors. Indeed, some evaluations of access performance group ILL and document delivery together.

A substantial literature has been published concerning access as a strategy for meeting patron information needs, covering the concept itself, interlibrary loan, document delivery, the cost-effectiveness of alternate strategies, and the impact of electronic resources, among other topics. This chapter concentrates on the subset of this literature pertinent to evaluation, focusing on significant methodological issues, the relative cost-effectiveness of access versus ownership, and evaluation of access performance. Included in the later would be studies of interlibrary loan in one or more libraries, evaluations of a commercial document delivery vendor, comparative evaluation of different vendors, and comparison of ILL with commercial document delivery. These studies tend to investigate one or more of four traditional performance criteria:

- Deliver speed or turnaround time

- Cost per item

- Fill rate

- User satisfaction

Excluded from this chapter are items that describe the access concept or simply argue its benefits and drawbacks, depict a specific library's or consortium's access program, outline the services offered by one or more document delivery supplier, evaluate SDI; or address vendor selection criteria. Note that a number of articles with "evaluation" in their title actually address vendor selection rather than reporting the results of an evaluation study and are thus beyond this review's scope.

Chapter 12 is organized into five sections, covering the cost-effectiveness of ILL/document delivery versus ownership, the evaluation of document delivery vendor performance, the evaluation of interlibrary loan, table of content service evaluation, and miscellaneous issues relating to the evaluation of access. (Entries that simultaneously address the evaluation of both commercial document delivery and traditional ILL are included in the section on document delivery.) The use of ILL/document delivery data for collection evaluation is covered in chapter 4 and for serials management in chapter 7.

EVALUATION OF COST-EFFECTIVENESS OF ACCESS VERSUS OWNERSHIP

Beam, Joan. "Document Delivery via UnCover: Analysis of a Subsidized Service." **Serials Review** 23 (winter 1997): 1–14.

The main thrust of Beam's article is on the evaluation of subsidized, unmediated document delivery from UnCover at the Colorado State University libraries during 1994 through 1997. The average cost per article was $12.26 during the three-year period. Of the 2,751 journal titles received between April 1994 and March 1996, 48 percent were requested only once, 15 percent more than five times, and 4 percent more than ten times. An examination of the 397 titles requested at least five times found that subscription was more cost-effective than document delivery for 16 percent ($1,896 versus $3,179 annual costs), but for the remaining 84 percent, annual subscription costs were $126,597 contrasted to $14,062 for document delivery. The overall cost of subscription for these titles outweighed document delivery by a ratio of 7.5 to 1. See Sellers and Beam entry for details (some of which are repeated in this article) about a 1994 pilot evaluation of UnCover by the Colorado State University Libraries.

Blagden, John. "Some Thoughts on the Access v. Holdings Debate." **Library Management** 17, no. 8 (1996): 28–29.

This brief item is worth noting because it provides some preliminary data concerning the BIODOC project at Cranfield University in the United Kingdom. In this experiment, the Biotechnology Centre cancelled all its journal subscriptions and substituted the UnCover table of contents service. After one year, ILL requests increased 166 percent and costs to the library increased 30 percent even when the savings from the serial cancellations were taken into account. Blagden observes that his ILL data is contrary to the national trend in British universities where, according to Standing Conference on National and University Libraries (SCONUL) annual statistics, ILL as a percentage of total circulation declined from 3.2 percent in 1992 to 2.8 percent in 1994. See Harrington, Evans, and Bevan for additional evaluative information about BIODOC.

Chappell, Mary Ann. "Meeting Undergraduate Literature Needs with ILL/Document Delivery." **Serials Review** 19 (spring 1993): 81–86, 94.

Written from the perspective of the James Madison University (JMU) library, this entry describes a three-way resource sharing agreement between JMU, Virginia Polytechnic Institute and State University, and the University of Virginia. Chappell recounts the program's background development and provides evaluative data for the faxing of serial articles during the 1991–92 academic year. JMU compiled a list of 500 journal titles (435 of which were owned by the other two partners) that the library would provide free to patrons through this agreement, termed the Document Express. The total yearly subscription price for these 500 titles was approximately $123,000 compared to JMU's cost of $43,115 for the program's first year. The average cost per article (including program start-up cost) was $12.68 during 1991–92, while it was estimated this cost would fall to $7.88 during the second year. Articles from journals not on the list were ordered from commercial vendors at a mean cost of $20.30. Because the turnaround time was 1.8 "working days," the advertised delivery time was increased from twenty-four to forty-eight hours. The author reports an "unfilled rate" of 25 percent. A table lists the twelve most frequently requested titles.

Currie, Debra L. "Serials Redesign: Using Electronic Document Delivery to Reshape Access to Agricultural Journal Literature." **Journal of Agricultural & Food Information** 3, no. 2 (1995): 13–22.

The LSU Library's Serials Redesign Project (which sought to substitute free document delivery though UnCover for subscription to lower priority journals) is described from the perspective of an agricultural reference librarian who participated in its early stages. Preliminary results from pilot studies with the Chemistry and Geography/Anthropology Departments are reported. UnCover's fill rate was 87 percent from July 1994 to January 1995. Moreover, 1,006 articles from 480 cancelled journals were acquired for $12,278.14: a "drop in the bucket" compared to the $207,000 subscription cost. The author describes her liaison role with six departments relating to agriculture after the project was extended to thirty-two science departments. Taking a candid approach, Currie acknowledges the project "did not receive the wholehearted support" of some agricultural department chairs or faculty, but concludes "there appears to be good reason for optimism." For further information on the Serials Redesign Project, see the entries by Hamaker plus Kleiner and Hamaker.

Duda, Andrea L., and Rosemary L. Meszaros. "Validating Journal Cancellation Decisions in the Sciences: A Report Card." **Issues in Science & Technology Librarianship** 19 (summer 1998). [Electronic Journal.] Available: http://www.istl.org/98-summer/article4.html (accessed August 30, 2003).

This entry analyzes the University of California at Santa Barbara (UCSB) library's experience from 1990 through 1997 using the University of California system's so-called "Fax Project," whereby science and engineering articles requested by patrons were faxed among the participating libraries. The authors focus on articles from journals cancelled by UCSB during five cancellation projects in 1987, 1989, 1991, 1994, and 1996. From 1991 to 1995, the percentage of faxed articles from cancelled journals ranged from 25.74 percent to 36.11 percent, jumping to 46.97 percent in 1997. For 15 of the 16 cancelled titles most frequently requested by UCSB patrons throughout the project, access (estimated at $15 per fax to cover staff, long distance charges, copyright, etc.) was far less expensive than subscription, based on hypothetical subscription costs since cancellation. One can calculate from data presented in a table that the total subscription cost for these 16 titles was $160,404, and the fax cost was $8,415 for a $151,989 savings.

Ferguson, Anthony W., and Kathleen Kehoe. "Access vs. Ownership: What Is Most Cost Effective in the Sciences." **Journal of Library Administration** 19, no. 2 (1993): 89–99.

Ferguson and Kehoe's investigation is structured on the 1,519 ILL/document delivery requests (15 percent monographs and 85 percent periodical articles) processed between January 1991 and September 1992 from faculty and graduate students in Columbia University's Biology, Physics, and Electrical Engineering Departments. A "fully-loaded," that is, including processing, cost of $27 for ILL and $39 for commercial document delivery was assumed. Ninety-two percent of the monographs and 72 percent of the periodicals received only a single request. Interestingly, subject specialists indicated 40 percent of the requested books and 80 percent of the periodical titles fell within the library's collecting parameters. The comparative cost of purchasing and borrowing was $33,370 versus $6,086 for monographs, $343,926 versus $28,674 for biology periodicals, $33,628 versus

$1,872 for physics periodicals, and $89,544 versus $6,264 for electrical engineering periodicals. Eight tables summarize the findings, and two appendices address costing methodology issues. An examination of ten periodical titles cancelled in 1987 found that access was more cost-effective than subscription for eight of them. This is an important study from a major university.

Fuseler, Elizabeth A. "Providing Access to Journals—Just in Time or Just in Case?" **College & Research Libraries News** 55 (March 1994): 130–32, 148.

Although ostensibly a description of the Colorado State University libraries Science and Technology Department's document delivery program, Fuseler's article includes significant evaluative information. A table of contents service was set up through ISI for forty-eight journals and needed articles from those journals were ordered through The Genuine Article. For the 263 articles requested from September 1990 through March 1992, the mean number of requests per title was 5.5 and the median 2 with eight journals not requested at all. During the years 1990–91 and 1991–92, total actual expenses for the document delivery service were $8,700 contrasted to a potential cost of $62,800 for subscriptions to the forty-eight journals. As a result of the study, the library decided it was cost-effective to subscribe to five of the forty-eight titles. The average turnaround time for the 112 articles ordered between December 1992 and June 1993 was five days, but ranged from one to twenty-one days. The cost per article was calculated as $26.06 in one time period and $23.88 in another, although the two periods are not clearly indicated.

Gossen, Eleanor A., and Suzanne Irving. "Ownership vs. Access and Low-Use Periodical Titles." **Library Resources & Technical Services** 39 (January 1995): 43–52.

Gossen and Irving examine the hypothetical cost of acquiring through ILL or document delivery the 609 periodical titles used five or fewer times between September 1991 and August 1992 at the SUNY at Albany Library. Using an average cost per borrowing figure of $18.62, they calculated the annual cost of providing access to these low-use titles was $25,622 compared to $128,601 for subscription.[2] However, the cost of access versus subscription for all SUNY at Albany periodical subscriptions was $2,900,456 contrasted to $1,273,531. Moreover, the low-use titles would be accessible if cancelled because 76 percent were covered by a document delivery vendor and current subscriptions to the others were held by at least one other library in New York state. A survey revealed that 50 percent of the faculty found that waiting three to seven days for an article was "acceptable." Offering a useful decision rule, the authors conclude it is cost-effective to rely on access for any periodical used fewer than six times per year.

Gossen, Eleanor A., and Sue Kaczor. "Variation in Interlibrary Loan Use by University at Albany Science Departments." **Library Resources & Technical Services** 41 (January 1997): 17–28.

The 412 ILL requests for journal articles by faculty, students, and staff in seven science departments at the University of Albany, SUNY, during the 1993–94 academic year form the basis of this detailed study. Scientists accounted for 9 percent of ILL requests but 18 percent of the FTE students and faculty at the university. Analysis by publication date revealed 1 percent of requests were to 1994 and 78 percent to 1984 through 1993, while 21 percent were more than ten years old and 12 percent more than twenty years. Of 291 requested titles, 79.7 percent were requested once, contrasted to only 6 requested more than five times. Subscriptions to the 209 journals for which price data were available would have cost $78,454, but the cost of borrowing the 318 articles from them would have been either $5,928 or $12,720—depending upon which of two average cost figures is used (the 1993 ARL/RLG cost study or the methodology of Ferguson and Kehoe [see entries in this chapter by Roche and by Ferguson and Kehoe]). It is interesting that 48 percent of the citations for requested items were identified through electronic tools and 32 percent through traditional ones. Further data is presented about requestors, the sources for filling requests, and other topics. The authors make a sophisticated effort to explain their findings in the context of previously published research.

Hamaker, Charles A. "Re-Designing Serials Collections." **Journal of Library Administration** 20, no. 1 (1994): 37–47.

Hamaker describes a pilot project (termed the Serials Redesign Project) undertaken with the LSU Chemistry Department in the spring of 1993 and the Geography/Anthropology Department later in the year to redefine the serials collection into titles that are owned and those that are accessed. Using a "zero based budget approach," faculty were asked to list the journals they use and indicate whether document delivery was sufficient to meet their needs. Among the variety of gathered data, these surveys demonstrated that access would be sufficient for 25 percent of the Chemistry journals owned by the library or wanted by faculty and for $17,740.50 of $54,026.50 geography/anthropology journals (32.8 percent).[3] Data is also presented on document delivery performance during the first half of 1993: an 87.7 percent fill rate, an average cost of $11.65, and a turnaround "close to 24 hours" compared to thirteen days for ILL.[4] Hamaker observes that the access/ownership phase implies the largest "paradigm shift" in librarianship since Fremont Rider proposed the use of microcards or microprint as the solution to the ever expanding size of research library collections in his classic 1944 book *The Scholar and the Future of the Research Library.*[5] See entries by Currie and Kleiner and Hamaker.

Hughes, Janet. "Can Document Delivery Compensate for Reduced Serials Holdings? A Life Sciences Library Perspective." **College & Research Libraries** 58 (September 1997): 421–31.

Hughes reports an evaluation of The Genuine Article service carried out in 1995 by the Pennsylvania State University Life Sciences Library. The fill rate was 93 percent for 120 requested articles, although the analysis was limited to items TGA indicated it could provide. The turnaround time averaged three to five days, using the U.S. mail option. Eight percent of the 112 received articles were from six previously cancelled journals, and their delivery cost was $128.95 compared to a 1994–95 subscription price of $4,630. Thirty-nine percent of the received articles (costing $817.51) were inaccessible or missing from thirty journals subscribed to by the library. Finally, 52.7 percent of the articles came from fifty-three journals that had never been owned by Pennsylvania State, these articles costing $1,007.89 in contrast to a $17,150 subscription price.[6] Further analysis showed that only 4 percent of the requests were more than five years old, and a single one predated 1990. Hughes concludes that commercial document delivery is a "viable alternative" to ownership but questions whether it would still be "acceptable" for core journals. This is a useful study, but the article itself is somewhat repetitive.

Kilpatrick, Thomas L., and Barbara G. Preece. "Serial Cuts and Interlibrary Loan: Filling the Gaps." **Interlending & Document Supply** 24, no. 1 (1996): 12–20.

After describing a 1990 serials cancellation project at the Southern Illinois University at Carbondale Library and reviewing the "serials crisis" literature, this entry evaluates the project's impact through analysis of the 124 ILL requests made from January through June 1994 for articles from the cancelled journal titles. Kilpatrick and Preece found that only 4.7 percent (58 of 1,241) cancelled titles were requested, 30 of these titles were requested just once, and 57 were available from at least two OCLC member libraries in Illinois.[7] Further analysis revealed 71 percent of the requested articles were in science, 47 percent were published outside the United States (compared to 69 percent of the cancelled titles), and only one article was not in English. The average "out-of-pocket" cost for the 124 articles was $6.24, while the mean document delivery turnaround time was 3.6 days compared to 14.6 days for ILL. The authors conclude, among other things, that ILL is quantifiable, but one can not accurately evaluate the serendipity factor of browsing.

Kingma, Bruce R. "Economic Issues in Document Delivery: Access Versus Ownership and Library Consortia." **Serials Librarian** 34, nos. 1–2 (1998): 203–11.

This entry explores, using graphs for illustration, the "break-even" point between ownership and access for scholarly journals. Assuming a subscription price of $500, shelving and processing costs of $63, a marginal in-house use cost of $0.94 for reshelving and photocopying by the patron, and a commercial document delivery cost of $16.47 plus $1.68 for the patron's time spent waiting, subscription becomes cost-effective when use exceeds 42 times per year. Using the same assumptions but substituting a $7.68 consortial delivery cost in place of commercial document delivery, the break-even point for subscription becoming the cost-effective alternative is 64. Kingma cites an unnamed academic library that could save $354,334 by canceling 453 journal titles and substituting ILL access. Examining the potential impact of rising subscription prices or copyright fees, the author concludes that increases in the former make access more cost-effective, whereas increases in the latter render subscription more economically attractive. This item is similar to and draws upon Kingma's 1997 article in *Library Trends.*

Kingma, Bruce R. "The Economics of Access Versus Ownership: The Costs and Benefits of Access to Scholarly Articles via Interlibrary Loan and Journal Subscriptions." In **The Economics of Information in the Networked Environment: Proceedings of the Conference; Challenging Marketplace Solutions to Prob-**

lems in the Economics of Information, Washington, DC, September 18–19, 1995, edited by Meredith A. Butler and Bruce R. Kingma, 99–110. Washington, DC: Association of Research Libraries, 1996. ISBN 0-918006-29-5. Also in **Journal of Library Administration** 26, nos. 1–2 (1998): 145–62.

Kingma provides preliminary results from his investigation at SUNY at Albany, Binghamton, Buffalo, and Stony Brook during the 1994–95 academic year—see the entry by Kingma with Irving for a more detailed, book-length report. A survey of patrons who submitted 2,747 science and mathematics ILL requests during the fall of 1994 (the response rate was 47.8 percent representing 76.3 percent of requested articles) found a willingness to pay an average of $2.55 for one-hour ILL delivery and $1.61 for one-day delivery. A table reveals the estimated savings from using ILL rather than subscription for these requests ranged from $137,225 at SUNY at Buffalo to $261,144 at SUNY at Stony Brook. Kingma explains there are three decision rules for access versus ownership, which consider the cost to the borrowing library; the cost to the borrowing library and the patron; and the cost to the borrowing library, the patron, and the lending library. The author states in an appended "questions and discussion" section that his analysis accounts for the patron receiving a free photocopy from ILL but not if the library subscribes to the journal.

Kingma, Bruce R. "Interlibrary Loan and Resource Sharing: The Economics of the SUNY Express Consortium." **Library Trends** 45 (winter 1997): 518–30.

Kingma's economic model for access versus ownership is applied to the SUNY Express consortium, composed of SUNY at Albany, Binghamton, Buffalo, and Stony Brook. Two graphs illustrate decision rules for determining the "break-even point" for subscription instead of access. In the first, assuming a subscription price of $500, shelving and processing costs of $63, marginal cost per use of $0.94, and marginal ILL cost of $16.47 per request, subscription is more efficient than ILL if expected lifetime use is thirty-five or more. In the second, assuming a marginal consortium delivery cost of $7.80 per article, the break-even point for subscription opposed to SUNY Express delivery is forty-nine. Observe that these break-even points differ from those in the 1998 Kingma entry because they do not include the cost of the patron's waiting time and the cost of consortial delivery varies slightly. Kingma then calculated that "a research library" could (assuming the 1993 ARL/RLG average ILL cost) cancel 453 titles for a net savings of $354,334, (assuming the cost of UnCover) cancel 565 titles for a $471,500 net savings, and (assuming the SUNY Express average delivery cost) cancel 218 for a $114,724 net savings.[8] However, he found the potential savings from cooperative collection development—$4,175 per library—were "unlikely" to cover the staffing and administrative costs of implementation. This paper provides practical illustrations of Kingma's methodology.

Kingma, Bruce R., and Natalia Mouravieva. "The Economics of Access Versus Ownership: The Library for Natural Sciences, Russian Academy of Sciences." **Interlending & Document Supply** 28, no. 1 (2000): 20–26.

After examining interlibrary loan/document delivery in a Russian context and the problems of contemporary Russian libraries, Kingma and Mouravieva apply the former's economic model to the Library for Natural Sciences (LNS) at the Russian Academy of Sciences. The cost of an international ILL borrowing transaction was calculated at $11.05, while noting salaries are "much lower" in Russian than U.S. libraries. ILL was found to be more cost-effective than subscription for 127 of 177 international journal subscriptions paid for by the LNS and would offer a potential savings of $223,109 (costing $131,277 instead of $354,386 for subscriptions). ILL was also more cost-effective for 57 of 99 international titles funded by the Soros Foundation with a potential savings of $64,793 ($27,434 versus $92,227). This item is significant because, as observed by the authors, the Russian results are "similar" to those found in the SUNY libraries.

Kingma, Bruce R., with Suzanne Irving. **The Economics of Access Versus Ownership: The Costs and Benefits of Access to Scholarly Articles via Interlibrary Loan and Journal Subscriptions.** New York: Haworth Press, 1996. ISBN 1-56024-809-2. Also published as **Journal of Interlibrary Loan, Document Delivery, & Information Supply,** 6, no. 3 (1996).

In this book, Kingma's economic model for choosing between subscription and ILL was applied at the SUNY at Albany, Binghamton, Buffalo, and Stony Brook Libraries. In the fall of 1994, ILL users were surveyed and the cost of ILL transactions and subscriptions calculated. According to the introduction, the major findings were as follows:

1. A patron waits an average of 12.95 days for an article to be delivered through ILL, representing a theoretical expense of $2.55 of time, reduced to $1.68 when the patron's cost of photocopying an article owned by the library is considered.

2. The average price patrons are willing to pay for priority delivery is $2.55, although "some" would pay $20 for one-hour and $8 for one-day delivery.

3. The mean cost of borrowing an article is either $31.23, $15.60, or $5.60 depending on delivery method.

4. The average cost of subscribing to a journal, exclusive of subscription price, is $62.96 with a marginal cost of $0.07 per use.

The following decision rule is offered for choosing between subscription or ILL access for a journal: subtract $62.96 from the subscription price, divide the result by all uses from a one-year study, and compare the cost per use with the cost of an ILL request. In summary, this is certainly an important and highly cited work.

Kleiner, Jane P., and Charles A. Hamaker. "Libraries 2000: Transforming Libraries Using Document Delivery, Needs Assessment, and Networked Resources." **College & Research Libraries** 58 (July 1997): 355–74.

This lengthy article begins with a literature review and a depiction of the Louisiana State University library serials environment in which 2,539 serials costing $738,885 were cancelled from 1986 to 1996. The primary focus falls on LSU's Serials Redesign Project whereby document delivery replaced subscription for marginal journals. Several pilot projects, conducted from 1993 through 1995 to test the approach in specific departments, are recounted. Only the most note-worthy of the numerous findings can be summarized here. During the 1995 fiscal year, the main supplier, UnCover, filled 94 percent of requests in 24 hours at an average cost of $12.72 while the fill rate for subsidiary suppliers (British Library Document Supply Centre [BLDSC], UMI, and Canada Institute for Scientific and Technical Information [CISTI]) ranged from 69 percent to 91 percent, the average cost per article from $11.72 to $16.07, and turnaround from two to seven days. The cost of document delivery for the 20 titles requested ten or more times was $5,629 compared to $28,229 for subscription. Kleiner and Hamaker also discuss how the library obtained $6 million in grants. The authors conclude that document delivery is preferable to subscription for high-cost, low-use journals and offer ten practical suggestions for incorporating it into collection development activity. This is the most comprehensive of the three entries about LSU's Serials Redesign Project. See also Currie and Hamaker.

Kohl, David F. "Revealing UnCover: Simple, Easy Article Delivery." **Online** 19 (May/June 1995): 52–60.

Kohl describes a bleak budgetary situation at the University of Cincinnati libraries whereby it was necessary in the fall of 1993 to cancel approximately 700 journals costing about $200,000. He then explains that during the 1993–94 aca-demic year, the library used UnCover to provide faculty free access to articles from half these titles (plus 10,000 others) for approximately $10,000. In the 1994–95 academic year, the service was extended to graduate students for a total cost of $20,000 and a $180,000 savings over the subscription price. Kohl notes that "nearly all articles" arrive within twenty-four hours. Much of the article focuses on a history of UnCover and the services it offers. Although primarily descriptive rather than evaluative, this entry is worth mentioning because the con-cept of document delivery as an alternative to subscription is presented along with general data to demonstrate the former's cost-effectiveness.

Payne, Valerie J. and Mary A. Burke. "A Cost-Effectiveness Study of Ownership Versus Access." **Serials Librarian** 32, nos. 3–4 (1997): 139–52.

Drawing upon the experience of St. Patrick's College in Maynooth, Ireland, during 1996, Payne and Burke explore the cost-effectiveness of three methods for procuring periodical articles: subscription, document delivery, and interlibrary loan. A section of the article addresses costing methodology, including direct and indirect, fixed and variable as well as relevant and irrelevant costs. Then, for twenty-one journals highly requested on ILL, total cost (subscription plus associ-ated expenses) was divided by anticipated lifetime use, estimated by the number of ILL requests between 1990 and 1994 (which the authors admit underestimates actual usage) to calculate cost per use. (This is a modified form of a methodology developed by Dorothy Milne and Bill Tiffany at Memorial University in New-foundland, Canada.)[9] The cost of various ILL/document delivery options was also ascertained (i.e., $16.75 for UnCover by fax, $11.25 for BLDSC via mail, etc).

The authors concluded that access was more cost-effective than subscription for twenty of the twenty-one titles in the study. They assert their methodology can be used by other libraries, but readers would probably be better served by the work of Kingma.

White, Gary W., and Gregory A. Crawford. "Cost-Benefit Analysis of Electronic Information: A Case Study." **College & Research Libraries** 59 (November 1998): 503–10.

The initial 40 percent of this entry explains cost-benefit analysis and its application to libraries. The remainder reports the results of a cost-benefit study of UMI's *Business Periodicals Ondisc* (part of *ABI/INFORM*) at the Pennsylvania State University at Harrisburg library. The cost of introducing the product in 1994 was calculated at $10,700, whereas the savings in ILL and copyright expenses, based on comparing 1993 and 1995 ILL expenditures accessing titles from BPO, was $9,091. The approximately $65,000 in 1995 subscription costs for the 215 BPO titles not subscribed to by the library are termed only a "potential benefit" because its unlikely the library would actually subscribe to them in any case. The researchers point out that apart from dollar costs, users received "nontangible benefits" such as immediate access to the articles. White and Crawford take a somewhat different approach by analyzing access through a full-text database instead of ILL or document delivery.

Wilson, Mary Dabney, and Whitney Alexander. "Automated Interlibrary Loan/Document Delivery Data Applications for Serials Collection Development." **Serials Review** 25, no. 4 (1999): 11–19.

This entry illustrates use of ILL data for dual purposes at Texas A & M University. First, to ascertain the cost-effectiveness of ILL versus subscription, ILL transactions through SAVEIT and Clio ILL-management software were analyzed for the 3,095 journal titles cancelled between 1990 and 1996. It was found that only 1.4 percent of these titles had been requested five or more times between May 1995 and January 1999. A lengthy table comparing total ILL costs with the 1999 subscription price shows that the latter was more cost-effective for only 4 of the 44 titles. Moreover, 1999 subscription costs would have been $53,344.31 compared to the $7,123.02 total for ILL. Secondly, the same ILL data was used to determine the 54 titles that TAMU would subscribe to rather than pay for on an article-by-article basis in PEAK—an experimental electronic journal pricing project sponsored by Elsevier. The authors conclude that ILL/document delivery statistics in combination with circulation data can provide "a powerful collection analysis tool."

EVALUATION OF DOCUMENT DELIVERY SERVICE PERFORMANCE

Anthes, Mary A. "An Experiment in Unmediated Document Delivery: EBSCOdoc at Witchita State University." **Library Collections, Acquisitions, & Technical Services** 23 (spring 1999): 1–13.

Following a description of Wichita State University library's implementation of EBSCOdoc to provide unmediated document delivery to faculty, this thorough entry focuses on evaluation of its performance during May 1996 through October 1997. Almost 85 percent of 1,447 orders were for journal articles, and 90 percent of ordered documents were published during the 1990s. Moreover, 72 percent of orders came from three science or engineering departments and 35 percent from just three faculty members. The average cost per order was $18 and the median cost $14.50, but the average cost increased to $24.46 if "customization and maintenance" expenses are added. The fill rate was 96 percent, but only items in EBSCO databases were ordered. Turnaround time between receipt of order by EBSCOdoc and shipment was two (median) or three (mean) days. A May 1997 survey of registered users (the survey instrument is appended) generated a 32 percent return rate and found an average overall satisfaction rating of 3.75 on a 1 (low) to 5 (high) scale. The subscription cost for the fifty-three journal titles requested five or more times would have been over $22,000 in 1997 compared to $4,034 in access fees. Ironically, a postscript states that EBSCO closed EBSCOdoc in September 1998 for economic reasons.

Association of Research Libraries. Office of Management Services. **Uses of Document Delivery Services,** compiled by Mary E. Jackson and Karen Croneis. Washington, DC: Association of Research Libraries, Office of Management Studies, 1994. 125p. (SPEC Kit 204). ISSN 0160-3582.

This SPEC (System and Procedures Exchange Center) kit is organized into five parts dealing with the following: selection of commercial suppliers; pilot evaluation projects; annual reports, evaluations, and statistics; flyers promoting document delivery; and descriptions of BLDSC, Chemical Abstracts, The Genuine Article, UMI, and UnCover. A brief annotated bibliography concerning document delivery is appended. The 56 pages devoted to pilot projects at the Universities of California, San Diego, Colorado, Houston, North Carolina at Chapel Hill, and Texas at Austin, as well as Temple and Rice, contain much evaluative data. For example, the Texas study found libraries had a 78 percent fill rate, a 13.51 day turnaround time between order and receipt, and a $5.19 mean cost compared to 43 percent, 17.35 day turnaround time, and $17.27 for commercial vendors. An attached survey of ninety ARL libraries (termed a SPEC flyer) reveals that speed was considered the most important criteria in selecting a document delivery supplier, while forty respondents perceived that commercial document deliver was faster than ILL, thirty thought it was "about the same," and three thought it was "worse." This entry, like most SPEC kits, is useful for its documents illustrating actual library practice.

Boyle, Frances, and Mary Davies. "Access Versus Holdings: Document Delivery Realities." **Electronic Library** 17 (April 1999): 105–13.

Boyle and Davies provide a preliminary report on an apparently ongoing evaluation project conducted in the United Kingdom at the University of Liverpool that initially included thirty document delivery vendors but then focused on five: British Library's (BL's) inside, BODOS (BIDS Online Document Ordering System), Ei Text from Elsevier Engineering Information, London and Manchester Document Access (LAMDA), and UnCover. Subject coverage (defined as the percentage of current and cancelled subscriptions offered by the service) ranged from 49 percent to 89 percent among the examined vendors. A pilot project, operated for four months in the Faculty of Science and two months in the Faculty of Engineering and Veterinary Science, found a 91 to 100 percent fill rate for 500 requests and "little [cost] discrepancy" with the average article costing between £10.93 and £12.30 by mail and £11.88 and £13.25 by fax. Moreover, 70 percent of the requested articles were published in the preceding four years and a "high level" were from cancelled journals. A separate section analyzing 100 requests sent through the LAMDA system found "overall... good" performance but a low fill-rate. Although the literature review is solid, unfortunately it contains incomplete and some inaccurate citations. Numerous tables summarize the findings by vendor and subject area. The authors conclude "in their current form document delivery services cannot be seen as a panacea for resolving the access versus holdings debate."

Chrzastowski, Tina E., and Mary A. Anthes. "Seeking the 99% Chemistry Library: Extending the Serial Collection Through the Use of Decentralized Document Delivery." **Library Acquisitions: Practice & Theory** 19 (summer 1995): 141–52.

A six and a half month pilot evaluation, conducted between October 15, 1994, and April 30, 1994, of the Chemical Abstracts Document Delivery Service by the University of Illinois at Urbana-Champaign Chemistry Library is this entry's focus. The fill rate for 234 articles, foreign patents, and conference proceedings requests stood at 85 percent with recent items, translated articles, and ambiguous citations most likely to be unfilled. The average cost for the article alone was $16.76 and $17.97 when staff costs are considered. The 136 requested titles (3 were requested four times, 27 two or three times, and 106 once) are listed in a table. Eighty-two percent of these titles had never been owned, whereas 18 percent had previously been cancelled. A survey of the ninety-four service users (40 percent responded) found they were "overwhelmingly satisfied" and that 66 percent of the respondents indicated willingness to pay a $3 to $7 fee per article to continue the service. This is a well-done study.

Clement, Elaine. "A Pilot Project to Investigate Commercial Document Suppliers." **Library Acquisitions: Practice & Theory** 20 (summer 1996): 137–46.

This entry describes a pilot evaluation of five commercial document suppliers conducted during the winter of 1993–94 in four branches of the Pennsylvania State University at University Park library. The five suppliers were Global Engineering Documents, used by the Engineering Library; Chemical Abstracts Service, used by the Physical Sciences Library; Mathdoc (of the American Mathematical Society), used in the Mathematics Library; Article Express, used by the Engineering Library; and GeoRef (of the American Geological Institute), used in the Earth and Mineral Sciences Library. The results are presented separately for each vendor. Based on 232 requests, the overall fill rate was 84.5 percent, the mean cost for an article stood at $16.48, and the mean delivery time was 10.8 days, compared to 16 for ILL. Furthermore, 89.2 percent of the requests were not held by PSU, 7.3 percent were missing, and 3.4 percent were "rush" orders while 61.6 percent were for journal articles and 21.1 percent for proceedings. Data beyond what normally appears in document delivery evaluation studies revealed 47.4 percent of the requests were for funded research, and the average number of pages in filled orders was 13.04. It was concluded that document supply is "timely and cost-effective," while having "minimal" impact on ILL. Clement provides a meticulously done investigation.

Crowley, Gwyneth H. "Unmediated Document Delivery: A Project Using First-Search and EBSCOdoc." **Interlending & Document Supply** 27, no. 3 (1999): 122–27.

An ummediated document delivery pilot project for the use of Agricultural Economics Department faculty and graduate students at Texas A & M University is reported here. The experiment was conducted during the summer and fall semesters of 1997, using BLDSC, EBSCOdoc, ISI's The Genuine Article, and UMI as suppliers. While forty-eight individuals registered for the project, only nine placed orders for ninety-three articles and dissertations. The average cost per item was $22.01, and the fill rate was 97.8 percent.[10] A survey (four users and four non-users returned complete responses) indicated satisfaction with the delivery speed, although data is not presented. Crowley believes unmediated document delivery has "potential." Unfortunately, this investigation is based on a small sample size.

Dade, Penny. "Electronic Information and Document Delivery: Final Report on the Pilot Trial of the UnCover Database." **Vine** 103 (1997): 43–45.

Dade offers a sketchy evaluation of UnCover based on a one-year trial (August 1994-July 1995) at the University of Hertfordshire during which the library funded faculty and staff access. Forty-six individuals requested 273 articles of which 34 percent were already owned by the library. Nearly half the articles (45.5 percent) were requested by staff from the Business School or the School of Art and Design.[11] A number of evaluative issues are discussed without offering data: it was "difficult to log on" to UnCover; the fax quality was "problematic;" the users guide arrived "too late to be of use;" and several publishers did not allow their articles to be provided. The author claims the provision of free electronic document delivery was "unique" in the United Kingdom.

Hunt, Jim. "(CARL) UnCover As a Substitute for or Supplement to Interlibrary Loan." **College & Undergraduate Libraries** 5, no. 1 (1998): 45–55.

This article describes UnCover and explores its potential use for ILL/document delivery at the California State University at Dominguez Hills library. Rather than basing the investigation on actual orders, UnCover's potential ability (apparently based on information provided by the company) to fill a "true random sample" of 174 previous ILL periodical requests was explored. The fill rate on the ILL requests had been 87.36 percent while the mean turnaround was a "disturbing and unexpected" 22.36 days. It was found that UnCover could fill only 39.66 percent of the sample requests at an estimated average cost of $17.88. The advertised twenty-four hour delivery time is noted. While explaining the UnCover fee structure, the author observes there is "no correlation" between a journal's subscription price and the copyright fee for an article from it, observing "outrageous fees [some exceed $100] are a publisher's perverse way of saying 'take your document delivery service and shove it.'" Hunt asserts that UnCover is not a "panacea," but "one way of improving services."

Kochan, Carol Ann, and John A. Elsweiler. "Testing the Feasibility of Unmediated Document Delivery Services with EBSCOdoc: The Utah State University Experience." **Journal of Interlibrary Loan, Document Delivery, & Information Supply** 9, no. 1 (1998): 67–77.

A pilot evaluation of EBSCOdoc for unmediated document delivery to ten Utah State University faculty members from two departments (Economics plus Animal, Dairy, and Veterinary Sciences) is described in this entry. From February 1, 1996, to June 8, 1996, 272 articles were received at an average cost of $17.55: 25 percent of these were already owned by the library. A table reveals 175 different journals were requested, of which 71.4 percent were requested a single time.[12] A survey of the participating faculty (receiving a 70 percent response rate) found an overall satisfaction rating of 3.83 on a 1 (low) to 5 (high) scale. The faculty also rated EBSCOdoc as superior to ILL in terms of ease of use (4.83) and timeliness (4.58), but were "dissatisfied" with EBSCO's fax quality (2.83). The survey (the instrument is reproduced in the appendix) is interesting but unfortunately based on a small sample size.

Kurosman, Kathleen, and Barbara Ammerman Durniak. "Document Delivery: A Comparison of Commercial Document Suppliers and Interlibrary Loan Services." **College & Research Libraries** 55 (March 1994): 129–39.

Vassar College Library's evaluation of traditional ILL and four commercial document delivery suppliers (UMI Article Clearinghouse, ISI's The Genuine Article, Information on Demand, and The Information Store) is described here. The study was based on fifty-two randomly selected requests sent between October 1991 and February 1992. The authors found that the "potential" fill rate (defined as the proportion of requests theoretically available) was 100 percent for ILL and from 23 to 100 percent for the four document suppliers, while the "actual" rate (the proportion of theoretically available articles actually provided) stood at 83 percent for ILL and 83 to 100 percent for the four vendors. The average delivery time was thirteen days for ILL and ranged from twelve to twenty-three for document delivery suppliers, while the average ILL cost was $0.56 and from $9.75 to $20.70 for the document delivery suppliers. Kurosman and Durniak conclude "conventional ILL compares favorably with the services of the commercial suppliers." Much detailed analysis is included in this first-rate and often-cited research piece.

Mancini, Alice Duhon. "Evaluating Commercial Document Suppliers: Improving Access to Current Journal Literature." **College & Research Libraries** 57 (March 1996): 123–31.

Mancini reports the University of Tennessee at Knoxville (UTK) library's evaluation of four commercial document delivery suppliers (UMI, CARL's

UnCover, ISI's The Genuine Article, and Faxon Finder) during a three-month period from September 12, 1994, through December 15, 1994. The study found the following: the mean fill rate for all four vendors stood at 76.57 percent, ranging from 35.29 percent for the worst performance to 96.16 percent for the best; the average cost for fax delivery ranged from $14.33 to $19.83; the mean turnaround time for fax delivery ranged from 1.72 to 3.25 days. Mancini also discusses staffing implications, access options for titles and services, and quality of reproduction. She concludes that commercial document delivery costs more than traditional ILL but offers faster turnaround time and that UMI and UnCover best met the needs of UTK.

Maxfield, Sandy. "Document Delivery Power for Faculty: An Experiment with UnCover." **Virginia Librarian** 39 (April/June 1993): 12–14.
   A test of UnCover to supply documents to faculty at George Madison University is recounted by Maxfield. The average cost of 431 articles requested by faculty between September 1992 and January 1993 was $9.93—quite similar to the $9.95 average cost for the 703 articles ILL received from UnCover between July 1992 and January 1993. A table summarizing faculty requests by academic unit reveals that library staff ordered more than any other area (14.2 percent of total faculty orders).[13] It is noted that "a few articles" were ordered from journals already owned by the library. Maxfield asserts "the early indications" are that UnCover is "effective."

McFarland, Robert T. "A Comparison of Science Related Document Delivery Services." **Science & Technology Libraries** 13 (fall 1992): 115–44.
   The author describes an evaluation by the Washington University library in St. Louis covering nine science document delivery services, including the John Crerar Library Photoduplication Service, Chemical Abstracts Document Delivery Service, the Linda Hall Library, ISI's The Genuine Article, and UMI's Article Clearinghouse. A Chemistry Library pilot study of 192 requests sent to the Chemical Abstracts Document Delivery Services between March and October 1991 found an average cost of $14.50 and an average delivery time of twenty-four hours by fax, six days by first-class mail, and two days by express mail. A comparative study of 95 requests sent to the nine vendors found an average cost of $14 (with the average per vendor ranging from $9 to $23) for regular orders and $23 for rush orders (with the vendor averages ranging from $14 to $31). The mean turnaround was seven days for regular orders (with a range of two to twelve days) and two days on rush orders, ranging from one to seven days, while the fill rate ranged from 95 to 100 percent for regular orders and 50 to 100 percent for rush orders. Additional criteria included cost-efficiency, that is, supplying "documents in the least amount of time at the lowest cost;" reliability, that is, supplying items within the advertised time frame; and responsiveness to problems.

Morris, Anne, and Emma Blagg. "Current Document Delivery Practices in UK Academic Libraries." **Library Management** 19, no. 4 (1998): 271–80.
   Morris and Blagg's investigation is based on 165 responses (a 60 percent rate) to a lengthy questionnaire sent to British academic libraries during 1996 and

early 1997. The survey focused on their use and perception of nine ILL/document delivery options (including BLDSC, UnCover, UMI, and the British Medical Association), but also included questions about collection size. Twelve tables contain detailed statistics on a variety of issues, including the subject and format of requests sent to the nine sources and the "best features" of each. Figures depict Likert scale scores of perceptions concerning ease of use, fulfillment of requests, reliability of service, and print quality. The most significant findings were as follows: 62 percent held more than 100,000 books and 8 percent fewer than 10,000; larger libraries had more ILL/document delivery requests; and BLSDC is perceived as supplying 57 percent of requests within a week. The authors conclude that BLDSC "has the most consistently good record" and that other suppliers "have a long way to go before they can compete." This entry is notable because it reports national-level perceptions of performance.

Morris, Anne, Julie Woodfield, and J. Eric Davies. "Experimental Evaluation of Selected Electronic Document Delivery Systems." **Journal of Librarianship & Information Science** 31 (September 1999): 135–44.

The Department of Information Science at Loughborough Information in the United Kingdom conducted an experimental evaluation of five document delivery systems: UMI ProQuest Direct, InfoTrac Search Bank (both full-text databases), British Library inside, Elsevier Engineering Information EiText, and the British Library Document Supply Centre. Two sets of articles, twenty dealing with business and twenty covering manufacturing engineering, were directed to multiple vendors at approximately the same time. The evaluative criteria were requesting and delivery time, costs, document quality, and coverage. Mean total time ranged from 8 minutes 18 seconds (for downloading from a full-text database) to 40 days, and mean cost ranged from £4.95 to £16.50. In a sophisticated approach, a panel of seven judges assessed document quality according to five readability variables: handling ease, layout, text quality, graphic quality, and navigational aids. The authors conclude the standard BLDSC service is "extremely good" for cost, coverage, and document quality, but not speed. A reasonably extensive literature review is included. This methodologically sophisticated entry differs from most others in this section because it reports a controlled experiment rather than actual library requests.

Orr, Debbie, and Cathy Dennis. "Unmediated Document Delivery and Academic Staff at Central Queensland University." **Interlending & Document Supply** 24, no. 4 (1996): 25–31.

Orr and Dennis write about an evaluative study of unmediated document delivery using several vendors conducted at Central Queensland University in Australia between March 1995 and March 1996. The average cost for articles was reported as $18.00 for UnCover, $25 for the British Library, and "generally $20.00" for the Chemical Abstracts service. A survey of 466 users, receiving a 24 percent response rate, found that a majority preferred UnCover. Fourteen journal titles requested eleven or more times are listed, but a majority of the titles (the number is not given) were ordered less than four times. "Resource duplication" was considered "a waste" as 538 of 3,423 documents (15.7 percent) ordered by users, representing about 10 percent of expenditures, were already in the collection.[14] For this and other reasons it was decided not to continue unmediated document delivery. While this article's major focus is on the evaluation of unmediated document delivery, it contains information pertinent to evaluation of vendor performance.

Pedersen, Wayne A., and David Gregory. "Interlibrary Loan and Commercial Document Delivery: Finding the Right Fit." **Journal of Academic Librarianship** 20 (November 1994): 263–72.

This article reports the evaluation by the Iowa State University library of six commercial document delivery suppliers accessible through the OCLC/ILL subsystem: UMI's Article Clearinghouse, ISI's The Genuine Article, Chemical Abstracts Document Delivery Service, Engineering Information's Article Express, The Information Store, and Information on Demand. The study was conducted during a six-week period in July and August 1993. A table summarizing the average results for the six vendors indicates the overall fill rate was 66 percent but ranged from 48 to 87 percent, the turnaround time ranged from nine to thirty-one days, and the cost from $8.36 to $29.95. Another lengthy table lists advantages and disadvantages associated with each of the six suppliers. Comparative data on ILL performance, based on five one-week sample periods between March 1992 and October 1993, indicated an eleven-day turnaround time and, from the week in October 1993, a 78 percent fill rate. The authors caution against comparing document delivery and ILL data because the latter represents "a group of libraries working in concert" rather than a single supplier.

Prabha, Chandra, and Elizabeth C. Marsh. "Commercial Document Suppliers: How Many of the ILL/DD Periodical Article Requests Can They Fulfill?" **Library Trends** 45 (winter 1997): 551–68.

A sample of 373 ILL periodical requests processed by OCLC's PRISM system between December 1994 and November 1995 is analyzed by Prabha and Marsh in terms of basic characteristics as well as availability from five suppliers—BLDSC, CISTI, Institute for Scientific Information, UMI, and UnCover. Among the considerable statistical details in this entry, the most noteworthy are the following: 8 percent of the articles were published in 1995, 21 percent in 1994, and 64 percent within the previous five years; 35 percent were in science and technology and 32 percent in the social sciences. Of 120 requested periodicals, 48 percent were asked for once, whereas 16 percent were requested more than five times. The majority of the periodicals were in English, published in Western countries by for-profit publishers and launched within the last twenty years. Based on vendor provided indexes, the authors found the percentage of available articles ranged from 39 to 81 percent for the five suppliers, while overall 92 percent of the articles could be provided by at least one service. This entry's voluminous statistics provide some insight into ILL periodical requests and document delivery vendor's potential ability to fill them.

Sekerak, Robert J., et al. "A Trial of Three Commercial Document Delivery Suppliers with Strong Holdings in Biomedicine." **Medical Reference Services Quarterly** 16 (summer 1997): 27–36.

Sekerak and his colleagues write about the University of Vermont Medical Library's evaluation, during a three-to-four month period in 1995, of three commercial document suppliers known to have strong biomedicine holdings: CISTI, EMDOCS (operated by Article Express), and UMI Article Clearinghouse. The research design used a sample of 150 requested articles (from 126 journals) not owned by the library. Based on examination of each vendor's catalog, the proportion of the 126 journals that could be supplied (in the order the service's are listed above) were 96 percent, 83 percent, and 55 percent. The respective figures for mean delivery time were 3.1, 8.1, and 2.6 days, and the respective average cost including copyright fee were $13.83, $20.13, and $11.73—composite data is not given. The authors decided that compared to ILL, commercial document delivery provides articles "in less time without substantially increased costs." Although this entry could be more rigorous, it is worth listing because of its focus on biomedicine.

Sellers, Minna, and Joan Beam. "Subsidizing Unmediated Document Delivery: Current Models and a Case Study." **Journal of Academic Librarianship** 21 (November 1995): 459–66.

After outlining a model for a "user-centered system for efficient document delivery," Sellers and Beam recount a pilot study of unmediated document delivery through UnCover2 at the Colorado State University (CSU) libraries during the spring semester of 1994. Transaction log analysis showed that 309 users requested 1,168 articles from 627 journals. Furthermore, 44 percent of the users ordered a single article, but 5 percent ordered 31 percent of the articles. Only 2.2 percent of the titles were requested by more than one user.[15] The average cost was $11.00 per article. That 23 percent of the requests were unfilled was considered a "significant problem." Disregarding unfilled orders, the mean delivery time was 1.6 days, and 93 percent were filled in four days. A satisfaction survey of the 264 users with known addresses, based on a 50 percent sample and obtaining a 68 percent response rate, found that 94 percent considered the service "important," 55 percent observed problems with quality of reproduction, 34 percent experienced difficulty using the system, and that 52 percent needed or expected articles "sooner" than they were received. This thoughtful article compares the CSU results with other reported findings and concludes "UnCover performed better and at a competitive cost." For a subsequent study of UnCover at Colorado State, see the article by Beam.

Thornton, Glenda A., and Yem Fong. "Exploring Document Delivery Options: A Pilot Study of the University of Colorado System." **Technical Services Quarterly** 12, no. 2 (1994): 1–12.

As an outgrowth of an administrative mandate to expedite ILL, five University of Colorado System libraries conducted a pilot evaluation of document delivery, focusing on UnCover but also including UMI and the British Library Document Supply Centre. The study, based on approximately 2,000 requests, was carried out from April 1, 1993, through approximately June 30, 1993. Within the five libraries, the fill rate ranged from 19 to 85 percent for both UnCover and the combined total for all vendors. Separately reported results by library and vendor revealed the turnaround ranged from 1.0 to 9.72 days, and the average cost from $8.49 to $13.83. A user survey (receiving 256 responses for a 25 percent return rate) found 88 percent would use document delivery service, but 50 percent would not pay for it. The authors concluded "libraries with small collections, large populations, and general patron needs could fill a high percentage of requests using commercial suppliers, while libraries with research or specialized needs experienced differing success rates."

Van Der Werff, Jane. "Which Document Delivery Service Best Serves Your Patron: UnCover2 or ILL?" **Journal of Interlibrary Loan, Document Delivery & Information Supply** 5, no. 1 (1994): 23–31.

The author offers "an informal study," from the perspective of Colorado libraries, concerning the relative benefits of UnCover2 versus traditional ILL. She focuses on three variables: "accessibility," that is, availability of the article; "how quickly it is needed;" and cost. As of 1993, UnCover2 offered articles, dating back to 1988, from 13,600 serial titles, whereas the OCLC ILL system accessed 1,360,441 serials without any time restrictions. Based on personal communication with other librarians, the author found UnCover2's twenty-four hour fill-rate was "about 80 percent" at the University of South Dakota, an estimated 95 percent at Montana State University, and "most...well within" twenty-four hours at Western Washington University. Van Der Werff recommends use of UnCover2 if ILL "can not deliver within the time frame needed" and the patron is willing to pay $10 to $12. Gathering data through informal contacts is not a rigorous research method, but it can be valid for decision-making purposes.

Walters, Sheila A. "User Behavior in a Non-Mediated Document Delivery Environment: The Direct Doc Pilot Project at Arizona State." **Computers in Libraries** 15 (October 1995): 22–24, 26.

This article describes a pilot evaluation concerning unmediated faculty use of three commercial document delivery systems conducted by the Arizona State University (ASU) libraries from March through December 1994. Over 100 faculty took part: 70 percent of the participants ordered from 7 to 152 documents with 15 as the median number. The library was surprised to find faculty "were willing to sacrifice speed for lower cost," but the fact that 76.5 percent of the 1,578 requested articles were already held by the ASU libraries constituted "the biggest surprise." Preliminary results indicated the average cost per document was $17.85 from OCLC FirstSearch, $16.50 from the RLG Eureka/CitaDel system, and $11.09 from UnCover. The mean delivery time was, using vendor reports, 1.3 days and, based on faculty reporting, 2.6 days. There were problems with 32 percent of the documents, of which the most frequent was "poor resolution" (13.8 percent). Walters concludes UnCover "met the needs of the majority of the faculty" and "posed the fewest problems."

Waltner, Robb M. "EBSCOdoc vs. CARL UnCover: A Comparison of Document Delivery Services at the University of Evansville Libraries." **Journal of Interlibrary Loan, Document Delivery & Information Supply** 7, no. 3 (1997): 21–28.

Between January and March 1996, only 39 percent of nineteen items needed by the University of Evansville libraries could be verified on the EBSCOdoc Web site, and delivery "often took several days" rather than the advertised twenty-four hours. In the January-April 1996 period, twenty-three of forty orders to EBSCOdoc required a $25 to $40 fee and one to four weeks delivery time. In twenty-two of the twenty-three cases, the patron then cancelled the request. Beginning April 1, 1996, the library began using CARL UnCover. During April, UnCover filled 46 percent of thirty-nine requests, all of which were provided within forty-eight hours at an average cost of $12.85. However, throughout the entire semester 59 percent of fifty-eight requests sent to UnCover were unavailable. Waltner concludes that EBSCOdoc provides comprehensive coverage with poor delivery speed, whereas UnCover offers speedy delivery but a low fill rate. This entry could have benefited by a better organized and more systematic presentation of the evaluation's results.

EVALUATION OF INTERLIBRARY LOAN

Bjarno, Helle. "Cost Finding and Performance Measures in ILL Management." **Interlending & Document Supply** 22, no. 2 (1994): 8–11.

Bjarno addresses the development of a model for evaluating ILL cost and performance in Danish academic libraries. To assist the project, the Danish National Library of Technology was used as a test site, and staff members from the Danish Loan Centre at the State University in Aarhus, Denmark, were interviewed. The author lists twenty-one "performance measures" divided into four categories: input cost measures, output measures, service effectiveness measures, and service domain measures, that is, characteristics of the service population. These are compressed into four "performance indicators:" productivity, cost per output, cost per use, and cost per attribute level (i.e., staff skill and experience). Methods for measuring performance and cost (staff costs, other costs, and output measures such as quantity) are then discussed. Originally presented at an international conference in Budapest, Hungary, in 1993, this article takes a somewhat theoretical approach.

Boyd, Norman. "Towards Access Services: Supply Times, Quality Control and Performance-Related Services." **Interlending & Document Supply** 25, no. 3 (1997): 118–23.

Boyd discusses the "True Supply Time" survey of ILL speed conducted from February 1 to March 31, 1996, among six unnamed public libraries in the United Kingdom's London and South Eastern Library Region. Although it was generally believed that ILL took an average of 60 days, the overall average was 23.8 days ranging from 17.72 to 38.6 days among the six libraries. The ILL process was divided into nine stages (from a patron submitting a request to actually picking it up at the library) and the amount of time required for each stage calculated for every participating library. For example, the mean number of days required for stage nine (the time elapsed between the library sending notification of an item's arrival and the patron collecting it) ranged from 1.71 to 3.56 with 28 days "the longest time registered." This entry is particularly notable for its micro evaluation of the time required to fill ILL requests.

Dobson, Cynthia, and Wayne A. Pedersen. "Document Delivery to Developing Countries." **Interlending & Document Supply** 26, no. 1 (1998): 3–9.

Dobson and Pedersen report an evaluation, conducted during the spring of 1995, concerning the Iowa State University library's ability to supply articles and book chapters to libraries and scholars in developing countries, including Colombia, Morocco, Russia, and Slovakia. The overall fill rate for 457 requests was 72.9 percent, ranging from 55.9 percent for Slovakia to 89.7 percent for Colombia. The average turnaround time for 233 requests with complete data was 16.3 days: 3 days for transmitting the request, 3.9 days for internal processing, and 9.7 days for delivering the item. The cost of fax was $1.18 per page contrasted to $10 per page for air mail. An analysis of supply options concluded that electronic request/electronic delivery offers the fastest turnaround, whereas air mail request/air mail delivery provides the slowest. The authors compare their results with those of other studies. This entry is notable because of the international focus and the emphasis on lending rather than borrowing.

Geiser, Cherie, and Rachel Miller. "GMRLC Negotiations for an Interstate Courier: History, Results, and Trends." **Journal of Library Administration** 23, nos. 1–2 (1996): 5–22.

The first part of this article describes the process in which the Greater Midwest Research Libraries Consortium (GMRLC) negotiated, from the fall of 1994 through January 1995, a contract with Federal Express for delivery of interlibrary loans among the consortium members. The second part presents evaluative data concerning the delivery service. During the nine-month period from January through September 1995, the average cost for the 2,747 volumes shipped by Federal Express was $2.58. Four libraries that conducted evaluations preceding and following implementation of Federal Express reported a two-day reduction in delivery time. In April 1995, mean delivery time among all GMRLC libraries was 12 days for Federal Express, 18.6 for the U.S. mail, 5.2 for fax, and 11.5 for Ariel. Geiser and Miller observe that shipping among libraries is far less expensive than ordering through commercial document delivery.

Hébert, Françoise. "Service Quality: An Unobtrusive Investigation of Interlibrary Loan in Large Public Libraries in Canada." **Library & Information Science Research** 16 (winter 1994): 3–21.

This article is devoted to the evaluation of ILL service in thirty-eight large Canadian public libraries. In each library "real" patrons, acting on Hébert's behalf, requested the same set of four books: "contrived" by the investigator, entered into the Canadian national database, and placed (thirty-eight copies) in the National Library and the University of Toronto from which they could be requested. The patrons then completed the SERVQUAL questionnaire to measure their expectations and perceptions concerning service quality. The overall fill rate was 52.3 percent for 130 requests. A breakdown of the causes of failure indicated that 31.5 percent of the requests could not be located and 10.8 percent had been refused by the local library. The median turnaround time was thirty-eight days, of which twenty-three days were spent on processing by the borrowing library. Analysis of SERVQUAL revealed a "serious gap" between customer expectations (a mean score of 5.65 on a 1–7 scale) and perception of service (a mean 5.22 score). The author both draws upon the LIS literature and successfully integrates concepts from the literature of management. This large-scale study should be commended for its methodologically rigorous and detailed analysis.

Higginbotham, Barbra Buckner, and Sally Bowdoin. "Evaluating the Access Program." In **Access Versus Assets: A Comprehensive Guide to Resource Sharing for Academic Librarians,** 275–83. Chicago: American Library Association, 1993. 399p. ISBN 0-8389-0607-9.

This section of a chapter from a major monograph succinctly addresses criteria for evaluating ILL performance. Ten factors (most of which do not require explanation) for evaluating borrowing are outlined and discussed:

1. Location finders (i.e., determining which other libraries hold the desired item)

2. Number of submitted requests

3. Service growth

4. Fill rate

5. Delivery speed

6. Document quality

7. Ease of use/flexibility

8. User satisfaction

9. Balance and fairness (i.e., are requests distributed evenly among partners?)

10. Costs

Nine factors for assessing a library's lending activity are similarly outlined. However, these are of minimal concern here because lending, unlike borrowing, does not directly relate to a library's ability to meet its patron's needs. The authors cite a 1989 ARL study that established an 84 percent borrowing fill rate as a benchmark for interlending effectiveness.[16] Not only Higginbotham & Bowdoin's book, but also this specific section, are often cited.

Jackson, Mary E. **Measuring the Performance of Interlibrary Loan Operations in North American Research and College Libraries: Results of a Study Funded by the Andrew W. Mellon Foundation.** Washington, DC: Association of Research Libraries, 1998. 122p. ISBN 0-918006-33-3.

This landmark study expands Roche's well-known 1993 investigation of ILL costs (see entry later in this section) by including other performance measures and college libraries. Data was gathered in 97 research libraries (mostly ARL members) plus 22 college library members of the Oberlin Group (a consortium of liberal arts colleges) from July 1995 through December 1997. The executive summary reports an average combined borrowing/lending cost of $27.83, a turnaround time of 15.6 calendar days, and an 85 percent borrowing fill rate for research libraries, while the corresponding figures for college libraries were $19.33, 10.8 calendar days, and 91 percent. The author expressed "disappointment" that no cause could be found for the statistically significant differences in performance between the two types of libraries. The characteristics associated with high performance lending and borrowing operations are outlined. One should mention, among the eight chapters, those that focus on findings for the 119 participating libraries, OhioLink libraries, Canadian research libraries, and comparison with the results of Roche's 1993 study—which shows that ILL costs have decreased. Thirteen appendices list participating institutions and include worksheets, definitions, scatter plots of results, and a brief annotated bibliography. This is undoubtedly the largest scale study of academic library ILL performance published to date.

Lacroix, Eve-Marie. "Interlibrary Loan in U.S. Health Sciences Libraries: Journal Article Use." **Bulletin of the Medical Library Association** 82 (October 1994): 363–68.

In the third publication in a long-term series, Lacroix reports a massive study of nearly four million ILL serial article requests entered into the NLM's DOCLINE system during the two fiscal years ending in September 30, 1992.[17] She found that 76 percent of the articles were used only once, 97 percent five or fewer times, and less than 1 percent ten or more times. Almost 99 percent of the articles were from English or multilingual titles containing English articles. Sixty-seven percent of the articles were from the most recent five years, 85 percent from the last ten years and 95 percent were published since 1970. Examination at the title level revealed that "nearly half" were used five or fewer times, while 10 percent were used more than 300 times a year. The author observes "the most heavily requested articles were not published in the most heavily used journals." A table lists the top ten journals during both the 1991 and 1992 fiscal years (nine of the ten overlapped). This exceedingly detailed study, as noted by Lacroix, has "significance" for document delivery in libraries.

Leishman, Joan. "Improving Interlibrary Loan Quality Through Bench Marking: A Case Study from the Health Science Information Consortium of Toronto." **Health Libraries Review** 12 (September 1995): 215–18.

This article reports two studies of interlibrary loan speed, conducted for benchmarking purposes, by the Health Science Information Consortium of

Toronto. Both studies analyzed turnaround for ILL requests sent from six different hospital libraries (out of forty consortium members) to their central supplier, the University of Toronto Science and Medicine Library, during one-week periods. The November 1993 study of 301 journal article requests found that 96 percent were received within three days with the average turnaround two days, while the March 1994 investigation of 229 requests discovered 65 percent were filled in three days, which was also the mean turnaround time. Leishman observes these evaluations led to changes in local procedures and provided a benchmark concerning "realistic" expectations, but does not explain why the second study showed a decline in performance.

Levene, Lee-Allison, and Wayne A. Pedersen. "Patron Satisfaction at Any Cost?: A Case Study of Interlibrary Loan in Two U.S. Research Libraries." **Journal of Library Administration** 23, nos. 1–2 (1996): 55–71.

The authors analyze data from a ten-library Greater Midwest Research Libraries Consortium study pertinent to the Iowa State University and the University of Arkansas, Fayetteville libraries. Sections contrasting access policies at the two institutions contained considerable evaluative data on ILL/document delivery performance at various times during the early 1990s. GMRLC data revealed that the University of Arkansas's delivery speed was almost twice Iowa State's (15.4000 versus 8.3896 days) but patron satisfaction levels on a 1 (high) to 5 (low) Likert scale were quite similar: 1.4000 for Iowa State and 1.3544 for Arkansas. The average cost per filled request was $1.46 for Iowa State and $2.11 at Arkansas. Statistical analysis found a "disparity" between actual delivery speed and user perception of delivery speed. Moreover, there was no statistically significant correlation between actual delivery speed and patron satisfaction at Iowa State and a "low correlation" (.22904) at the University of Arkansas. For further details about the GMRLC study and its methodology see the entry by Weaver-Meyers and Stolt.

McKnight, Michelynn. "Interlibrary Loan Availability of Nursing Journals Through DOCLINE and OCLC: A Five-State Survey." **Bulletin of the Medical Library Association** 88 (July 2000): 254–55.

McKnight analyzes the availability of a core list of nursing journals through the OCLC and DOCLINE interlibrary loan systems in the five states of Texas, Arkansas, Louisiana, Oklahoma, and New Mexico.[18] She found that 153 of 165 titles (92.7 percent) were available in the region, while 165 OCLC libraries and 114 DOCLINE participants made at least two titles available.[19] Altogether 284 libraries offered nursing journals, 161 exclusively through OCLC and 93 exclusively through DOCLINE. The author concludes that libraries not participating in both systems may be paying unnecessary commercial document delivery fees. By focusing on journal availability rather than actual ILL performance, this "brief communication" takes a somewhat different approach to ILL evaluation than other entries in this section.

Medina, Sue O. "Improving Document Delivery in a Statewide Network." **Journal of Interlibrary Loan & Information Supply** 2, no. 3 (1992): 7–14.

Medina investigates interlibrary loan delivery speed among the 30 libraries belonging to the Network of Alabama Academic Libraries (NALL). In 1986, mean turnaround time for member libraries ranged from nine to nineteen days. In 1987, when all requests were filled through the U.S. mail, the mean delivery time within the NAAL stood at 9.0 days. However, it is interesting that photocopied items required 10.1 days compared to 7.9 days for original items. After the libraries began faxing requests in 1988, the average turnaround declined to 5.7 days for all items and 4.8 days for photocopied ones. The mean turnaround was 5.1 days in 1990 after a courier service was instigated in October 1989. The average time between sending the request and shipping the item fell from 3.2 days in 1987 to 2.0 in 1990, even though total ILL volume increased from 14,794 in 1986–87 to 33,827 in 1989–90. This serves as a useful, if somewhat dated, study of ILL turnaround at the state level.

Naylor, Ted E. "The Cost of Interlibrary Loan Services in a Medium-Sized Academic Library." **Journal of Interlibrary Loan, Document Delivery & Information Supply** 8, no. 2 (1997): 51–61.

The application of the ARL/RLG methodology for calculating ILL cost (see entry by Roche) to the Wichita State University library is described here. After gathering data for the 1995–96 fiscal year, average cost figures for the following transactions were ascertained: a filled borrowing request, $8.51; an unfilled borrowing request, $4.68; a filled lending request, $2.47; an unfilled lending request, $1.36. Moreover, 11,480 of 13,340 (86.1 percent) borrowing requests were successfully filled.[20] Separate sections present cost data for staff salaries and benefits, networks and communications, delivery, photocopy expenses, equipment, and supplies. It is no surprise that 70.7 percent of total costs were for staff. Commercial document delivery (based on 165 items obtained from UnCover, National Technical Information Service (NTIS), and Chemical Abstracts) cost on average 80 percent more (i.e., $15.27 per item) but delivered within an average of twenty-four hours rather than seven days for ILL. Naylor stresses that this investigation can be a "starting point" for evaluation of ILL costs in medium-sized academic libraries because the 1993 ARL/RLG study was oriented toward large research institutions.

Perrault, Anna H., and Marjo Arseneau. "User Satisfaction and Interlibrary Loan Service: A Study at Louisiana State University." **RQ** 35 (fall 1995): 90–100.

As part of an accreditation cycle self-study, ILL users at the LSU library were surveyed in order to assess their expectations and satisfaction with the service. The ten-question survey instrument, sent to a 20 percent random sample of all faculty and graduate student ILL users during a six-month period in 1992, received a 69.73 percent response rate. On a 1 to 5 Likert scale (1 = unsatisfactory, 5 = excellent), 93.26 percent of respondents rated the service as satisfactory to excellent (3–5) and 69.66 percent as above satisfactory (4–5). A major portion of the article is devoted to comparing faculty and graduate student survey responses, but the authors found "the differences are mainly a matter of degree." Significantly, 65.30 percent of faculty and 60 percent of graduate students placed the highest priority on "obtaining material regardless of speed and cost," while the respective percentages were 32.65

and 20 percent for "speed" and 2.04 and 13.33 percent for "cost." It was "surprising" that only 14.28 percent of faculty and 13.33 percent of graduate students needed the item within a week. A thorough literature review revealed no previously published survey of satisfaction with ILL in an academic library.

Roche, Marilyn M. **ARL/RLG Interlibrary Loan Cost Study: A Joint Effort by the Association of Research Libraries and the Research Libraries Group.** Washington, DC: Association of Research Libraries, 1993. 64p. ISBN 0-918006-70-8.

Implemented in seventy-six North American research libraries during 1991, this is probably the best-known and largest scale study devoted exclusively to ILL costs. The following cost components were addressed: staff, network and communications, delivery, photocopying, supplies, software and equipment, rental and maintenance, plus direct and indirect borrowing costs. The study's objective was to provide benchmark data and a management tool. The most frequently quoted finding was that a research library's average cost to borrow an item stood at $18.62 and $10.93 to lend one for a total ILL transaction expense of $29.55. Data is also reported at the 10th, 25th, 75th, and 90th percentiles for all institutions as well as separately for Big Ten and Big Eight libraries. Not unexpectedly, 77 percent of the costs are for staff. Numerous tables, graphs, and bar charts analyze the data from a variety of perspectives. The eight appendices are an outstanding feature of this entry, containing, among other things, a statistical summary of the results, a brief description of the data gathering methodology, a list of the participating institutions, and the survey instrument plus worksheets. The foreword's assertion that this is "the most extensive data available on the costs incurred by libraries in interlibrary lending and borrowing operations" remained true until the publication of Jackson's study in 1998 (see entry earlier in the section).

Seaman, Scott. "An Examination of Unfilled OCLC Lending and Photocopy Requests." **Information Technology & Libraries** 11 (September 1992): 229–35.

An investigation of ILL requests the Ohio State University libraries were unable to fill is reported by Seaman. The article, which contains a useful literature review, is based on 15,147 requests sent through the OCLC ILL subsystem between May 1, 1990, and November 30, 1990. Overall, Ohio State filled 51.8 percent of 7,846 copy requests (i.e., for a reproduction of the original) and 48.2 percent of 7,301 loan requests (for the actual item). Detailed analysis of unfilled requests revealed that 38 percent of the loan requests and 22 percent of the copy requests were unavailable, most commonly "not on the shelf." This finding has important implications for the evaluation of both collections and interlibrary loan performance because it provides evidence that owned resources may nevertheless be unavailable. Other reasons for failure (policy prohibits loan, bad citation, etc.) are less relevant to this book's focus on collections and access.

Sellen, Mary. "Turnaround Time and Journal Article Delivery: A Study of Four Delivery Systems." **Journal of Interlibrary Loan, Document Delivery, & Information Supply** 9, no. 4 (1999): 65–72.

A study of ILL turnaround time, using four delivery methods, conducted at an unnamed undergraduate academic institution in Southern California, is reported here. The investigation was based on a sample of 400 requests during the slow activity months of June, July, and August and another sample of 200 requests from the busier months of January, February, and March. Because no statistically significant difference was found between the two samples, Sellen infers that ILL performance is "not dependent on the time of year." Totaling both samples, the mean delivery time was 9.85 days by mail, 3.65 days by Ariel, 2.94 by fax, and 2.52 by courier. The overall mean was 4.79 days, compared to 13.76 days in Budd's 1986 study.[21] Thus, the author concludes, "Recent technological developments have significantly decreased turnaround time in the delivery of periodical articles."

Siddiqui, Moid A. "A Statistical Study of Interlibrary Loan Use at a Science and Engineering Academic Library." **Library Resources & Technical Services** 43 (October 1999): 233–46.

Siddiqui investigates patterns in the 1,280 ILL requests processed at King Fahd University of Petroleum and Minerals library in Saudi Arabia during the year 1997. Five of eighteen departments produced 61 percent of the requests. However, "no clear relationship" was observed between the number of ILL requests from a department and departmental size or the number of its journal subscriptions. Nearly half the customers (48 percent) requested a single item, while only 2 percent requested more than ten. Further analysis revealed the following: 84 percent of the requests were periodical articles and 16 percent monographs; of 694 periodicals, 72 percent were requested only once and 16 percent twice; 11 percent of all requests were to periodicals cancelled in 1997; and the $2,224 cost (a mean of $16 per article) to fill requests from cancelled titles represented a savings of $115,373 over the subscription price. Sixty-four percent of the requests were filled within four weeks, and the mean turnaround time was 14.2 days. Although not explicitly stated by the author while reviewing other studies, these patterns are generally consistent with findings from North American libraries.

Stolt, Wilbur A., Pat L. Weaver-Meyers, and Molly Murphy. "Interlibrary Loan and Customer Satisfaction: How Important is Delivery Speed?" In **Continuity and Transformation; The Promise of Confluence: Proceedings of the Seventh National Conference of the Association of College and Research Libraries, Pittsburgh, Pennsylvania, March 29-April 1, 1995,** edited by Richard AmRhein, 365–71. Chicago: Association of College and Research Libraries, 1995. ISBN 0-8389-7786-3.

This presentation at an ACRL national conference reports a "recent" survey of ILL customer satisfaction completed at the University of Oklahoma Library. Two hundred questionnaires generated a 37.5 percent response rate.[22] The authors found "no significant correlation" between satisfaction with the service and turnaround time (an average of 10.47 days), leading to the conclusion "a disproportionate emphasis has been placed on delivery speed." The survey also found that "only" 24 percent of users would be willing to pay $10 for forty-eight hour service. Data from the previous year revealed an 82 percent fill rate (8 percent were already owned and 10 percent cancelled) and a $14.72 cost per item. See the next entry (Weaver-Meyers and Stolt) for a similar study on a larger scale.

Weaver-Meyers, Pat L., and Wilbur A. Stolt. "Delivery Speed, Timeliness, and Satisfaction: Patrons' Perceptions About ILL Service." **Journal of Library Administration** 23, nos. 1–2 (1996): 23–42.

This article reports a survey of patron perceptions concerning ILL service, conducted by ten of the eighteen member libraries in the Greater Midwest Research Libraries Consortium. ILL patrons were surveyed in April 1995 concerning their overall satisfaction with the service and whether they received the requested item "in a timely manner." The mean delivery time for all institutions was 15.46 days, ranging from 8.38 to 19.14 days. Fifty percent of the requests were received in 12 days and 90 percent in 27 days. The delivery time included a mean of 2.67 days between the institution's and the patron's receipt of the item.

Following considerable statistical analysis (Pearson Correlation Coefficient, multiple regression analysis, and ANOVA [ANalysis of VAriance between groups]) on their data, Weaver-Meyers and Stolt conclude the following: there is "little relationship" between patron satisfaction and actual delivery speed; patron satisfaction and their perception of timeliness are "strongly" correlated; and only 17 percent of a patron's perception of timeliness can be predicted from actual speed. Weaver-Meyers and Stolt conclude that "materials received within two weeks satisfy the average academic's 'window of usefulness.'" This methodologically sophisticated investigation has intriguing implications. See the Levene and Pedersen entry for GMRLC study data pertinent to Iowa State University and the University of Arkansas.

Wiley, Lynn, and Tina E. Chrzastowski. "The State of ILL in the State of IL: The Illinois Interlibrary Loan Assessment Project." **Library Collections, Acquisitions & Technical Services** 25 (spring 2001): 5–20.

The authors analyze ILL serial requests by the twenty-six largest libraries in Illinois (the Chicago Public Library, the Illinois State Library, and twenty-four academic libraries) during the eleven months from July 1996 through May 1997. OCLC's Prism Inter Library Loan Reports (PILLR), which later evolved into the OCLC Management Statistics Service, was used to gather and tabulate the data. They found 58 percent of 89,316 ILL requests were filled by libraries in Illinois, while 42 percent were filled out of state. A breakdown of the requested items by LC class ranges found that the sciences were requested over the social sciences and humanities by an almost two-to-one ratio. A core group of 113 titles borrowed out of state more than twenty times was identified. It is interesting that 54 percent of these had been cancelled by an Illinois library, 29 percent were still owned in Illinois, whereas 17 percent were never held. Most of the requests (43.7 percent of those filled in-state and over 60 percent of the ones filled outside Illinois) were from journal titles needed only once. Wiley and Chrzastowski emphasize that statewide ILL analysis can facilitate cost-effective collection management.

Willemse, John. "Improving Interlending Through Goal Setting and Performance Measurement." **Interlending & Document Supply** 21, no. 1 (1993): 13–17.

An ongoing assessment of ILL performance at the University of South Africa during the late 1980s and early 1990s is narrated here. The investigation focuses on the fill rate and delivery time of four sources: the Southern African Interlending Schemes (SAIS), the British Library Document Supply Centre, the international lending system, and Data-Search (a commercial vendor). It was found that in 1991, 21.8 percent of the total requests were filled in seven days, 61.4 percent within fourteen days, and 73.9 percent by the end of twenty-one days—raw data are not provided. SAIS had the best seven-day fill rate (28.2 percent), but BLDSC had the highest rate after twenty-one days (84.4 percent). A table, summarizing the findings for each year from 1988 through 1991, indicates overall improvement. Willemse then discusses a number of factors responsible for this improvement as well as the pros and cons of using fax, mail, and telex for ILL activity. A useful analysis and evaluation of ILL in a South African context is provided by this article.

EVALUATION OF TABLE OF CONTENTS SERVICES

Davies, Mary, Frances Boyle, and Susan Osborne. "CAS-IAS Services: Where Are We Now?" **Electronic Library** 16 (February 1998): 37–48.

This item's major contribution relates to evaluation of table of contents service currency, although the term "current alerting service" (CAS) is used. The methodology consisted of comparing the information provided by eight services, including the British Library's Inside Information and Swets' SwetScan, and some publisher Web pages with journal issues on the shelf (for samples of fourteen and then nineteen titles) to ascertain which was most up-to-date. Ten such comparisons were conducted between September 1993 and March 1997 at the Imperial Cancer Research Fund in London. In 1993 and 1994, the shelf issues were more current than the services, but by March 1997, the services were more current than the shelves by a 47 to 16 percent ratio with the two equally current for 37 percent of the sample (data was not presented for individual services). The authors briefly note other evaluative criteria for alerting services such as coverage, format, and cost. Next, sixteen criteria (including both performance and technological issues) for evaluating document delivery are listed in outline format. A lengthy appendix tabulates basic information (i.e., subject coverage, cost, etc.) concerning approximately twenty-five table of contents and document supply services as of mid-1997. Davies, Boyle, and Osborne conclude that Current Alerting Service/Individual Article Supply (CAS-IAS) services have not "delivered their early promise" and monitoring their performance "will have to continue."

Goodyear, Mary Lou, and Jane Dodd. "From the Library of Record to the Library as Gateway: An Analysis of Three Electronic Table-of-Contents Services." **Library Acquisitions: Practice & Theory** 18 (fall 1994): 253–64.

The authors begin by discussing four environmental changes impacting libraries (the political climate, scholarly communication, the concept of a library, and technology) and the process of seeking user input regarding electronic resources at Texas A & M University. The entry's major focus falls on evaluating the coverage of three electronic table-of-contents services: OCLC Article First, UnCover, and Faxon Finder. Tables present for each service, as of mid-1993, the numbers and percentages for the following:

1. Serial titles covered according to twenty-one letters of the Library of Congress classification system

2. Titles listed in seven major indexes, such as *Business Periodicals Index* and *Index Medicus,* that are covered by the service—this is a variation of the checklist approach, although that term is not used

3. Unique titles (i.e., not held by the other two services) in seven broad subject areas

It was found that Article First is strong in business, Faxon Finder and UnCover are strong in the humanities, Article First and Faxon Finder show strength in science, social science coverage is similar among the three, veterinary medicine is not well covered by any, and UnCover has the most unique titles. Goodyear and Dodd observe, "The same skills used to evaluate collections can be applied to electronic information services."

Jaguszewski, Janice M., and Jody L. Kempf. "Four Current Awareness Databases: Coverage and Currency Compared." **Database** 18 (February/March 1995): 34–44.

An evaluation at the University of Minnesota-Twin Cities Campus Science and Engineering Library of the Current Contents on Diskette, CARL UnCover2, Inside Information, and ContentsFirst table of contents databases is depicted here. The four services are described and their strengths and weaknesses analyzed. Lists of fifty chemistry and fifty mathematics journals—compiled from the RLG Long-Term Serials Project—were checked against the four databases twice (in January and May 1994) for holdings and to ascertain if the most current issue matched the most current issue in the University of Minnesota OPAC.[23] The authors found the coverage of the fifty mathematics journals ranged from 16 to 92 percent in the four services, while the corresponding figures for chemistry titles ranged from 80 to 93 percent. Among the four databases, the percentage of covered titles that listed the most recent issue in both searches ranged from 11 to 72 percent for mathematics and 17 to 75 percent in chemistry. Two lengthy tables summarize the findings. This is an exceptionally thoughtful and well-done study.

MISCELLANEOUS ISSUES

Harrington, John, Janet Evans, and Simon J. Bevan. "BIODOC: A Preliminary User Analysis." **Serials** 9 (July 1996): 170–77.

Drawing heavily upon a user study from an unpublished master's thesis by Emma Nicholls, this entry provides a preliminary evaluation of Cranfield University's BIODOC project after approximately six months.[24] (See also the entry by

Blagden.) In 1994, the Biotechnology Centre subscribed to 16 journals and obtained 559 different titles through ILL. Beginning January 1995, all subscriptions were cancelled and replaced by an electronic table of contents service (UnCover Reveal) and "new...fast" document delivery. The mean delivery time for five document delivery suppliers, including UnCover and BLDSC, ranged from approximately two to seven days. Nicholls found, based on twenty-three interviews during the summer of 1995, the following: 28 percent rated the current awareness service as effective, 44 percent satisfactory, 28 percent less than satisfactory, 25 percent were "very satisfied" with delivery speed, 62 percent "satisfied," whereas 13 percent considered the performance "not sufficient." Harrington, Evans, and Bevan conclude, "BIODOC appears very unlikely to offer real cost savings."

Kingma, Bruce R. "Access to Journal Articles: A Model of the Cost Efficiency of Document Delivery and Library Consortia." In **ASIS 94: Proceedings of the 57th ASIS Annual Meeting; Alexandria, VA, October 17–20, 1994,** edited by Bruce Maxian, 8–16. Medford, NJ: Published for the American Society for Information Science by Learned Information, 1994. ISBN 0-938734-93-8. ISSN 0044-7870.

The author explains his economic model for determining the relative cost-effectiveness of subscription, commercial document delivery, or consortium document delivery for procuring journals. Both "fixed" (i.e., subscription, acquisition, shelf space plus overhead) as well as "marginal" (i.e., labor for reshelving and depreciation with use) are considered. Most of the item is devoted to complex equations that can be used to calculate a "tipping-point" at which one option becomes more cost-effective than another. Some of the assumptions (e.g., "all patrons are identical") used to simplify the equations may be questionable. Note that the model can be expanded to include other issues, such as the patron's time. The author observes that an option can be "cost-efficient" but not "economically-efficient" if patrons are dissatisfied with speed and service. This entry is recommended for readers interested in a sophisticated mathematical explanation of Kingma's methodology. For applications of this model at SUNY and elsewhere see the numerous other entries by Kingma in this chapter.

Kinnucan, Mark T. "Demand for Document Delivery and Interlibrary Loan in Academic Settings." **Library & Information Science Research** 15 (fall 1993): 355–74.

Kinnucan employs conjoint analysis (a "widely used" marketing technique for measuring consumer preferences) to assess the attitude of academic users toward ILL and document delivery. The research was based on surveying and interviewing seventy-nine faculty and graduate students (76 percent of those contacted responded) at Ohio State University, Ohio University, and Wright State University in which they indicated preferences regarding cost, delivery speed, and delivery method. Regression analysis, scatter plots, and histograms are used in the methodologically sophisticated analysis of the results. The major finding was that for most users, price was more important than delivery speed and other variables. Note that users "are willing to pay... [but] not willing to pay much"—58 percent of respondents reported a fifty-fifty chance they would pay $4 for document delivery. Ironically, 94 percent said they would use ILL if it were free, but only 47 percent reported actually using it within the last year even though all three institutions provided free ILL. This meticulously detailed investigation represents, according to the author, the first application of conjoint analysis to document delivery.

Mitchell, Eleanor, and Sheila A. Walters. "Evaluating Document Delivery Service." In **Document Delivery Services: Issues and Answers,** 117–47. Medford, NJ: Learned Information, Inc, 1995. ISBN 1-57387-003-X.

This chapter from a monograph concerning document delivery is organized into two parts: a discussion of evaluative criteria and a summary of eighteen performance evaluation studies reported between 1985 and 1993. The initial section contains an exceedingly sophisticated discussion of seven criteria, with a focus on factors influencing performance rather than methodology per se: turnaround time; cost; fill rate; quality, that is, readability; reliability, that is, can the vendor deliver what is supposedly in inventory; user satisfaction; and value-added services. Interestingly, the authors observe a value-added service might "count against a supplier," that is, mail copy follow-ups to faxes might result in unidentified "orphan documents" that cause confusion. The second part employs an outline format to succinctly summarize published and unpublished evaluations of supplier performance, using such headings as type of library, suppliers, time frame, sample, method of shipment, methodology, turnaround, fill rate, costs, and results, although every heading is not used in each summary. This item should be especially helpful for a reader seeking an introductory overview.

Murdoch, Jean. "Remote Document Supply Demand from Subscribers to Scientific Journals." **Interlending & Document Supply** 25, no. 1 (1997): 25–26.

In this intriguing investigation, the names of the libraries or organizations sending, during a twelve-month period, requests to the BLDSC for articles from an unidentified science journal were compared to a list of subscribers provided by the publisher, Blackwell's. It was found that 16 percent of U.K. subscribers to the journal (accounting for 22 percent of the total document delivery requests) also ordered its articles from the British Library Document Supply Centre and that the organization with the most document delivery requests was also a subscriber. Furthermore, 18 percent of overseas subscribers also requested articles from the title. Murdoch concludes that her results "offer little support for the hypothesis that interlending and document supply are used as a cheap alternative to taking out a subscription." She speculates that libraries with a subscription may still need document delivery due to gaps in holdings, local unavailability, or the inconvenience of using the local collection. This short item is particularly significant because it strongly suggests that a library subscribing to a journal still may not have all issues available for patrons.

Roberts, Elizabeth P. "ILL/Document Delivery as an Alternative to Local Ownership of Seldom-Used Scientific Journals." **Journal of Academic Librarianship** 18 (March 1992): 30–34.

This entry begins with a discussion, including a literature review, that concludes ILL is still needed but should incorporate new technologies. Accordingly, Roberts emphasizes the importance of developing effective document delivery systems. The article's major contribution is a survey of chemistry, physics, and biochemistry department faculty attitudes toward ILL/document delivery at two ARL institutions: Washington State University and Arizona State University. The results revealed that 74 percent use ILL to obtain items not locally available, 66 percent use ILL one to three times annually, and that 42 percent are willing to wait no more than one or two weeks for an item. The most frequent reason for non-use (cited by 44 percent) was "it takes too long." It is interesting that 19 percent of respondents would not pay for twenty-four to forty-eight hour delivery, 27 percent would pay $1–$2, 20 percent would pay $5, and only 3 percent would pay $10 or more. This study would have more credibility if the sampling methodology, sample size, and response rate had been reported.

Truesdell, Cheryl B. "Is Access a Viable Alternative to Ownership? A Review of Access Performance." **Journal of Academic Librarianship** 20 (September 1994): 200–206.

This analytical literature review synthesizes several dozen items published from the late 1970s through the mid-1990s dealing with performance evaluation of document delivery/ILL. The focus is on the three familiar criteria of cost, delivery speed, and fill rate. The author offers many perceptive insights: cost studies may not be correlated with performance levels; average turnaround time reports "mask a high level of variability;" and the ability to designate five potential lenders in the OCLC system exaggerates fill rate (termed the most "unpredictable variable") for ILL compared to document delivery. Studies show commercial document delivery costs more than ILL but "is not necessarily ... more effective or efficient." Emphasizing that generally agreed upon standards of performance must be developed, Truesdell advocates a "general consensus" for three service levels: "rush," twenty-four to forty-eight hours; "normal," three to five days; and "research," one to two weeks. Moreover, turnover should be measured by the calendar days between the patron requesting and receiving the item. In summary, this is a sophistical and useful review.

Wessels, R.H.A. "Optimizing the Size of Journal Collections in Libraries." **Interlending & Document Supply** 23, no. 3 (1995): 18–21.

A model for determining a local library collection's optimum number of journal subscriptions is proposed by a director of a library consortium in the Netherlands. The model assumes that 80 percent of requests are fulfilled with 35 percent of the serials budget and that document delivery is "guaranteed." The model's four parameters are the annual number of articles required by a library's patrons, the average cost of filling a document delivery request, "the total number of journals that could possibly be acquired," and the average subscription price. Several graphs illustrate the model's application to a small university library and then a research institute. The author states his model could "assist librarians in their development of access and holdings strategies" and also be used to demonstrate the serials acquisitions budget is inadequate. This model is certainly interesting from a theoretical perspective but gathering the necessary data could be difficult.

Wright, Sally, and Mike Gollop. "Estimating Non-Market Costs in Providing Information Services: Developing an Economic Model." **Vine** 103 (1996): 38–42.

Wright and Gollop analyze the "non-market" cost of ILL, that is, indirect cost to the university because staff must wait for needed documents. Data was gathered through a Stated Preference Survey in which respondents indicated their preferences regarding "wait time" for ILL requests and the monetary figure charge to their hypothetical budget. The questionnaire was sent to 293 academics (every third one) in the Science and Engineering Departments of the University of Leeds, United Kingdom, generating a 63 percent response rate. The cost of a day's "wait time" for the user was calculated at £1.43, extrapolated to £14.77 for each ILL request, based on the 10.33 day turnaround time during 1993–94. The authors conclude that for every £20.59 increase in a journal's subscription cost, its yearly use must increase by "one" to justify a subscription. This item is important because it attempts to quantify an often overlooked dimension of the "access versus ownership" debate—the cost of the user's time.

NOTES

1. Thomas L. Kilpatrick, "Interlibrary Loan: Past, Present, Future," *Advances in Library Resource Sharing* 1 (1990): 22–38.

2. Marilyn M. Roche, *ARL/RLG Interlibrary Loan Cost Study* (Washington, DC: Association of Research Libraries, 1993).

3. Percentage is Nisonger's calculation.

4. Calculated from Hamaker's statement that 606 of 691 were filled.

5. Fremont Rider, *The Scholar and the Future of the Research Library: A Problem and Its Solution* (New York: Hadham Press, 1944).

6. The percentage calculated by Nisonger.

7. The percentage calculated by Nisonger.

8. Roche, *ARL/RLG Interlibrary Loan Cost Study.*

9. Dorothy Milne and Bill Tiffany, "A Cost-Per-Use Method for Evaluating the Cost-Effectiveness of Serials: A Detailed Discussion of Methodology," *Serials Review* 17 (summer 1991): 7–19; Milne and Tiffany, "A Survey of the Cost-Effectiveness of Serials: A Cost-Per-Use Method and Its Results," *Serials Librarian* 19, nos. 3–4 (1991): 137–49.

10. Nisonger's calculation from author's statement that all but 2 of 93 requests were filled.

11. The percentage is Nisonger's calculation from Dade's data.

12. This percentage is Nisonger's calculation.

13. The percentage is Nisonger's calculation from Maxfield's data that 61 of 431 articles were requested by library staff.

14. Percentage is Nisonger's calculation.

15. Percentage calculated by Nisonger from Sellers and Beam's data.

16. Pat L. Weaver-Meyers et al., *Interlibrary Loan in Academic and Research Libraries: Workload and Staffing* (Washington, DC: Association of Research Libraries, 1989).

17. Eve-Marie Lacroix and Gale A Dutcher, "A Comparison of Interlibrary Loan Requests Received by the National Library of Medicine: 1959 and 1984," *Bulletin of the*

Medical Library Association 75 (January 1987): 7–13; Lacroix and Dutcher, "Impact of DOCLINE on Interlibrary Loan Service at the National Library of Medicine," *Bulletin of the Medical Library Association* 77 (January 1989): 42–47.

18. Margaret Allen, *Key Nursing Journals: Characteristics and Database Coverage.* (Stratford, WI: unpublished manuscript, 1998).

19. Nisonger's calculation from McKnight's data.

20. The percentage is Nisonger's calculation.

21. John M. Budd, "Interlibrary Loan Service: A Study of Turnaround Time," *RQ* 26 (fall 1986): 75–80.

22. Nisonger's calculation from the authors' data.

23. Lists of important journals for which at least one RLG member would maintain a subscription on a permanent basis. They were identified in 1990 and organized by subject.

24. Emma Nicholls, "BIODOC an Interim Evaluation of a Rapid Document Delivery and Electronic Current Awareness Service" (master's thesis, University of Sheffield, 1995).

Index

About the Author

THOMAS E. NISONGER is Associate Professor, School of Library and Information Science, Indiana University, Bloomington.